Stress-Related Disorders

SOURCEBOOK

Fourth Edition

Health Reference Series

Fourth Edition

Stress-Related Disorders

SOURCEBOOK

Basic Consumer Health Information about Stress and Stress-Related Disorders, Including Signs, Symptoms, Types and Sources of Acute and Chronic Stress, the Impact of Stress on the Body and Mental Health Problems Associated with Stress, Such as Depression, Anxiety Disorders, Bipolar Disorder, Obsessive-Compulsive Disorder, Substance Abuse, Post-Traumatic Stress Disorder, and Suicide

Along with Tips for Managing Stress, Assistance for Coping with Stress-Related Disorders using Complementary and Alternative Medicine Therapies, a Glossary of Related Terms, and a Directory of Resources for Additional Help and Information

OMNIGRAPHICS

155 W. Congress, Suite 200 Detroit, MI 48226

Bibliographic Note

Because this page cannot legibly accommodate all the copyright notices, the Bibliographic Note portion of the Preface constitutes an extension of the copyright notice.

* * *

Omnigraphics, Inc.

Editorial Services provided by Omnigraphics, Inc., a division of Relevant Information, Inc.

Keith Jones, *Managing Editor*

* * *

Library of Congress Cataloging-in-Publication Data

Stress-related disorders sourcebook : basic consumer health information about stress and stress-related disorders, including signs, symptoms, types, and sources of acute and chronic stress, the impact of stress on the body, and mental health problems associated with stress, such as depression, anxiety disorders, bipolar disorder, obsessive-compulsive disorder, substance abuse, posttraumatic stress disorder, and suicide; along with advice about getting help for stress-related disorders, managing stress and coping with trauma, a glossary of stress-related terms, and a directory of resources for additional help and information / Keith Jones, managing editor. – Fourth edition

   pages cm. – (Health reference series)

  Includes bibliographical references and index.

  Summary: "Provides basic consumer health information about types of stress and the stress response, the physical and mental health effects of stress, along with facts about treatment for stress-related disorders, and stress management techniques for adults and children. Includes index, glossary of related terms, and other resources"– Provided by publisher.

  ISBN 978-0-7808-1380-9 (hardcover : alk. paper) – ISBN 978-0-7808-1406-6 (ebook)

  1. Stress management--Popular works. 2. Stress (Physiology)–Popular works. 3. Stress (Psychology)--Popular works. I. Omnigraphics, Inc.

  RA785.S78 2015

  155.9'042–dc23

                                                                    2015030052

Table of Contents

Part II: How Stress Affects the Body

Part III: How Stress Affects Mental Health

Part VI: Additional Help and Information

Preface

About This Book

While recent surveys show a decrease in the overall stress level of people in the Untied States it still hovers above healthy levels, especially with young adults. Money and work lead the list of major stressors, followed by concerns about family responsibilities and health. Stress takes its toll on the body by eroding sleep quality and mental focus, leaving its victims impatient, irritable, fatigued, and prone to overeating and substance abuse. Prolonged stress adversely affects immune system function, worsening conditions such as cancer, chronic pain disorders, diabetes, heart problems and even pregnancy. Mental health disorders, including depression, anxiety, and posttraumatic stress disorder, are also linked to serious problems coping with stress. As stress levels in adults rise, so do those in children and adolescents who struggle to cope with worries about family and school.

Stress-Related Disorders Sourcebook, Fourth Edition provides updated information about the origins and types of stress and describes physical and mental health disorders that may develop during and after stressful situations. Readers will learn about how stress worsens asthma, headache, digestive disorders and chronic pain. The *Sourcebook* also discusses how stress contributes to mental health problems and addiction to tobacco, alcohol, and drugs. Information about trauma, loss, and grief is presented, along with suggestions for managing stressful situations, such as caregiver stress, economic hardship, holiday stress, return from active military duty, and occupational stress. Tips on helping children and teens cope with stress are also offered, along with a glossary of related terms and a directory of resources.

How to Use This Book

This book is laid out as parts, chapters, and sections. Parts cover broad areas of the subject and are divided into chapters that focus on individual topics. Each chapter may be subdivided into sections containing closely related content.

Part I: Introduction to Stress and Stress-Related Disorders identifies signs and symptoms of acute, chronic, and posttraumatic stress and discusses life events and risk factors that increase vulnerability to developing stress-related disorders. Age-related stress, factors that influence reactivity to stress, and occupational stress are also included.

Part II: How Stress Affects the Body provides information about health conditions exacerbated by stress. These include Alzheimer's disease, cancer, diabetes, gastrointestinal problems, headache, multiple sclerosis, heart and cardiovascular diseases, sleep disorders, and chronic pain disorders.

Part III: How Stress Affects Mental Health discusses how stress erodes emotional well-being and contributes to the development of mental health disorders, such as depression, anxiety disorders, bipolar disorder, binge eating, obsessive-compulsive disorder, and substance abuse and addiction. Trauma survivors and their families will also find information about common reactions after trauma and types of stress-related disorders that develop after exposure to violence, disaster, assault or war.

Part IV: Treating Stress-Related Disorders offers information about treatments for stress-related disorders, including psychological therapies, medications, and complementary and alternative medicine. For people coping with a loved one's stress-related responses, this part offers tips on helping someone with posttraumatic stress disorder and recognizing when someone needs help from mental health and other medical professionals.

Part V: Stress Management identifies strategies for combating stress in everyday life. People coping with emotional and physical reactions to stress will find suggestions on healthy habits that alleviate stress and tips for coping with stressful situations at home, at work and on road. Information about developing resilience to stress is also included, along with tips on stress management for children, teens, families, older adults, and specifically for survivors of a disaster or any other traumatic event.

Part VI: Additional Help and Information provides a glossary of important terms related to stress and stress-related disorders. A directory of organizations that provide health information about stress-related disorders is also included.

Bibliographic Note

This volume contains documents and excerpts from publications issued by the following U.S. government agencies: Centers for Disease Control and Prevention (CDC); Federal Bureau of Investigation (FBI); National Cancer Institute (NCI); National Center for Posttraumatic Stress Disorder (NCPTSD); National Heart, Lung, and Blood Institute (NHLBI); National Institute of Arthritis and Musculoskeletal and Skin Diseases (NIAMS); National Institute of Diabetes and Digestive and Kidney Diseases (NIDDK); National Institute on Aging (NIA); National Institute on Alcohol Abuse and Alcoholism (NIAAA); National Institute on Drug Abuse (NIDA); National Institutes of Health (NIH); Office on Women's Health (OWH); Substance Abuse and Mental Health Services Administration (SAMHSA); and the U.S. Food and Drug Administration (FDA).

It may also contain original material produced by Omnigraphics, Inc. and reviewed by medical consultants.

About the Health Reference Series

The *Health Reference Series* is designed to provide basic medical information for patients, families, caregivers, and the general public. Each volume takes a particular topic and provides comprehensive coverage. This is especially important for people who may be dealing with a newly diagnosed disease or a chronic disorder in themselves or in a family member. People looking for preventive guidance, information about disease warning signs, medical statistics, and risk factors for health problems will also find answers to their questions in the *Health Reference Series*. The *Series*, however, is not intended to serve as a tool for diagnosing illness, in prescribing treatments, or as a substitute for the physician/patient relationship. All people concerned about medical symptoms or the possibility of disease are encouraged to seek professional care from an appropriate health care provider.

A Note about Spelling and Style

Health Reference Series editors use *Stedman's Medical Dictionary* as an authority for questions related to the spelling of medical terms and the *Chicago Manual of Style* for questions related to grammatical structures, punctuation, and other editorial concerns. Consistent adherence is not always possible, however, because the individual volumes within the *Series* include many documents from a wide variety of different producers, and the editor's primary goal is to present material from each source as accurately as is possible. This sometimes means that information in different chapters or sections may follow other guidelines and alternate spelling authorities.

Medical Review

Omnigraphics contracts with a team of qualified, senior medical professionals who serve as medical consultants for the Health Reference Series. As necessary, medical consultants review reprinted and originally written material for currency and accuracy. Citations including the phrase, "Reviewed (month, year)" indicate material reviewed by this team. Medical consultation services are provided to the Health Reference Series editors by:

Dr. Vijayalakshmi, MBBS, DGO, MD
Dr. Senthil Selvan, MBBS, DCH, MD

Our Advisory Board

We would like to thank the following board members for providing guidance to the development of this Series:

- Dr. Lynda Baker, Associate Professor of Library and Information Science, Wayne State University, Detroit, MI

- Nancy Bulgarelli, William Beaumont Hospital Library, Royal Oak, MI

- Karen Imarisio, Bloomfield Township Public Library, Bloomfield Township, MI

- Karen Morgan, Mardigian Library, University of Michigan-Dearborn, Dearborn, MI

- Rosemary Orlando, St. Clair Shores Public Library, St. Clair Shores, MI

Health Reference Series Update Policy

The inaugural book in the *Health Reference Series* was the first edition of Cancer Sourcebook published in 1989. Since then, the Series has been enthusiastically received by librarians and in the medical community. In order to maintain the standard of providing high-quality health information for the layperson the editorial staff at Omnigraphics felt it was necessary to implement a policy of updating volumes when warranted.

Medical researchers have been making tremendous strides, and it is the purpose of the *Health Reference Series* to stay current with the most recent advances. Each decision to update a volume is made on an individual basis. Some of the considerations include how much new information is available and the feedback we receive from people who use the books. If there is a topic you would like to see added to the update list, or an area of medical concern you feel has not been adequately addressed, please write to:

Managing Editor
Health Reference Series
Omnigraphics, Inc.
155 W. Congress, Suite 200
Detroit, MI 48226

Part One

Introduction to Stress and Stress-Related Disorders

Chapter 1

Stress – An Overview

What is Stress?

- Stress is a normal psychological and physical reaction to demands in our lives. It is the way our bodies react physically, emotionally, mentally, and behaviorally to any change in the status quo. Even imagined change can cause stress.

- Stress is highly individual. A situation that one person may find stressful may not bother another person. Stress occurs when something happens that we feel imposes a demand on us. When we perceive that we cannot cope, or feel inadequate to meet the demand, we begin to feel stress.

- Stress is not entirely bad. We need a certain amount of stress in our lives because it is stimulating and motivating. It gives us the energy to try harder and keeps us alert.

- When we find ourselves in situations that challenge us too much, we react with the "fight or flight" stress response.

- Stress actually begins in our brains and it is expressed in our body. Once we perceive stress, our body sends out chemical messengers in the form of stress hormones to help our bodies handle the stress.

This chapter includes excerpts from "Stress Fact Sheet," Mental Illness Research, Education and Clinical Centers (MIRECC), July 2013; and text from "Stress and your health fact sheet," Office on Women's Health (OWH), July 16, 2012.

What are Possible Symptoms of Stress?

- **Mental Symptoms:** forgetfulness, nervousness, confusion, poor concentration, lethargy, negativity, overly busy mind

- **Physical Symptoms:** tension, fatigue, insomnia, muscle aches, digestive upset, appetite change, headaches, restlessness

- **Emotional Symptoms:** anxiety, mood swings, irritability, depression, resentment, anger, impatience, worrying, feeling pressured

- **Social or Behavioral Symptoms:** lashing out, decreased sex drive, lack of intimacy, isolation, intolerance, loneliness, avoiding social situations, overuse of alcohol, tobacco, and/or drugs

- **Spiritual Symptoms:** apathy, loss of direction, emptiness, loss of life's meaning, unforgiving, no sense of purpose

How Does Stress Affect Our Health and Our Lives?

- 75 to 90% of all medical office visits are for stress-related ailments and complaints

- stress is linked to the 6 leading causes of death in America – heart disease, cancer, lung ailments, accidents, cirrhosis of the liver, and suicide

- stress is also implicated in hypertension, smoking, obesity, alcoholism, drug abuse, gastrointestinal problems, arthritis, immune system disturbances, skin disorders, neurological conditions, etc.

What Can You Do about Stress?

Your reaction to stress is determined by a combination of factors including your physiology, past successes/failures in coping with stress, and interpretations of stressful events in your life. Managing stress effectively is a complex skill – one you can learn with time and active participation. Cultivating constructive thinking, maintaining an optimistic and hopeful outlook, and altering patterns of negative thinking are some of the more important strategies.

The following strategies also can be of value:

- **Physical techniques:**

  Exercise regularly and aim for 20 to 30 minutes at least three times each week

Eat in moderation and choose a healthy diet

Stop smoking

Reduce alcohol

Limit caffeine

Get adequate rest

- **Psychological techniques:**

Learn to relax both mind and body – try deep/abdominal breathing, progressive muscle relaxation, and visualizing positive outcomes

Build some fun into your routine

Use humor

Learn to look differently at situations that cause stress

Learn to get along better with others

Find ways to manage your time effectively

Establish realistic expectations for yourself and others

- **Environmental techniques:**

Develop a social support network

Maintain a neat, clean, and comfortable work area

Improve lighting

Reduce noise

Open windows if possible

Ban smoking

Consider a humidifier

Maintain indoor plants

When Is It Time to Ask for Help?

- If you feel trapped, as though there's nowhere to turn
- If you worry excessively and can't concentrate

- *Do women react to stress differently from men?*

One recent survey found that women were more likely to experience physical symptoms of stress than men. But we don't have enough proof to say that this applies to all women. We do know that women often cope with stress in different ways than men. Women "tend and befriend," taking care of those closest to them, but also drawing support from friends and family. Men are more likely to have the "fight or flight" response. They cope by "escaping" into a relaxing activity or other distraction.

Chapter 2

Stressful Life Events

Chapter Contents

Section 2.1

How Teens Can Deal with Loss and Grief

Text in this section is excerpted from "Dealing with loss and grief,"
Office on Women's Health (OWH), January 7, 2015.

Everyone faces something very upsetting at some point in their lives. Teens may have to deal with the death of someone they love, their parents' divorce, violence, or abuse, for example. These very upsetting experiences can bring up lots of feelings. There are ways to cope, though, and we have information that can help.

What is grief?

"Grief" and "grieving" are used to describe the feelings a person has after a death or other loss. You also may feel grief after a really hard experience (sometimes called a trauma) like being attacked or your home getting destroyed. That is because the experience has caused you to lose important parts of the way your life used to be.

Feeling grief is normal. Every person has her own reactions to loss. Here are some reactions you might have if you are grieving:

- Strong emotions, such as sadness, anger, worry, or guilt

- Few or no feelings, like you are emotionally numb

- Crying spells or feeling like there's a lump in your throat

- Physical reactions, such as having stomach aches or not sleeping

- Spiritual reactions, like feeling disappointed in your religion or feeling even more connected to it

Grief can go on for many months, but it should lessen over time. Everyone is different, but you should expect to feel at least a little better after a couple of months. If your grief doesn't get better over time, you may need the help of a therapist. Also, you should reach out for help without waiting if you have signs of depression. These include feeling worthless, having trouble functioning in your life, or thinking about hurting yourself.

Real help

Dealing with grief can be very hard. You don't have to face it alone. Get support by phone, text, chat, or email from a special helpline for teens. If you are looking for escape in things like drinking or drugs, remember that they can cause big problems. Keep in mind that if you don't find healthy ways to cope, your grief can get even worse.

How can I deal with grief?

Grief can be hard to handle. If you're feeling grief after a serious trauma like a violent attack, talk to an adult you trust and see if therapy may help you feel better. Check out the list below for other tips on handling grief.

Different people handle grief in different ways. Ways of handling grief include the following:

- Find comfort in good memories. Looking through old photo albums is one way to do this.

- Stay busy to keep your mind off the sadness. You might try taking up a new hobby or activity.

- Talk about your loss. Some people do this naturally and easily with friends and family, while others talk to a professional therapist.

- Exercise every day. Whether you play sports, walk, jog, swim, or get moving some other way, physical activity can help you feel better.

- Put your feelings into words or pictures. Try blogging, writing in a journal, or drawing. If it's hard for you to talk about your feelings, putting them on paper can help you feel better.

- Listen to music. Try singing along to songs that have meaning for you.

What to do when parents divorce

If your parents are getting divorced, it's normal to feel grief. So much of your life may be changing, and you may not have much control over what happens. You may feel angry, sad, lonely, scared, and lots of other emotions. All this can take time to heal.

There are many things you can do to feel better about a divorce. For starters, you can remember that divorce is never a child's fault.

Talk to your parents about how you're feeling. Tell them what would make the divorce easier on you. Get help from friends. You might also consider joining a support group for kids of divorcing parents. Your parents, school nurse, school counselor, or other adults can help you look for one. Also, see if you can think about any personal strengths that helped you in hard times before. And check out some of our tips for dealing with grief.

How to deal with loss and military life

If you have a family member in the military, you may have losses even if your relative never gets hurt. You may miss your relative when that person is away, or feel sad, worried, or angry a lot. And it can be hard to adjust when that person comes back.

You can use our general tips for handling grief, plus some special ways military kids can cope:

- Ask about how things are going to change when your family member gets deployed. Find out about any new responsibilities or privileges you may have.

- Try not to put your life on hold while your family member is deployed. Set goals and make plans for yourself.

- Figure out how and when you're going to stay in touch with the family member who is away.

- Keep track of important moments to share with your family member. Make a film, write a blog, or create a photo journal.

- Help your family keep up important traditions. Consider creating new ones.

- Connect with other people who can relate. You might look into a support group or even a camp for military kids.

- Spend special time together when your family member comes back. Keep plans simple, though. Expect it to take time for that person to fit back into home life.

Section 2.2

Mourning the Death of a Spouse

Text in this section is excerpted from "Mourning the Death of a Spouse," National Institute on Aging (NIA), March 2013.

When your spouse dies, your world changes. You are in mourning—feeling grief and sorrow at the loss. You may feel numb, shocked, and fearful. You may feel guilty for being the one who is still alive. If your spouse died in a nursing home, you may wish that you had been able to care for him or her at home. At some point, you may even feel angry at your spouse for leaving you. All these feelings are normal. There are no rules about how you should feel. There is no right or wrong way to mourn.

When you grieve, you can feel both physical and emotional pain. People who are grieving often cry easily and can have:

- Trouble sleeping

- Little interest in food

- Problems with concentration

- A hard time making decisions

If you are grieving, in addition to dealing with feelings of loss, you may also need to put your own life back together. This can be hard work. Some people may feel better sooner than they expect. Others may take longer. As time passes, you may still miss your spouse, but for most people, the intense pain will lessen. There will be good and bad days. You will know that you are feeling better when the good days begin to outnumber the bad.

For some people, mourning can go on so long that it becomes unhealthy. This can be a sign of serious depression and anxiety. If sadness keeps you from carrying on with your day-to-day life, talk to your doctor.

What Can You Do?

In the beginning, you may find that taking care of details and keeping busy helps. For a while, family and friends may be around to assist

11

you. But, there comes a time when you will have to face the change in your life.

Here are some ideas to keep in mind:

- **Take care of yourself.** Grief can be hard on your health. Try to eat right, make exercise a part of your daily routine, take your medicine, and get enough sleep. Bad habits, such as drinking too much alcohol or smoking, can put your health at risk. Keep up with your usual visits to your healthcare provider.

- **Talk to caring friends.** Let family and friends know when you want to talk about your husband or wife. It may help to be with people who let you say what you're feeling.

- **Join a grief support group.** Sometimes it helps to talk to people who are also grieving. Check with hospitals, religious communities, and local agencies to find out about support groups.

- **Try not to make any major changes right away.** It's a good idea to wait for a while before making big decisions like moving or changing jobs.

- **See your doctor.** If you're having trouble taking care of your everyday activities, like getting dressed or fixing meals, talk to your healthcare provider.

- **Don't be afraid to seek professional help.** Sometimes short-term talk therapy with a counselor can help.

- **Remember your children are grieving, too.** You may find that your relationship with your children has changed. It will take time for the whole family to adjust to life without your spouse.

- **Mourning takes time.** It's common to have rollercoaster emotions for a while.

Do Men and Women Feel the Same Way?

Andrew, age 73, felt like the wind had been knocked out of him when his wife died. He began sleeping all day and staying up at night watching TV. Meals were mostly snacks like cookies and chips. He knew it wasn't healthy, but he didn't know what to do. Across town, Alice woke up in a panic. It had been 5 weeks since Jeff, her husband of 41 years, died. She cared for him during his long illness. How was she going to cope with the loneliness?

12

Men and women share many of the same feelings when their spouse dies. Both may deal with the pain of loss, and both may worry about the future. But, there can also be differences. Often, married couples divide up their household tasks. One person may pay bills and handle car repairs. The other person may cook meals and mow the lawn. Splitting up jobs often works well until there is only one person who has to do it all. Learning to manage new tasks, from chores to household repairs to finances, takes time, but it can be done.

Being alone can increase concerns about safety. It's a good idea to make sure there are working locks on the doors and windows. If you need help, ask your family or friends.

Facing the future without a husband or wife can be scary. Many people have never lived alone. Those who are both widowed and retired may feel very lonely and become depressed. Talk to your doctor about how you are feeling.

Taking Charge of Your Life

After years of being part of a couple, it can be upsetting to be alone. Many people find it helps to have things to do every day. Write down your weekly plans. You might:

- Take a walk with a friend.
- Go to the library to check out books.
- Volunteer at a local school as a tutor or playground aide.
- Join a community exercise class or a senior swim group.
- Join a singing group.
- Sign up for bingo or bridge at a nearby recreation center.
- Think about a part-time job.
- Join a bowling league.
- Offer to babysit.
- Consider adopting a pet.
- Take a class from the recreation center or local college.
- Learn a new skill.

Some widowed people lose interest in cooking and eating. It may help to have lunch with friends at a senior center or cafeteria. Sometimes eating at home alone feels too quiet. Turning on a radio or TV during meals can help. For information on nutrition and cooking for one, look for helpful books at your local library or bookstore.

Is There More to Do?

When you feel stronger, you should think about:

- Writing a new will
- Looking into a durable power of attorney for legal matters and a power of attorney for health care in case you are unable to make your own medical decisions
- Putting joint property (such as a house or car) in your name
- Checking on your health insurance as well as your current life, car, and homeowner's insurance
- Signing up for Medicare by your 65th birthday
- Making a list of bills you will need to pay in the next few months; for instance, State and Federal taxes, rent, or mortgage

When you are ready, go through your spouse's clothes and other personal items. It may be hard to give away these belongings. Instead of parting with everything at once, you might make three piles: one to keep, one to give away, and one "not sure." Ask your children or others to help. Think about setting aside items like a special piece of clothing, watch, favorite book, or picture to give to your children or grandchildren as personal reminders of your spouse.

What about Going Out?

Lillian felt lost. Widowed at age 71, she went out with the same couples that she and her husband, Ray, had always liked. But, without Ray, she felt out of place. How could she enjoy going out when she felt like a fifth-wheel?

Having a social life can be tough. It may be hard to think about going to parties alone. It can be hard to think about coming home alone. You may be anxious about dating. Many people miss the feeling of closeness that marriage brings. After time, some are ready to have a social life again.

Here are some things to remember:

- Go slowly. There's no rush.
- It's okay to make the first move when it comes to planning things to do.

14

- Try group activities. Invite friends for a potluck dinner or go to a senior center.

- With married friends, think about informal outings like walks or picnics rather than couples events that remind you of the past.

- Find an activity you like. You may have fun and meet people who like to do the same thing.

- Many people find that pets provide important companionship.

- You can develop meaningful relationships with friends and family members of all ages.

Don't Forget

Take care of yourself. Get help from your family or professionals if you need it. Be open to new experiences. Don't feel guilty if you laugh at a joke or enjoy a visit with a friend. You are adjusting to life without your spouse.

Chapter 3

Stress in Children and Teens

Some people believe that babies and young children are not affected by events that take place when they are very young, but what we do in the first three years has a tremendous impact on children's future development.

Understanding of the Developing Brain

Recent research and technological advances have changed our understanding of the developing brain. With this new information, parents and educators have the opportunity to provide children with interactions and settings that will allow them to reach their greatest potential. We now have a greater appreciation for the fact that the early years are a very fertile period in the child's life. We need to make conscious choices about how we treat children so that impact can be positive.

Research has demonstrated that there is an interaction between one's genetic endowment (nature) and the environment (nurture). Structural, hormonal, and chemical influences that are present during pregnancy affect the growth and development of the fetus. As early as three weeks after conception, a baby's brain cells begin to form. These nerve cells then migrate to sections of the brain that will eventually control the reflexes, voluntary body movement, perception, language

---

This chapter includes excerpts from "Stress and the Developing Brain," Office of the Administration for Children and Families Early Childhood Learning & Knowledge Center (ECLKC), May 29, 2015; and text from "Feeling stressed," Office on Women's Health (OWH), January 7, 2015."

and thought. These structural changes–the cellular linkages being made–are unique to each individual infant. The linkages form as a result of the infant's experiences, both in the womb and once they are born.

Far-Reaching Harmful Effects of Stress

Medical science continues to demonstrate the far-reaching harmful effects of stress. Stress is defined as an emotional reaction that elevates cognitive and physiological activity levels. It places demands upon the system for physical or cognitive productivity. When those demands are activated over a period of time, it progresses to a series of changes leading to exhaustion.

The degree of stress experienced by a woman while she is pregnant can have a negative affect on the fetus. When maternal hormones, such as corticosterone and tryptophan, become overstimulated due to her own stressful conditions, there is a harmful chemical effect on the fetus' brain development.

The adult "fight or flight" response to stress is not an option for an infant or young child. Exposure to intense anger, loud screaming, or physical violence creates fear within the child that floods the brain with stress hormones. Being left alone and crying when hungry or wet are also conditions that create fear and stress in a young child. Various types of unpredictable, traumatic, chaotic, or neglectful environments physically change the brain by over-activating the neural pathways. As a result, there may be an increase in the child's muscle tone, profound sleep difficulties, an increased startle response, and significant anxiety. These responses, in turn, can lead to a permanent state of high alert, a tendency to misperceive the intentions and behavior of others, and the tendency to react with aggression.

Conscious memories of the first years of life are lost but the emotional part of the brain, referred to as the limbic system, and the body remember. An infant's first sense of what the world is like is recorded in the body. Without intervention, young children who have experienced high levels of stress will be at serious risk for emotional, behavioral, and learning difficulties.

Early Learning

Neuroscientist Dr. James LeDoux (1993) agrees that events early in life, experienced with strong emotions, can and do remain an influence throughout our lives. He suggests that what we feel is processed before what we think. Feelings experienced precognitively and preverbally continue to play out in later life even though the individual may have no conscious memory of the association. A significant trauma that takes place often or intensely enough can rob a child of the ability to learn normally by pulling away brain circuitry meant for other tasks.

An area of the brain, referred to as the amygdala, is central in understanding how stress affects learning. The amygdala governs attention, memory, planning, and behavior–all skills necessary for the child to be able to take in and process information. Difficulties in attention often include distractibility and impulsivity, which impair problem solving. In social situations, children who are overly active, impulsive, and unable to focus tend to have trouble reading others' social cues and responding appropriately to others in the environment.

Role of Relationships

Research links the external environmental influences on brain development with the quality of stimulation and degree to which the caregiver is attuned to the needs of the infant. Social interaction with an empathetic and attuned caregiver plays the major role in the growth and regulation of the child's nervous system and in helping the child develop the strength needed to become socially competent and able to learn. The consistent experience of empathy that takes place with an emotionally available caregiver gradually builds the child's capacity to empathize with others.

Relationships that a child experiences provide the foundations for approaches to learning, which, hopefully, will be enthusiastic, curious, and persistent. Stanley Greenspan (1997), a noted child psychiatrist, explains that the capacity to feel a full range of emotions–learned through relationships–allows children to organize events and ideas before they have the words to express them. Children learn how to think by creating ideas based on their experiences and how it feels to engage in those experiences. For example, young children become more focused and interactive through being able to enjoy the excitement of reciprocal play. The playful and creative give and take with an emotionally present, verbal adult motivates the development of language and encourages the child toward discriminating, generalizing, categorizing, and organizing her experiences. This is the basis for the ability to think first concretely and then abstractly.

The Abecedarian Project at the University of Alabama found that when at-risk young children were exposed to a stimulating environment, appropriate toys, playmates, and good nutrition, they developed less mental retardation than the control group. Early intervention in infancy, when the neurological circuits for learning are being formed, resulted in higher IQs in comparison to the control group. The conclusion was that early enrollment in a high quality, enriched day care setting is paramount to the children's significant and long-lasting improvements.

Feeling Stressed

Schoolwork, chores, dating dramas, fights with friends, and more— so many things can stress you out! But what exactly is stress, and how can you handle it? Keep reading to learn more.

What is stress?

Stress is what you feel when you react to pressure. The pressure can come from events in your life, from other people, or even from yourself. Things that cause stress are called stressors.

What are ways to handle stress?

Put your body in motion

Physical activity is a great way to beat stress. It can clear your head and lift your spirits. Physical activity increases endorphins, which are natural "feel-good" chemicals in the body. You may like games of football, tennis, or basketball, or you may prefer walks with family and friends. Whatever you choose, get up, get out, and get moving!

Fuel up

When you take a car for a long drive, you fill up the gas tank first. You also need to fuel your body each day.

Balanced nutrition gives you the energy you need to handle hectic days. Don't be fooled by the jolt of energy you get from sodas and sugary snacks. The boost is short, and when it wears off, you may feel even more tired. Start the day with a healthy breakfast. If you don't feel like eating when you wake up, grab a healthy snack like a banana, string cheese, or nuts so you can fuel up on the go.

LOL!

Laughter may not be the best medicine, but it sure can help. Lots of laughing can help your body make natural "feel-good" chemicals called endorphins. And the good feeling can last after the giggling stops. So, beat stress with a funny movie, cartoons, or jokes.

We all do things we think are pretty silly or stupid at times. When you do, try not to get mad at yourself. Instead, see if you can find the funny in what you did.

Have fun with friends

Being with people you like is a good way to ditch your stress. Get a group together to watch a movie, shoot some hoops, listen to music — or just hang out and talk. Friends can help you remember the brighter side of life.

Spill to someone you trust

Instead of keeping your feelings bottled up, talk to someone you trust about what's bothering you. It could be a friend, a parent, a teacher, or a friend's parent. The person may have some great advice or a different way to look at things. Plus, just getting support can feel good. Remember, you don't have to handle stress alone!

Take time to chill

Pick a comfy spot to sit and read, daydream, or take a nap. Listen to your favorite music. Work on a relaxing project like doing a puzzle or making jewelry.

Stress can sometimes make you feel like a rubber band pulled tight. If this happens, take a few deep breaths. If you're in the middle of an impossible homework problem, take a break! Taking time to relax after (and sometimes during) a hectic day can make a big difference.

Catch some sleep

Being stressed out can affect your sleep, which can make you feel cranky or fuzzy-headed. Being tired can mess up schoolwork, sports, friendships, and more. All that can add to your stress!

Sleep is a big deal for teens. Because your body and mind are changing, you need more sleep to recharge for the next day. Most teens should aim for a little more than 9 hours of sleep each night.

Keep a journal

Having a hard day? You can write about what's going on and how you feel. Writing is a great way to get things off your chest. You also can write a plan for how to handle problems and responsibilities. Then, you might go back and reread what you wrote a couple of weeks later to see how you got through a tough time. You can create your own journal.

Get it together

Feeling overwhelmed or forgetful? Being unprepared for school, practice, or other activities can make for a very stressful day. Having a plan and getting organized can really help. You can learn ways to manage your time well.

Lend a hand

Helping someone can help you feel capable and strong. And it can remind you that everyone faces some kind of challenge at some point. Helping others also is a great way to find out about talents you never knew you had!

You can help in simple ways, like smiling at someone who looks sad or helping an older neighbor with packages. If you want to join a volunteer group, try contacting a local recreation center or after-school program.

Learn ways to better deal with anger

It is totally normal to be angry sometimes. And as a teen, the changing hormones in your body may make you feel mad for what seems like no good reason. The important thing is to deal with your anger in a healthy way. If you do, you'll feel calmer, and your relationships can be a lot less stressful.

When your anger starts to boil, try to cool down with some deep breaths. Try to think about what exactly upset you and some possible solutions to the problem.

What causes stress?

Different people are stressed by different things. For example, you might get very stressed about a test, but your friend might feel fine. Your sister might think moving is terrifying, but you may think it's exciting. There are no right or wrong things to stress over.

Some things that might cause stress include:
- Schoolwork
- Changes in your body or weight

- Problems with friends or other relationships
- Being bullied
- Living in a dangerous neighborhood
- Peer pressure to dress or act a certain way, or to smoke, drink, or use drugs
- Feeling like you don't fit in
- Desire to please your parents or other important adults
- Sick family member
- Changing schools
- Conflict at home
- Taking on too many activities at once

Of course, other things may cause stress for you that are not listed above. Even fun things, like starring in the school play or starting to date, can get you stressed.

Some things that cause stress are the same things that cause grief. These include things like your parents getting divorced or the death of someone you love.

Sometimes, people have a lot of stress because of money worries. If your family is having money problems, you can look together at a website about ways to cope during tough financial times.

Is stress always bad?

A little bit of stress can help you. During a sports competition, stress might push you to perform better, for example. Also, the stress of deadlines can get you to finish work on time.

A lot of stress or stress that lasts a long time can hurt you. It can cause problems for your physical and emotional health, like stomach aches, sleep problems, and trouble concentrating.

If your stress is getting to be too much, take steps to tackle it. Check out our tips on how to handle stress. Also, turn to a parent or another adult you trust for advice and support.

Don't try to lower your stress in unhealthy ways. Things like taking drugs, drinking, cutting back on your sleep, or eating a lot or very little will only cause more problems. Treat yourself with the respect you deserve.

In a recent survey, 1 out of 3 teens said their stress went up during the past year. 1 out of 10 teens said they never set aside time to manage stress. And during the school year, teens report more stress than adults.

What are signs of being stressed out?

Sometimes, stress just comes and goes. But if you are facing a lot of pressure or problems, you may start to feel like you're often too stressed out.

Signs that you are getting too stressed may include:

- Feeling down or tired
- Feeling angry or edgy
- Feeling sad or worried
- Having trouble concentrating
- Having headaches or stomach aches
- Having trouble sleeping
- Laughing or crying for no reason
- Wanting to be alone a lot
- Having tense muscles
- Not being able to see the positive side of a situation
- Not enjoying activities that you used to enjoy
- Feeling like you have too many things you have to do

Some of these signs can also be signs of depression, which needs treatment.

How does my body act when stressed?

Your body has a built-in response to stressors. Your palms may sweat, your mouth may get dry, and your stomach may twist. This is all normal! Of course, stress doesn't feel very good. When your body is hit by stress, try to calm it down. Taking some deep breaths can help. You also can try yoga, going for a walk, or some other physical activity.

Can stress lead to more serious problems?

Stress that's too much for you to handle may play a role in some serious problems. These problems include eating disorders, hurting yourself, depression, anxiety disorders, alcohol and drug abuse, smoking, and even suicide. If you are facing any of these problems, talk to an adult you trust right away!

Chapter 4

Stress and Aging

Have you ever looked at side-by-side photos of a person before and after a particularly trying time in his or her life, for instance, before and a few years after starting a highly demanding job? The person likely appears much older in the later photo. The stress of the job is thought to contribute to the prematurely aged appearance. You might feel stress from work or other aspects of your daily life, too. Stress is everywhere. Even when you feel relaxed, your body is still experiencing considerable stress—biological stress. And, it is this type of stress that is widely studied by gerontologists for its effects on aging and longevity.

Biological stress begins with the very basic processes in the body that produce and use energy. We eat foods and we breathe, and our body uses those two vital elements (glucose from food and oxygen from the air) to produce energy, in a process known as metabolism. You may already think of metabolism as it pertains to eating—"My metabolism is fast, so I can eat dessert," or "My metabolism has slowed down over the years, so I'm gaining weight." Since metabolism is all about energy, it also encompasses breathing, circulating blood, eliminating waste, controlling body temperature, contracting muscles, operating the brain and nerves, and just about every other activity associated with living.

This chapter includes excerpts from "METABOLISM: Does stress really shorten your life?," National Institute on Aging (NIA), January 22, 2015; and text from "Forgetfulness: Knowing When to Ask for Help," National Institute on Aging (NIA), May 2015."

These everyday metabolic activities that sustain life also create "metabolic stress," which, over time, results in damage to our bodies. Take breathing—obviously, we could not survive without oxygen, but oxygen is a catalyst for much of the damage associated with aging because of the way it is metabolized inside our cells. Tiny parts of the cell, called mitochondria, use oxygen to convert food into energy. While mitochondria are extremely efficient in doing this, they produce potentially harmful by-products called oxygen free radicals.

A variety of environmental factors, including tobacco smoke and sun exposure, can produce them, too. The oxygen free radicals react with and create instability in surrounding molecules. This process, called oxidation, occurs as a chain reaction: the oxygen free radical reacts with molecule "A" causing molecule "A" to become unstable; molecule "A" attempts to stabilize itself by reacting with neighboring molecule "B"; then molecule "B" is unstable and attempts to become stable by reacting with neighboring molecule "C"; and so on. This process repeats itself until one of the molecules becomes stable by breaking or rearranging itself, instead of passing the instability on to another molecule.

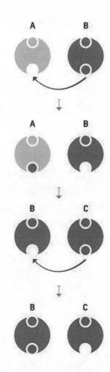

Figure 4.1. _Free Radicals: Oxidation Chain Reaction_

Some free radicals are beneficial. The immune system, for instance, uses oxygen free radicals to destroy bacteria and other harmful organisms. Oxidation and its by-products also help nerve cells in the brain communicate. But, in general, the outcome of free radicals is damage (breaks or rearrangements) to other molecules, including proteins and DNA. Because mitochondria metabolize oxygen, they are particularly prone to free radical damage. As damage mounts, mitochondria may become less efficient, progressively generating less energy and more free radicals.

Scientists study whether the accumulation of oxidative (free radical) damage in our cells and tissues over time might be responsible for many of the changes we associate with aging. Free radicals are already implicated in many disorders linked with advancing age, including cancer, atherosclerosis, cataracts, and neurodegeneration.

Fortunately, free radicals in the body do not go unchecked. Cells use substances called antioxidants to counteract them. Antioxidants include nutrients, such as vitamins C and E, as well as enzyme proteins produced naturally in the cell, such as superoxide dismutase (SOD), catalase, and glutathione peroxidase.

Many scientists are taking the idea that antioxidants counter the negative effects of oxygen free radicals a step further. Studies have tested whether altering the antioxidant defenses of the cell can affect the lifespan of animal models. These experiments have had conflicting results. NIA-supported researchers found that inserting extra copies of the SOD gene into fruit flies extended the fruit flies' average lifespan by as much as 30 percent. Other researchers found that immersing roundworms in a synthetic form of SOD and catalase extended their lifespan by 44 percent. However, in a comprehensive set of experiments, increasing or decreasing antioxidant enzymes in laboratory mice had no effect on lifespan. Results from a limited number of human clinical trials involving antioxidants generally have not supported the premise that adding antioxidants to the diet will support longer life. Antioxidant supplementation remains a topic of continuing investigation.

Heat Shock Proteins

In the early 1960s, scientists discovered that fruit flies exposed to a burst of heat produced proteins that helped their cells survive the temperature change. Over the years, scientists have found these "heat shock proteins" in virtually every living organism, including plants, bacteria, worms, mice, and even humans. Scientists have learned

29

that, despite their name, heat shock proteins are produced when cells are exposed to a variety of stresses, not just heat. The proteins can be triggered by oxidative stress and by exposure to toxic substances (for example, some chemicals). When heat shock proteins are produced, they help cells dismantle and dispose of damaged proteins and help other proteins keep their structure and not become unraveled by stress. They also facilitate making and transporting new proteins in the body.

Heat shock response to stress changes with age. Older animals have a higher everyday level of heat shock proteins, indicating that their bodies are under more biological stress than younger animals. On the other hand, older animals are unable to produce an adequate amount of heat shock proteins to cope with fleeting bouts of stress from the environment.

Heat shock proteins are being considered as a possible aging biomarker—something that could predict lifespan or development of age-related problems—in animal models like worms and fruit flies. However, the exact role heat shock proteins play in the human aging process is not yet clear.

The Future of Aging Research: Stress

The first C. elegans worm genetically manipulated to have a longer lifespan was resistant to stress caused by heat. Subsequently, researchers learned that a common thread among all long-lived animals is that their cells (and in some cases the animals as a whole) are more resistant to a variety of stresses, compared to animals with an average or shorter lifespan.

Scientists also found that age-related damage to DNA and proteins is often reversible and does not cause problems until the damage evokes a stress response. This suggests that the stress response, rather than the damage itself, is partially responsible for age-related deterioration.

Some biologists have started looking at stress resistance when choosing animal models to study as examples of successful aging. Researchers can test stress resistance in young animals and then continue studying only those animals demonstrating high resistance. Ongoing studies will determine if there is a direct cause-effect relationship between stress resistance and longevity, and if these longer-lived animals are resistant to all or only certain sources of stress.

In addition, researchers are studying the relationship between psychological stress and aging. In one study, mothers of severely and chronically sick children had shorter telomeres, relative to other women. In other research, caregivers of people with Alzheimer's disease were found to have shortened telomeres. These findings could suggest that emotional or psychological stress might affect the aging process. More research on the mechanisms involved is needed before scientists can make any conclusions about clinical implications.

Keeping Your Memory Sharp

People with some forgetfulness can use a variety of techniques that may help them stay healthy and maintain their memory and mental skills. Here are some tips:

- Plan tasks, make "to do" lists, and use memory aids like notes and calendars. Some people find they remember things better if they mentally connect them to other meaningful things, such as a familiar name, song, book, or TV show.
- Develop interests or hobbies and stay involved in activities that can help both the mind and body.
- Engage in physical activity and exercise. Several studies have associated exercise (such as walking) with better brain function, although more research is needed to say for sure whether exercise can help to maintain brain function or prevent or delay symptoms of Alzheimer's.
- Limit alcohol use. Although some studies suggest that moderate alcohol use has health benefits, heavy or binge drinking over time can cause memory loss and permanent brain damage.

Find activities, such as exercise or a hobby, to relieve feelings of stress, anxiety, or depression. If these feelings last for a long time, talk with your doctor.

Chapter 5

Factors That Influence Response to Stress

Chapter Contents

Section 5.1

Stress Response and How It Can Affect You

Text in this section is excerpted from "The Stress Response and How it Can Affect You," U.S. Department of Veterans Affairs (VA), July 2013.

Stress Response

The *stress response*, or "fight or flight" response, is the emergency reaction system of the body. It is there to keep you safe in emergencies. The stress response includes physical and thought responses to your perception of various situations. When the stress response is turned on, your body may release substances like adrenaline and cortisol. Your organs are programmed to respond in certain ways to situations that are viewed as challenging or threatening.

The stress response can work against you. You can turn it on when you don't really need it and, as a result, perceive something as an emergency when it's really not. It can turn on when you are just thinking about past or future events. Harmless, chronic conditions can be intensified by the stress response activating too often, with too much intensity, or for too long. Stress responses can be different for different individuals. Below is a list of some common stress related responses people have.

Physical Responses

- Muscle Aches
- ↑ Heart rate
- Weight Gain
- Constipation
- Muscle Twitching
- Low Energy
- Tight Chest

- Dizziness
- Stomach Cramps
- Insomnia
- Headache
- Nausea
- Dry Mouth
- Weight Loss

- Weakness
- Diarrhea
- Trembling
- Chills
- Sweating
- Choking Feeling
- Leg Cramps
- Hot Flashes
- Pounding Heart
- Chest Pain
- Numb or Tingling Hands/ Feet
- ↑ Blood Pressure
- Dry Throat
- Face Flushing
- Feeling Faint
- Neck Pain
- ↑ Urination
- Light Headedness

Emotional and Thought Responses

- Restlessness
- Agitation
- Worthlessness
- Depression
- Guilt
- Anger
- Nightmares
- Sensitivity
- Numbness
- Mood Swings
- Low Concentration
- Preoccupation
- Insecurity
- Anxiety
- Depression
- Hopelessness
- Defensiveness
- Racing Thoughts
- Intense Thinking
- Expecting the Worst
- Lack of Motivation
- Forgetfulness
- Rigidity
- Intolerance

Behavioral Responses

- Avoidance
- Neglect
- ↑ Smoking
- Poor Appearance
- ↑ Spending
- ↓ Eating
- Nail Biting
- ↑ Talking

3

- Sexual Problems
- Fidgeting
- ↓ Exercise
- Aggressive Speaking
- ↑ Sleeping
- ↓ Relaxing Activities
- Withdrawal
- ↑ Alcohol Use
- ↑ Eating
- Arguing

- Poor Hygiene
- Seeking Reassurance
- Skin Picking
- ↑ Body Checking
- Foot Tapping
- Rapid Walking
- Teeth Clenching
- Multitasking
- ↓ Fun Activities

The parasympathetic nervous system in your body is designed to turn on your body's *relaxation response.* Your behaviors and thinking can keep your body's natural relaxation response from operating at its best.

Getting your body to relax on a daily basis for at least brief periods can help decrease unpleasant stress responses. Learning to relax your body, through specific breathing and relaxation exercises as well as by minimizing stressful thinking, can help your body's natural relaxation system be more effective. Your Behavioral Health Provider can assist you with learning relaxation techniques.

Section 5.2

Personality and Stress

"Personality and Stress," © 2015 Omnigraphics, Inc.
Reviewed September 2015.

The stress response, sometimes known as the "fight-or-flight" response, mobilizes the body's reserves to overcome a perceived threat. It evolved to protect people from danger and is considered essential to survival. When confronted with a stressful situation, the body increases its production of the chemicals cortisol, adrenaline, and noradrenaline. These chemicals trigger a faster heart rate, rapid breathing, muscle tension, and alertness. At the same time, the chemicals slow down nonessential body functions, such as the digestive and immune systems.

Stress can broadly be classified as physiological or psychological. Physiological stress refers to the adaptive mechanisms the body uses to respond to physical challenges, such as a broken bone or exposure to extreme cold. Psychological stress, on the other hand, refers to a disparity between an external stressor and the person's mental, emotional, or social resources. Examples might include feelings of anxiety about an upcoming test or worry about meeting a work deadline.

Even though the sources of psychological stress may not be life threatening, the body responds to them in much the same way as it responds to physiological stressors. These responses, while designed to protect the body, can actually have harmful effects on both physical and mental health when they recur frequently over prolonged periods of time. Chronic stress has been linked to a multitude of health conditions, including depression, digestive problems, fatigue, headaches, heart disease, high blood pressure, insomnia, muscle aches, and obesity.

Personality Types

The response to stress is a complex and highly personalized mechanism involving many interrelated biological, psychological, and social factors. Studies have shown that an individual's personality—as determined by inherited characteristics, life experiences, and cognitive predispositions—strongly influences how they interpret and deal with stressful situations. People who demonstrate certain personality traits, such as resilience and adaptability, tend to respond better to adversity and be less susceptible to stress.

Researchers have developed the Five Factor Model as a way to classify different personality types. The "Big Five" personality characteristics in this model include:

- Openness to new experiences, as opposed to closed-mindedness

- Conscientiousness, as opposed to disorganization

- Extraversion, as opposed to introversion

- Agreeableness, as opposed to disagreeableness

- Neuroticism, as opposed to emotional stability

Although age, gender, intellect, and other factors can influence a person's sensitivity to stressors, studies have shown that personality type is an important factor in determining an individual's reaction to stress. In fact, personality traits can help explain how some people can handle huge amounts of stress for long periods of time, while others may feel overwhelmed when faced with small amounts of stress on a temporary basis.

An individual's personality influences every stage of the stress response, from evaluating whether or not a situation is stressful to choosing coping methods. In general, individuals with strong scores in extraversion tend to be optimistic and develop good problem-solving and coping strategies. They can reappraise potentially stressful situations in a positive way—for instance, as a challenge and an opportunity for growth and personal development—and effectively seek social support to help them deal with the stressor. On the other hand, individuals with strong scores in neuroticism tend to be pessimistic. They can become overwhelmed by potentially stressful situations, which can take a toll on their life satisfaction and physical health.

Type A and Type B Behavior

The theory of Type A behavior was developed in the 1950s by American cardiologist Meyer Friedman, who noticed a link between a certain personality type and the risk of heart disease. His 1974 book on the theory opened up a new field of research that looked beyond the well-known risk factors of diet and cholesterol and examined the mind-body connection to heart disease. The term "Type A personality" soon became a national buzzword to refer to high-stress personalities who tended to be driven, impatient, and competitive. This personality type was considered to be in opposition to Type B personalities, who tended to be calm, steady, relaxed, and less vulnerable to stress.

Type A personalities are believed to have an overactive sympathetic nervous system pathway. This pathway is responsible for stimulating the "fight-or-flight" response, which is associated with increased secretions of the emergency hormones that elevate the heart and respiratory rates and may contribute to hypertension and heart disease. In Type B personalities, the parasympathetic nervous system pathway is dominant. This pathway is associated with a lower metabolic rate and the release of "feel-good" neurotransmitters like endorphin, melatonin, and serotonin.

Critics argue, however, that human behaviour is too complex to be categorized within the narrow parameters outlined by Friedman.

Modern-day psychologists generally refrain from drawing a clear distinction between the two extreme personality types, preferring to regard them as points on a continuum. In addition, some psychologists argue that personality and experiences do not necessarily condition people to respond to stress in a certain way. Instead, they claim that people can learn to manage stress effectively through training programs that help them build self-confidence, develop problem-solving skills, and face the everyday challenges of life in a more positive manner.

Reference:

McLeod, Saul. "Type A Personality." *Simply Psychology,* 2011.

Section 5.3

Gender Differences in Stress Response

"Gender Differences in Stress Response," © 2015 Omnigraphics, Inc. Reviewed September 2015.

It has long been recognized that men and women react differently to stress. Researchers have noted, for example, that women have a higher incidence of stress-related illnesses like post-traumatic stress disorder (PTSD), depression, and anxiety than men. Studies on gender differences in stress response have also shown that the classic, action-oriented "fight-or-flight" response is more typical of men, whereas women are more likely to exhibit a socially oriented "tend-and-befriend" response.

Scientists believe that such differences may have a biological basis. A 2010 study on the brains of rats—which have the same basic neural structure as those of humans—found that females were more sensitive to a certain stress hormone than males, and also less able to adapt to high levels of it. In addition, a 2012 study on humans found that men's and women's brains processed stress differently and suggested that a single gene may be responsible for this gender variation.

Gender Differences in the Brain's Response to Stress

The 2010 study focused on corticotropin releasing factor (CRF), a hormone released by the hypothalamus region of the brain in response to stress. CRF acts as a neurotransmitter, helping to carry signals between brain cells. In response to a stressor, CRF binds to receptors on cells in the locus ceruleus, a cluster of neurons in the brainstem. The CRF signals the neurons to secrete norepinephrine and cortisol, the main hormones responsible for mobilizing the body's energy reserves and producing the fight-or-flight stress response.

In the presence of these hormones, the nervous system goes into a state of hyperarousal, which is characterized by a faster heart rate, rapid breathing, muscle tension, and alertness. Although hyperarousal is a natural part of the body's stress response, research has shown that long-term and excessive activation of the CRF receptors can lead to stress-related disorders, such as anxiety and PTSD.

In the study of rats, scientists observed that the stress signalling system was more responsive in females than in males, so the receptors in the female brains bound more tightly to CRF. Moreover, the CRF receptors remained activated much longer in response to stress in the female brains, thereby prolonging their exposure to CRF. The male brains, on the other hand, quickly adapted to the higher levels of stress hormones by reducing the number of receptors through a process called internalization, thus limiting their exposure to CRF.

Researchers believe that these gender differences in the stress response may help explain why women have a higher incidence of stress-related mood and anxiety disorders than men. Although the biological mechanism may be different in humans than in animals, the possibility that gender may influence CRF exposure has clinical and therapeutic implications for many psychiatric disorders.

Gender Differences in the Behavioral Response to Stress

In the twenty-first century, many psychologists have begun to question the longstanding belief that humans universally exhibit the fight-or-flight response to stress. A growing number have argued that while this response is common for men, women are more likely to exhibit a tend-and-befriend response. Instead of preparing to fight back or run away when faced with danger, many women demonstrate affiliative social behavior—either by seeking social support to deal with the situation or by trying to defuse the situation through relationship-building.

Research has found that in addition to releasing stress hormones like norepinephrine, women's brains respond to stress by secreting endorphins—so-called "feel-good" chemicals that help alleviate pain and create positive emotions about social interactions. Scientists have theorized that this chemical response may have evolved out of women's historic role in nurturing offspring and affiliating with social groups in times of adversity.

The 2012 study suggested that this gender difference might be connected to the SRY gene, which men carry on the Y chromosome. The SRY gene produces proteins that regulate the secretion of norepinephrine and other hormones involved in the fight-or-flight response to stress. Since women do not have the SRY gene, their responses to stress are regulated by other genes. Although all of the biological mechanisms involved are not fully understood, recognizing that gender plays a role in the response to stress can help people develop positive coping strategies.

References:

1. Goldstein, Jill M., et al. "Sex Differences in Stress Response Circuitry Activation Dependent on Female Hormonal Cycle." Journal of Neuroscience 30(2), January 13, 2010.

2. Maestripieri, Dario. "Gender Differences in Responses to Stress: It Boils Down to a Single Gene." Psychology Today, March 17, 2012.

3. National Institutes of Health. "Stress Hormone Receptors Less Adaptive in Female Brain." Science News, August 9, 2010.

4. "Study: Why Women Are More Sensitive to Stress." Live Science, June 18, 2010.

Section 5.4

Chronic Stress and Loneliness Affect Health

Since human beings are a social species, forming and maintaining satisfying social relationships is vital to their physical and mental well-being. The lack of such relationships can lead to loneliness, which is a much more complex psychiatric condition than simply "being alone." Studies have shown that chronic loneliness can take a toll on an individual's physical and mental health, compromising the immune system, impairing cognitive performance, and increasing the risk of depression, heart disease, and other conditions. In fact, research suggests that people who experience chronic loneliness have a 45 percent higher risk of early death, while those with strong social connections have a 50 percent lower risk of dying over any given period of time.

Loneliness and Stress

Everyone feels lonely at some point in their lives. Some psychologists claim that people first experience loneliness in infancy, when they are left alone by their parents. Transient loneliness, which is caused by environmental factors like moving to a new city, starting at a new school, or ending a romantic relationship, is a temporary situation that is generally relieved over time. Chronic loneliness, on the other hand, can occur independently of environmental factors and persist over long periods of time. This type of loneliness can affect people even in the absence of social isolation.

Loneliness and stress are closely related, with each condition often contributing to the other. Loneliness can be a significant stressor. Since social relationships are fundamental to human existence, a strain or break in social relationships can rank among the most stressful experiences in life. In addition, healthy and varied social relationships serve as a protective mechanism that increases stress resistance, as people rely on the comforting support of family and friends to help them cope with stressful situations.

As a result of these factors, lonely people experience higher levels of perceived stress as compared to non-lonely people when exposed to the same types of stressors. People who lack social connections tend to react more strongly to the stressors of daily life, which may lead to the development of chronic stress and all of the health problems associated with it.

Health Consequences of Loneliness

Studies have shown that loneliness initiates a series of physiological processes that can negatively affect people's health and well-being. Overwhelming and consistent feelings of loneliness often result in low self-worth, depression, anxiety, irritability, and suicidal behavior.

Loneliness can also contribute to the development of such conditions as insomnia, obesity, and substance abuse.

By stimulating the stress response, long-term, persistent loneliness can also lead to a variety of stress-related health issues, including hypertension, cardiovascular disease, and immune system dysfunction. Studies have also shown that loneliness is one of the major causes of motor decline in old age. Elderly people who are lonely are also more likely to experience memory loss and cognitive decline, leading to an increased risk of developing clinical dementia and Alzheimer's disease.

Managing Loneliness

Many aspects of modern life—such as technology replacing face-to-face interaction—leave people feeling disconnected, which has made loneliness a growing public health concern. On the plus side, though, loneliness is a treatable condition. Experts have developed methods of behavioral training to help lonely people improve their capacity to socialize. They have also come up with strategies to help people control their expectations and view their situations differently, so that they no longer perceive being alone as stressful.

One of the first steps in managing loneliness involves improving social skills to help people maintain existing relationships or form new ones. For people who experience loneliness due to changing circumstances, such as the loss of a loved one, treatment might include various means of enhancing social support. Individuals can take steps to relieve their own feelings of loneliness by engaging in activities to keep busy, joining groups that share a common interest, volunteering to help others, and sharing feelings or discussing problems with other people.

References:

1. Derbyshire, David. "Loneliness Is a Killer." *Daily Mail,* July 28, 2010.

2. Tiwari, Sarvada Chandra. "Loneliness: A Disease?" *Indian Journal of Psychiatry* 55(4), October-December 2013, p. 320.

Section 5.5

Media Coverage Linked to Stress

Text in this section is excerpted from "Media Coverage of Traumatic
Events: Research on Effects," U.S. Department of Veterans
Affairs (VA), August 17, 2015.

Many people are unable to resist news coverage of traumatic events,
such as disasters and terrorist attacks. As horrific as they are to watch
on television and read about in newspapers and magazines, many still
find it nearly impossible to turn away. It is difficult to know why the
information is so hard to resist. Some say that people are hoping for
information because they are fearful of future events and want to be
prepared; others say that people are watching and reading in an effort
to digest and process the event; still others say the media is intentionally creating seductive and addictive images almost like those seen in
an action movie.

Whatever the reason, it is important to understand the effects on
the community that this type of exposure may have. Research generally finds an association between watching media coverage of traumatic events and stress symptoms. However, most studies cannot
answer the important question of whether watching television of the
event makes people worse or if people who have more severe stress
reactions are the ones who choose to watch more television coverage
of the event.

Research from the September 11, 2001 attacks

Adults

In a national survey of U.S. adults, three to five days after the
September 11, 2001, attacks, people reported watching an average of
eight hours of television related to the attacks. Those who watched
the most coverage had more substantial stress reactions than those
who watched less television coverage.

Children

In the same national survey, parents reported that their children watched an average of three hours of television related to the bombing, with older adolescents watching more than younger children. Children who watched the most coverage were reported to have more stress symptoms than those who watched less coverage.

Research from the Oklahoma City bombing

Before September 11, 2001, the bombing of the Alfred P. Murrah Federal Building in 1995 was the most deadly terrorist act perpetrated on US soil. One hundred sixty-eight people were killed, over 700 were injured, and more than 16,000 individuals in the downtown area were affected by the blast. In addition, approximately 12,000 people were involved in the rescue effort in a variety of different contexts. Because of the serious nature of this event, the media covered the bombing extensively.

Adults

In a study of 85 adults seeking mental-health services six months after the bombing, the number of hours of bomb-related television watched did not correlate with increased PTSD symptoms.

Children

Two-thirds of a large group of Oklahoman school children in grades 6 through 12 reported that, in the seven weeks after the bombing, "most" or "all" of their television viewing was bomb related. Children in this group who watched bomb-related television reported more PTSD symptoms seven weeks after the bombing than children who did not watch as much bomb-related television. This was true for children who lost an immediate family member and for those who did not lose a close family member. However, children who were related to a deceased victim reported more difficulty calming down after watching bomb-related television than children who did not lose a close family member.

Similar results were found in a sample of over 2,000 middle-school children (grades 6-8) from Oklahoma. Again, approximately two-thirds reported that "most" or "all" of their television viewing was bomb related. Interestingly, television exposure was directly related to PTSD only in children who did not see, hear, or feel the explosion and who did not know anyone who was killed or injured in the explosion.

These findings suggest two different possibilities. The first is that watching bomb-related television may contribute to an increase in PTSD symptoms. Alternately, it may be that the children who were the most distressed chose to watch bomb-related television.

Information from other sources

Adults

Two hundred thirty-seven Israeli adults were divided into two groups. One group was exposed to television clips of terrorism and political violence; the other group was exposed to news clips unrelated to national threat. Individuals who watched the terrorism clips reported more anxiety than those who watched clips unrelated to terrorism.

In a sample of adults, those who had an intimate friend or relative killed in the Mount St. Helens tragedy reported that the media was a hindrance to their recovery. Adults who suffered property loss reported that the media was neither a help nor a hindrance.

Dr. Neal Cohen was New York City's mental health commissioner at the time of the crash of TWA Flight 800 and one of the psychiatrists who provided services to family members. In an article in *Psychiatric Services*, Dr. Cohen wrote, "The mourners involvement with the media had both positive and negative impacts. Certainly the media helped to allay the feelings of powerlessness that frequently afflict those stricken by a tragedy. However, the presence of reporters and cameras also imposed a heavy burden on family members. The most personal aspects of mourning could too easily become the subject of a television news feature.

In a letter to the *Medical Journal of Australia* (1986) about the effects of trauma-related media on adult trauma victims, psychiatrist Alexander McFarlane wrote, "media exposure following a trauma may reinforce the victims' feelings of vulnerability and fixate their images of death and destruction." Media exposure also "may increase the risk of the development and maintenance of chronic PTSD following a trauma."

Children

Sixty-five percent of a small sample of children from Kuwait reported viewing televised images of violence, death, and grotesque mutilation related to the Gulf War. This type of television exposure was associated with increases in PTSD symptoms.

Clearly, the media plays a critical role in the aftermath of a traumatic event. The media provides needed information, makes announcements, and gives instructions regarding services that are available to victims and their families. They are a resource for the community and can provide a source of hope.

However, too much trauma-related television viewing may have a negative impact, especially on children. Providers should tell patients:

- If you find that you feel anxious or stressed after watching a news program, if you feel you cannot turn off the television or participate in recreational activities, or if you have trouble sleeping, you may want to consider limiting the amount and type of media coverage that you are viewing.

- Some strategies that may be useful include limiting viewing just prior to bedtime, reading newspaper and journal articles rather than watching television, and talking to people about the attack as a means of gathering information.

Literature regarding children and television more clearly asserts that too much viewing of disaster-related television could be harmful. Statistics from before September 11 tell us that televisions in the average American household are on for more than seven hours a day. This doesn't necessarily mean that one person is watching TV for seven hours straight, but, nonetheless, the TV is on. Different people may watch at different times, or the TV may be on as someone is cooking or engaging in some other activity. As such, children in most American households are probably being exposed to images of traumatic events for many hours each day even though no one has made a conscious decision to expose these children to these images.

Guidance providers can give children and their parents

If parents allow young children to watch the news at all, experts suggest that parents watch the news WITH their children and talk about what they are seeing. For example, if parents allowed their children to watch coverage of the September 11(th) attacks, children may have needed it explained to them that despite seeing the plane crash into the building over and over again, this was a single incident on one day. Also, parents can help their children put the news into context by explaining that:

- There are many good people who will do their best to keep them safe if something bad happens (focus on the firemen and rescue teams and not just on the attack).

- The news often tells us bad things that happen in the world, but most of the country is safe and most people who fly in airplanes land safely on the ground and have no problems at all.

Unfortunately, it is true that most reported news is bad news. We don't hear about the plane that landed safely or the car that made it to and from its destination without incident. Children need to be reminded that what they see on the news does not represent the way things are everywhere.

Most importantly, parents need to allow and even encourage children to ask questions. Children may have irrational fears after watching a news report because they misunderstand something. If they share those fears or ask clarifying questions, parents can help alleviate their anxiety. Parents can tell the child that a lot of people are working hard to make the situation safer for the future. If a child seems to be watching too much news coverage of a traumatic event, the parent can redirect the child's attention to other more productive and positive activities.

Chapter 6

Occupational Stress

Chapter Contents

Section 6.1

Stress in the Workplace

Text in this section is excerpted from "Stress At Work," Centers for
Disease Control and Prevention (CDC), June 6, 2014.

The nature of work is changing at whirlwind speed. Perhaps now
more than ever before, job stress poses a threat to the health of workers and, in turn, to the health organizations. This chapter highlights
knowledge about the causes of stress at work and outlines steps that
can be taken to prevent job stress.

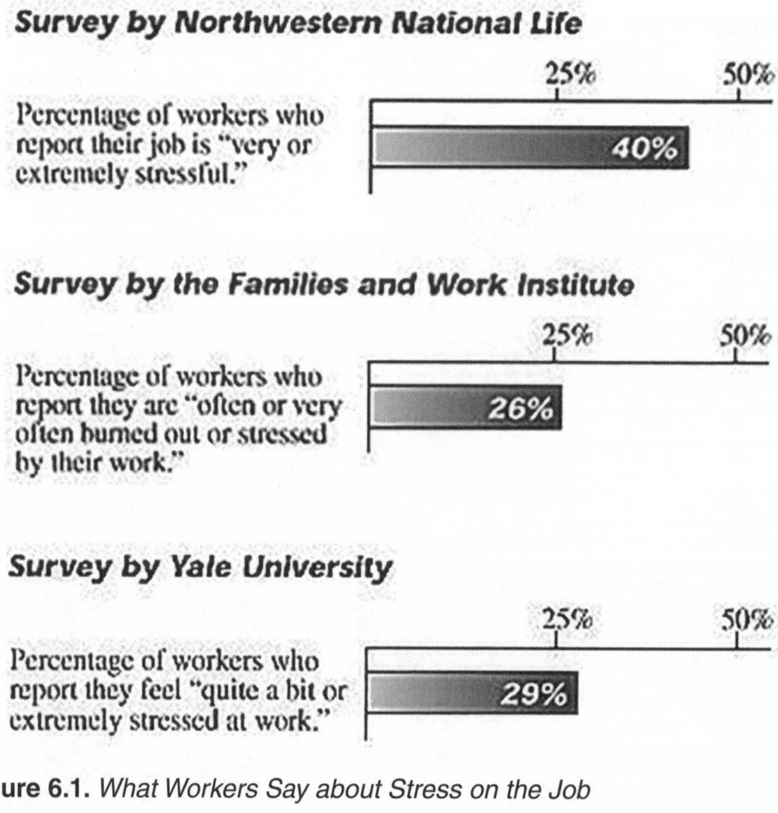

Survey by Northwestern National Life

Percentage of workers who report their job is "very or extremely stressful."

40%

Survey by the Families and Work Institute

Percentage of workers who report they are "often or very often burned out or stressed by their work."

26%

Survey by Yale University

Percentage of workers who report they feel "quite a bit or extremely stressed at work."

29%

Figure 6.1. *What Workers Say about Stress on the Job*

Scope of Stress in the American Workplace

Job stress has become a common and costly problem in the American workplace, leaving few workers untouched. For example, studies report the following:

- One-fourth of employees view their jobs as the number one stressor in their lives.

- Three-fourths of employees believe the worker has more on-the-job stress than a generation ago.

- Problems at work are more strongly associated with health complaints than are any other life stressor-more so than even financial problems or family problems.

Fortunately, research on job stress has greatly expanded in recent years. But in spite of this attention, confusion remains about the causes, effects, and prevention of job stress. This booklet summarizes what is known about job stress and what can be done about it.

What Is Job Stress?

Job stress can be defined as the harmful physical and emotional responses that occur when the requirements of the job do not match the capabilities, resources, or needs of the worker. Job stress can lead to poor health and even injury.

The concept of job stress is often confused with challenge, but these concepts are not the same. Challenge energizes us psychologically and physically, and it motivates us to learn new skills and master our jobs. When a challenge is met, we feel relaxed and satisfied. Thus, challenge is an important ingredient for healthy and productive work. The importance of challenge in our work lives is probably what people are referring to when they say "a little bit of stress is good for you."

> Job stress results when the requirements of the job do not match the capabilities, resources, or needs of the worker.

What are the Causes of Job Stress?

Nearly everyone agrees that job stress results from the interaction of the worker and the conditions of work. Views differ, however, on the importance of worker characteristics versus working conditions as the primary cause of job stress. These differing viewpoints are important because they suggest different ways to prevent stress at work.

According to one school of thought, differences in individual characteristics such as personality and coping style are most important in predicting whether certain job conditions will result in stress-in other words, what is stressful for one person may not be a problem for someone else. This viewpoint leads to prevention strategies that focus on workers and ways to help them cope with demanding job conditions.

Although the importance of individual differences cannot be ignored, scientific evidence suggests that certain working conditions are stressful to most people. The excessive workload demands and conflicting expectations described in David's and Theresa's stories are good examples. Such evidence argues for a greater emphasis on working conditions as the key source of job stress, and for job redesign as a primary prevention strategy.

In 1960, a Michigan court upheld a compensation claim by an automotive assembly line worker who had difficulty keeping up with the pressures of the production line. To avoid falling behind, he tried to work on several assemblies at the same time and often got parts mixed up. As a result, he was subjected to repeated criticism from the foreman. Eventually he suffered a psychological breakdown.

By 1995, nearly one-half of the States allowed worker compensation claims for emotional disorders and disability due to stress on the job [note, however, that courts are reluctant to uphold claims for what can be considered ordinary working conditions or just hard work].

NIOSH Approach to Job Stress

On the basis of experience and research, NIOSH favors the view that working conditions play a primary role in causing job stress. However, the role of individual factors is not ignored. According to the NIOSH view, exposure to stressful working conditions (called job stressors) can have a direct influence on worker safety and health. But as shown below, individual and other situational factors can intervene to strengthen or weaken this influence. Examples of individual and situational factors that can help to reduce the effects of stressful working conditions include the following:

- Balance between work and family or personal life

- A support network of friends and coworkers

- A relaxed and positive outlook

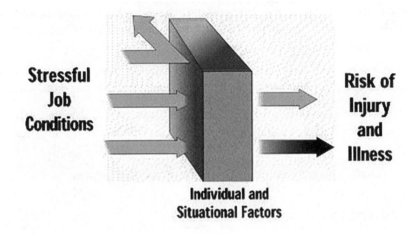

Figure 6.2. *NIOSH Approach to Job Stress*

Job Conditions That May Lead to Stress

The Design of Tasks. Heavy workload, infrequent rest breaks, long work hours and shiftwork; hectic and routine tasks that have little inherent meaning, do not utilize workers' skills, and provide little sense of control.

Management Style. Lack of participation by workers in deci- sion- making, poor communication in the organization, lack of fami- ly-friendly policies.

Example: Theresa needs to get the boss's approval for everything, and the company is insensitive to her family needs.

Interpersonal Relationships. Poor social environment and lack of support or help from coworkers and supervisors.

Example: Theresa's physical isolation reduces her opportunities to interact with other workers or receive help from them.

Work Roles. Conflicting or uncertain job expectations, too much responsibility, too many "hats to wear."

Example: Theresa is often caught in a difficult situation trying to satisfy both the customer's needs and the company's expectations.

Career Concerns. Job insecurity and lack of opportunity for growth, advancement, or promotion; rapid changes for which workers are unprepared.

Example: Since the reorganization at David's plant, everyone is worried about their future with the company and what will happen next.

Environmental Conditions. Unpleasant or dangerous physical conditions such as crowding, noise, air pollution, or ergonomic problems.

Example: David is exposed to constant noise at work.

Job Stress and Health

Stress sets off an alarm in the brain, which responds by preparing the body for defensive action. The nervous system is aroused and hormones are released to sharpen the senses, quicken the pulse, deepen respiration, and tense the muscles. This response (sometimes called the fight or flight response) is important because it helps us defend against threatening situations. The response is preprogrammed biologically. Everyone responds in much the same way, regardless of whether the stressful situation is at work or home.

Short-lived or infrequent episodes of stress pose little risk. But when stressful situations go unresolved, the body is kept in a constant state of activation, which increases the rate of wear and tear to biological systems. Ultimately, fatigue or damage results, and the ability of the body to repair and defend itself can become seriously compromised. As a result, the risk of injury or disease escalates.

In the past 20 years, many studies have looked at the relationship between job stress and a variety of ailments. Mood and sleep disturbances, upset stomach and headache, and disturbed relationships with family and friends are examples of stress-related problems that are quick to develop and are commonly seen in these studies. These early signs of job stress are usually easy to recognize. But the effects of job stress on chronic diseases are more difficult to see because chronic diseases take a long time to develop and can be influenced by many factors other than stress. Nonetheless, evidence is rapidly accumulating to suggest that stress plays an important role in several types of chronic health problems-especially cardiovascular disease, musculoskeletal disorders, and psychological disorders.

Health care expenditures are nearly 50% greater for workers who report high levels of stress.

Early Warning Signs of Job Stress

Headache

Sleep disturbances

Difficulty in concentrating

Short temper

Upset stomach

Job dissatisfaction

Low morale

Job Stress and Health:

What the Research Tells Us

Cardiovascular Disease

Many studies suggest that psychologically demanding jobs that allow employees little control over the work process increase the risk of cardiovascular disease.

Musculoskeletal Disorders

On the basis of research by NIOSH and many other organizations, it is widely believed that job stress increases the risk for development of back and upper- extremity musculoskeletal disorders.

Psychological Disorders

Several studies suggest that differences in rates of mental health problems (such as depression and burnout) for various occupations are due partly to differences in job stress levels. (Economic and lifestyle differences between occupations may also contribute to some of these problems.)

Workplace Injury

Although more study is needed, there is a growing concern that stressful working conditions interfere with safe work practices and set the stage for injuries at work.

Suicide, Cancer, Ulcers, and Impaired Immune Function

Some studies suggest a relationship between stressful working conditions and these health problems. However, more research is needed before firm conclusions can be drawn.

Stress, Health, and Productivity

Some employers assume that stressful working conditions are a necessary evil-that companies must turn up the pressure on workers and set aside health concerns to remain productive and profitable in today's economy. But research findings challenge this belief. Studies show that stressful working conditions are actually associated with increased absenteeism, tardiness, and intentions by workers to quit their jobs-all of which have a negative effect on the bottom line.

Recent studies of so-called healthy organizations suggest that policies benefiting worker health also benefit the bottom line. A healthy organization is defined as one that has low rates of illness, injury, and disability in its workforce and is also competitive in the marketplace. NIOSH research has identified organizational characteristics associated with both healthy, low-stress work and high levels of productivity. Examples of these characteristics include the following:

- Recognition of employees for good work performance

- Opportunities for career development

- An organizational culture that values the individual worker

- Management actions that are consistent with organizational values

Stress Prevention and Job Performance

St. Paul Fire and Marine Insurance Company conducted several studies on the effects of stress prevention programs in hospital settings. Program activities included (1) employee and management education on job stress, (2) changes in hospital policies and procedures to reduce organizational sources of stress, and (3) establishment of employee assistance programs.

In one study, the frequency of medication errors declined by 50% after prevention activities were implemented in a 700-bed hospital. In a second study, there was a 70% reduction in malpractice claims in 22 hospitals that implemented stress prevention activities. In contrast, there was no reduction in claims in a matched group of 22 hospitals that did not implement stress prevention activities.

According to data from the Bureau of Labor Statistics, workers who must take time off work because of stress, anxiety, or a related disorder will be off the job for about 20 days.

What Can Be Done about Job Stress?

The examples of Theresa and David illustrate two different approaches for dealing with stress at work.

Stress Management. Theresa's company is providing stress management training and an employee assistance program (EAP) to improve the ability of workers to cope with difficult work situations. Nearly one-half of large companies in the United States provide some type of stress management training for their workforces. Stress management programs teach workers about the nature and sources of stress, the effects of stress on health, and personal skills to reduce stress-for example, time management or relaxation exercises. (EAPs provide individual counseling for employees with both work and personal problems.) Stress management training may rapidly reduce stress symptoms such as anxiety and sleep disturbances; it also has the advantage of being inexpensive and easy to implement. However, stress management programs have two major disadvantages:

- The beneficial effects on stress symptoms are often short-lived.

- They often ignore important root causes of stress because they focus on the worker and not the environment.

Organizational Change. In contrast to stress management training and EAP programs, David's company is trying to reduce job stress by bringing in a consultant to recommend ways to improve working conditions. This approach is the most direct way to reduce stress at work. It involves the identification of stressful aspects of work (e.g., excessive workload, conflicting expectations) and the design of strategies to reduce or eliminate the identified stressors. The advantage of this approach is that it deals directly with the root causes of stress at work. However, managers are sometimes uncomfortable with this approach because it can involve changes in work routines or production schedules, or changes in the organizational structure.

As a general rule, actions to reduce job stress should give top priority to organizational change to improve working conditions. But even the most conscientious efforts to improve working conditions are unlikely to eliminate stress completely for all workers. For this reason, a combination of organizational change and stress management is often the most useful approach for preventing stress at work.

Section 6.2

Heat Stress in the Workplace

Text in this section is excerpted from "Heat Stress," Centers for
Disease Control and Prevention (CDC), July 30, 2015.

Workers who are exposed to extreme heat or work in hot environments may be at risk of heat stress. Exposure to extreme heat can result in occupational illnesses and injuries. Heat stress can result in heat stroke, heat exhaustion, heat cramps, or heat rashes. Heat can also increase the risk of injuries in workers as it may result in sweaty palms, fogged-up safety glasses, and dizziness. Burns may also occur as a result of accidental contact with hot surfaces or steam.

Workers at risk of heat stress include outdoor workers and workers in hot environments such as firefighters, bakery workers, farmers, construction workers, miners, boiler room workers, factory workers, and others. Workers at greater risk of heat stress include those who are 65 years of age or older, are overweight, have heart disease or high blood pressure, or take medications that may be affected by extreme heat.

Prevention of heat stress in workers is important. Employers should provide training to workers so they understand what heat stress is, how it affects their health and safety, and how it can be prevented.

Types of Heat-Related Illnesses

Heat Stroke

Heat stroke is the most serious heat-related disorder. It occurs when the body becomes unable to control its temperature: the body's temperature rises rapidly, the sweating mechanism fails, and the body is unable to cool down. When heat stroke occurs, the body temperature can rise to 106 degrees Fahrenheit or higher within 10 to 15 minutes. Heat stroke can cause death or permanent disability if emergency treatment is not given.

Symptoms

Symptoms of heat stroke include:

- Hot, dry skin or profuse sweating
- Hallucinations
- Chills
- Throbbing headache
- High body temperature
- Confusion/Dizziness
- Slurred speech

First Aid

Take the following steps to treat a worker with heat stroke:

- Call 911 and notify their supervisor.
- Move the sick worker to a cool shaded area.
- Cool the worker using methods such as:
- Soaking their clothes with water.
- Spraying, sponging, or showering them with water.
- Fanning their body.

Heat Exhaustion

Heat exhaustion is the body's response to an excessive loss of the water and salt, usually through excessive sweating. Workers most prone to heat exhaustion are those that are elderly, have high blood pressure, and those working in a hot environment.

Symptoms

Symptoms of heat exhaustion include:

- Heavy sweating
- Extreme weakness or fatigue
- Dizziness, confusion
- Nausea
- Clammy, moist skin
- Pale or flushed complexion

- Muscle cramps
- Slightly elevated body temperature
- Fast and shallow breathing

First Aid

- Treat a worker suffering from heat exhaustion with the following:
- Have them rest in a cool, shaded or air-conditioned area.
- Have them drink plenty of water or other cool, nonalcoholic beverages.
- Have them take a cool shower, bath, or sponge bath.

Heat Syncope

Heat syncope is a fainting (syncope) episode or dizziness that usually occurs with prolonged standing or sudden rising from a sitting or lying position. Factors that may contribute to heat syncope include dehydration and lack of acclimatization.

Symptoms

Symptoms of heat syncope include:

- Light-headedness
- Dizziness
- Fainting
- First Aid
- Workers with heat syncope should:
    - Sit or lie down in a cool place when they begin to feel symptoms.
    - Slowly drink water, clear juice, or a sports beverage.

Heat Cramps

Heat cramps usually affect workers who sweat a lot during strenuous activity. This sweating depletes the body's salt and moisture levels. Low salt levels in muscles causes painful cramps. Heat cramps may also be a symptom of heat exhaustion.

Symptoms

Muscle pain or spasms usually in the abdomen, arms, or legs.

First Aid

Workers with heat cramps should:

- Stop all activity, and sit in a cool place.
- Drink clear juice or a sports beverage.
- Do not return to strenuous work for a few hours after the cramps subside because further exertion may lead to heat exhaustion or heat stroke.
- Seek medical attention if any of the following apply:
  - The worker has heart problems.
  - The worker is on a low-sodium diet.
  - The cramps do not subside within one hour.

Heat Rash

- Heat rash is a skin irritation caused by excessive sweating during hot, humid weather.

Symptoms

Symptoms of heat rash include:

- Heat rash looks like a red cluster of pimples or small blisters.
- It is more likely to occur on the neck and upper chest, in the groin, under the breasts, and in elbow creases.

First Aid

Workers experiencing heat rash should:

- Try to work in a cooler, less humid environment when possible.
- Keep the affected area dry.
- Dusting powder may be used to increase comfort.

Recommendations for Employers

Employers should take the following steps to protect workers from heat stress:

- Schedule maintenance and repair jobs in hot areas for cooler months.

- Schedule hot jobs for the cooler part of the day.
- Acclimatize workers by exposing them for progressively longer periods to hot work environments.
- Reduce the physical demands of workers.
- Use relief workers or assign extra workers for physically demanding jobs.
- Provide cool water or liquids to workers.
- Avoid alcohol, and drinks with large amounts of caffeine or sugar.
- Provide rest periods with water breaks.
- Provide cool areas for use during break periods.
- Monitor workers who are at risk of heat stress.
- Provide heat stress training that includes information about:
- Worker risk
- Prevention
- Symptoms
- The importance of monitoring yourself and coworkers for symptoms
- Treatment
- Personal protective equipment

Recommendations for Workers

Workers should avoid exposure to extreme heat, sun exposure, and high humidity when possible. When these exposures cannot be avoided, workers should take the following steps to prevent heat stress:

- Wear light-colored, loose-fitting, breathable clothing such as cotton.
- Avoid non-breathing synthetic clothing.
- Gradually build up to heavy work.
- Schedule heavy work during the coolest parts of day.
- Take more breaks in extreme heat and humidity.
- Take breaks in the shade or a cool area when possible.

- Drink water frequently. Drink enough water that you never become thirsty. Approximately 1 cup every 15–20 minutes.

- Avoid alcohol, and drinks with large amounts of caffeine or sugar.

- Be aware that protective clothing or personal protective equipment may increase the risk of heat stress.

- Monitor your physical condition and that of your coworkers.

Section 6.3

Cold Stress in the Workplace

Text in this section is excerpted from "Cold Stress," Centers for Disease Control and Prevention (CDC), July 30, 2015.

Workers who are exposed to extreme cold or work in cold environments may be at risk of cold stress. Extreme cold weather is a dangerous situation that can bring on health emergencies in susceptible people, such as those without shelter, outdoor workers, and those who work in an area that is poorly insulated or without heat. What constitutes cold stress and its effects can vary across different areas of the country. In regions relatively unaccustomed to winter weather, near freezing temperatures are considered factors for "cold stress." Whenever temperatures drop decidedly below normal and as wind speed increases, heat can more rapidly leave your body. These weather-related conditions may lead to serious health problems.

Types of Cold-related Illnesses and Injuries

Hypothermia

When exposed to cold temperatures, your body begins to lose heat faster than it can be produced. Prolonged exposure to cold will eventually use up your body's stored energy. The result is hypothermia, or abnormally low body temperature. A body temperature that is too low affects the brain, making the victim unable to think clearly or move well. This makes hypothermia particularly dangerous because a person may not know it is happening and will not be able to do anything about it.

Symptoms

Symptoms of hypothermia can vary depending on how long you have been exposed to the cold temperatures.

Early Symptoms

- Shivering
- Fatigue
- Loss of coordination
- Confusion and disorientation

Late Symptoms

- No shivering
- Blue skin
- Dilated pupils
- Slowed pulse and breathing
- Loss of consciousness

First Aid

Take the following steps to treat a worker with hypothermia:

- Alert the supervisor and request medical assistance.
- Move the victim into a warm room or shelter.
- Remove their wet clothing.
- Warm the center of their body first-chest, neck, head, and groin-using an electric blanket, if available; or use skin-to-skin contact under loose, dry layers of blankets, clothing, towels, or sheets.
- Warm beverages may help increase the body temperature, but do not give alcoholic beverages. Do not try to give beverages to an unconscious person.

- After their body temperature has increased, keep the victim dry and wrapped in a warm blanket, including the head and neck.

- If victim has no pulse, begin cardiopulmonary resuscitation (CPR).

Cold Water Immersion

Cold water immersion creates a specific condition known as immersion hypothermia. It develops much more quickly than standard hypothermia because water conducts heat away from the body 25 times faster than air. Typically people in temperate climates don't consider themselves at risk from hypothermia in the water, but hypothermia can occur in any water temperature below 70°F. Survival times can be lengthened by wearing proper clothing (wool and synthetics and not cotton), using a personal flotation device (PFD, life vest, immersion suit, dry suit), and having a means of both signaling rescuers (strobe lights, personal locator beacon, whistles, flares, waterproof radio) and having a means of being retrieved from the water. Below you will find links with information about cold water survival and cold water rescue.

Frostbite

Frostbite is an injury to the body that is caused by freezing. Frostbite causes a loss of feeling and color in the affected areas. It most often affects the nose, ears, cheeks, chin, fingers, or toes. Frostbite can permanently damage body tissues, and severe cases can lead to amputation. In extremely cold temperatures, the risk of frostbite is increased in workers with reduced blood circulation and among workers who are not dressed properly.

Symptoms

Symptoms of frostbite include:

- Reduced blood flow to hands and feet (fingers or toes can freeze)

- Numbness

- Tingling or stinging

- Aching

- Bluish or pail, waxy skin

First Aid

Workers suffering from frostbite should:

- Get into a warm room as soon as possible.

- Unless absolutely necessary, do not walk on frostbitten feet or toes-this increases the damage.

- Immerse the affected area in warm-not hot-water (the temperature should be comfortable to the touch for unaffected parts of the body).

- Warm the affected area using body heat; for example, the heat of an armpit can be used to warm frostbitten fingers.

- Do not rub or massage the frostbitten area; doing so may cause more damage.

- Do not use a heating pad, heat lamp, or the heat of a stove, fireplace, or radiator for warming. Affected areas are numb and can be easily burned.

Trench Foot

Trench foot, also known as immersion foot, is an injury of the feet resulting from prolonged exposure to wet and cold conditions. Trench foot can occur at temperatures as high as 60°F if the feet are constantly wet. Injury occurs because wet feet lose heat 25 times faster than dry feet. Therefore, to prevent heat loss, the body constricts blood vessels to shut down circulation in the feet. Skin tissue begins to die because of lack of oxygen and nutrients and due to the buildup of toxic products.

Symptoms

Symptoms of trench foot include:

- Reddening of the skin

- Numbness

- Leg cramps

- Swelling

- Tingling pain

- Blisters or ulcers

- Bleeding under the skin

- Gangrene (the foot may turn dark purple, blue, or gray)

First Aid

Workers suffering from trench foot should:

- Remove shoes/boots and wet socks.

- Dry their feet.

- Avoid walking on feet, as this may cause tissue damage.

Chilblains

Chilblains are caused by the repeated exposure of skin to temperatures just above freezing to as high as 60 degrees F. The cold exposure causes damage to the capillary beds (groups of small blood vessels) in the skin. This damage is permanent and the redness and itching will return with additional exposure. The redness and itching typically occurs on cheeks, ears, fingers, and toes.

Symptoms

Symptoms of chilblains include:

- Redness

- Itching

- Possible blistering

- Inflammation

- Possible ulceration in severe cases

First Aid

Workers suffering from chilblains should:

- Avoid scratching

- Slowly warm the skin

- Use corticosteroid creams to relieve itching and swelling

- Keep blisters and ulcers clean and covered

Recommendations for Employers

Employers should take the following steps to protect workers from cold stress:

- Schedule maintenance and repair jobs in cold areas for warmer months.

- Schedule cold jobs for the warmer part of the day.

- Reduce the physical demands of workers.

- Use relief workers or assign extra workers for long, demanding jobs.

- Provide warm liquids to workers.

- Provide warm areas for use during break periods.

- Monitor workers who are at risk of cold stress.

- Provide cold stress training that includes information about:

- Worker risk

- Prevention

- Symptoms

- The importance of monitoring yourself and coworkers for symptoms

- Treatment

- Personal protective equipment

Recommendations for Workers

Workers should avoid exposure to extremely cold temperatures when possible. When cold environments or temperatures cannot be avoided, workers should follow these recommendations to protect themselves from cold stress:

- Wear appropriate clothing.

- Wear several layers of loose clothing. Layering provides better insulation.

- Tight clothing reduces blood circulation. Warm blood needs to be circulated to the extremities.

- When choosing clothing, be aware that some clothing may restrict movement resulting in a hazardous situation.

- Make sure to protect the ears, face, hands and feet in extremely cold weather.

- Boots should be waterproof and insulated.

- Wear a hat; it will keep your whole body warmer. (Hats reduce the amount of body heat that escapes from your head.)

- Move into warm locations during work breaks; limit the amount of time outside on extremely cold days.

- Carry cold weather gear, such as extra socks, gloves, hats, jacket, blankets, a change of clothes and a thermos of hot liquid.

- Include a thermometer and chemical hot packs in your first aid kit.

- Avoid touching cold metal surfaces with bare skin.

- Monitor your physical condition and that of your coworkers.

Section 6.4

Occupation Specific Stress: Law Enforcement

This section includes excerpts from "Officer Work Hours, Stress and Fatigue," National Institute of Justice (NIJ), August 13, 2012; text from "Causes of Officer Stress and Fatigue," National Institute of Justice (NIJ), January 24, 2012; and text from "Preventing Office Fatigue," National Institute of Justice (NIJ), January 24, 2012.

Law enforcement officers commonly work extended hours in ever-changing environments that can cause great mental and physical stress.

Enduring fatigue for a long period of time may lead to chronic fatigue syndrome, a health problem characterized by extreme fatigue that does not improve with bed rest and continues to worsen with physical and mental activity.

Fatigue can:

- Impair an officer's mental and physical ability.

- Create a cycle of fatigue.

- Limit job performance.

- Damage an officer's health.

Disrupted sleep
increases fatigue

Fatigue diminishes ability
to cope with stressors
in a healthy way

Inability to cope
with stressors
disrupts sleep

Figure 6.3. *Cycle of Fatigue*

Fatigue arises primarily from inadequate sleep—both the quantity and quality of sleep.

Officers get inadequate sleep when they experience a break in their circadian rhythms, the sleep/wake cycle all living organisms require to maintain good health.

Circadian rhythms impact a person's biochemical, physiological and behavioral processes. External cues such as daylight or noise help modulate a person's circadian rhythms, generating a series of internal responses that cause sleeping and waking. Changes in external cues can effect a person's mental and physical disposition — one common example is the experience of jet lag.

Continual breaks in circadian rhythm can cause serious mental and physical fatigue. This fatigue diminishes people's mental and physical health, and impairs their ability to deal with stressful situations. For police officers, this gives way to a **cycle of fatigue** that decreases their ability to perform their job effectively.

Causes of Officer Stress and Fatigue

Enduring stress for a long period of time can lead to anxiety, depression or post-traumatic stress disorder (PTSD). PTSD is a psychological condition marked by an inability to be intimate, inability to sleep, increased nightmares, increased feelings of guilt and reliving the event.

For law enforcement officers, stress can increase fatigue to the point that decision-making is impaired and officers cannot properly protect themselves or citizens.

Factors That Can Cause Stress and Fatigue for Law Enforcement Officers

Work-related factors might include:

- Poor management.

- Inadequate or broken equipment.

- Excessive overtime.

- Frequent rotating shifts (see 10-Hour Shifts Offer Cost Savings and Other Benefits to Law Enforcement Agencies).

- Regular changes in duties — for example, spending one day filling out paperwork and the next intervening in a violent domestic dispute.

Individual factors might include:

- Family problems.

- Financial problems.

- Health problems.

- Taking second jobs to make extra income.

Preventing Office Fatigue

Law enforcement officers usually do not speak up about how stress affects their lives. Most departments have an unspoken code of silence about the stress and strain that comes with police work. For most officers, the work ethic and culture of law enforcement appears to accept fatigue as part of the job.

Additionally, managers do not always see how overtime causes work-related injuries and accidents. And many police officers are willing to risk their health because overtime provides additional income.

Some police agencies are trying to avoid officer fatigue by:

- Encouraging officers to engage in physical activity.

- Encouraging officers to take time away from work.

- Avoiding mandatory overtime hours.

- Discouraging officers from taking on second jobs or moonlighting.

- Creating schedules and policies that minimize overtime and shift rotation.

- Using technology or policies that reduce overtime. These technological changes might include:

- Using laptop devices in cars to write reports.

- Using a "call in" reporting system to deal with certain calls for service.

- Allowing officers to process paperwork on calls for service at a later time.

Section 6.5

Occupation Specific Stress: Aviation

Text in this section is excerpted from "Aircrew Safety & Health," Centers for Disease Control and Prevention (CDC), March 10, 2015.

Job Stress

What you need to know

When job stress is high due to heavy demands and pressures or in response to a traumatic event, your body and mind can experience the "flight or fight" response. Your job performance and health may decline if your job stress is very high or lasts a long time. Here you can learn more about how to recognize and manage job stress.

What are job stressors?

Workplace conditions or events that cause job stress are called job stressors. Aircrew may face job stress from:

- occasional or repeated heavy job demands

- working long and irregular hours

- sleep disruption

- job insecurity

- encounters with uncooperative or unpleasant passengers or co-workers/managers

- unpredictable schedule disruptions

- extended time away from home and loved ones

- traumatic events, such as in-flight emergencies or disasters

Why might aircrew be concerned about job stress?

Job stress can interfere with your work performance and can have both short and long-term health consequences.

What types of job stress are there?

Acute stress

Acute stress can occur when job demands, pressures, or uncertainties are higher over a relatively short period of time. This is generally followed by a return to low or more moderate levels. Examples might include working back-to-back flight segments with full passenger loads, flying during bad weather, or if a passenger medical event occurs in-flight. The symptoms of acute stress are generally mild to moderate and temporary. They can include:

- physical and/or emotional tension

- digestive or sleep disturbances

- fear and anxiety

- irritability

- needing time to unwind after work before interacting with family and friends

- sleep disturbance

Chronic stress

Chronic or prolonged stress can develop from experiencing heavy demands and pressures over an extended period of time. There is also little or no control over those demands, limited resources to meet those demands, and/or limited relief or "down-time." Symptoms of chronic stress can range from mild to high and are generally persistent. Those with chronic stress may experience the symptoms associated with acute stress listed above, as well as:

- difficulty making decisions
- loss of interest in normal activities
- sleep problems
- feeling powerless
- difficulty with relationships
- feeling sad and having other symptoms of depression

Traumatic incident stress

Aircrew are responsible for the safety of passengers and must respond quickly to medical, mechanical or other in-flight emergencies. Such emergencies can be considered traumatic incidents if they involve damage to physical structures or spaces, bodily injury, or death. Traumatic incident stress may occur at the time of the event or weeks or months later. It may include severe acute physical symptoms such as difficulty breathing, symptoms of shock, or chest pain that requires immediate medical attention.

What can be done to reduce or eliminate job stress?

What employees can do

Times of stress can be overwhelming, and may lead to pleasure-seeking in the form of unhealthy choices that may worsen the effects of stress. You can be proactive by taking steps to reduce the effects of job stress by finding support and making healthy choices. Evidence shows that supportive relationships can reduce stress levels, along with taking better care of yourself. Here are some things you can do:

- Find support. Seek help from a trusted partner, family member, friend, counselor, doctor, or clergyperson. Consider using programs offered by your employer if available.

- Connect socially with others.

- Talk with your supervisor, a union steward, or a trusted senior member of your organization about work conditions that may be causing or aggravating your stress. When discussing issues it

74

may help to seek clarification about roles and priorities, available resources, and options for doing things differently that may not be apparent.

- Start or resume routines that are comforting or soothing to you especially if you've been stressed or your schedule has been disrupted. For example, practice yoga or find other activities that may help you relax, such as taking a warm bath.

- Make time to do things that make you happy – even if for brief periods of time.

- Limit time spent watching television, in front of computer screens or other electronic devices.

- Choose healthier meal options and pack healthy snacks.

- Go for walks or exercise regularly.

- Get enough sleep.

- Avoid drugs and alcohol.

What managers can do

Just as it is necessary to design jobs in a way that protects workers from toxic chemicals, jobs should also be designed to reduce worker exposure to job stressors. While some stressors such as shiftwork, long work hours, or schedule delays due to weather or mechanical issues cannot be eliminated, airline management should make extra efforts to identify, evaluate and implement work schedule practices that aid crewmember recovery following long flights. Additionally, programs should be developed to provide employees exposed to work-related traumatic incidents with mental health debriefings and to direct them to needed resources. Here is what managers can do to help reduce their crewmembers' job stress:

- Set fair and reasonable expectations.

- Clearly define workers' roles and responsibilities.

- Recognize and reward employee contributions.

- Permit employees to have a say and participate in decisions affecting their jobs

- Give workers opportunities to participate in decisions and actions affecting their jobs.

- Improve communication–reduce uncertainty about career development and future employment.

- Balance workload by ensuring adequate resources (staff, time) to accommodate flight demands.

- Design jobs to provide meaning, stimulation, and opportunities for applying skills.

- Permit work schedule flexibility to enable crewmembers to better balance job demands and responsibilities with those outside the job, including childcare.

- Establish and maintain an effective and proactive workforce protection program that is automatically activated for personnel involved in work-related traumatic incidents.

Part Two

How Stress Affects the Body

Chapter 7

Alzheimer's Disease

Chapter Contents

Section 7.1

What is Alzheimer's Disease?

Text in this section is excerpted from "Alzheimer's Disease Fact
Sheet," National Institute on Aging (NIA), May 2015.

Alzheimer's disease is an irreversible, progressive brain disorder
that slowly destroys memory and thinking skills, and eventually the
ability to carry out the simplest tasks. In most people with Alzheimer's,
symptoms first appear in their mid-60s. Estimates vary, but experts
suggest that more than 5 million Americans may have Alzheimer's.

Alzheimer's disease is currently ranked as the sixth leading cause
of death in the United States, but recent estimates indicate that the
disorder may rank third, just behind heart disease and cancer, as a
cause of death for older people.

Alzheimer's is the most common cause of dementia among older
adults. Dementia is the loss of cognitive functioning—thinking, remembering, and reasoning—and behavioral abilities to such an extent that
it interferes with a person's daily life and activities. Dementia ranges
in severity from the mildest stage, when it is just beginning to affect a
person's functioning, to the most severe stage, when the person must
depend completely on others for basic activities of daily living.

The causes of dementia can vary, depending on the types of brain
changes that may be taking place. Other dementias include Lewy
body dementia, frontotemporal disorders, and vascular dementia. It is
common for people to have mixed dementia—a combination of two or
more disorders, at least one of which is dementia. For example, some
people have both Alzheimer's disease and vascular dementia.

Alzheimer's disease is named after Dr. Alois Alzheimer. In 1906,
Dr. Alzheimer noticed changes in the brain tissue of a woman who had
died of an unusual mental illness. Her symptoms included memory
loss, language problems, and unpredictable behavior. After she died,
he examined her brain and found many abnormal clumps (now called
amyloid plaques) and tangled bundles of fibers (now called neurofibrillary, or tau, tangles).

These plaques and tangles in the brain are still considered some of
the main features of Alzheimer's disease. Another feature is the loss

80

of connections between nerve cells (neurons) in the brain. Neurons transmit messages between different parts of the brain, and from the brain to muscles and organs in the body.

Changes in the Brain

Scientists continue to unravel the complex brain changes involved in the onset and progression of Alzheimer's disease. It seems likely that damage to the brain starts a decade or more before memory and other cognitive problems appear. During this preclinical stage of Alzheimer's disease, people seem to be symptom-free, but toxic changes are taking place in the brain. Abnormal deposits of proteins form amyloid plaques and tau tangles throughout the brain, and once-healthy neurons stop functioning, lose connections with other neurons, and die.

The damage initially appears to take place in the hippocampus, the part of the brain essential in forming memories. As more neurons die, additional parts of the brain are affected, and they begin to shrink. By the final stage of Alzheimer's, damage is widespread, and brain tissue has shrunk significantly.

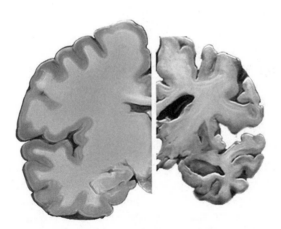

Cross sections of the brain show atrophy, or shrinking, of brain tissue caused by Alzheimer's disease.

Figure 7.1. *Healthy Brain and Severe Alzheimer's*

Signs and Symptoms

Memory problems are typically one of the first signs of cognitive impairment related to Alzheimer's disease. Some people with memory problems have a condition called mild cognitive impairment (MCI). In MCI, people have more memory problems than normal for their age, but their symptoms do not interfere with their everyday lives. Movement difficulties and problems with the sense of smell have also been linked to MCI. Older people with MCI are at greater risk for developing Alzheimer's, but not all of them do. Some may even go back to normal cognition.

The first symptoms of Alzheimer's vary from person to person. For many, decline in non-memory aspects of cognition, such as word-finding, vision/spatial issues, and impaired reasoning or judgment, may signal the very early stages of Alzheimer's disease. Researchers are studying biomarkers (biological signs of disease found in brain images, cerebrospinal fluid, and blood) to see if they can detect early changes in the brains of people with MCI and in cognitively normal people who may be at greater risk for Alzheimer's. Studies indicate that such early detection may be possible, but more research is needed before these techniques can be relied upon to diagnose Alzheimer's disease in everyday medical practice.

Mild Alzheimer's Disease

As Alzheimer's disease progresses, people experience greater memory loss and other cognitive difficulties. Problems can include wandering and getting lost, trouble handling money and paying bills, repeating questions, taking longer to complete normal daily tasks, and personality and behavior changes. People are often diagnosed in this stage.

Moderate Alzheimer's Disease

In this stage, damage occurs in areas of the brain that control language, reasoning, sensory processing, and conscious thought. Memory loss and confusion grow worse, and people begin to have problems recognizing family and friends. They may be unable to learn new things, carry out multistep tasks such as getting dressed, or cope with new situations. In addition, people at this stage may have hallucinations, delusions, and paranoia and may behave impulsively.

Severe Alzheimer's Disease

Ultimately, plaques and tangles spread throughout the brain, and brain tissue shrinks significantly. People with severe Alzheimer's cannot communicate and are completely dependent on others for their care. Near the end, the person may be in bed most or all of the time as the body shuts down.

What Causes Alzheimer's

Scientists don't yet fully understand what causes Alzheimer's disease in most people. In people with early-onset Alzheimer's, a genetic mutation is usually the cause. Late-onset Alzheimer's arises from a complex series of brain changes that occur over decades. The causes probably include a combination of genetic, environmental, and lifestyle factors. The importance of any one of these factors in increasing or decreasing the risk of developing Alzheimer's may differ from person to person.

The Basics of Alzheimer's

Scientists are conducting studies to learn more about plaques, tangles, and other biological features of Alzheimer's disease. Advances in brain imaging techniques allow researchers to see the development and spread of abnormal amyloid and tau proteins in the living brain, as well as changes in brain structure and function. Scientists are also exploring the very earliest steps in the disease process by studying changes in the brain and body fluids that can be detected years before Alzheimer's symptoms appear. Findings from these studies will help in understanding the causes of Alzheimer's and make diagnosis easier.

One of the great mysteries of Alzheimer's disease is why it largely strikes older adults. Research on normal brain aging is shedding light on this question. For example, scientists are learning how age-related changes in the brain may harm neurons and contribute to Alzheimer's damage. These age-related changes include atrophy (shrinking) of certain parts of the brain, inflammation, production of unstable molecules called free radicals, and mitochondrial dysfunction (a breakdown of energy production within a cell).

Genetics

Most people with Alzheimer's have the late-onset form of the disease, in which symptoms become apparent in their mid-60s. The apolipoprotein E (APOE) gene is involved in late-onset Alzheimer's. This gene has several forms. One of them, APOE ε4, increases a person's risk of developing the disease and is also associated with an earlier age of disease onset. However, carrying the APOE ε4 form of the gene does not mean that a person will definitely develop Alzheimer's disease, and some people with no APOE ε4 may also develop the disease.

Also, scientists have identified a number of regions of interest in the genome (an organism's complete set of DNA) that may increase a person's risk for late-onset Alzheimer's to varying degrees.

Early-onset Alzheimer's occurs in people age 30 to 60 and represents less than 5 percent of all people with Alzheimer's. Most cases are caused by an inherited change in one of three genes, resulting in a type known as early-onset familial Alzheimer's disease, or FAD. For others, the disease appears to develop without any specific, known cause, much as it does for people with late-onset disease.

Most people with Down syndrome develop Alzheimer's. This may be because people with Down syndrome have an extra copy of chromosome 21, which contains the gene that generates harmful amyloid.

Health, Environmental, and Lifestyle Factors

Research suggests that a host of factors beyond genetics may play a role in the development and course of Alzheimer's disease. There is a great deal of interest, for example, in the relationship between cognitive decline and vascular conditions such as heart disease, stroke, and high blood pressure, as well as metabolic conditions such as diabetes and obesity. Ongoing research will help us understand whether and how reducing risk factors for these conditions may also reduce the risk of Alzheimer's.

A nutritious diet, physical activity, social engagement, and mentally stimulating pursuits have all been associated with helping people stay healthy as they age. These factors might also help reduce the risk of cognitive decline and Alzheimer's disease. Clinical trials are testing some of these possibilities.

Diagnosis of Alzheimer's Disease

Doctors use several methods and tools to help determine whether a person who is having memory problems has "possible Alzheimer's dementia" (dementia may be due to another cause) or "probable Alzheimer's dementia" (no other cause for dementia can be found).

To diagnose Alzheimer's, doctors may:

- Ask the person and a family member or friend questions about overall health, past medical problems, ability to carry out daily activities, and changes in behavior and personality

- Conduct tests of memory, problem solving, attention, counting, and language

- Carry out standard medical tests, such as blood and urine tests, to identify other possible causes of the problem

- Perform brain scans, such as computed tomography (CT), magnetic resonance imaging (MRI), or positron emission tomography (PET), to rule out other possible causes for symptoms.

These tests may be repeated to give doctors information about how the person's memory and other cognitive functions are changing over time.

Alzheimer's disease can be *definitely* diagnosed only after death, by linking clinical measures with an examination of brain tissue in an autopsy.

People with memory and thinking concerns should talk to their doctor to find out whether their symptoms are due to Alzheimer's or another cause, such as stroke, tumor, Parkinson's disease, sleep disturbances, side effects of medication, an infection, or a non-Alzheimer's dementia. Some of these conditions may be treatable and possibly reversible.

If the diagnosis is Alzheimer's, beginning treatment early in the disease process may help preserve daily functioning for some time, even though the underlying disease process cannot be stopped or reversed. An early diagnosis also helps families plan for the future. They can take care of financial and legal matters, address potential safety issues, learn about living arrangements, and develop support networks.

In addition, an early diagnosis gives people greater opportunities to participate in clinical trials that are testing possible new treatments for Alzheimer's disease or other research studies.

Treatment of Alzheimer's Disease

Alzheimer's disease is complex, and it is unlikely that any one drug or other intervention can successfully treat it. Current approaches focus on helping people maintain mental function, manage behavioral symptoms, and slow or delay the symptoms of disease. Researchers hope to develop therapies targeting specific genetic, molecular, and cellular mechanisms so that the actual underlying cause of the disease can be stopped or prevented.

Maintaining Mental Function

Several medications are approved by the U.S. Food and Drug Administration to treat symptoms of Alzheimer's. Donepezil (Aricept®), rivastigmine (Exelon®), and galantamine (Razadyne®) are used to treat mild to moderate Alzheimer's (donepezil can be used for severe

Alzheimer's as well). Memantine (Namenda®) is used to treat moderate to severe Alzheimer's. These drugs work by regulating neurotransmitters, the chemicals that transmit messages between neurons. They may help maintain thinking, memory, and communication skills, and help with certain behavioral problems. However, these drugs don't change the underlying disease process. They are effective for some but not all people, and may help only for a limited time.

Managing Behavior

Common behavioral symptoms of Alzheimer's include sleeplessness, wandering, agitation, anxiety, and aggression. Scientists are learning why these symptoms occur and are studying new treatments—drug and non-drug—to manage them. Research has shown that treating behavioral symptoms can make people with Alzheimer's more comfortable and makes things easier for caregivers.

Looking for New Treatments

Alzheimer's disease research has developed to a point where scientists can look beyond treating symptoms to think about addressing underlying disease processes. In ongoing clinical trials, scientists are developing and testing several possible interventions, including immunization therapy, drug therapies, cognitive training, physical activity, and treatments used for cardiovascular and diabetes.

Support for Families and Caregivers

Caring for a person with Alzheimer's disease can have high physical, emotional, and financial costs. The demands of day-to-day care, changes in family roles, and decisions about placement in a care facility can be difficult. There are several evidence-based approaches and programs that can help, and researchers are continuing to look for new and better ways to support caregivers.

Becoming well-informed about the disease is one important long-term strategy. Programs that teach families about the various stages of Alzheimer's and about ways to deal with difficult behaviors and other caregiving challenges can help.

Good coping skills, a strong support network, and respite care are other ways that help caregivers handle the stress of caring for a loved one with Alzheimer's disease. For example, staying physically active provides physical and emotional benefits.

Some caregivers have found that joining a support group is a critical lifeline. These support groups allow caregivers to find respite, express concerns, share experiences, get tips, and receive emotional comfort. Many organizations sponsor in-person and online support groups, including groups for people with early-stage Alzheimer's and their families.

Section 7.2

Link between Alzheimer's and Stress

Text in this section is excerpted from "Understanding the Biology
of Alzheimer's Disease and the Aging Brain," National Institute on
Aging (NIA), December 2012.

How Tau Pathology May Spread in the Alzheimer's Brain

Neurofibrillary tangles are a hallmark of Alzheimer's disease. Tangles are composed of misfolded forms of the protein tau—a structural change that results in tau clumping into insoluble fibrils that, under the microscope, resemble threadlike fibers. What causes tau to misfold and lose function has long been a mystery.

A University of Pennsylvania, Philadelphia, study using kidney cells suggests a "domino effect" in which misfolded tau causes normal tau to misfold. The researchers found that minute quantities of misfolded tau introduced into cultured cells expressing normal tau caused the tau to form fibrils like those seen in the Alzheimer's brain. In addition, the researchers found that the cells soaked up the misfolded tau from the fluid surrounding them. Assuming that brain cells also take up tau, this study suggests a route by which tau pathology could spread from one neuron to another, as it appears to do in Alzheimer's disease.

As Alzheimer's disease progresses, tau pathology spreads from one brain region to another in a consistent pattern Tangles appear first in the entorhinal cortex, next in the hippocampus, and then in the cerebral cortex. These brain regions are connected to one another via synapses that create communication networks.

Research groups at Columbia University, New York City, and Harvard University, Cambridge, MA, have now shown that abnormal tau spreads from one brain region to the next by moving across synapses. Each research group performed similar experiments in which they created experimental mice that expressed mutant human tau only in the entorhinal cortex. As the mice aged, the mutant tau gradually spread across the connected brain regions. As the abnormal human tau appeared in each brain region, it clumped together with normal mouse tau to form tangles and damage synapses.

These studies demonstrate one mechanism by which Alzheimer's pathology can spread from one brain region to another. They also suggest a possible target for therapies that might delay or prevent disease onset and progression.

Mitchondrial Dysfunction in Alzheimer's Disease

Mitochondria are the "powerhouses" of the cell, generating the energy needed to function and survive. In Alzheimer's disease, abnormal levels of beta-amyloid damage brain mitochondria, leading to neuronal dysfunction. A team led by investigators at Columbia University, New York City, found that beta-amyloid interacts with mitochondria by binding to a mitochondrial enzyme called ABAD (beta-amyloid-binding alcohol dehydrogenase). Treating Alzheimer's model mice with a peptide that blocks beta-amyloid binding to ABAD improved mitochondrial function and also alleviated the mice's memory deficits. This study strongly implicates mitochondrial beta-amyloid as a critical player in the development of Alzheimer's disease.

Synapses depend on nearby mitochondria to generate the energy needed for proper functioning. A study led by Harvard University, Cambridge, MA, researchers showed that abnormal forms of tau disrupt this process. In mice expressing a mutant form of human tau, neurons lacked the mitochondria needed for proper functioning; similar abnormalities were seen at autopsy in people diagnosed with Alzheimer's. The researchers also found that tau does not have to form thread-like fibrils to disrupt mitochondria from delivering energy to synapses. Rather, reduced levels of normal tau in mouse models are enough to disrupt the process.

Working Memory Loss in Normal Aging

Working memory is the ability of the brain to store and manipulate information over brief periods of time. It is critical to tasks of daily living such as planning dinner and keeping the list of ingredients in mind while pulling them out of the refrigerator. Many of the cognitive changes experienced by normal adults (forgetfulness, distractibility, reduced efficiency in carrying out tasks) result from declines in working memory. Research now shows that multitasking impairs working memory performance, especially as we age.

University of California, San Francisco, researchers used functional magnetic resonance imaging scanning to study brain networks in younger and older adults who were asked to perform a working memory task. The researchers then intentionally distracted the participants during the task. Both younger and older adults redirected their brain networks from the assigned task to the interruption. However, unlike younger adults, older adults failed to disengage their attention from the interruption and failed to reestablish functional connections with the memory network originally engaged in the task. The inability to disengage from distraction is likely to impact a wide range of life activities, particularly in the information age, which requires increasing organizational skill to deal with even basic needs such as medical care and paying bills.

To understand the cellular changes underlying age-related decline in working memory, researchers from Yale University, New Haven, CT, studied rhesus monkeys. Like humans, they may develop problems with working memory in their senior years. The researchers showed that this loss is tied to changes in a specific network of neurons in the prefrontal cortex, the brain region responsible for working memory. In younger animals, these prefontal cortex neurons continue to fire in response to an environmental signal after the signal is removed. However, with age, the researchers found, the firing rates of these neurons declined steeply.

Taking the experiment a step further, they found that the decline could be reversed in the monkeys by directly delivering drugs to the brain that inhibit cyclic AMP, an intracellular signaling molecule. The beneficial response suggests that declines in age-related working memory may be reversible. One of the cyclic AMP inhibitors used in this study, guanafacine, is already approved by the U.S. Food and Drug Administration to treat high blood pressure. A pilot clinical trial is now underway to see if this medication can improve working memory in cognitively normal older people.

Brain neurons have a remarkable capacity to remodel their connections with other neurons in response to changes in the environment. This phenomenon, known as "synaptic plasticity," is critical for memory processes and for behavioral adaptation to changes in the environment. However, Mt. Sinai Medical Center, New York City, researchers found that in rats, the remodeling capacity of neurons diminishes with age in the prefrontal cortex, a brain region involved in learning and memory.

When young rats experienced 3 weeks of behavioral stress, neurons in their prefrontal cortex responded by retracting and/or reshaping their dendritic spines. In contrast, the dendritic spines of middle-aged and aged rats did not remodel during stress. Since the prefrontal cortex plays a central role in working memory, loss of synaptic plasticity in this brain region may contribute to age-related loss of working memory function.

Astrocytes and Blood Vessels in Aging and Alzheimer's Disease

Neurons do not function in isolation, but in close collaboration with blood vessels and glial cells, which support and protect brain cells. Like neurons, glial cells and blood vessels show changes in structure and function in both Alzheimer's disease and normal aging. These changes can impair healthy brain function.

Astrocytes, a type of glial cell, are star-shaped cells that surround and help regulate, support, and protect neurons and blood vessels. One of many critical functions astrocytes perform is to secrete growth factors that stimulate neurogenesis, or the birth of new neurons. Recognizing that neurogenesis declines as the brain ages, researchers at Rosalind Franklin University, Chicago, studied how aging impacts astrocytes.

They found that astrocytes in the brains of aging rats showed signs of structural changes similar to those seen during mild brain inflammation and decreased levels of neuronal growth factors. Importantly, the brain regions in which these astrocyte changes were seen included parts of the hippocampus, where new neurons are generated. These findings indicate that decreased availability of astrocyte-derived growth factors may contribute to age-related declines in neurogenesis.

Another important function astrocytes perform is to protect neurons against damage by free radicals. Free radicals are highly reactive molecules that can build up inside cells due to aging or other factors and cause cellular damage, a condition known as "oxidative stress." Astrocytes protect neurons from oxidative stress by generating antioxidants, molecules that neutralize free radicals and render them harmless.

University of Michigan, Ann Arbor, researchers exposed cultured mouse astrocytes to beta-amyloid, which causes oxidative stress in neurons. Beta-amyloid disrupted astrocyte antioxidant production pathways and simultaneously interfered with the astrocytes' ability to protect neurons against beta-amyloid toxicity. These results suggest the possibility of developing Alzheimer's disease therapeutics by enhancing astrocyte antioxidant production pathways.

Researchers are interested in finding out how physical exercise may influence cognitive health into late age. University of Kentucky, Lexington, researchers showed that exercise benefits aging glial cells (which support and protect neurons), blood vessel cells, and neurons. The researchers compared the brains of middle-aged female mice with and without access to exercise wheels. (Mice provided with exercise wheels tend to run on them without encouragement.) After only 6 weeks, the exercising mice showed significant reductions in markers of glial and blood vessel cell aging compared with the sedentary mice.

Chapter 8

Panic Attacks

What is a panic attack?

You may have had a panic attack if you experienced four or more of the symptoms listed below coming on abruptly and peaking in about 10 minutes.

Panic Symptoms

- Pounding heart
- Sweating
- Trembling or shaking
- Shortness of breath
- Feeling of choking
- Chest pain
- Nausea or abdominal distress
- Feeling dizzy, unsteady, lightheaded, or faint
- Feelings of unreality or being detached from yourself
- Fear of losing control or going crazy

Text in this chapter is excerpted from "Panic Attacks," Mental Illness Research, Education and Clinical Centers (MIRECC) at the U.S. Department of Veterans Affairs (VA), July 2013.

- Fear of dying

- Numbness or tingling

- Chills or hot flashes

Panic attacks are sometimes accompanied by avoidance of certain places or situations. These are often situations that would be difficult to escape from or in which help might not be available. Examples might include crowded shopping malls, public transportation, restaurants, or driving.

Why do panic attacks occur?

Panic attacks are the body's alarm system gone awry. All of us have a built-in alarm system, powered by adrenaline, which increases our heart rate, breathing, and blood flow in response to danger. Ordinarily, this 'danger response system' works well. In some people, however, the response is either out of proportion to whatever stress is going on, or may come out of the blue without any stress at all.

For example, if you are walking in the woods and see a bear coming your way, a variety of changes occur in your body to prepare you to either fight the danger or flee from the situation. Your heart rate will increase to get more blood flow around your body, your breathing rate will quicken so that more oxygen is available, and your muscles will tighten in order to be ready to fight or run. You may feel nauseated as blood flow leaves your stomach area and moves into your limbs. These bodily changes are all essential to helping you survive the dangerous situation.

After the danger has passed, your body functions will begin to go back to normal. This is because your body also has a system for "recovering" by bringing your body back down to a normal state when the danger is over.

As you can see, the emergency response system is adaptive when there is, in fact, a "true" or "real" danger (e.g., bear). However, sometimes people find that their emergency response system is triggered in "everyday" situations where there really is no true physical danger (e.g., in a meeting, in the grocery store, while driving in normal traffic, etc.).

What triggers a panic attack?

Sometimes particularly stressful situations can trigger a panic attack. For example, an argument with your spouse or stressors at work can cause a stress response (activating the emergency response system) because you perceive it as threatening or overwhelming, even if there is no direct risk to your survival.

Sometimes panic attacks don't seem to be triggered by anything in particular – they may "come out of the blue." Somehow, the natural "fight or flight" emergency response system has gotten activated when there is no real danger. Why does the body go into "emergency mode" when there is no real danger?

Often, people with panic attacks are frightened or alarmed by the physical sensations of the emergency response system. First, unexpected physical sensations are experienced (tightness in your chest or some shortness of breath). This then leads to feeling fearful or alarmed by these symptoms ("Something's wrong!", "Am I having a heart attack?", "Am I going to faint?") The mind perceives that there is a danger even though no real danger exists. This, in turn, activates the emergency response system ("fight or flight"), leading to a "full blown" panic attack. In summary, panic attacks occur when we misinterpret physical symptoms as signs of impending death, craziness, loss of control, embarrassment, or fear of fear. Sometimes you may be aware of thoughts of danger that activate the emergency response system (for example, thinking "I'm having a heart attack" when you feel chest pressure or increased heart rate). At other times, however, you may not be aware of such thoughts. After several incidences of being afraid of physical sensations, anxiety and panic can occur in response to the initial sensations without conscious thoughts of danger. Instead, you just feel afraid or alarmed. In other words, the panic or fear may seem to occur "automatically" without you consciously telling yourself anything.

After having had one or more panic attacks, you may also become more focused on what is going on inside your body. You may scan your body and be more vigilant about noticing any symptoms that might

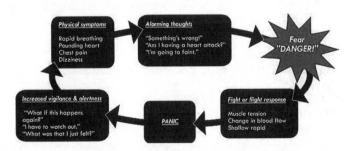

Figure 8.1. *Panic Attack*

signal the start of a panic attack. This makes it easier for panic attacks to happen again because you pick up on sensations you might otherwise not have noticed, and misinterpret them as something dangerous. A panic attack may then result.

How do I cope with panic attacks?

An important part of overcoming panic attacks involves re-interpreting your body's physical reactions and teaching yourself ways to decrease the physical arousal. This can be done through practicing the cognitive and behavioral interventions below.

Behavioral Interventions

1. Breathing Retraining

Research has found that over half of people who have panic attacks show some signs of hyperventilation or over breathing. This can produce initial sensations that alarm you and lead to a panic attack. Over breathing can also develop as part of the panic attack and make the symptoms worse. When people hyperventilate, certain blood vessels in the body become narrower. In particular, the brain may get slightly less oxygen. This can lead to the symptoms of dizziness, confusion, and lightheadedness that often occur during panic attacks. Other parts of the body may also get a bit less oxygen, which may lead to numbness or tingling in the hands or feet or the sensation of cold, clammy hands. It also may lead the heart to pump harder. Although these symptoms may be frightening and feel unpleasant, it is important to remember that hyperventilating is not dangerous. However, you can help overcome the unpleasantness of over breathing by practicing Breathing Retraining.

Practice this basic technique three times a day, every day

- **Inhale.** With your shoulders relaxed, inhale as slowly and deeply as you can while you count to six. If you can, use your diaphragm to fill your lungs with air.
- **Hold.** Keep the air in your lungs as you slowly count to four.
- **Exhale.** Slowly breathe out as you count to six.
- **Repeat.** Do the inhale-hold-exhale cycle several times. Each time you do it, exhale for longer counts.

Like any new skill, Breathing Retraining requires practice. Try practicing this skill twice a day for several minutes. Initially, do not try this technique in specific situations or when you become frightened or have a panic attack. Begin by practicing in a quiet environment to build up your skill level so that you can later use it in time of "emergency."

2. Decreasing Avoidance

Regardless of whether you can identify why you began having panic attacks or whether they seemed to come out of the blue, the places where you began having panic attacks often can become triggers themselves. It is not uncommon for individuals to begin to avoid the places where they have had panic attacks. Over time, the individual may begin to avoid more and more places, thereby decreasing their activities and often negatively impacting their quality of life. To break the cycle of avoidance, it is important to first identify the places or situations that are being avoided, and then to do some "relearning."

To begin this intervention, first create a list of locations or situations that you tend to avoid. Then choose an avoided location or situation that you would like to target first. Now develop an "exposure hierarchy" for this situation or location. An "exposure hierarchy" is a list of actions that make you feel anxious in this situation. Order these actions from least to most anxiety-producing. It is often helpful to have the first item on your hierarchy involve thinking or imagining part of the feared/avoided situation.

Here is an example of an exposure hierarchy for decreasing avoidance of the grocery store. Note how it is ordered from the least amount of anxiety (at the top) to the most anxiety (at the bottom):

- Think about going to the grocery store alone.

- Go to the grocery store with a friend or family member.

- Go to the grocery store alone to pick up a few small items (5–10 minutes in the store).

- Shopping for 10–20 minutes in the store alone.

- Doing the shopping for the week by myself (20–30 minutes in the store).

Your homework is to "expose" yourself to the lowest item on your hierarchy and use your breathing relaxation and coping statements to help you remain in the situation. Practice this several times during the upcoming week. Once you have mastered each item with minimal anxiety, move on to the next higher action on your list.

Cognitive Interventions

1. Identify your negative self-talk

Anxious thoughts can increase anxiety symptoms and panic. The first step in changing anxious thinking is to identify your own negative, alarming self-talk. Some common alarming thoughts:

- I'm having a heart attack.
- I must be going crazy.
- I think I'm dying.
- People will think I'm crazy.
- I'm going to pass out.
- Oh no – here it comes.
- I can't stand this.
- I've got to get out of here!

2. Use positive coping statements

Changing or disrupting a pattern of anxious thoughts by replacing them with more calming or supportive statements can help to divert a panic attack. Some common helpful coping statements:

- This is not an emergency.
- I don't like feeling this way, but I can accept it.
- I can feel like this and still be okay.
- This has happened before, and I was okay. I'll be okay this time, too.
- I can be anxious and still deal with this situation.
- I can handle these symptoms or sensations.

Chapter 9

Cancer and Stress

What is psychological stress?

Psychological stress describes what people feel when they are under mental, physical, or emotional pressure. Although it is normal to experience some psychological stress from time to time, people who experience high levels of psychological stress or who experience it repeatedly over a long period of time may develop health problems (mental and/or physical).

Stress can be caused both by daily responsibilities and routine events, as well as by more unusual events, such as a trauma or illness in oneself or a close family member. When people feel that they are unable to manage or control changes caused by cancer or normal life activities, they are in distress. Distress has become increasingly recognized as a factor that can reduce the quality of life of cancer patients. There is even some evidence that extreme distress is associated with poorer clinical outcomes. Clinical guidelines are available to help doctors and nurses assess levels of distress and help patients manage it.

How does the body respond during stress?

The body responds to physical, mental, or emotional pressure by releasing stress hormones (such as epinephrine and norepinephrine) that increase blood pressure, speed heart rate, and raise blood sugar

Text in this chapter is excerpted from "Psychological Stress and Cancer," National Cancer Institute (NCI), December 10, 2012.

levels. These changes help a person act with greater strength and speed to escape a perceived threat.

Research has shown that people who experience intense and long-term (i.e., chronic) stress can have digestive problems, fertility problems, urinary problems, and a weakened immune system. People who experience chronic stress are also more prone to viral infections such as the flu or common cold and to have headaches, sleep trouble, depression, and anxiety.

Can psychological stress cause cancer?

Although stress can cause a number of physical health problems, the evidence that it can cause cancer is weak. Some studies have indicated a link between various psychological factors and an increased risk of developing cancer, but others have not.

Apparent links between psychological stress and cancer could arise in several ways. For example, people under stress may develop certain behaviors, such as smoking, overeating, or drinking alcohol, which increase a person's risk for cancer. Or someone who has a relative with cancer may have a higher risk for cancer because of a shared inherited risk factor, not because of the stress induced by the family member's diagnosis.

How does psychological stress affect people who have cancer?

People who have cancer may find the physical, emotional, and social effects of the disease to be stressful. Those who attempt to manage their stress with risky behaviors such as smoking or drinking alcohol or who become more sedentary may have a poorer quality of life after cancer treatment. In contrast, people who are able to use effective coping strategies to deal with stress, such as relaxation and stress management techniques, have been shown to have lower levels of depression, anxiety, and symptoms related to the cancer and its treatment. However, there is no evidence that successful management of psychological stress improves cancer survival.

Evidence from experimental studies does suggest that psychological stress can affect a tumor's ability to grow and spread. For example, some studies have shown that when mice bearing human tumors were kept confined or isolated from other mice—conditions that increase stress—their tumors were more likely to grow and spread (metastasize). In one set of experiments, tumors transplanted into the mammary fat pads of mice had much higher rates of spread to the lungs and lymph nodes if the mice were chronically stressed than if the mice were not stressed. Studies in mice and in human cancer cells grown in the laboratory have found that the stress hormone norepinephrine, part of the body's fight-or-flight response system, may promote angiogenesis and metastasis.

In another study, women with triple-negative breast cancer who had been treated with neoadjuvant chemotherapy were asked about their use of beta blockers, which are medications that interfere with certain stress hormones, before and during chemotherapy. Women who reported using beta blockers had a better chance of surviving their cancer treatment without a relapse than women who did not report beta blocker use. There was no difference between the groups, however, in terms of overall survival.

Although there is still no strong evidence that stress directly affects cancer outcomes, some data do suggest that patients can develop a sense of helplessness or hopelessness when stress becomes overwhelming. This response is associated with higher rates of death, although the mechanism for this outcome is unclear. It may be that people who feel helpless or hopeless do not seek treatment when they become ill, give up prematurely on or fail to adhere to potentially helpful therapy, engage in risky behaviors such as drug use, or do not maintain a healthy lifestyle, resulting in premature death.

How can people who have cancer learn to cope with psychological stress?

Emotional and social support can help patients learn to cope with psychological stress. Such support can reduce levels of depression, anxiety, and disease- and treatment-related symptoms among patients. Approaches can include the following:

- Training in relaxation, meditation, or stress management
- Counseling or talk therapy
- Cancer education sessions
- Social support in a group setting
- Medications for depression or anxiety
- Exercise

Some expert organizations recommend that all cancer patients be screened for distress early in the course of treatment. A number also recommend re-screening at critical points along the course of care. Health care providers can use a variety of screening tools, such as a distress scale or questionnaire, to gauge whether cancer patients need help managing their emotions or with other practical concerns. Patients who show moderate to severe distress are typically referred to appropriate resources, such as a clinical health psychologist, social worker, chaplain, or psychiatrist.

Chapter 10

Diabetes and Stress

How Is Diabetes Linked to Mental Illness?

Diabetes has a complex and reciprocal relationship with mental illness and shares metabolic features with certain mental disorders. For example, insulin resistance and impaired glucose regulation, which are features of diabetes, have been separately observed in patients with mental disorders such as schizophrenia and depression.

Mental illness reduces the likelihood that a person with diabetes will be properly treated, just as mental illness is associated with other disparities in care.

Rates of severe psychological distress are twice as high in people with diabetes compared with the rates among those without the disease. In addition, severe psychological distress is negatively associated with processes of diabetes care (e.g., access to prevention services) and outcomes. For young people with type 1 diabetes, previous psychiatric referral is a significant risk factor for death from acute diabetes-related events such as hypoglycemia or coma. Relationships between diabetes and some specific mental illnesses are described below.

Depression

Diabetes increases risk for depression and depressive symptoms. CDC reports that people with diabetes have roughly a doubled risk of

Text in this chapter is excerpted from "Diabetes Care for Clients in Behavioral Health Treatment," Substance Abuse and Mental Health Services Administration (SAMHSA), 2013.

also having depression compared with those who do not have diabetes. Similarly, a person with depression faces a 60-percent increase in risk for type 2 diabetes. A depressive disorder typically precedes a type 1 diagnosis and follows a type 2 diagnosis. Long-term use of antidepressant medications has been implicated in higher risk for type 2 diabetes, although these findings remain controversial.

Among all people with depression, recurrence and longer episodes are more common in people with diabetes than in those without the disease. Even at mild levels, depression can adversely affect glycemic control and a person's ability to perform diabetes self-care.

Anxiety disorders

People with diabetes have an elevated risk for anxiety disorders compared with the general population. Anxieties may be triggered by the burdens of having a chronic disease and by diabetes-specific factors such as having to inject insulin and living with the threat of acute diabetic symptoms and long-term complications. Such stressors may trigger generalized anxiety, obsessivecompulsive behavior, or phobic avoidance of activities necessary to managing diabetes such as checking blood glucose levels or injecting insulin.

Schizophrenia

People with schizophrenia have higher rates of hyperglycemia and type 2 diabetes than the general population, and diabetes is a leading cause of illness and death for people affected by schizophrenia-related disorders. Antipsychotic medications used to treat schizophrenia and, increasingly, nonpsychotic emotional disorders, are associated with increased risk for type 2 diabetes.

Deficits in learning, attention, memory, and other cognitive functions have been detected in type 1 and type 2 diabetes patients through neurocognitive testing. Deficits may result from a variety of factors, including hypoglycemia, hyperglycemia, and insulin resistance. These cognitive effects can be exacerbated in people who also have schizophrenia, which presents its own risks to cognition.

Eating disorders

Compared with the general public, people with diabetes are more likely to develop eating disorders, which are more likely to occur in young women. Eating disorders increase the risk for poor glycemic control and resulting acute diabetes symptoms.

How Is Diabetes Linked to Stress?

Stress, which can be experienced without a diagnosis of a mental disorder, increases risk for diabetes symptoms and complications. Hormones that are activated in response to stress (e.g., epinephrine, norepinephrine, cortisol, growth hormone) cause blood glucose levels to increase. Substantial evidence exists that stress can adversely affect the course of diabetes (whether it also can trigger the onset of diabetes is not established). Stress also can interfere with diabetes self-management, although the effects may depend on how the stress is perceived (that is, as positive or negative) and whether psychosocial or psychological support is available.

Chapter 11

Erectile Dysfunction

What is Erectile Dysfunction (ED)?

Erectile dysfunction (also known as impotence) is the inability to get and keep an erection firm enough for sex. Having erection trouble from time to time isn't necessarily a cause for concern. But if erectile dysfunction is an ongoing problem, it may cause stress, cause relationship problems or affect your self-confidence.

Even though it may seem awkward to talk with your doctor about erectile dysfunction, go in for an evaluation. Problems getting or keeping an erection can be a sign of a health condition that needs treatment, such as heart disease or poorly controlled diabetes. Treating an underlying problem may be enough to reverse your erectile dysfunction. If treating an underlying condition doesn't help your erectile dysfunction, medications or other direct treatments may work.

What are the causes of ED?

Male sexual arousal is a complex process that involves the brain, hormones, emotions, nerves, muscles and blood vessels. Erectile dysfunction can result from a problem with any of these. Likewise, stress and mental health problems can cause or worsen erectile dysfunction. Sometimes a combination of physical and psychological issues causes erectile dysfunction. For instance, a minor physical problem that slows

Text in this chapter is excerpted from "Erectile Dysfunction (ED)," United States Department of Veterans Affairs (VA), July 2013.

your sexual response may cause anxiety about maintaining an erection. The resulting anxiety can lead to or worsen erectile dysfunction.

Physical causes of ED.

In most cases, erectile dysfunction is caused by something physical. Common causes include:

- Heart disease
- Clogged blood vessels (atherosclerosis)
- High blood pressure
- Diabetes
- Obesity
- Metabolic syndrome, a condition involving increased blood pressure, high insulin levels, body fat around the waist and high cholesterol
- Parkinson's disease
- Multiple sclerosis
- Low testosterone
- Peyronie's disease, development of scar tissue inside the penis
- Certain prescription medications
- Tobacco use
- Alcoholism and other forms of substance abuse
- Treatments for prostate cancer or enlarged prostate
- Surgeries or injuries that affect the pelvic area or spinal cord

Psychological causes of ED.

The brain plays a key role in triggering the series of physical events that cause an erection, starting with feelings of sexual excitement. A number of things can interfere with sexual feelings and cause or worsen erectile dysfunction. These include:

- Depression, anxiety or other mental health conditions
- Stress
- Fatigue
- Relationship problems due to stress, poor communication or other concerns

What are the risk factors for ED?

As you get older, erections may take longer to develop and may not be as firm. You may need more direct touch to your penis to get and keep an erection. This isn't a direct consequence of getting older. Usually it's a result of underlying health problems or taking medications, which is more common as men age.

A variety of risk factors can contribute to erectile dysfunction. They include:

- Medical conditions, particularly diabetes or heart problems.
- Using tobacco, which restricts blood flow to veins and arteries. Over time tobacco use can cause chronic health problems that lead to erectile dysfunction.
- Being overweight, especially if you're very overweight (obese).
- Certain medical treatments, such as prostate surgery or radiation treatment for cancer.
- Injuries, particularly if they damage the nerves that control erections.
- Medications, including antidepressants, antihistamines and medications to treat high blood pressure, pain or prostate cancer.
- Psychological conditions, such as stress, anxiety or depression.
- Drug and alcohol use, especially if you're a long-term drug user or heavy drinker.
- Prolonged bicycling, which can compress nerves and affect blood flow to the penis —leading to temporary erectile dysfunction.

What are the tests used to diagnose ED?

For many men, a physical exam and answering questions (medical history) are all that's needed before a doctor is ready to recommend a treatment. If your doctor suspects that underlying problems may be involved, or you have chronic health problems, you may need further tests or you may need to see a specialist.

Tests for underlying problems may include:

- Physical exam. This may include careful examination of your penis and testicles and checking your nerves for feeling.
- Blood tests. A sample of your blood may be sent to a lab to check for signs of heart disease, diabetes, low testosterone levels and other health problems.

- Urine tests (urinalysis). Like blood tests, urine tests are used to look for signs of diabetes and other underlying health conditions.

- Ultrasound. This test can check blood flow to your penis. It involves using a wand-like device (transducer) held over the blood vessels that supply the penis. It creates a video image to let your doctor see if you have blood flow problems. This test is sometimes done in combination with an injection of medications into the penis to determine if blood flow increases normally.

- Overnight erection test. Most men have erections during sleep without remembering them. This simple test involves wrapping special tape around your penis before you go to bed. If the tape is separated in the morning, your penis was erect at some time during the night. This indicates the cause is of your erectile dysfunction is most likely psychological and not physical.

What are the treatments and medications for ED?

A variety of options exist for treating erectile dysfunction. The cause and severity of your condition, and underlying health problems, are important factors in your doctor's recommending the best treatment or treatments for you. Your doctor can explain the risks and benefits of each treatment, and will consider your preferences. Your partner's preferences also may play a role in treatment choices.

Oral medications. Oral medications are a successful erectile dysfunction treatment for many men. They include:

- Sildenafil (Viagra)

- Tadalafil (Cialis)

- Vardenafil (Levitra)

All three medications work in much the same way. These drugs enhance the effects of nitric oxide, a natural chemical your body produces that relaxes muscles in the penis. This increases blood flow and allows you to get an erection in response to sexual stimulation. These medications vary in dosage, how long they work and their side effects. Your doctor will take into account your particular situation to determine which medication may work best.

Don't expect these medications to fix your erectile dysfunction immediately. You may need to work with your doctor to find the right medication and dose for you.

Before taking any prescription erectile dysfunction medication (including over-the-counter supplements or herbal remedies), get your doctor's OK. Although these medications can help many people, not all men should take them to treat erectile dysfunction. These medications may not work or may be dangerous for you if you:

- Take nitrate drugs for angina, such as nitroglycerin (Nitro-Bid, others), isosorbide mononitrate (Imdur) and isosorbide dinitrate (Isordil)

- Take a blood-thinning (anticoagulant) medication, alpha blockers for enlarged prostate (benign prostatic hyperplasia) or high blood pressure medications

- Have heart disease or heart failure

- Have had a stroke

- Have very low blood pressure (hypotension) or uncontrolled high blood pressure (hypertension)

- Have uncontrolled diabetes

Other medications. Other medications for erectile dysfunction include:

- Alprostadil self-injection. With this method, you use a fine needle to inject alprostadil (Alprostadil, Caverject Impulse, Edex) into the base or side of your penis. In some cases, medications generally used for other conditions are used for penile injections on their own or in combination. Examples include papaverine, alprostadil and phentolamine. Each injection generally produces an erection in five to 20 minutes that lasts about an hour. Because the needle used is very fine, pain from the injection site is usually minor. Side effects can include bleeding from the injection, prolonged erection and formation of fibrous tissue at the injection site.

- Alprostadil penis suppository. Alprostadil intraurethral (MUSE) therapy involves placing a tiny alprostadil suppository inside your penis. You use a special applicator to insert the suppository about two inches down into your penis. Side effects can include pain, minor bleeding in the urethra, dizziness and formation of fibrous tissue inside your penis.

- Testosterone replacement. Some men have erectile dysfunction caused by low levels of the hormone testosterone, and may need testosterone replacement therapy.

Penis pumps, surgery, and implants. Medications may not work or may not be a good choice for you. If this is the case, your doctor may recommend a different treatment. Other treatments include:

- Penis pumps. A penis pump (vacuum constriction device) is a hollow tube with a hand-powered or battery-powered pump. The tube is placed over your penis, and then the pump is used to suck out the air inside the tube. This creates a vacuum that pulls blood into your penis. Once you get an erection, you slip a tension ring around the base of your penis to hold in the blood and keep it firm. You then remove the vacuum device. The erection typically lasts long enough for a couple to have sex. You remove the tension ring after intercourse.

- Penile implants. This treatment involves surgically placing devices into the two sides of the penis. These implants consist of either inflatable or semirigid rods made from silicone or polyurethane. The inflatable devices allow you to control when and how long you have an erection. The semirigid rods keep the penis firm but bendable. This treatment can be expensive and is usually not recommended until other methods have been tried first. As with any surgery, there is a risk of complications such as infection.

- Blood vessel surgery. In rare cases, a leaking blood vessel can cause erectile dysfunction and surgery is necessary to repair it.

Psychological counseling. If your erectile dysfunction is caused by stress, anxiety or depression, your doctor may suggest that you, or you and your partner, visit a psychologist or counselor. Even if it is caused by something physical, erectile dysfunction can create stress and relationship tension.

What are some things I can do about ED?

For many men, erectile dysfunction is caused or worsened by lifestyle choices. Here are some things you can do that may help:

- If you smoke, quit. If you have trouble quitting, get help. Try nicotine replacement (such as gum or lozenges), available over-the-counter, or ask your doctor about prescription medication that can help you quit.

- Lose weight. Being overweight can cause — or worsen — erectile dysfunction.

- Get regular exercise. This can help with underlying problems that play a part in erectile dysfunction in a number of ways, including reducing stress, helping you lose weight and increasing blood flow.

- Get treatment for alcohol or drug problems. Drinking too much or taking certain illicit drugs can worsen erectile dysfunction directly or by causing long-term health problems.

- Work through relationship issues. Improve communication with your partner and consider couples or marriage counseling if you're having trouble working through problems on your own.

Chapter 12

Gastrointestinal Problems

Chapter Contents

Section 12.1

Irritable Bowel Syndrome

This section includes excerpts from "Definition and Facts for Irritable
Bowel Syndrome," National Institute of Diabetes and Digestive and
Kidney Diseases (NIDDK), February 23, 2015; text from "Symptoms
and Causes of Irritable Bowel Syndrome," National Institute of
Diabetes and Digestive and Kidney Diseases (NIDDK), February
23, 2015; and text from "Brief Psychological and Educational
Therapy Improves Symptoms of Irritable Bowel Syndrome," National
Institute of Diabetes and Digestive and Kidney Diseases (NIDDK),
December 3, 2012.

What is irritable bowel syndrome (IBS)?

Irritable bowel syndrome (IBS) is a group of symptoms—including
pain or discomfort in your abdomen and changes in your bowel movement patterns—that occur together. Doctors call IBS a functional
gastrointestinal (GI) disorder. Functional GI disorders happen when
your GI tract behaves in an abnormal way without evidence of damage
due to a disease.

What are the symptoms of IBS?

The most common symptoms of irritable bowel syndrome (IBS)
include pain or discomfort in your abdomen and changes in how often
you have bowel movements or how your stools look. The pain or discomfort of IBS may feel like cramping and have at least two of the following:

- Your pain or discomfort improves after a bowel movement.
- You notice a change in how often you have a bowel movement.
- You notice a change in the way your stools look.

IBS is a chronic disorder, meaning it lasts a long time, often years.
However, the symptoms may come and go. You may have IBS if:

- You've had symptoms at least three times a month for the past 3
  months.
- Your symptoms first started at least 6 months ago.

People with IBS may have diarrhea, constipation, or both. Some people with IBS have only diarrhea or only constipation. Some people have symptoms of both or have diarrhea sometimes and constipation other times. People often have symptoms soon after eating a meal.

Other symptoms of IBS are

- bloating
- the feeling that you haven't finished a bowel movement
- whitish mucus in your stool

Women with IBS often have more symptoms during their menstrual periods.

While IBS can be painful, IBS doesn't lead to other health problems or damage your gastrointestinal (GI) tract.

What causes IBS?

Doctors aren't sure what causes IBS. Experts think that a combination of problems can lead to IBS.

Physical Problems

Brain-Gut Signal Problems

Signals between your brain and the nerves of your gut, or small and large intestines, control how your gut works. Problems with brain-gut signals may cause IBS symptoms.

GI Motility Problems

If you have IBS, you may not have normal motility in your colon. Slow motility can lead to constipation and fast motility can lead to diarrhea. Spasms can cause abdominal pain. If you have IBS, you may also experience hyperreactivity—a dramatic increase in bowel contractions when you feel stress or after you eat.

Pain Sensitivity

If you have IBS, the nerves in your gut may be extra sensitive, causing you to feel more pain or discomfort than normal when gas or stool is in your gut. Your brain may process pain signals from your bowel differently if you have IBS.

Infections

A bacterial infection in the GI tract may cause some people to develop IBS. Researchers don't know why infections in the GI tract

117

lead to IBS in some people and not others, although abnormalities of the GI tract lining and mental health problems may play a role.

Small Intestinal Bacterial Overgrowth

Normally, few bacteria live in your small intestine. Small intestinal bacterial overgrowth is an increase in the number or a change in the type of bacteria in your small intestine. These bacteria can produce extra gas and may also cause diarrhea and weight loss. Some experts think small intestinal bacterial overgrowth may lead to IBS. Research continues to explore a possible link between the two conditions.

Neurotransmitters (Body Chemicals)

People with IBS have altered levels of neurotransmitters—chemicals in the body that transmit nerve signals—and GI hormones. The role these chemicals play in IBS is unclear.

Younger women with IBS often have more symptoms during their menstrual periods. Post-menopausal women have fewer symptoms compared with women who are still menstruating. These findings suggest that reproductive hormones can worsen IBS problems.

Genetics

Whether IBS has a genetic cause, meaning it runs in families, is unclear. Studies have shown IBS is more common in people with family members who have a history of GI problems.

Food Sensitivity

Many people with IBS report that foods rich in carbohydrates, spicy or fatty foods, coffee, and alcohol trigger their symptoms. However, people with food sensitivity typically don't have signs of a food allergy. Researchers think that poor absorption of sugars or bile acids may cause symptoms.

Mental Health Problems

Psychological, or mental health, problems such as panic disorder, anxiety, depression, and post-traumatic stress disorder are common in people with IBS. The link between mental health and IBS is unclear. GI disorders, including IBS, are sometimes present in people who have reported past physical or sexual abuse. Experts think people who have been abused tend to express psychological stress through physical symptoms.

If you have IBS, your colon may respond too much to even slight conflict or stress. Stress makes your mind more aware of the sensations in your colon. IBS symptoms can also increase your stress level.

Researchers have found that patients with irritable bowel syndrome (IBS) show an improvement in symptoms following a short course of group therapy involving psychological and educational approaches. IBS is a collection of symptoms, including abdominal pain or discomfort (such as cramping), along with diarrhea, constipation, or both. A primary reason why IBS is dificult to treat is that its exact causes are not well understood, although it is believed to have both physical and mental origins. One possible cause is a problem with communication between the brain and the gut, which could lead to changes in bowel habits. Based on this likely mind-body connection, some successful treatment of IBS has been achieved using psychological counseling and education-based therapies to help patients control the activity of their own nervous systems and gastrointestinal tracts, but variable results, along with cost issues, unavailability of trained clinicians, and a general preference for pharmaceutical remedies, have hindered the implementation of psychological therapy as a standard of treatment.

To determine if a combination of psychological and educational therapy can lead to a sustained improvement in IBS symptoms and an increase in the quality of life for patients, a team of scientists performed a clinical trial where IBS patients in the intervention group attended a ive-week series of two-hour group classes co-led by a gastroenterologist and therapist to promote self-eficacy and teach relaxation techniques. As a basis for comparison, a control group of patients was monitored while on the waiting list for the group classes. Patients who attended the group classes learned about the linkage between emotions, stress, and abdominal symptoms with an emphasis on their ability to control the activity of their own bodies. They were also taught about the connection between mood, stress, and GI symptoms, and the difference between ineffective coping styles, such as panicking during moments of anxiety, and more effective responses, such as arriving at conscious, rational solutions during stressful situations.

The classes also instructed patients on deep breathing techniques and progressive muscle relaxation, including homework assignments consisting of at least 15 minutes of relaxation exercises twice a day. During and after the trial, the class participants and control patients were asked to monitor and document their symptoms in relationship with their mood states, stressors, and diets. The results of this trial suggested that patients who underwent the group psychological and educational therapy had a reduction in IBS symptoms and a better quality of life, lasting for at least three months after the trial, than those who did not participate in the class.

The therapy was particularly helpful for those individuals who had a low or average quality of life prior to starting the intervention, although it had less of an effect for those whose quality of life was higher at the beginning of the study. This study demonstrated an effective, low-cost method of treating IBS symptoms, especially for those with low or average health-related quality of life, and could pave the way for the adoption of such an approach as an alternative to, or a supplement for, pharmacological therapy.

Section 12.2

Gastritis

Text in this section is excerpted from "Gastritis," National Institute of Diabetes and Digestive and Kidney Diseases (NIDDK), September 2014.

What is gastritis?

Gastritis is a condition in which the stomachlining—known as the mucosa—is inflamed, or swollen. The stomach lining contains glands that produce stomach acid and an enzyme called pepsin. The stomach acid breaks down food and pepsin digests protein. A thick layer of mucus coats the stomach lining and helps prevent the acidic digestive juice from dissolving the stomach tissue. When the stomach lining is inflamed, it produces less acid and fewer enzymes. However, the stomach lining also produces less mucus and other substances that normally protect the stomach lining from acidic digestive juice.

Gastritis may be acute or chronic:

- Acute gastritis starts suddenly and lasts for a short time.

- Chronic gastritis is long lasting. If chronic gastritis is not treated, it may last for years or even a lifetime.

Gastritis can be erosive or nonerosive:

- Erosive gastritis can cause the stomach lining to wear away, causing erosions—shallow breaks in the stomach lining—or ulcers—deep sores in the stomach lining.

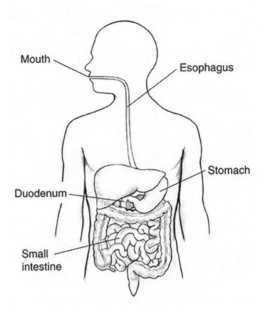

Figure 12.1. *The upper gastrointestinal (GI) tract*

- Nonerosive gastritis causes inflammation in the stomach lining; however, erosions or ulcers do not accompany nonerosive gastritis.

A health care provider may refer a person with gastritis to a gastroenterologist—a doctor who specializes in digestive diseases.

What causes gastritis?

Common causes of gastritis include

- *Helicobacter pylori (H. pylori)* infection
- damage to the stomach lining, which leads to reactive gastritis
- an autoimmune response

H. pylori infection. *H. pylori* is a type of bacteria—organisms that may cause an infection. *H. pylori* infection

- causes most cases of gastritis
- typically causes nonerosive gastritis
- may cause acute or chronic gastritis

H. pylori infection is common, particularly in developing countries, and the infection often begins in childhood. Many people who are infected with *H. pylori* never have any symptoms. Adults are more likely to show symptoms when symptoms do occur.

Researchers are not sure how the *H. pylori* infection spreads, although they think contaminated food, water, or eating utensils may transmit the bacteria. Some infected people have *H. pylori* in their saliva, which suggests that infection can spread through direct contact with saliva or other body fluids.

Damage to the stomach lining, which leads to reactive gastritis. Some people who have damage to the stomach lining can develop reactive gastritis.

Reactive gastritis

- may be acute or chronic

- may cause erosions

- may cause little or no inflammation

Reactive gastritis may also be called reactive gastropathy when it causes little or no inflammation.

The causes of reactive gastritis may include

- nonsteroidal anti-inflammatory drugs (NSAIDs), a type of over-the-counter medication. Aspirin and ibuprofen are common types of NSAIDs.

- drinking alcohol.

- using cocaine.

- exposure to radiation or having radiation treatments.

- reflux of bile from the small intestine into the stomach. Bile reflux may occur in people who have had part of their stomach removed.

- a reaction to stress caused by traumatic injuries, critical illness, severe burns, and major surgery. This type of reactive gastritis is called stress gastritis.

An autoimmune response. In autoimmune gastritis, the immune system attacks healthy cells in the stomach lining. The immune system normally protects people from infection by identifying and destroying bacteria, viruses, and other potentially harmful foreign substances. Autoimmune gastritis is chronic and typically nonerosive.

122

Less common causes of gastritis may include

- Crohn's disease, which causes inflammation and irritation of any part of the gastrointestinal (GI) tract.

- sarcoidosis, a disease that causes inflammation that will not go away. The chronic inflammation causes tiny clumps of abnormal tissue to form in various organs in the body. The disease typically starts in the lungs, skin, and lymph nodes.

- allergies to food, such as cow's milk and soy, especially in children.

- infections with viruses, parasites, fungi, and bacteria other than *H. pylori,* typically in people with weakened immune systems.

What are the signs and symptoms of gastritis?

Some people who have gastritis have pain or discomfort in the upper part of the abdomen—the area between the chest and hips. However, many people with gastritis do not have any signs and symptoms. The relationship between gastritis and a person's symptoms is not clear. The term "gastritis" is sometimes mistakenly used to describe any symptoms of pain or discomfort in the upper abdomen.

When symptoms are present, they may include

- upper abdominal discomfort or pain

- nausea

- vomiting

Seek Help for Symptoms of Bleeding in the Stomach

Erosive gastritis may cause ulcers or erosions in the stomach lining that can bleed. Signs and symptoms of bleeding in the stomach include

- shortness of breath
- dizziness or feeling faint
- red blood in vomit
- black, tarry stools
- red blood in the stool
- weakness
- paleness

A person with any signs or symptoms of bleeding in the stomach should call or see a health care provider right away.

What are the complications of chronic and acute gastritis?

The complications of chronic gastritis may include

- peptic ulcers. Peptic ulcers are sores involving the lining of the stomach or duodenum, the first part of the small intestine. NSAID use and *H. pylori* gastritis increase the chance of developing peptic ulcers.

- atrophic gastritis. Atrophic gastritis happens when chronic inflammation of the stomach lining causes the loss of the stomach lining and glands. Chronic gastritis can progress to atrophic gastritis.

- anemia. Erosive gastritis can cause chronic bleeding in the stomach, and the blood loss can lead to anemia. Anemia is a condition in which red blood cells are fewer or smaller than normal, which prevents the body's cells from getting enough oxygen. Red blood cells contain hemoglobin, an iron-rich protein that gives blood its red color and enables the red blood cells to transport oxygen from the lungs to the tissues of the body. Research suggests that *H. pylori* gastritis and autoimmune atrophic gastritis can interfere with the body's ability to absorb iron from food, which may also cause anemia.

- vitamin B12 deficiency and pernicious anemia. People with autoimmune atrophic gastritis do not produce enough intrinsic factor. Intrinsic factor is a protein made in the stomach and helps the intestines absorb vitamin B12. The body needs vitamin B12 to make red blood cells and nerve cells. Poor absorption of vitamin B12 may lead to a type of anemia called pernicious anemia.

- growths in the stomach lining. Chronic gastritis increases the chance of developing benign, or noncancerous, and malignant, or cancerous, growths in the stomach lining. Chronic *H. pylori* gastritis increases the chance of developing a type of cancer called gastric mucosa-associated lymphoid tissue (MALT) lymphoma.

In most cases, acute gastritis does not lead to complications. In rare cases, acute stress gastritis can cause severe bleeding that can be life threatening.

How is gastritis diagnosed?

A health care provider diagnoses gastritis based on the following:

- medical history
- physical exam

- upper GI endoscopy
- other tests

Medical History

Taking a medical history may help the health care provider diagnose gastritis. He or she will ask the patient to provide a medical history. The history may include questions about chronic symptoms and travel to developing countries.

Physical Exam

A physical exam may help diagnose gastritis. During a physical exam, a health care provider usually

- examines a patient's body
- uses a stethoscope to listen to sounds in the abdomen
- taps on the abdomen checking for tenderness or pain

Upper GI Endoscopy

Upper GI endoscopy is a procedure that uses an endoscope—a small, flexible camera with a light—to see the upper GI tract. A health care provider performs the test at a hospital or an outpatient center. The health care provider carefully feeds the endoscope down the esophagus and into the stomach and duodenum. The small camera built into the endoscope transmits a video image to a monitor, allowing close examination of the GI lining. A health care provider may give a patient a liquid anesthetic to gargle or may spray anesthetic on the back of the patient's throat before inserting the endoscope. A health care provider will place an intravenous (IV) needle in a vein in the arm to administer sedation. Sedatives help patients stay relaxed and comfortable. The test may show signs of inflammation or erosions in the stomach lining.

The health care provider can use tiny tools passed through the endoscope to perform biopsies. A biopsy is a procedure that involves taking a piece of tissue for examination with a microscope by a pathologist—a doctor who specializes in examining tissues to diagnose diseases. A health care provider may use the biopsy to diagnose gastritis, find the cause of gastritis, and find out if chronic gastritis has progressed to atrophic gastritis.

Other Tests

A health care provider may have a patient complete other tests to identify the cause of gastritis or any complications. These tests may include the following:

- **Upper GI series.** Upper GI series is an X-ray exam that provides a look at the shape of the upper GI tract. An X-ray technician performs this test at a hospital or an outpatient center, and a radiologist—a doctor who specializes in medical imaging—interprets the images. This test does not require anesthesia. A patient should not eat or drink before the procedure, as directed by the health care provider. Patients should check with their health care provider about what to do to prepare for an upper GI series. During the procedure, the patient will stand or sit in front of an X-ray machine and drink barium, a chalky liquid. Barium coats the esophagus, stomach, and small intestine so the radiologist and health care provider can see these organs' shapes more clearly on X-rays. A patient may experience bloating and nausea for a short time after the test. For several days afterward, barium liquid in the GI tract may cause white or light-colored stools. A health care provider will give the patient specific instructions about eating and drinking after the test.

- **Blood tests.** A health care provider may use blood tests to check for anemia or *H. pylori*. A health care provider draws a blood sample during an office visit or at a commercial facility and sends the sample to a lab for analysis.

- **Stool test.** A health care provider may use a stool test to check for blood in the stool, another sign of bleeding in the stomach, and for *H. pylori* infection. A stool test is an analysis of a sample of stool. The health care provider will give the patient a container for catching and storing the stool. The patient returns the sample to the health care provider or a commercial facility that will send the sample to a lab for analysis.

- **Urea breath test.** A health care provider may use a urea breath test to check for *H. pylori* infection. The patient swallows a capsule, liquid, or pudding that contains urea—a waste product the body produces as it breaks down protein. The urea is "labeled" with a special carbon atom. If *H. pylori* are present, the bacteria will convert the urea into carbon dioxide. After a few minutes, the patient breathes into a container, exhaling carbon dioxide. A nurse or technician will perform this test at a health care provider's office or a commercial facility and send the samples to a lab. If the test detects the labeled carbon atoms in the exhaled breath, the health care provider will confirm an *H. pylori* infection in the GI tract.

How is gastritis treated?

Health care providers treat gastritis with medications to

- reduce the amount of acid in the stomach
- treat the underlying cause

Reduce the Amount of Acid in the Stomach

The stomach lining of a person with gastritis may have less protection from acidic digestive juice. Reducing acid can promote healing of the stomach lining. Medications that reduce acid include

- **antacids,** such as Alka-Seltzer, Maalox, Mylanta, Rolaids, and Riopan. Many brands use different combinations of three basic salts—magnesium, aluminum, and calcium—along with hydroxide or bicarbonate ions to neutralize stomach acid. Antacids, however, can have side effects. Magnesium salt can lead to diarrhea, and aluminum salt can cause constipation. Magnesium and aluminum salts are often combined in a single product to balance these effects. Calcium carbonate antacids, such as Tums, Titralac, and Alka-2, can cause constipation.

- **H2 blockers,** such as cimetidine (Tagamet HB), famotidine (Pepcid AC), nizatidine (Axid AR), and ranitidine (Zantac 75). H2 blockers decrease acid production. They are available in both over-the-counter and prescription strengths.

- **proton pump inhibitors (PPIs)** include omeprazole (Prilosec, Zegerid), lansoprazole (Prevacid), dexlansoprazole (Dexilant), pantoprazole (Protonix), rabeprazole (AcipHex), and esomeprazole (Nexium). PPIs decrease acid production more effectively than H2 blockers. All of these medications are available by prescription. Omeprazole and lansoprazole are also available in over-the-counter strength.

Treat the Underlying Cause

Depending on the cause of gastritis, a health care provider may recommend additional treatments.

- Treating *H. pylori* infection with antibiotics is important, even if a person does not have symptoms from the infection. Curing the infection often cures the gastritis and decreases the chance of developing complications, such as peptic ulcer disease, MALT lymphoma, and gastric cancer.

- Avoiding the cause of reactive gastritis can provide some people with a cure. For example, if prolonged NSAID use is the cause of the gastritis, a health care provider may advise the patient to stop taking the NSAIDs, reduce the dose, or change pain medications.

- Health care providers may prescribe medications to prevent or treat stress gastritis in a patient who is critically ill or injured. Medications to protect the stomach lining include sucralfate (Carafate), H2 blockers, and PPIs. Treating the underlying illness or injury most often cures stress gastritis.

- Health care providers may treat people with pernicious anemia due to autoimmune atrophic gastritis with vitamin B12 injections.

How can gastritis be prevented?

People may be able to reduce their chances of getting gastritis by preventing *H. pylori* infection. No one knows for sure how *H. pylori* infection spreads, so prevention is difficult. To help prevent infection, health care providers advise people to

- wash their hands with soap and water after using the bathroom and before eating

- eat food that has been washed well and cooked properly

- drink water from a clean, safe source

Eating, Diet, and Nutrition

Researchers have not found that eating, diet, and nutrition play a major role in causing or preventing gastritis.

Chapter 13

Headache and Its Link to Stress

You're sitting at your desk, working on a difficult task, when it suddenly feels as if a belt or vice is being tightened around the top of your head. Or you have periodic headaches that occur with nausea and increased sensitivity to light or sound. Maybe you are involved in a routine, non-stressful task when you're struck by head or neck pain.

Sound familiar? If so, you've suffered one of the many types of headache that can occur on its own or as part of another disease or health condition.

Anyone can experience a headache. Nearly 2 out of 3 children will have a headache by age 15. More than 9 in 10 adults will experience a headache sometime in their life. Headache is our most common form of pain and a major reason cited for days missed at work or school as well as visits to the doctor. Without proper treatment, headaches can be severe and interfere with daily activities.

Certain types of headache run in families. Episodes of headache may ease or even disappear for a time and recur later in life. It's possible to have more than one type of headache at the same time.

This chapter includes excerpts from "Headache: Hope Through Research," National Institute of Neurological Disorders and Stroke (NINDS), July 17, 2015; and text from "Migraine fact sheet," Office on Women's Health (OWH), July 16, 2012.

Primary headaches occur independently and are not caused by another medical condition. It's uncertain what sets the process of a primary headache in motion. A cascade of events that affect blood vessels and nerves inside and outside the head causes pain signals to be sent to the brain. Brain chemicals called *neurotransmitters* are involved in creating head pain, as are changes in nerve cell activity (called *cortical spreading depression*). Migraine, cluster, and tension-type headache are the more familiar types of primary headache.

Secondary headaches are symptoms of another health disorder that causes pain-sensitive nerve endings to be pressed on or pulled or pushed out of place. They may result from underlying conditions including fever, infection, medication overuse, stress or emotional conflict, high blood pressure, psychiatric disorders, head injury or trauma, stroke, tumors, and nerve disorders (particularly trigeminal neuralgia, a chronic pain condition that typically affects a major nerve on one side of the jaw or cheek).

Headaches can range in frequency and severity of pain. Some individuals may experience headaches once or twice a year, while others may experience headaches more than 15 days a month. Some headaches may recur or last for weeks at a time. Pain can range from mild to disabling and may be accompanied by symptoms such as nausea or increased sensitivity to noise or light, depending on the type of headache.

Why Headaches Hurt

Information about touch, pain, temperature, and vibration in the head and neck is sent to the brain by the trigeminal nerve, one of 12 pairs of cranial nerves that start at the base of the brain.

The nerve has three branches that conduct sensations from the scalp, the blood vessels inside and outside of the skull, the lining around the brain (*the meninges*), and the face, mouth, neck, ears, eyes, and throat.

Brain tissue itself lacks pain-sensitive nerves and does not feel pain. Headaches occur when pain-sensitive nerve endings called *nociceptors* react to headache triggers (such as stress, certain foods or odors, or use of medicines) and send messages through the *trigeminal* nerve to the thalamus, the brain's "relay station" for pain sensation from all over the body. The thalamus controls the body's sensitivity to light and noise and sends messages to parts of the brain that manage awareness of pain and emotional response to it. Other parts of the brain may also be part of the process, causing nausea, vomiting, diarrhea, trouble concentrating, and other neurological symptoms.

When to see a doctor

Not all headaches require a physician's attention. But headaches can signal a more serious disorder that requires prompt medical care. Immediately call or see a physician if you or someone you're with experience any of these symptoms:

- Sudden, severe headache that may be accompanied by a stiff neck.

- Severe headache accompanied by fever, nausea, or vomiting that is not related to another illness.

- "First" or "worst" headache, often accompanied by confusion, weakness, double vision, or loss of consciousness.

- Headache that worsens over days or weeks or has changed in pattern or behavior.

- Recurring headache in children.

- Headache following a head injury.

- Headache and a loss of sensation or weakness in any part of the body, which could be a sign of a stroke.

- Headache associated with convulsions.

- Headache associated with shortness of breath.

- Two or more headaches a week.

- Persistent headache in someone who has been previously headache-free, particularly in someone over age 50.

- New headaches in someone with a history of cancer or HIV/ AIDS.

Diagnosing Your Headache

How and under what circumstances a person experiences a headache can be key to diagnosing its cause. Keeping a headache journal can help a physician better diagnose your type of headache and determine the best treatment. After each headache, note the time of day when it occurred; its intensity and duration; any sensitivity to light, odors, or sound; activity immediately prior to the headache; use of prescription and nonprescription medicines; amount of sleep the previous night; any stressful or emotional conditions; any influence from weather or daily activity; foods and fluids consumed in the past 24 hours; and any known health conditions at that time. Women should record the days of their menstrual cycles. Include notes about other family members who have a history of headache or other disorder. A pattern may emerge that can be helpful to reducing or preventing headaches.

Once your doctor has reviewed your medical and headache history and conducted a physical and neurological exam, lab screening and diagnostic tests may be ordered to either rule out or identify conditions that might be the cause of your headaches. Blood tests and urinalysis can help diagnose brain or spinal cord infections, blood vessel damage, and toxins that affect the nervous system. Testing a sample of the fluid that surrounds the brain and spinal cord can detect infections, bleeding in the brain (called a brain hemorrhage), and measure any buildup of pressure within the skull. Diagnostic imaging, such as with Computed Tomography (CT) and Magnetic Resonance Imaging (MRI), can detect irregularities in blood vessels and bones, certain brain tumors and cysts, brain damage from head injury, brain hemorrhage, inflammation, infection, and other disorders. Neuroimaging also gives doctors a way to see what's happening in the brain during headache attacks. An electroencephalogram (EEG) measures brain wave activity and can help diagnose brain tumors, seizures, head injury, and inflammation that may lead to headaches.

Stress causing headaches

Stress can trigger both migraine and tension-type headache. Events like getting married, moving to a new home, or having a baby can cause stress. But studies show that everyday stresses — *not* major life changes—cause most headaches. Juggling many roles, such as being a mother and wife, having a career, and financial pressures, can be daily stresses for women.

Making time for yourself and finding healthy ways to deal with stress are important. Some things you can do to help prevent or reduce stress include:

• Eating healthy foods

• Being active (at least 30 minutes most days of the week is best)

• Doing relaxation exercises

• Getting enough sleep

132

Try to figure out what causes you to feel stressed. You may be able to cut out some of these stressors. For example, if driving to work is stressful, try taking the bus or subway. You can take this time to read or listen to music, rather than deal with traffic. For stressors you can't avoid, keeping organized and doing as much as you can ahead of time will help you to feel in control.

Chapter 14

Heart and Cardiovascular Problems

Chapter Contents

Section 14.1

PTSD and Heart Disease

Text in this section is excerpted from "Heart-mind mystery," Office
of Research and Development (ORD), February 28, 2014; and text
from "Emotional stress and heart disease in women: an interview
with Dr. Viola Vaccarino," National Heart, Lung, and Blood Institute
(NHLBI), July 12, 2014.

So how exactly does post-traumatic stress disorder (PTSD) affect the heart?

While most experts agree there's a strong link, maybe even a causal
one, between PTSD and heart disease, theories abound as to how
exactly that disease process works. Is the main culprit stress hormones
that damage blood vessels over time? The bad health habits that tend
to go along with PTSD, such as smoking and not exercising? Or poor
sleep quality, which can thwart the immune system? In all likelihood,
it's all of these and more, all interacting in complex ways.

Another question: Is there something unique about PTSD's effects
on the heart, or is the same impact seen with related emotional problems, such as depression, anxiety, and hostility?

The links between those mental conditions and heart disease are
well-documented. One recent study looked at the records of more than
236,000 Veterans and found a higher incidence of heart failure among
those with depression or anxiety alone, or the combination of both.
Past studies have found similar links to heart attack. Teasing out the
impact of those conditions, versus that of PTSD alone, can be difficult.
The consensus so far is that PTSD exerts an effect independent of any
other conditions.

Dr. Mary Whooley , at the San Francisco VA Medical Center and
UCSF, leads the Heart and Soul Study, which followed more than
1,000 heart patients for a decade. Her research has focused mainly on
depression, not PTSD, but there are clear parallels.

She calls the relationship between depression and heart disease
"complex and bidirectional," and suggests the same could be said of
PTSD.

A couple of her papers have used a graphic that shows a circle with five boxes, with arrows going from one to the next. At the top is depression. The condition itself leads to harmful behaviors: inactivity, poor eating habits, social isolation, smoking, lack of adherence to medication regimens. These habits unleash a cascade of biological changes. They center on the autonomic nervous system, which controls heart rate and blood pressure, and which also triggers a release of stress hormones, involving the hypothalamus in the brain and the pituitary and adrenal glands. Other effects: Inflammation rises, blood vessels constrict, platelets clump together in the blood, raising the risk of clots.

This all contributes to cardiovascular disease. And that, in turn creates, physical health problems, difficulty with everyday tasks, money trouble, emotional distress.

The circle ends up back at depression. The cycle starts over again.

Says Whooley, "It's pretty obvious at this point that it goes both ways," referring to the link between depression and heart disease.

It wasn't always so obvious. For years, she says, the main focus of research was post-heart attack depression. It was clear that heart disease could cause depression. There was far less recognition of depression as a primary driver of heart disease in the first place. That view has changed.

PTSD and depression—some parallels, some differences

What's getting the most attention now as a factor in heart disease, says Whooley, is the behavioral dimension of depression. A few of her studies have suggested that poor health habits "strongly contribute" to the development of heart disease.

"The emphasis is now on, well maybe this is a health behavior issue that can be modified, rather than a biological consequence we can't do anything about."

A similar dynamic, she notes, may apply in PTSD, with some key differences.

"Certainly there are different things that cause PTSD versus depression. And each may have different physiological responses that contribute to cardiovascular disease in different ways. For example, patients with depression often suffer from chronic anxiety, but patients with PTSD also tend to experience acute sensations of stress and panic that can impair blood flow to the heart. So stress-induced ischemia— low blood flow to the heart—is probably a more significant mechanism in PTSD than in depression."

At the same time, says Whooley, "There is likely to be significant overlap as far as how the two conditions are linked with heart disease. PTSD patients also have poor health behaviors, and these behavioral changes are linked to elevated inflammation and norepinephrine." Norepinephrine, also called noradrenaline, is a hormone released in response to stress.

The neurobiology of PTSD

Whooley's depression model, with its focus on poor health habits driving biological changes, may help explain, to a large extent, how PTSD damages the heart. But others place equal emphasis on how the emotional state of PTSD itself may *directly* vex the cardiovascular system.

One hallmark of PTSD is hyperarousal—feeling keyed up, on the lookout for danger. Another is mentally reliving the trauma, through flashbacks or nightmares. These symptoms, along with others, might set in motion the body's stress response, starting in the brain and orchestrated by the autonomic nervous system. Norepinephrine and other hormones are secreted, triggering changes throughout the tissues and organs of the body.

It's the "fight or flight" response, which is how the body responds to danger and threats. The heart beats faster, arteries constrict, blood pressure increases. The platelets in the blood become stickier, in preparation for clotting a potential wound. More glucose is pumped into the bloodstream, for quick energy. This can all save your life if you're being chased by a tiger. But when the process happens repeatedly over time, in response to chronic emotional stress, the lining of the arteries gets damaged. The heart muscle weakens. The effect is destructive, not protective.

A theory to tie it all together

Schnurr believes these direct biological links have a lot to do with PTSD's role in heart disease and other medical problems. But she doesn't discount the other mechanisms: poor health habits, for example, or related psychological conditions, such as depression or hostility.

The bottom line is, no one single mechanism seems to account for the relatively huge impact of PTSD on heart health and mortality. "We have links between stress and health," says Schnurr, "but we don't have the type of direct one-to-one links you might expect. And so it's hard to get from point A to point B."

To tie it all together, she likes to cite the "allostatic load" theory, first proposed in the late 1980s. "It seems like a good way to connect the dots," says Schnurr.

Allostatic load refers to the cumulative burden of stress. Every time the body goes through these many physiological changes to adapt to stress—some of them small and subtle—the experience adds to the overall wear and tear on the organism. It's like adding miles on your car and all its parts. Eventually, says Schnurr, "we pay a price.

"For the most part, the biological changes we see are not clinically remarkable. So it's hard to argue that any by themselves could lead to the types of physical health changes we see in PTSD. So conceptually, this theory makes sense."

What is the current state of the science regarding the relationship between emotional stress and heart disease in women?

There is growing recognition of the importance of emotional stress as a risk factor for heart disease. Compared to men, women have higher levels of psychological risk factors such as early life adversity, post-traumatic stress disorder, and depression. In addition, women are more prone to develop mental problems as a result of stress. Emotional or psychological stress potentially contributes to heart disease in many ways, from influencing heart disease risk factors, to affecting the development of atherosclerosis (hardening of the arteries), to triggering heart attacks. It also may impair the recovery, future health, and quality of life of patients who have already developed the disease.

Emerging evidence suggests that young women are especially vulnerable to the negative effects of stress on the heart, which may result in earlier onset of heart disease or more negative health outcomes if the disease is already present.*

What are the key findings from the Myocardial Infarction and Mental Stress Study (MIMS) related to young women and emotional stress?

The aim of the study was to determine whether it is more common for young women to have myocardial ischemia (reduced blood flow to the heart that can lead to heart attacks) after an emotional stressor compared with men of the same age. Ninety-eight post-heart attack patients (49 women and 49 men) ages 38 to 60 years participated. When exposed to an emotional stressor in the laboratory, women age

50 or younger showed approximately twice the levels of myocardial ischemia compared to men of the same age with similar characteristics. This higher level of what we refer to as mental stress-induced myocardial ischemia continued even after overall health status, heart disease severity, and depression were taken into account. Interestingly, we did not find this gender difference in men and women over age 50. There is something specific about these younger women that makes them particularly vulnerable to emotional/mental stress. This increased vulnerability may result from the fact that these women had a high burden of life stressors and challenging social conditions, such as poverty, depression and history of abuse. Although these conditions did not explain their higher rate of reduced blood flow to the heart, these life stressors may have signaled a higher vulnerability towards emotional stress.

Participants were exposed to an emotional stressor using a standardized mental stress test. First they were placed in a quiet room for 30 minutes to rest. Then they were asked to imagine a stressful life situation, such as a family member being mistreated, and to present the story within three minutes in front of a video camera to an intimidating audience of people wearing white coats. To further increase stress, they were told that their speech would be evaluated by staff. Subsequently, pictures of the heart were taken to examine whether reduced blood flow (ischemia) occurred during mental stress. On a separate day, participants underwent an exercise stress test by walking on a treadmill, and pictures of the heart were taken in a similar way to examine whether there was reduced blood flow with physical stress as a comparison. Compared with age-matched men, women 50 years or younger had twice the rate of mental stress induced myocardial ischemia (52 percent versus 25 percent). Unlike mental stress, we did not see gender differences in ischemia after physical stress tests.

These results are particularly intriguing given that the women tended to have less severe heart disease than men as determined by the degree of blockage in their coronary arteries. We think that abnormal constriction of the coronary arteries, especially the smaller arteries, played a role in mental stress-induced ischemia in these young women rather than coronary blockage. In fact, microvascular dysfunction –constriction of the small blood vessels that lead to the heart– is thought to be more common in women than men, and has been linked to emotional stress and mental stress-induced ischemia.

Ischemia triggered by mental stress has been associated with a doubling of risk for future heart attacks and death in cardiac patients. It could explain why young women (under age 50) who have a heart attack die twice as often as men of the same age despite having less severe heart disease.

What do you see as potential future directions for research into the role of emotional stress in heart disease in women?

Our ultimate goal is to translate this research so that it can be used in clinical practice and prevention. We hope to show that mental stress testing may be a good way to identify those at risk earlier on so that interventions can take place to improve prognosis of heart disease in these patients, or even long before a heart attack ever happens.

Future research needs to focus on younger women and men to better understand the risk pathways that link emotional stress to heart disease risk and allow for prevention before it is too late. In particular, we need to focus more on women under age 50, a group that is rarely studied, so that we can uncover the factors that drive their increased vulnerability to stress. Once we better understand these factors and pathways, we can develop tailored interventions.

"This work is important in helping us gain clues about the processes in the body that contribute to gender differences in health outcomes associated with heart disease," explained Catherine M. Stoney, Ph.D., program director in the Division of Cardiovascular Sciences at the NIH's National Heart, Lung, and Blood Institute.

Section 14.2

Stress and Coronary Heart Disease

Text in this section is excerpted from "What Is Coronary Heart Disease?" National Heart, Lung, and Blood Institute (NHLBI), September 29, 2014.

What Is Coronary Heart Disease?

Coronary heart disease (CHD) is a disease in which a waxy substance called plaque (plak) builds up inside the coronary arteries. These arteries supply oxygen-rich blood to your heart muscle.

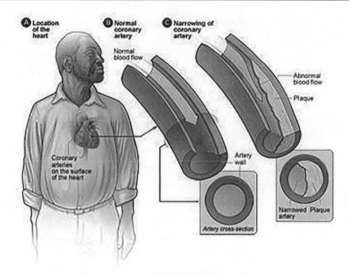

Figure 14.1. *Atherosclerosis Figure A shows the location of the heart in the body. Figure B shows a normal coronary artery with normal blood flow. The inset image shows a cross-section of a normal coronary artery. Figure C shows a coronary artery narrowed by plaque. The buildup of plaque limits the flow of oxygen-rich blood through the artery. The inset image shows a cross-section of the plaque-narrowed artery.*

When plaque builds up in the arteries, the condition is called atherosclerosis (ATH-er-o-skler-O-sis). The buildup of plaque occurs over many years.

Over time, plaque can harden or rupture (break open). Hardened plaque narrows the coronary arteries and reduces the flow of oxygen-rich blood to the heart.

If the plaque ruptures, a blood clot can form on its surface. A large blood clot can mostly or completely block blood flow through a coronary artery. Over time, ruptured plaque also hardens and narrows the coronary arteries.

Overview

If the flow of oxygen-rich blood to your heart muscle is reduced or blocked, angina (an-JI-nuh) or a heart attack can occur.

Angina is chest pain or discomfort. It may feel like pressure or squeezing in your chest. The pain also can occur in your shoulders, arms, neck, jaw, or back. Angina pain may even feel like indigestion.

A heart attack occurs if the flow of oxygen-rich blood to a section of heart muscle is cut off. If blood flow isn't restored quickly, the section of heart muscle begins to die. Without quick treatment, a heart attack can lead to serious health problems or death.

Over time, CHD can weaken the heart muscle and lead to heart failure and arrhythmias (ah-RITH-me-ahs). Heart failure is a condition in which your heart can't pump enough blood to meet your body's needs. Arrhythmias are problems with the rate or rhythm of the heartbeat.

Outlook

CHD is the most common type of heart disease. In the United States, CHD is the #1 cause of death for both men and women. Lifestyle changes, medicines, and medical procedures can help prevent or treat CHD. These treatments may reduce the risk of related health problems.

Who Is at Risk for Coronary Heart Disease?

In the United States, coronary heart disease (CHD) is a leading cause of death for both men and women. Each year, about 375,000 Americans die from CHD.

Certain traits, conditions, or habits may raise your risk for CHD. The more risk factors you have, the more likely you are to develop the disease.

You can control many risk factors, which may help prevent or delay CHD.

Major Risk Factors

- Unhealthy blood cholesterol levels. This includes high LDL cholesterol (sometimes called "bad" cholesterol) and low HDL cholesterol (sometimes called "good" cholesterol).

- High blood pressure. Blood pressure is considered high if it stays at or above 140/90 mmHg over time. If you have diabetes or chronic kidney disease, high blood pressure is defined as 130/80 mmHg or higher. (The mmHg is millimeters of mercury—the units used to measure blood pressure.)

- Smoking. Smoking can damage and tighten blood vessels, lead to unhealthy cholesterol levels, and raise blood pressure. Smoking also can limit how much oxygen reaches the body's tissues.

143

- Insulin resistance. This condition occurs if the body can't use its own insulin properly. Insulin is a hormone that helps move blood sugar into cells where it's used for energy. Insulin resistance may lead to diabetes.

- Diabetes. With this disease, the body's blood sugar level is too high because the body doesn't make enough insulin or doesn't use its insulin properly.

- Overweight or obesity. The terms "overweight" and "obesity" refer to body weight that's greater than what is considered healthy for a certain height.

- Metabolic syndrome. Metabolic syndrome is the name for a group of risk factors that raises your risk for CHD and other health problems, such as diabetes and stroke.

- Lack of physical activity. Being physically inactive can worsen other risk factors for CHD, such as unhealthy blood cholesterol levels, high blood pressure, diabetes, and overweight or obesity.

- Unhealthy diet. An unhealthy diet can raise your risk for CHD. Foods that are high in saturated and *trans* fats, cholesterol, sodium (salt), and sugar can worsen other risk factors for CHD.

- Older age. Genetic or lifestyle factors cause plaque to build up in your arteries as you age. By the time you're middle-aged or older, enough plaque has built up to cause signs or symptoms. In men, the risk for CHD increases after age 45. In women, the risk for CHD increases after age 55.

- Family history of early heart disease. Your risk increases if your father or a brother was diagnosed with CHD before 55 years of age, or if your mother or a sister was diagnosed with CHD before 65 years of age.

- Although older age and a family history of early heart disease are risk factors, it doesn't mean that you'll develop CHD if you have one or both. Controlling other risk factors often can lessen genetic influences and help prevent CHD, even in older adults.

Emerging Risk Factors

Researchers continue to study other possible risk factors for CHD. High levels of a protein called C-reactive protein (CRP) in the blood may raise the risk of CHD and heart attack. High levels of CRP are a sign of inflammation in the body.

Inflammation is the body's response to injury or infection. Damage to the arteries' inner walls may trigger inflammation and help plaque grow.

Research is under way to find out whether reducing inflammation and lowering CRP levels also can reduce the risk of CHD and heart attack.

High levels of triglycerides (tri-GLIH-seh-rides) in the blood also may raise the risk of CHD, especially in women. Triglycerides are a type of fat.

Other Risks Related to Coronary Heart Disease

Other conditions and factors also may contribute to CHD, including:

- Sleep apnea. Sleep apnea is a common disorder in which you have one or more pauses in breathing or shallow breaths while you sleep. Untreated sleep apnea can increase your risk for high blood pressure, diabetes, and even a heart attack or stroke.

- Stress. Research shows that the most commonly reported "trigger" for a heart attack is an emotionally upsetting event, especially one involving anger.

- Alcohol. Heavy drinking can damage the heart muscle and worsen other CHD risk factors. Men should have no more than two drinks containing alcohol a day. Women should have no more than one drink containing alcohol a day.

- Preeclampsia (pre-e-KLAMP-se-ah). This condition can occur during pregnancy. The two main signs of preeclampsia are a rise in blood pressure and excess protein in the urine. Preeclampsia is linked to an increased lifetime risk of heart disease, including CHD, heart attack, heart failure, and high blood pressure.

Section 14.3

Stress and Broken Heart Syndrome

Text in this section is excerpted from "What is Broken Heart
Syndrome," National Heart, Lung, and Blood Institute (NHLBI),
October 8, 2014.

What is Broken Heart Syndrome

Broken heart syndrome is a condition in which extreme stress can
lead to heart muscle failure. The failure is severe, but often short-term.

Most people who experience broken heart syndrome think they may
be having a heart attack, a more common medical emergency caused
by a blocked coronary (heart) artery. The two conditions have similar
symptoms, including chest pain and shortness of breath. However,
there's no evidence of blocked coronary arteries in broken heart syndrome, and most people have a full and quick recovery.

Overview

Broken heart syndrome is a recently recognized heart problem. It
was originally reported in the Asian population in 1990 and named
takotsubo cardiomyopathy (KAR-de-o-mi-OP-ah-thee). In this condition, the heart is so weak that it assumes a bulging shape ("tako tsubo"
is the term for an octopus trap, whose shape resembles the bulging
appearance of the heart during this condition). Cases have since been
reported worldwide, and the first reports of broken heart syndrome in
the United States appeared in 1998. The condition also is commonly
called stress-induced cardiomyopathy.

The cause of broken heart syndrome is not fully known. In most
cases, symptoms are triggered by extreme emotional or physical stress,
such as intense grief, anger, or surprise. Researchers think that the
stress releases hormones that "stun" the heart and affect its ability to
pump blood to the body. (The term "stunned" is often used to indicate
that the injury to the heart muscle is only temporary.)

People who have broken heart syndrome often have sudden intense
chest pain and shortness of breath. These symptoms begin just a few
minutes to hours after exposure to the unexpected stress. Many seek

emergency care, concerned they are having a heart attack. Often, patients who have broken heart syndrome have previously been healthy.

Women are more likely than men to have broken heart syndrome. Researchers are just starting to explore what causes this disorder and how to diagnose and treat it.

Broken Heart Syndrome versus Heart Attack

Symptoms of broken heart syndrome can look like those of a heart attack.

Most heart attacks are caused by blockages and blood clots forming in the coronary arteries, which supply the heart with blood. If these clots cut off the blood supply to the heart for a long enough period of time, heart muscle cells can die, leaving the heart with permanent damage. Heart attacks most often occur as a result of coronary heart disease (CHD), also called coronary artery disease.

Broken heart syndrome is quite different. Most people who experience broken heart syndrome have fairly normal coronary arteries, without severe blockages or clots. The heart cells are "stunned" by stress hormones but not killed. The "stunning" effects reverse quickly, often within just a few days or weeks. In most cases, there is no lasting damage to the heart.

Because symptoms are similar to a heart attack, it is important to seek help right away. You, and sometimes emergency care providers, may not be able to tell that you have broken heart syndrome until you have some tests.

All chest pain should be checked by a doctor. If you think you or someone else may be having heart attack symptoms or a heart attack, don't ignore it or feel embarrassed to call for help. Call 9–1–1 for emergency medical care. In the case of a heart attack, acting fast at the first sign of symptoms can save your life and limit damage to your heart.

Outlook

Research is ongoing to learn more about broken heart syndrome and its causes.

The symptoms of broken heart syndrome are treatable, and most people who experience it have a full recovery, usually within days or weeks. The heart muscle is not permanently damaged, and the risk of broken heart syndrome happening again is low.

Chapter 15

Stress and Multiple Sclerosis

What is Multiple Sclerosis?

An unpredictable disease of the central nervous system, multiple sclerosis (MS) can range from relatively benign to somewhat disabling to devastating, as communication between the brain and other parts of the body is disrupted. Many investigators believe MS to be an auto-immune disease—one in which the body, through its immune system, launches a defensive attack against its own tissues. In the case of MS, it is the nerve-insulating myelin that comes under assault. Such assaults may be linked to an unknown environmental trigger, perhaps a virus.

Most people experience their first symptoms of MS between the ages of 20 and 40; the initial symptom of MS is often blurred or double vision, red-green color distortion, or even blindness in one eye. Most MS patients experience muscle weakness in their extremities and difficulty with coordination and balance. These symptoms may be severe enough to impair walking or even standing. In the worst cases, MS can produce partial or complete paralysis. Most people with MS also exhibit paresthesias, transitory abnormal sensory feelings such as numbness, prickling, or "pins and needles" sensations. Some may also experience pain. Speech impediments, tremors, and dizziness are

This chapter includes excerpts from "Multiple Sclerosis Information Page," National Institute of Neurological Disorders and Stroke (NINDS), July 17, 2015; and text from "Multiple Sclerosis Centers of Excellence," United States Depart-ment of Veterans Affairs (VA), June 3, 2015.

other frequent complaints. Occasionally, people with MS have hearing loss. Approximately half of all people with MS experience cognitive impairments such as difficulties with concentration, attention, memory, and poor judgment, but such symptoms are usually mild and are frequently overlooked. Depression is another common feature of MS.

Is there any treatment?

There is as yet no cure for MS. Many patients do well with no therapy at all, especially since many medications have serious side effects and some carry significant risks. However, three forms of beta interferon (Avonex, Betaseron, and Rebif) have now been approved by the Food and Drug Administration for treatment of relapsing-remitting MS. Beta interferon has been shown to reduce the number of exacerbations and may slow the progression of physical disability. When attacks do occur, they tend to be shorter and less severe. The FDA also has approved a synthetic form of myelin basic protein, called copolymer I (Copaxone), for the treatment of relapsing-remitting MS. Copolymer I has few side effects, and studies indicate that the agent can reduce the relapse rate by almost one third. Other FDA approved drugs to treat relapsing forms of MS in adults include teriflunomide and dimethyl fumarate. An immunosuppressant treatment, Novantrone (mitoxantrone), is approved by the FDA for the treatment of advanced or chronic MS. The FDA has also approved dalfampridine (Ampyra) to improve walking in individuals with MS.

One monoclonal antibody, natalizumab (Tysabri), was shown in clinical trials to significantly reduce the frequency of attacks in people with relapsing forms of MS and was approved for marketing by the U.S. Food and Drug Administration (FDA) in 2004. However, in 2005 the drug's manufacturer voluntarily suspended marketing of the drug after several reports of significant adverse events. In 2006, the FDA again approved sale of the drug for MS but under strict treatment guidelines involving infusion centers where patients can be monitored by specially trained physicians.

While steroids do not affect the course of MS over time, they can reduce the duration and severity of attacks in some patients. Spasticity, which can occur either as a sustained stiffness caused by increased muscle tone or as spasms that come and go, is usually treated with muscle relaxants and tranquilizers such as baclofen, tizanidine, diazepam, clonazepam, and dantrolene. Physical therapy and exercise can help preserve remaining function, and patients may find that various aids—such as foot braces, canes, and walkers—can help them remain independent and mobile. Avoiding excessive activity and avoiding heat are probably the most important measures patients can take to counter physiological fatigue. If psychological symptoms of fatigue such as depression or apathy are evident, antidepressant medications may help. Other drugs that may reduce fatigue in some, but not all, patients include amantadine (Symmetrel), pemoline (Cylert), and the still-experimental drug aminopyridine. Although improvement of optic symptoms usually occurs even without treatment, a short course of treatment with intravenous methylprednisolone (Solu-Medrol) followed by treatment with oral steroids is sometimes used.

How is MS affected by Stress?

People with MS talk about stress all the time. Not everybody says that they have stress but an overwhelming number of people talk about it as an important piece of their lives. There are many reasons why that may be the case. There is a lot of uncertainty and unpredictability associated with living with MS. The disease progresses in different ways for different people. You may have periods of the onset and remission of disability in ways that you can't always plan for. MS comes with impairments that are both visible and invisible and these are stressful to different people in different ways. It can be stressful when gait impairment is noticed by others. Handling cognitive impairment can also be stressful.

MS requires that people are constantly needing to adjust and readjust that they're changing circumstances and figure out how to get by on a day-to-day basis. It may have significant financial implications, employment implications, impact relationships. If people have significant cognitive impairment, it may affect their decision making and their ability to navigate through the world. All these things can be stressful.

We all know that exercise is a good thing. Certainly, exercise is good for cardiac health, for heart health. It improves pulmonary function which can be something that is very important. It is something that's very important for people with MS. Again, exercise by putting stress on bones can promote increased bone density again, which can protect patients with MS from developing fractures should they fall.

Exercise promotes cognitive skills. We would expect that that would be because blood flow tends to increase when we're exercising and nutrients can better go to the brain but it's also been demonstrated that specific chemicals, proteins can be produced and secreted by people who exercise that are both neuro protective and also can promote regeneration of damaged nerve cells in the brain.

All of us who exercise will acknowledge the fact that exercise can help you relax. You can imagine that exercise can promote better mood. Strength, endurance, balance are other things that can be improved by exercise and certainly can benefit patients with Multiple Sclerosis.

Chapter 16

Stress and Back Pain

What Is Back Pain?

Back pain is an all-too-familiar problem that can range from a dull, constant ache to a sudden, sharp pain that leaves you incapacitated. It can come on suddenly—from an accident, a fall, or lifting something heavy—or it can develop slowly, perhaps as the result of age-related changes to the spine. Regardless of how back pain happens or how it feels, you know it when you have it. And chances are, if you don't have back pain now, you will eventually.

What Are the Causes of Back Pain?

It is important to understand that back pain is a symptom of a medical condition, not a diagnosis itself. Medical problems that can cause back pain include the following:

Mechanical problems: A mechanical problem is a problem with the way your spine moves or the way you feel when you move your spine in certain ways. Perhaps the most common mechanical cause of back pain is a condition called intervertebral disk degeneration, which simply means that the disks located between the vertebrae of

This chapter includes excerpts from "Handout on Health: Back Pain," National Institute of Arthritis and Musculoskeletal and Skin Diseases (NIAMS), March 2015; and text from "Chronic Pain and PTSD: A Guide for Patients," United States Department of Veterans Affairs (VA), January 3, 2014.

the spine are breaking down with age. As they deteriorate, they lose their cushioning ability. This problem can lead to pain if the back is stressed. Other mechanical causes of back pain include spasms, muscle tension, and ruptured disks, which are also called herniated disks.

Injuries: Spine injuries such as sprains and fractures can cause either short-lived or chronic pain. Sprains are tears in the ligaments that support the spine, and they can occur from twisting or lifting improperly. Fractured vertebrae are often the result of osteoporosis. Less commonly, back pain may be caused by more severe injuries that result from accidents or falls.

Acquired conditions and diseases: Many medical problems can cause or contribute to back pain. They include scoliosis, a curvature of the spine that does not usually cause pain until middle age; spondylolisthesis; various forms of arthritis, including osteoarthritis, rheumatoid arthritis, and ankylosing spondylitis; and spinal stenosis, a narrowing of the spinal column that puts pressure on the spinal cord and nerves. Although osteoporosis itself is not painful, it can lead to painful fractures of the vertebrae. Other causes of back pain include pregnancy; kidney stones or infections; endometriosis, which is the buildup of uterine tissue in places outside the uterus; and fibromyalgia, a condition of widespread muscle pain and fatigue.

Infections and tumors: Although they are not common causes of back pain, infections can cause pain when they involve the vertebrae, a condition called osteomyelitis, or when they involve the disks that cushion the vertebrae, which is called diskitis. Tumors also are relatively rare causes of back pain. Occasionally, tumors begin in the back, but more often they appear in the back as a result of cancer that has spread from elsewhere in the body.

Although the causes of back pain are usually physical, emotional stress can play a role in how severe pain is and how long it lasts. Stress can affect the body in many ways, including causing back muscles to become tense and painful.

Chronic Pain and Stress-Related Disorders

What is chronic pain?

Chronic pain is when a person suffers from pain in a particular area of the body (for example, in the back or the neck) for at least three to six months. It may be as bad as, or even worse than, short-term pain, but it can feel like more of a problem because it lasts a longer time. Chronic pain lasts beyond the normal amount of time that an injury takes to heal.

Chronic pain can come from many things. Some people get chronic pain from normal wear and tear of the body or from aging. Others have chronic pain from various types of cancer, or other chronic medical illnesses. In some cases, the chronic pain may be from an injury that happened during an accident or an assault. Some chronic pain has no explanation.

What is the experience of chronic pain like physically?

There are many forms of chronic pain, including pain felt in: the low back (most common); the neck; the mouth, face, and jaw (TMJ); the pelvis; or the head (e.g., tension and migraine headaches). Of course, each type of condition results in different experiences of pain.

People with chronic pain are less able to function well in daily life than those who do not suffer from chronic pain. They may have trouble with things such as walking, standing, sitting, lifting light objects, doing paperwork, standing in line at a grocery store, going shopping, or working. Many patients with chronic pain cannot work because of their pain or physical limitations.

What is the experience of chronic pain like psychologically?

Research has shown that many patients who experience chronic pain (up to 100% of these patients) tend to also be diagnosed with depression. Because the pain and disability are always there and that may even become worse over time, many of them think suicide is the only way to end their pain and frustration. They think they have no control over their life. This frustration may also lead the person to use drugs or have unneeded surgery.

Chronic pain and PTSD

Some people's chronic pain stems from a traumatic event, such as a physical or sexual assault, a motor vehicle accident, or some type of disaster. Under these circumstances the person may experience both chronic pain and PTSD. The person in pain may not even realize the connection between their pain and a traumatic event. Approximately 15% to 35% of patients with chronic pain also have PTSD. Only 2% of people who do not have chronic pain have PTSD. One study found that 51% of patients with chronic low back pain had

PTSD symptoms. For people with chronic pain, the pain may actually serve as a reminder of the traumatic event, which will tend to make the PTSD even worse. Survivors of physical, psychological, or sexual abuse tend to be more at risk for developing certain types of chronic pain later in their lives.

Chapter 17

Stress and Pregnancy

Will stress during pregnancy affect my baby?

It is normal to feel some stress during pregnancy. Your body is going through many changes, and as your hormones change, so do your moods. Too much stress can cause you to have trouble sleeping, headaches, loss of appetite, or a tendency to overeat—all of which can be harmful to you and your developing baby.

High levels of stress can also cause high blood pressure, which increases your chance of having preterm labor or a low-birth-weight infant.

You should talk about stress with your health care provider and loved ones. If you are feeling stress because of uncertainty or fear about becoming a mother, experiencing work-related stress, or worrying about miscarriage, talk to your health care provider during your prenatal visits.

Emotional Stress and the Infant

Current research, particularly the work of Megan Gunnar (1998), demonstrates the negative effects that emotional stress has on the

This chapter includes excerpts from "Will stress during pregnancy affect my baby?" National Institute of Child Health and Human Development (NICHD), November 30, 2012; text from "The Psychological Work of Pregnancy," Early Childhood Learning & Knowledge Center (ECLKC), May 29, 2015; and text from "Depression during and after pregnancy fact sheet," Office on Women's Health (OWH), July 16, 2012.

developing fetus. Those who provide services to pregnant women and their families need to help expectant parents talk openly and fully about positive and negative feelings associated with pregnancy and their role as parents, including fears about the pain of childbirth. They need to explore how the new child will affect their relationship with extended family and discuss boundary issues that may arise if a family member is perceived as too helpful, too distant, or too critical. Important discussions can occur about the values that each parent holds, such as around discipline or religious matters. Older siblings also need to be prepared for the new baby and helped to deal with the anxious and jealous feelings before and after the birth.

Women need to be educated about maternal depression and its consequences for the development of their child. Support groups for pregnant women, a doula (a labor and post-childbirth support person), non-medical childbirth coaching, mother/baby groups, and father/baby groups can be useful in providing the needed support and in assessing potential difficulties. Pairing more experienced mothers with new, young mothers who can mentor and be positive role models may also be useful.

Teaching parents about the stages of development allows them to anticipate the joys and challenges that they will face as their child grows. In those situations where the mother's emotional difficulties require more than community support, or a child's temperamental or constitutional factors lead to a difficult fit between parent and child, referrals to early intervention or qualified infant mental health practitioners can be necessary.

Helping our Head Start families become emotionally prepared during pregnancy can go a long way in preventing emotional difficulties after the baby is born. We know that times of change can bring great opportunities. The birth of a new baby should be a joyful time. For many of our families who have severe external stressors, such as financial difficulties, young or unwanted pregnancies, traumatic abuse, or substance abuse histories, this is a time when our active intervention can open up unseen possibilities and provide much needed insight and support.

What causes depression? What about postpartum depression?

There is no single cause. Rather, depression likely results from a combination of factors:

- Depression is a mental illness that tends to run in families. Women with a family history of depression are more likely to have depression.

- Changes in brain chemistry or structure are believed to play a big role in depression.

- Stressful life events, such as death of a loved one, caring for an aging family member, abuse, and poverty, can trigger depression.

- Hormonal factors unique to women may contribute to depression in some women. We know that hormones directly affect the brain chemistry that controls emotions and mood. We also know that women are at greater risk of depression at certain times in their lives, such as puberty, during and after pregnancy, and during perimenopause. Some women also have depressive symptoms right before their period.

Depression after childbirth is called postpartum depression. Hormonal changes may trigger symptoms of postpartum depression. When you are pregnant, levels of the female hormones estrogen (ESS-truh-jen) and progesterone (proh-JESS-tur-ohn) increase greatly. In the first 24 hours after childbirth, hormone levels quickly return to normal. Researchers think the big change in hormone levels may lead to depression. This is much like the way smaller hormone changes can affect a woman's moods before she gets her period.

Levels of thyroid hormones may also drop after giving birth. The thyroid is a small gland in the neck that helps regulate how your body uses and stores energy from food. Low levels of thyroid hormones can cause symptoms of depression. A simple blood test can tell if this condition is causing your symptoms. If so, your doctor can prescribe thyroid medicine.

Other factors may play a role in postpartum depression. You may feel:

- Tired after delivery

- Tired from a lack of sleep or broken sleep

- Overwhelmed with a new baby

- Doubts about your ability to be a good mother

- Stress from changes in work and home routines

- An unrealistic need to be a perfect mom

- Loss of who you were before having the baby

- Less attractive

- A lack of free time

159

Are some women more at risk for depression during and after pregnancy?

Certain factors may increase your risk of depression during and after pregnancy:

- A personal history of depression or another mental illness
- A family history of depression or another mental illness
- A lack of support from family and friends
- Anxiety or negative feelings about the pregnancy
- Problems with a previous pregnancy or birth
- Marriage or money problems
- Stressful life events
- Young age
- Substance abuse

Women who are depressed during pregnancy have a greater risk of depression after giving birth.

Did you know?

If you take medicine for depression, stopping your medicine when you become pregnant can cause your depression to come back. Do not stop any prescribed medicines without first talking to your doctor. Not using medicine that you need may be harmful to you or your baby.

What should I do if I have symptoms of depression during or after pregnancy?

Call your doctor if:

- Your baby blues don't go away after 2 weeks
- Symptoms of depression get more and more intense
- Symptoms of depression begin any time after delivery, even many months later
- It is hard for you to perform tasks at work or at home

- You cannot care for yourself or your baby

- You have thoughts of harming yourself or your baby

Your doctor can ask you questions to test for depression. Your doctor can also refer you to a mental health professional who specializes in treating depression.

Some women don't tell anyone about their symptoms. They feel embarrassed, ashamed, or guilty about feeling depressed when they are supposed to be happy. They worry they will be viewed as unfit parents.

Any woman may become depressed during pregnancy or after having a baby. It doesn't mean you are a bad or "not together" mom. You and your baby don't have to suffer. There is help.

Here are some other helpful tips:

- Rest as much as you can. Sleep when the baby is sleeping.

- Don't try to do too much or try to be perfect.

- Ask your partner, family, and friends for help.

- Make time to go out, visit friends, or spend time alone with your partner.

- Discuss your feelings with your partner, family, and friends.

- Talk with other mothers so you can learn from their experiences.

- Join a support group. Ask your doctor about groups in your area.

- Don't make any major life changes during pregnancy or right after giving birth. Major changes can cause unneeded stress. Sometimes big changes can't be avoided. When that happens, try to arrange support and help in your new situation ahead of time.

Chapter 18

Stress and Skin Problems

Chapter Contents

Section 18.1

Stress and Psoriasis

This chapter includes excerpts from "Questions and Answers about Psoriasis," National Institute of Arthritis and Musculoskeletal and Skin Diseases (NIAMS) at the National Institute of Health (NIH), October 2013; and text from "New Insights Into How Psoriasis Arises and How It Heals," from National Institute of Arthritis and Musculoskeletal and Skin Diseases (NIAMS) at the National Institute of Health (NIH), January 2015..

What Is Psoriasis?

Psoriasis is a chronic (long-lasting) skin disease of scaling and inflammation that affects greater than 3 percent of the U.S. population, or more than 5 million adults. Although the disease occurs in all age groups, it primarily affects adults. It appears about equally in males and females.

Psoriasis occurs when skin cells quickly rise from their origin below the surface of the skin and pile up on the surface before they have a chance to mature. Usually this movement (also called turnover) takes about a month, but in psoriasis it may occur in only a few days.

In its typical form, psoriasis results in patches of thick, red (inflamed) skin covered with silvery scales. These patches, which are sometimes referred to as plaques, usually itch or feel sore. They most often occur on the elbows, knees, other parts of the legs, scalp, lower back, face, palms, and soles of the feet, but they can occur on skin anywhere on the body. The disease may also affect the fingernails, the toenails, and the soft tissues of the genitals, and inside the mouth. Although it is not unusual for the skin around affected joints to crack, some people with psoriasis experience joint inflammation that produces symptoms of arthritis. This condition is called psoriatic arthritis.

How Does Psoriasis Affect Quality of Life?

Individuals with psoriasis may experience significant physical discomfort and some disability. Itching and pain can interfere with basic functions, such as self-care, walking, and sleep. Plaques on hands and feet can prevent individuals from working at certain occupations, playing some sports, and caring for family members or a home. The frequency of medical care is costly and can interfere with an employment or school schedule. People with moderate to severe psoriasis may feel self-conscious about their appearance and have a poor self-image that stems from fear of public rejection and concerns about intimate relationships. Psychological distress can lead to significant depression and social isolation.

What Causes Psoriasis?

Psoriasis is a skin disorder driven by the immune system, especially involving a type of white blood cell called a T cell. Normally, T cells help protect the body against infection and disease. In the case of psoriasis, T cells are put into action by mistake and become so active that they trigger other immune responses, which lead to inflammation and to rapid turnover of skin cells.

In many cases, there is a family history of psoriasis. Researchers have studied a large number of families affected by psoriasis and identified genes linked to the disease. Genes govern every bodily function and determine the inherited traits passed from parent to child.

People with psoriasis may notice that there are times when their skin worsens, called flares, then improves. Conditions that may cause flares include infections, stress, and changes in climate that dry the skin. Also, certain medicines, including beta-blockers, which are prescribed for high blood pressure, and lithium may trigger an outbreak or worsen the disease. Sometimes people who have psoriasis notice that lesions will appear where the skin has experienced trauma. The trauma could be from a cut, scratch, sunburn, or infection.

How Is Psoriasis Diagnosed?

Occasionally, doctors may find it difficult to diagnose psoriasis, because it often looks like other skin diseases. It may be necessary to confirm a diagnosis by examining a small skin sample under a microscope.

There are several forms of psoriasis. Some of these include:

Plaque psoriasis. Skin lesions are red at the base and covered by silvery scales.

165

- **Guttate psoriasis.** Small, drop-shaped lesions appear on the trunk, limbs, and scalp. Guttate psoriasis is most often triggered by upper respiratory infections (for example, a sore throat caused by streptococcal bacteria).

- **Pustular psoriasis.** Blisters of noninfectious pus appear on the skin. Attacks of pustular psoriasis may be triggered by medications, infections, stress, or exposure to certain chemicals.

- **Inverse psoriasis.** Smooth, red patches occur in the folds of the skin near the genitals, under the breasts, or in the armpits. The symptoms may be worsened by friction and sweating.

- **Erythrodermic psoriasis.** Widespread reddening and scaling of the skin may be a reaction to severe sunburn or to taking corticosteroids (cortisone) or other medications. It can also be caused by a prolonged period of increased activity of psoriasis that is poorly controlled. Erythrodermic psoriasis can be very serious and requires immediate medical attention.

Another condition in which people may experience psoriasis is psoriatic arthritis. This is a form of arthritis that produces the joint inflammation common in arthritis and the lesions common in psoriasis. The joint inflammation and the skin lesions don't necessarily have to occur at the same time.

How Is Psoriasis Treated?

Doctors generally treat psoriasis in steps based on the severity of the disease, size of the areas involved, type of psoriasis, where the psoriasis is located, and the patient's response to initial treatments. Treatment can include:

- medicines applied to the skin (topical treatment)
- light treatment (phototherapy)
- medicines by mouth or injection (systemic therapy).

Over time, affected skin can become resistant to treatment, especially when topical corticosteroids are used. Also, a treatment that works very well in one person may have little effect in another. Thus, doctors often use a trial-and-error approach to find a treatment that works, and they may switch treatments periodically if a treatment does not work or if adverse reactions occur.

Topical Treatment

Treatments applied directly to the skin may improve its condition. Doctors find that some patients respond well to ointment or cream forms of corticosteroids, vitamin D3, retinoids, coal tar, or anthralin. Bath solutions and lubricants may be soothing, but they are seldom strong enough to improve the condition of the skin. Therefore, they usually are combined with stronger remedies.

- **Topical corticosteroids.** These drugs reduce inflammation and the turnover of skin cells, and they suppress the immune system. Corticosteroids are typically recommended for active outbreaks of psoriasis. Long-term use or overuse of highly potent (strong) corticosteroids can cause thinning of the skin, internal side effects, and resistance to the treatment's benefits.

- **Vitamin D analogs.** Synthetic forms of vitamin D control the speed of turnover of skin cells. Excessive use of these creams may raise the amount of calcium in the body to unhealthy levels.

- **Retinoids.** Topical retinoids are synthetic forms of vitamin A. Because of the risk of birth defects, women of childbearing age must take measures to prevent pregnancy when using retinoids.

- **Coal tar.** Preparations containing coal tar (gels and ointments) may be applied directly to the skin, added (as a liquid) to the bath, or used on the scalp as a shampoo. Coal tar products are available in different strengths, and many are sold over the counter (not requiring a prescription). The most potent form of coal tar may irritate the skin, is messy, has a strong odor, and may stain the skin or clothing.

- **Anthralin.** Anthralin reduces the increase in skin cells and inflammation. Doctors may prescribe daily application of anthralin ointment, cream, or paste for brief periods to treat chronic psoriasis lesions. Afterward, anthralin must be washed off the skin to prevent irritation. It discolors skin, bathtub, sink, clothing, and most surfaces.

- **Salicylic acid.** This peeling agent, which is available in many forms such as ointments, creams, gels, and shampoos, can be applied to reduce scaling of the skin or scalp.

- **Bath solutions.** People with psoriasis may find that adding oil when bathing, then applying a lubricant, soothes their skin. Also, individuals can remove scales and reduce itching by soaking in water containing a coal tar solution, oiled oatmeal, Epsom salts, or Dead Sea salts.

- **Lubricants.** When applied regularly over a long period, lubricants have a soothing effect. Preparations that are thick and greasy usually work best because they seal water in the skin, reducing scaling and itching.

Light Therapy

Natural ultraviolet (UV) light from the sun and controlled delivery of artificial UV light are used in treating psoriasis. It is important that light therapy be administered by a doctor. Spending time in the sun or a tanning bed can cause skin damage, increase the risk of skin cancer, and worsen symptoms.

- **Sunlight.** Much of sunlight is composed of bands of different wavelengths of UV light. When absorbed into the skin, UV light suppresses the process leading to disease, causing activated T cells in the skin to die. This process reduces inflammation and slows the turnover of skin cells that causes scaling.

- **Ultraviolet B (UVB) phototherapy.** UVB is light with a short wavelength that is absorbed in the skin's epidermis. An artificial source can be used to treat mild and moderate psoriasis. Some physicians will start treating patients with UVB instead of topical agents. A UVB phototherapy, called broadband UVB, can be used for a few small lesions, to treat widespread psoriasis, or for lesions that resist topical treatment. This type of phototherapy is normally given in a doctor's office by using a light panel or light box. Some patients use UVB light boxes at home under a doctor's guidance.

Another type of UVB, called narrowband UVB, emits the part of the UV light spectrum band that is most helpful for psoriasis. Narrowband UVB treatment is superior to broadband UVB, but it is less effective than PUVA treatment (see next paragraph). At first, patients may require several treatments of narrowband UVB spaced close together to improve their skin. Once the skin has shown improvement, a maintenance treatment may be all that is necessary. However, narrowband UVB treatment is not without risk. It can cause more severe and longer lasting burns than broadband treatment.

- **Psoralen and ultraviolet A (UVA) phototherapy (PUVA).** This treatment combines oral or topical administration of a medicine called psoralen with exposure to UVA light. UVA has a long wavelength that penetrates deeper into the skin than UVB. Psoralen makes the skin more sensitive to this light. Compared with broadband UVB treatment, PUVA treatment taken two to three times a week clears psoriasis more consistently and in fewer treatments. However, it is associated with more short-term side effects, including nausea, headache, fatigue, burning, and itching. Care must be taken to avoid sunlight after ingesting psoralen to avoid severe sunburns, and the eyes must be protected with UVA-absorbing glasses. Long-term treatment is associated with an increased risk of squamous-cell and, possibly, melanoma skin cancers.

Systemic Treatment

For more severe forms of psoriasis, doctors sometimes prescribe medicines that are taken internally by pill or injection. This is called systemic treatment.

- **Methotrexate.** Like cyclosporine, methotrexate slows cell turnover by suppressing the immune system. It can be taken by pill or injection. Patients taking methotrexate must be closely monitored because it can cause liver damage and/or decrease the production of oxygen-carrying red blood cells, infection-fighting white blood cells, and clot-enhancing platelets. As a precaution, doctors do not prescribe the drug for people who have had liver disease or anemia (an illness characterized by weakness or tiredness due to a reduction in the number or volume of red blood cells that carry oxygen to the tissues). Methotrexate should not be used by pregnant women, or by women who are planning to get pregnant, because it may cause birth defects.

- **Retinoids.** Oral retinoids are compounds with vitamin A-like properties that may be prescribed for severe cases of psoriasis that do not respond to other therapies. Because these medications also may cause birth defects, women must protect themselves from pregnancy.

- **Cyclosporine.** Taken orally, cyclosporine acts by suppressing the immune system to slow the rapid turnover of skin cells. It may provide quick relief of symptoms, but the improvement stops when treatment is discontinued. Its rapid onset of action is helpful in avoiding hospitalization of patients whose psoriasis is rapidly progressing. Cyclosporine may impair kidney function or cause high blood pressure (hypertension). Therefore, patients must be carefully monitored by a doctor. Also, cyclosporine is not recommended for patients who have a weak immune system or those who have had skin cancers as a result of PUVA treatments in the past.

- **Biologic response modifiers.** Biologics are made from proteins produced by living cells instead of chemicals. They interfere with specific immune system processes which cause the overproduction of skin cells and inflammation. These drugs are injected (sometimes by the patient). Patients taking these treatments need to be monitored carefully by a doctor. Because these drugs suppress the immune system response, patients taking these drugs have an increased risk of infection, and the drugs may also interfere with patients taking vaccines. Also, some of these drugs have been associated with other diseases (like central nervous system disorders, blood diseases, cancer, and lymphoma) although their role in the development of or contribution to these diseases is not yet understood. Some are approved for adults only, and their effects on pregnant or nursing women are not known.

Combination Therapy

Combining various topical, light, and systemic treatments often permits lower doses of each and can result in increased effectiveness. There are many approaches for treating psoriasis. Ask the doctor about the best options for you. Find out:

- How long the treatment may last.
- How long it will take to see results.
- What the possible side effects are.
- What to do if the side effects are severe.

Psychological Support

Some individuals with moderate to severe psoriasis may benefit from counseling or participation in a support group to reduce self-consciousness about their appearance or relieve psychological distress resulting from fear of social rejection.

What Research Is Being Conducted on Psoriasis?

Researchers are trying to learn how skin cells form in order to create healthy skin. At the same time, others are looking at the cells and mechanisms which cause lesions in the skin. If any of these mechanisms can be interrupted, researchers may find a way to stop the disease process.

Significant progress has been made in understanding the inheritance of psoriasis. A number of genes involved in psoriasis are already known or suspected. In a multifactor disease (involving genes, environment, and other factors), variations in one or more genes may produce a greater likelihood of getting the disease. Researchers are continuing to study the genetic aspects of psoriasis, and some studies are looking at the nervous system to determine the genes responsible for the circuitry that causes itching.

Since discovering that inflammation in psoriasis is triggered by T cells, researchers have been studying new treatments that quiet immune system reactions in the skin. Among these are treatments that block the activity of T cells or block cytokines (proteins that promote inflammation). If researchers find a way to target only the disease-causing immune reactions while leaving the rest of the immune system alone, resulting treatments could benefit psoriasis patients as well as those with other autoimmune diseases.

Research has suggested that psoriasis patients may be at greater risk of cardiovascular problems, especially if the psoriasis is severe, as well as obesity, high blood pressure, and diabetes. Researchers are trying to determine the reasons for these associations and how best to treat patients.

Nervous System Connection

Scientists are increasingly uncovering evidence of cross-talk between the nervous system and the immune system in many diseases, including psoriasis. Emotional stress can exacerbate psoriatic symptoms, while local anesthetics or nerve injury often reduce inflammation and induce remission.

Curious about the nervous system connection to psoriasis, scientists led by Ulrich von Andrian, M.D., Ph.D., of Harvard Medical School, focused their attention on a subset of pain-sensing neurons abundant in skin that confer the sensations of uncomfortable heat, cold and inflammatory pain. Working with a mouse model, they reasoned that if these neurons were involved in promoting psoriasis, removing them would ease symptoms of the condition.

They found that after removing these neurons, mice were less responsive to a compound called imiquimod, which normally triggers a psoriasis-like condition. The imiquimod-treated site was less swollen and inflamed than in control mice, and it contained less IL-23, a molecule known to mediate inflammation.

"From these results we knew that pain-sensing neurons, when exposed to imiquimod, trigger inflammation by stimulating the production of IL-23," said Jose Ordovas-Montanes, a NIAMS-supported graduate student at Harvard Medical School and co-first author of the study. "But we didn't know where the IL-23 was coming from."

Further experiments identified the source of IL-23 to be immune cells called dermal dendritic cells (DDCs), and revealed that these cells are located in close proximity to pain-sensing neurons in mouse skin.

The researchers concluded that when mice are treated with imiquimod, pain-sensing nerve cells in their skin stimulate DDCs to make IL-23. IL-23, in turn, elicits an inflammatory cascade that ultimately produces the lesions that characterize psoriasis.

"By uncovering a role for the nervous system in psoriasis, we've discovered an entirely new pathway that we can explore for therapeutic purposes," said Dr. von Andrian. "By targeting these pain-sensing neurons, we may be able to develop new medicines for treating psoriasis and possibly other inflammatory skin diseases."

Section 18.2

Is Acne Linked to Stress?

Text in this section is excerpted from "Questions and Answers about Acne," National Institute of Arthritis and Musculoskeletal and Skin Diseases (NIAMS) at the National Institute of Health (NIH), May 2013.

Acne is a disorder resulting from the action of hormones and other substances on the skin's oil glands (sebaceous glands) and hair follicles. These factors lead to plugged pores and outbreaks of lesions commonly called pimples or zits. Acne lesions usually occur on the face, neck, back, chest, and shoulders. Although acne is usually not a serious health threat, it can be a source of significant emotional distress. Severe acne can lead to permanent scarring.

How Does Acne Develop?

Doctors describe acne as a disease of the pilosebaceous units (PSUs). Found over most of the body, pilosebaceous units consist of a sebaceous gland connected to a canal, called a follicle, that contains a fine hair. These units are most numerous on the face, upper back, and chest. The sebaceous glands make an oily substance called sebum that normally empties onto the skin surface through the opening of the follicle, commonly called a pore. Cells called keratinocytes line the follicle.

The hair, sebum, and keratinocytes that fill the narrow follicle may produce a plug, which is an early sign of acne. The plug prevents sebum from reaching the surface of the skin through a pore. The mixture of oil and cells allows bacteria *Propionibacterium acnes (P. acnes)* that normally live on the skin to grow in the plugged follicles. These bacteria produce chemicals and enzymes and attract white blood cells that cause inflammation. (Inflammation is a characteristic reaction of tissues to disease or injury and is marked by four signs: swelling, redness, heat, and pain.) When the wall of the plugged follicle breaks down, it spills everything into the nearby skin—sebum, shed skin cells, and bacteria—leading to lesions or pimples.

People with acne frequently have a variety of lesions, some of which are shown in the illustrations below. The basic acne lesion, called the comedo (KOM-e-do), is simply an enlarged and plugged hair follicle. If the comedo stays beneath the skin, it is called a closed comedo and

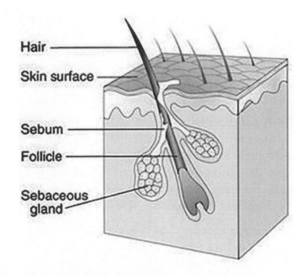

Figure 18.1. *Normal Pilosebaceous Unit*

173

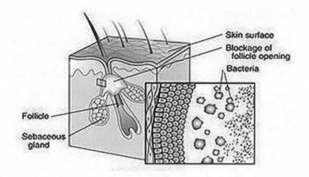

Figure 18.2. *A) Microcomedo Types of Lesions*

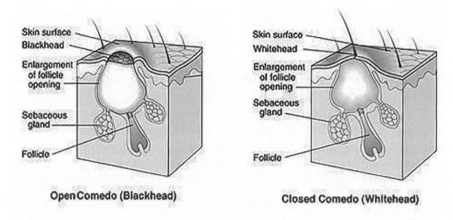

Figure 18.3. *B) Open Comedo (Blackhead) Types of Lesions*

Figure 18.4. *C) Closed Comedo (Whitehead) Types of Lesions*

produces a white bump called a whitehead. A comedo that reaches the surface of the skin and opens up is called an open comedo or blackhead because it looks black on the skin's surface. This black discoloration is due to changes in sebum as it is exposed to air. It is not due to dirt. Both whiteheads and blackheads may stay in the skin for a long time.

Other troublesome acne lesions can develop, including the following:

- **Papules.** Inflamed lesions that usually appear as small, pink bumps on the skin and can be tender to the touch.

- **Pustules (pimples).** Papules topped by white or yellow pus-filled lesions that may be red at the base.

- **Nodules.** Large, painful, solid lesions that are lodged deep within the skin.

- **Cysts.** Deep, painful, pus-filled lesions that can cause scarring.

What Causes Acne?

The exact cause of acne is unknown, but doctors believe it results from several related factors. One important factor is an increase in hormones called androgens (male sex hormones). These increase in both boys and girls during puberty and cause the sebaceous glands to enlarge and make more sebum. Hormonal changes related to pregnancy or starting or stopping birth control pills can also cause acne.

Another factor is heredity or genetics. Researchers believe that the tendency to develop acne can be inherited from parents. For example, studies have shown that many school-age boys with acne have a family history of the disorder. Certain drugs, including androgens and lithium, are known to cause acne. Greasy cosmetics may alter the cells of the follicles and make them stick together, producing a plug.

Factors That Can Make Acne Worse

Factors that can cause an acne flare include:

- stress

- changing hormone levels in adolescent girls and adult women 2 to 7 days before their menstrual period starts

- oil from skin products (moisturizers or cosmetics) or grease encountered in the work environment (for example, a kitchen with fry vats)

- pressure from sports helmets or equipment, backpacks, tight collars, or tight sports uniforms

- environmental irritants, such as pollution and high humidity

- squeezing or picking at blemishes

- hard scrubbing of the skin

Myths about the Causes of Acne

There are many myths about what causes acne. Chocolate and greasy foods are often blamed, but there is little evidence that foods have much effect on the development and course of acne in most people.

175

Another common myth is that dirty skin causes acne; however, black-heads and other acne lesions are not caused by dirt. Stress doesn't cause acne, but research suggests that for people who have acne, stress can make it worse.

Who Gets Acne?

People of all races and ages get acne. It is most common in adolescents and young adults. An estimated 80 percent of all people between the ages of 11 and 30 have acne outbreaks at some point. For most people, acne tends to go away by the time they reach their thirties; however, some people in their forties and fifties continue to have this skin problem.

How Is Acne Treated?

Acne is often treated by dermatologists, who are doctors who specialize in skin problems. These doctors treat all kinds of acne, particularly severe cases. Doctors who are general or family practitioners, pediatricians, or internists may treat patients with milder cases of acne.

The goals of treatment are to heal existing lesions, stop new lesions from forming, prevent scarring, and minimize the psychological stress and embarrassment caused by this disease. Drug treatment is aimed at reducing several problems that play a part in causing acne:

- abnormal clumping of cells in the follicles
- increased oil production
- bacteria
- inflammation.

Depending on the extent of the problem, the doctor may recommend one of several over-the-counter (OTC) medicines and/or prescription medicines. Some of these medicines may be topical (applied to the skin), and others may be oral (taken by mouth). The doctor may suggest using more than one topical medicine or combining oral and topical medicines.

Treatment for Blackheads, Whiteheads, and Mild Inflammatory Acne

Doctors usually recommend an OTC or prescription topical medicine for people with mild signs of acne. Topical medicine is applied directly to the acne lesions or to the entire area of affected skin.

There are several OTC topical medicines used for mild acne. Each works a little differently. Following are the most common ones:

- **Benzoyl peroxide.** Kills P. acnes, and may also reduce oil production

- **Resorcinol.** Can help break down blackheads and whiteheads

- **Salicylic acid.** Helps break down blackheads and whiteheads. Also helps cut down the shedding of cells lining the hair follicles

- **Sulfur.** Helps break down blackheads and whiteheads.

Topical OTC medicines are available in many forms, such as gels, lotions, creams, soaps, or pads. In some people, OTC acne medicines may cause side effects such as skin irritation, burning, or redness, which often get better or go away with continued use of the medicine. If you experience severe or prolonged side effects, you should report them to your doctor.

OTC topical medicines are somewhat effective in treating acne when used regularly; however, it may take up to 8 weeks before you see noticeable improvement.

Treatment for Moderate-to-Severe Inflammatory Acne

People with moderate-to-severe inflammatory acne may be treated with prescription topical or oral medicines, alone or in combination.

Prescription Topical Medicines

Several types of prescription topical medicines are used to treat acne. They include:

- **Antibiotics.** Help stop or slow the growth of bacteria and reduce inflammation

- **Vitamin A derivatives (retinoids).** Unplug existing comedones (plural of comedo), allowing other topical medicines, such as antibiotics, to enter the follicles. Some may also help decrease the formation of comedones. These drugs contain an altered form of vitamin A.

- **Others.** May destroy P. acnes and reduce oil production or help stop or slow the growth of bacteria and reduce inflammation.

Like OTC topical medicines, prescription topical medicines come as creams, lotions, solutions, gels, or pads. Your doctor will consider your skin type when prescribing a product. Creams and lotions provide moisture and tend to be good choices for people with sensitive skin. If you have very oily skin or live in a hot, humid climate, you may prefer an alcohol-based gel or solution, which tends to dry the skin. Your doctor will tell you how to apply the medicine and how often to use it.

For some people, prescription topical medicines cause minor side effects including stinging, burning, redness, peeling, scaling, or discoloration of the skin. With some medicines, these side effects usually decrease or go away after the medicine is used for a period of time. If side effects are severe or don't go away, notify your doctor.

Prescription Oral Medicines

For patients with moderate-to-severe acne, doctors often prescribe oral antibiotics. Oral antibiotics are thought to help control acne by curbing the growth of bacteria and reducing inflammation. Prescription oral and topical medicines may be combined. Common antibiotics used to treat acne are tetracycline, minocycline, and doxycycline.

Other oral medicines less commonly used are clindamycin, erythromycin, or sulfonamides. Some people taking these antibiotics have side effects, such as an upset stomach, dizziness or lightheadedness, changes in skin color, and increased tendency to sunburn. Because tetracyclines may affect tooth and bone formation in fetuses and young children, these drugs are not given to pregnant women or children under age 14. There is some concern, although it has not been proven, that tetracycline and minocycline may decrease the effectiveness of birth control pills. Therefore, a backup or another form of birth control may be needed. Prolonged treatment with oral antibiotics may be necessary to achieve the desired results.

Treatment for Severe Nodular or Cystic Acne

People with nodules or cysts should be treated by a dermatologist. For patients with severe inflammatory acne that does not improve with medicines such as those described above, a doctor may prescribe isotretinoin, a retinoid (vitamin A derivative). Isotretinoin is an oral drug that is usually taken once or twice a day with food for 15 to 20 weeks. It markedly reduces the size of the oil glands so that much less oil is produced. As a result, the growth of bacteria is decreased.

Advantages of Isotretinoin

Isotretinoin is a very effective medicine that can help prevent scarring. After 15 to 20 weeks of treatment with isotretinoin, acne completely or almost completely goes away in most patients. In those patients where acne recurs after a course of isotretinoin, the doctor may institute another course of the same treatment or prescribe other medicines.

Disadvantages of Isotretinoin

Isotretinoin can cause birth defects in the developing fetus of a pregnant woman. **It is important that women of childbearing age are not pregnant and do not get pregnant while taking this medicine.** Women must use two separate effective forms of birth control at the same time for 1 month before treatment begins, during the entire course of treatment, and for 1 full month after stopping the drug. You should ask your doctor when it is safe to get pregnant after you have stopped taking isotretinoin.

Some people with acne become depressed by the changes in the appearance of their skin. Changes in mood may be intensified during treatment or soon after completing a course of medicines like isotretinoin. There have been a number of reported suicides and suicide attempts in people taking isotretinoin; however, the connection between isotretinoin and suicide or depression is not known. Nevertheless, if you or someone you know feels unusually sad or has other symptoms of depression, such as loss of appetite, loss of interest in once-loved activities, or trouble concentrating, it's important to consult your doctor.

Talk to your doctor or pharmacist about the side effects of isotretinoin. You can also visit the Food and Drug Administration (FDA) website. To determine if isotretinoin should be stopped if side effects occur, your doctor may test your blood before you start treatment and periodically during treatment. Side effects usually go away after the medicine is stopped.

Treatments for Hormonally Influenced Acne in Women

In some women, acne is caused by an excess of androgen (male) hormones. Clues that this may be the case include hirsutism (excessive growth of hair on the face or body), premenstrual acne flares, irregular menstrual cycles, and elevated blood levels of certain androgens.

The doctor may prescribe one of several drugs to treat women with this type of acne:

- **Birth control pills.** To help suppress the androgen produced by the ovaries

- **Low-dose corticosteroid drugs, such as prednisone or dexamethasone.** To help suppress the androgen produced by the adrenal glands

- **Antiandrogen drugs such as spironolactone.** To reduce the excessive oil production.

Other Treatments for Acne

Doctors may use other types of procedures in addition to drug therapy to treat patients with acne. For example, the doctor may remove the patient's comedones during office visits. Sometimes the doctor will inject corticosteroids directly into lesions to help reduce the size and pain of inflamed cysts and nodules.

Early treatment is the best way to prevent acne scars. Once scarring has occurred, the doctor may suggest a medical or surgical procedure to help reduce the scars. A superficial laser may be used to treat irregular scars. Dermabrasion (or microdermabrasion), which is a form of "sanding down" scars, is sometimes used. Another treatment option for deep scars caused by cystic acne is the transfer of fat from another part of the body to the scar. A doctor may also inject a synthetic filling material under the scar to improve its appearance.

How Should People With Acne Care for Their Skin?

Clean Skin Gently

If you have acne, you should gently wash your face with a mild cleanser, once in the morning and once in the evening, as well as after heavy exercise. Wash your face from under the jaw to the hairline and be sure to thoroughly rinse your skin.

Ask your doctor or another health professional for advice on the best type of cleanser to use.

Using strong soaps or rough scrub pads is not helpful and can actually make the problem worse. Astringents are not recommended unless the skin is very oily, and then they should be used only on oily spots.

It is also important to shampoo your hair regularly. If you have oily hair, you may want to wash it every day.

Avoid Frequent Handling of the Skin

Avoid rubbing and touching skin lesions. Squeezing, pinching or picking blemishes can lead to the development of scars or dark blotches.

Shave Carefully

Test both electric and safety razors to see which is more comfortable. When using a safety razor, make sure the blade is sharp and soften the hair thoroughly with soap and water before applying shaving cream. Shave gently and only when necessary to reduce the risk of nicking blemishes.

Avoid a Sunburn or Suntan

Many of the medicines used to treat acne can make you more prone to sunburn. A sunburn that reddens the skin or suntan that darkens the skin may make blemishes less visible and make the skin feel drier. However, these benefits are only temporary, and there are known risks of excessive sun exposure, such as more rapid skin aging and a risk of developing skin cancer.

Choose Cosmetics Carefully

While undergoing acne treatment, you may need to change some of the cosmetics you use. All cosmetics and hair-care products should be oil free. Choose products labeled noncomedogenic (meaning they don't promote the formation of closed pores). In some people, however, even these products may make acne worse.

For the first few weeks of treatment, applying foundation evenly may be difficult because the skin may be red or scaly, particularly with the use of topical tretinoin or benzoyl peroxide.

What Research Is Being Conducted on Acne?

Medical researchers are working on new drugs to treat acne, particularly topical antibiotics to replace some of those in current use. As with many other types of bacterial infections, doctors are finding that, over time, the bacteria that are associated with acne are becoming resistant to treatment with certain antibiotics, though it is not clear how significant a problem this resistance represents.

Scientists are also trying to better understand the mechanisms involved in acne so that they can develop new treatments that work on those mechanisms. For example, one group of NIAMS-supported researchers is studying the mechanisms that regulate the development of the sebaceous glands. Another group is trying to understand how P. acnes activates the immune system in order to identify possible immunologic interventions. Other areas of research involve examining the effects of isotretinoin (a potent drug for acne) on the sebaceous glands. Moreover, a new drug called isoprenylcysteine is currently being evaluated for the treatment of P. acnes-induced inflammation and overproduction of sebum.

Chapter 19

Stress and Sleep Disorders

What is insomnia?

Insomnia is a common sleep disorder. If you have insomnia, you may:

- Lie awake for a long time and have trouble falling asleep
- Wake up a lot and have trouble returning to sleep
- Wake up too early in the morning
- Feel like you haven't slept at all

Lack of or poor quality sleep causes other symptoms that can affect daytime function. You may feel very sleepy and have low energy throughout the day. You may have trouble thinking clearly or staying focused. Or, you might feel depressed or irritable.

Insomnia is defined as short and poor quality sleep that affects your functioning during the day. Although the amount of sleep a person needs varies, most people need between 7 and 8 hours of sleep a night to feel refreshed.

Insomnia can be mild to severe and varies in how often it occurs and how long it lasts. Acute insomnia is a short-term sleep problem that is generally related to a stressful or traumatic life event and lasts from a few days to a few weeks. Acute insomnia might happen from

Text in this chapter is excerpted from "Insomnia fact sheet," Office on Women's Health (OWH), July 16, 2012.

time to time. With chronic insomnia, sleep problems occur at least 3 nights a week for more than a month.

Insomnia tends to increase as women and men age.

What are the different types of insomnia and what causes them?

There are 2 types of insomnia:

- **Primary insomnia** is not a symptom or side-effect of another medical condition. It is its own disorder. It may be life-long or triggered by travel, shift work, stressful life events, or other factors that disrupt your sleep routine. Primary insomnia may end once the issue is resolved, or can last for years. Some people tend to be prone to primary insomnia.

- **Secondary insomnia** has an underlying cause, so it's a symptom or side-effect of something else. It is the most common type. Secondary insomnia may have a medical cause, such as:

- Depression or anxiety

- Chronic pain such as from fibromyalgia, migraine, or arthritis

- Gastrointestinal problems such as heartburn

- Sleep disorders, such as sleep apnea or restless leg syndrome

- Stroke

- Alzheimer's disease

- Menopause

  Secondary insomnia also can result from:

- Some medicines, such as those that treat asthma, heart problems, allergies, and colds

- Caffeine, tobacco, and alcohol

- Poor sleep environment (such as too much light or noise, or a bed partner who snores)

Secondary insomnia often goes away once the underlying cause is treated, but may become a primary insomnia.

Some people with primary or secondary insomnia form habits to deal with the lack of sleep, such as worrying about sleep or going to bed too early. These habits can make insomnia worse or last longer.

How is insomnia treated?

If insomnia is caused by a short-term change in the sleep/wake schedule, as with jet lag, your sleep schedule may return to normal on its own. Making lifestyle changes to help you sleep better can also help. If your insomnia makes it hard for you to function during the day, talk to your doctor.

Treatment for chronic insomnia begins by:

- Finding and treating any medical or mental health problems

- Stopping or reducing behaviors that may lead to the insomnia or make it worse, like drinking moderate to large amounts of alcohol at night

Other treatments are:

- Cognitive behavioral therapy (CBT)

- Medication

Cognitive behavioral therapy (CBT)

Research shows that CBT is an effective and lasting treatment of insomnia. CBT helps you change thoughts and actions that get in the way of sleep. This type of therapy is also used to treat conditions such as depression, anxiety, and eating disorders.

CBT consists of one or more approaches. These are:

- **Cognitive control and psychotherapy** — Controlling or stopping negative thoughts and worries that keep you awake.

- **Sleep hygiene** — Taking steps to make quality sleep more likely, such as going to bed and waking up at the same time each day, not smoking, avoiding drinking too much coffee or alcohol late in the day, and getting regular exercise.

- **Sleep restriction** — Matching the time spent in bed with the amount of sleep you need. This is achieved by limiting the amount of time spent in your bed not sleeping. You go to bed later and get up earlier then you would normally, and then slowly increase the time in bed until you are able to sleep all night.

- **Stimulus control** — Conditioning a positive response with getting into bed. For example, using the bed only for sleep and sex.

- **Relaxation training** — Reducing stress and body tension. This can include meditation, hypnosis, or muscle relaxation.

- **Biofeedback** — Measuring body actions, such as muscle tension and brain wave frequency, to help you control them.

- **Remain passively awake** — Trying not to fall asleep, thereby stopping any worries you might have about falling asleep easily.

Medication

In some cases, insomnia is treated with medicine:

- **Prescription sleep medicines** — Prescription sleep medicines can help some people get much-needed rest. Most sleep medicines are used for short-term treatment, though some people with severe chronic insomnia may benefit from longer treatment. It is important to understand the risks before using a sleep medicine. In some cases, sleep medicines may:

  - Become habit-forming

  - Mask medical problems that may be causing the insomnia, and delay treatment

  - Interact with other medicines you use and cause serious health problems

  - Cause grogginess or rebound insomnia, where the sleeping problems get worse

  - Uncommon side-effects of sleep medicines include:

  - Severe allergic reactions or facial swelling

  - High blood pressure, dizziness, weakness, nausea, confusion, or short-term memory loss

  - Complex sleep-related behaviors, such as binge eating or driving while asleep

- **Over-the-counter (OTC) sleep aids** — OTC sleep aids may help on an occasional sleepless night, but they are not meant for regular or long-term use. Most OTC sleep aids contain antihistamines (ant-ih-HISS-tuh-meenz). Antihistamines are not safe for some people to use. OTC sleep aids also can have some unpleasant side-effects, such as dry mouth, dizziness, and prolonged grogginess.

Some dietary supplements claim to help people sleep. Some are "natural" products like melatonin (mel-uh-TOH-nuhn). Others are food supplements such as valerian (an herb) teas or extracts. The U.S. Food and Drug Administration does not regulate dietary supplements as it does medicine. It is unclear if these products are safe or if they actually work.

Talk to your doctor about sleep problems before using an OTC sleep aid. You may have a medical issue that needs to be treated. Also, the insomnia may be better treated in other ways.

If you decide to use a sleep medicine, experts advise you to:

- Read the Medication Guide first.

- Use the medicine at the time of day directed by your doctor.

- Do not drive or engage in activities that require you to be alert.

- Always take the dose prescribed by your doctor.

- Tell your doctor about other medicines you use.

- Call your doctor right away if you have any problems while using the medicine.

- Avoid drinking alcohol and using drugs.

- Talk to your doctor if you want to stop using the sleep medicine. Some medicines must be stopped gradually.

What can I do to sleep better?

- Try to go to sleep at the same time each night and get up at the same time each morning. Do not take naps after 3 p.m.

- Avoid caffeine, nicotine, and alcohol late in the day or at night.

- Get regular physical activity. But exercise or physical activity done too close to bed time can make it hard to fall asleep. Make sure you eat dinner at least 2 to 3 hours before bedtime.

- Keep your bedroom dark, quiet, and cool. If light is a problem, try a sleeping mask. If noise is a problem, try earplugs, a fan, or a "white noise" machine to cover up the sounds.

- Follow a routine to help relax and wind down before sleep, such as reading a book, listening to music, or taking a bath.

- If you can't fall asleep within 20 minutes or don't feel drowsy, get out of bed and sit in your bedroom or another room. Read or do a quiet activity until you feel sleepy. Then try going back to bed.

- If you lay awake worrying about things, try making a to-do list before you go to bed so that you don't use time in bed for worry.

- Use your bed only for sleep and sex.

- See your doctor or a sleep specialist if you think that you have insomnia or another sleep problem.

Chapter 20

Teeth Grinding (Bruxism)

Bruxism is a disorder characterized by grinding, gnashing, and clenching of the teeth. Although it can have many different causes, it is often related to stress. Bruxism is widely prevalent, affecting an estimated 30 to 40 million people in the United States. People with bruxism may unconsciously clench their jaws during the day or grind their teeth while they are asleep at night. In most cases, bruxism is treatable with proper care and attention.

Symptoms and Diagnosis

Bruxism is usually diagnosed through a visit to a dentist. During a regular dental checkup, a dentist will look for and inquire about the following symptoms:

- Damaged teeth

- Unusual teeth sensitivity

- Swelling and pain in the jaw or facial muscles around the mouth

- Tongue indentations

- Headaches or earaches

- Frequent awakening or poor quality of sleep

If the patient shows signs of bruxism, the dentist may prescribe a splint or mouthguard to prevent the teeth from grinding together. If the problem seems to be stress-related, the patient may be referred

"Bruxism," © 2015 Omnigraphics, Inc. Reviewed September 2015.

to a therapist or a counselor who will suggest methods for modifying the patient's behavior and sleep patterns.

Causes

Although various factors may contribute to bruxism, it is often related to the patient's emotional and psychological state. Nearly 70 percent of cases of bruxism can be traced to stress and anxiety. For children, the stress may be due to such causes as school exams, bullying by classmates, scolding from parents, or moving to a new neighborhood. Some small children may grind their teeth as part of the teething process or due to frequent earaches. Among children, bruxism often appears between the ages of three and ten years and then disappears on its own at puberty.

For adults, common sources of stress may include workplace tensions, family problems, relationship issues, or anxiety about health conditions. Certain personality types tend to be more vulnerable to stress-related bruxism, including those who are highly aggressive, competitive, or hyperactive.

Certain lifestyle factors can increase the risk of developing bruxism, such as smoking, alcohol consumption, and drug use. Some dental disorders can also aggravate bruxism, such as improper teeth alignment or jaw movement. Bruxism may also develop as a side effect of certain medications, or as a symptom of neurological disorders like Huntington's disease and Parkinson's disease. Finally, bruxism is often related to sleep disorders, such as excessive snoring, pauses in breathing, or obstructive sleep apnea.

Treatments

Treatments for bruxism should be selected to best fit the individual patient and the underlying cause of the disorder. When a dental problem is determined to be the cause of bruxism, a dental appliance such as a splint or mouthguard might alleviate the condition. These devices help prevent the teeth from grinding together and also help protect the tooth enamel from further damage. Various dental procedures can also be performed to correct misalignment of the teeth and jaw or address damage to the teeth from clenching and grinding.

Behavioral therapy can also help patients deal with improper mouth and jaw alignment. Correcting the position and placement of the tongue, teeth, and lips can bring about a significant improvement in the condition. Biofeedback is another treatment method used to assess and alter the movement of the muscles around the mouth and jaw. The doctor may use monitoring equipment to help guide the patient toward overcoming the habit of clenching the jaw or grinding the teeth.

If the primary cause of bruxism is determined to be psychological in nature, a number of behavioral and related therapies may help alleviate the condition. Stress management is the foremost issue to be addressed in people with bruxism. Counseling sessions with experts can help patients develop coping strategies. Other popular means of reducing stress include meditation, relaxation, exercise, and music. Hypnosis is a proven method of treatment for people who tend to grind their teeth at night. Most people with bruxism respond well with the proper treatment.

References:

1.   Bruxism Association. "Causes of Bruxism," n.d.

2.   KidsHealth. "Bruxism." Nemours Foundation, 2015.

Part Three

How Stress Affects Mental Health

Chapter 21

Depression

Do you feel very tired, helpless, and hopeless? Are you sad most of the time and take no pleasure in your family, friends, or hobbies? Are you having trouble working, sleeping, eating, and functioning? Have you felt this way for a long time?

If so, you may have depression.

What is depression?

Everyone feels sad sometimes, but these feelings usually pass after a few days. When you have depression, you have trouble with daily life for weeks at a time. Depression is a serious illness that needs treatment.

What are the different forms of depression?

There are several forms of depression.

Major depression—severe symptoms that interfere with your ability to work, sleep, study, eat, and enjoy life. An episode can occur only once in a person's lifetime, but more often, a person has several episodes.

Text in this section is excerpted from "Depression," National Institute of Mental Health (NIMH), 2013.

Dysthymic disorder, or dysthymia—depressive symptoms that last a long time (2 years or longer) but are less severe than those of major depression.

Minor depression—similar to major depression and dysthymia, but symptoms are less severe and may not last as long.

What are the signs and symptoms of depression?

Different people have different symptoms. Some symptoms of depression include:

- Feeling sad or "empty"
- Feeling hopeless, irritable, anxious, or guilty
- Loss of interest in favorite activities
- Feeling very tired
- Not being able to concentrate or remember details
- Not being able to sleep, or sleeping too much
- Overeating, or not wanting to eat at all
- Thoughts of suicide, suicide attempts
- Aches or pains, headaches, cramps, or digestive problems.

What causes depression?

Several factors, or a combination of factors, may contribute to depression.

Genes—people with a family history of depression may be more likely to develop it than those whose families do not have the illness.

Brain chemistry—people with depression have different brain chemistry than those without the illness.

Stress—loss of a loved one, a difficult relationship, or any stressful situation may trigger depression.

Does depression look the same in everyone?

No. Depression affects different people in different ways.

Women experience depression more often than men. Biological, life cycle, and hormonal factors that are unique to women may be linked to women's higher depression rate. Women with depression typically have symptoms of sadness, worthlessness, and guilt.

Men with depression are more likely to be very tired, irritable, and sometimes even angry. They may lose interest in work or activities they once enjoyed, and have sleep problems.

Older adults with depression may have less obvious symptoms, or they may be less likely to admit to feelings of sadness or grief. They also are more likely to have medical conditions like heart disease or stroke, which may cause or contribute to depression. Certain medications also can have side effects that contribute to depression.

Children with depression may pretend to be sick, refuse to go to school, cling to a parent, or worry that a parent may die. Older children or teens may get into trouble at school and be irritable. Because these signs can also be part of normal mood swings associated with certain childhood stages, it may be difficult to accurately diagnose a young person with depression.

How is depression treated?

The first step to getting the right treatment is to visit a doctor or mental health professional. He or she can do an exam or lab tests to rule out other conditions that may have the same symptoms as depression. He or she can also tell if certain medications you are taking may be affecting your mood.

The doctor should get a complete history of symptoms, including when they started, how long they have lasted, and how bad they are. He or she should also know whether they have occurred before, and if so, how they were treated. He or she should also ask if there is a history of depression in your family.

Medications called antidepressants can work well to treat depression. They can take several weeks to work.

Antidepressants can have side effects including:

- Headache
- Nausea—feeling sick to your stomach
- Difficulty sleeping or nervousness
- Agitation or restlessness
- Sexual problems.

Most side effects lessen over time. **Talk to your doctor about any side effects you have.**

It's important to know that although antidepressants can be safe and effective for many people, they may present serious risks to some, especially children, teens, and young adults. A "black box"—the most serious type of warning that a prescription drug can have—has been added to the labels of antidepressant medications. These labels warn people that antidepressants may cause some people, especially those who become agitated when they first start taking the medication and before it begins to work, to have suicidal thoughts or make suicide attempts. Anyone taking antidepressants should be monitored closely, especially when they first start taking them. For most people, though, the risks of untreated depression far outweigh those of antidepressant medications when they are used under a doctor's careful supervision.

Psychotherapy can also help treat depression. Psychotherapy helps by teaching new ways of thinking and behaving, and changing habits that may be contributing to the depression. Therapy can help you understand and work through difficult relationships or situations that may be causing your depression or making it worse.

Electroconvulsive therapy. For severe depression that is very difficult to treat and does not respond to medication or therapy, electroconvulsive therapy (ECT) is sometimes used. Although ECT once had a bad reputation, it has greatly improved and can provide relief for people for whom other treatments have not worked. ECT may cause side effects such as confusion and memory loss. Although these effects are usually short-term, they can sometimes linger.

How can I help a loved one who is depressed?

If you know someone who has depression, first help him or her see a doctor or mental health professional.

- Offer support, understanding, patience, and encouragement.

- Talk to him or her, and listen carefully.

- Never ignore comments about suicide, and report them to your loved one's therapist or doctor.

- Invite him or her out for walks, outings, and other activities.

- Remind him or her that with time and treatment, the depression will lift.

How can I help myself if I am depressed?

As you continue treatment, gradually you will start to feel better. Remember that if you are taking an antidepressant, it may take several weeks for it to start working. Try to do things that you used to enjoy before you had depression. Go easy on yourself. Other things that may help include:

- Breaking up large tasks into small ones, and doing what you can as you can. Try not to do too many things at once.

- Spending time with other people and talking to a friend or relative about your feelings.

- Once you have a treatment plan, try to stick to it. It will take time for treatment to work.

- Do not make important life decisions until you feel better. Discuss decisions with others who know you well.

Where can I go for help?

If you are unsure where to go for help, ask your family doctor. You can also check the phone book for mental health professionals. Hospital doctors can help in an emergency.

What if I or someone I know is in crisis?

If you or someone you know is in crisis, get help quickly.

- Call your doctor.
- Call 911 for emergency services.
- Go to the nearest hospital emergency room.
- Call the toll-free, 24-hour hotline of the National Suicide Prevention Lifeline at 1-800-273-TALK (1-800-273-8255); TTY: 1-800-799-4TTY (4889)

Chapter 22

Anxiety Disorders

Anxiety is a normal reaction to stress. It helps you deal with a tense situation in the office, study harder for an exam, or keep focused on an important speech. In general, it helps you cope. But when anxiety becomes an excessive, irrational dread of everyday things, it can be disabling.

Anxiety disorders affect about 40 million American adults age 18 years and older (about 18 percent). It's not the same as the mild stress you may feel when you have to speak in public, or the butter-flies you may feel in your stomach when going on a first date. Anxiety disorders can last at least six months and can get worse if they are not treated.

What are Anxiety Disorders?

Occasional anxiety is a normal part of life. You might feel anxious when faced with a problem at work, before taking a test, or making an important decision. Anxiety disorders involve more than temporary worry or fear. For a person with an anxiety disorder, the anxiety does not go away and can get worse over time. These feelings can inter-fere with daily activities such as job performance, school work, and relationships.

This chapter includes excerpts from "Anxiety disorders fact sheet," Office on Women's Health (OWH), February 12, 2015; and text from "What are Anxiety Disorders?" is excerpted from "Anxiety Disorders," National Institute of Mental Health (NIMH) at the National Institutes of Health (NIH), May 2015.

There are a variety of anxiety disorders. Collectively, they are among the most common mental disorders.

Types of Anxiety Disorders

There are three types of anxiety disorders:

1. Generalized Anxiety Disorder (GAD)

2. Panic Disorder

3. Social Anxiety Disorder (Social Phobia)

What Is Generalized Anxiety Disorder?

"I always thought I was just a worrier. I'd feel keyed up and unable to relax. At times it would come and go, and at times it would be constant. It could go on for days. I'd worry about what I was going to fix for a dinner party, or what would be a great present for somebody. I just couldn't let something go."

"I'd have terrible sleeping problems. There were times I'd wake up wired in the middle of the night. I had trouble concentrating, even reading the newspaper or a novel. Sometimes I'd feel a little light-headed. My heart would race or pound. And that would make me worry more. I was always imagining things were worse than they really were. When I got a stomachache, I'd think it was an ulcer."

"I was worried all the time about everything. It didn't matter that there were no signs of problems, I just got upset. I was having trouble falling asleep at night, and I couldn't keep my mind focused at work. I felt angry at my family all the time."

All of us worry about things like health, money, or family problems. But people with generalized anxiety disorder (GAD) are extremely worried about these and many other things, even when there is little or no reason to worry about them. They are very anxious about just getting through the day. They think things will always go badly. At times, worrying keeps people with GAD from doing everyday tasks.

Causes

GAD sometimes runs in families, but no one knows for sure why some people have it while others don't. Researchers have found that several parts of the brain are involved in fear and anxiety. By learning more about fear and anxiety in the brain, scientists may be able to create better treatments. Researchers are also looking for ways in which stress and environmental factors may play a role.

Signs and Symptoms

People with GAD can't seem to get rid of their concerns, even though they usually realize that their anxiety is more intense than the situation warrants. They can't relax, startle easily, and have difficulty concentrating. Often they have trouble falling asleep or staying asleep. Physical symptoms that often accompany the anxiety include fatigue, headaches, muscle tension, muscle aches, difficulty swallowing, trembling, twitching, irritability, sweating, nausea, lightheadedness, having to go to the bathroom frequently, feeling out of breath, and hot flashes.

GAD develops slowly. It often starts during the teen years or young adulthood. Symptoms may get better or worse at different times, and often are worse during times of stress.

When their anxiety level is mild, people with GAD can function socially and hold down a job. Although they don't avoid certain situations as a result of their disorder, people with GAD can have difficulty carrying out the simplest daily activities if their anxiety is severe.

Who Is at Risk?

Generalized anxiety disorders affect about 3.1% American adults age 18 years and older (about 18%) in a given year, causing them to be filled with fearfulness and uncertainty. The average age of onset is 31 years old.

GAD affects about 6.8 million American adults, including twice as many women as men. The disorder develops gradually and can begin at any point in the life cycle, although the years of highest risk are between childhood and middle age.

Diagnosis

GAD is diagnosed when a person worries excessively about a variety of everyday problems for at least 6 months.

People with GAD may visit a doctor many times before they find out they have this disorder. They ask their doctors to help them with headaches or trouble falling asleep, which can be symptoms of GAD but they don't always get the help they need right away. It may take doctors some time to be sure that a person has GAD instead of something else.

First, talk to your doctor about your symptoms. Your doctor should do an exam to make sure that another physical problem isn't causing the symptoms. The doctor may refer you to a mental health specialist.

Treatments

GAD is generally treated with psychotherapy, medication, or both.

Psychotherapy. A type of psychotherapy called cognitive behavior therapy is especially useful for treating GAD. It teaches a person different ways of thinking, behaving, and reacting to situations that help him or her feel less anxious and worried.

Medication. Doctors also may prescribe medication to help treat GAD. Two types of medications are commonly used to treat GAD—anti-anxiety medications and antidepressants. Anti-anxiety medications are powerful and there are different types. Many types begin working right away, but they generally should not be taken for long periods.

Antidepressants are used to treat depression, but they also are helpful for GAD. They may take several weeks to start working. These medications may cause side effects such as headache, nausea, or difficulty sleeping. These side effects are usually not a problem for most people, especially if the dose starts off low and is increased slowly over time. **Talk to your doctor about any side effects you may have.**

It's important to know that although antidepressants can be safe and effective for many people, they may be risky for some, especially children, teens, and young adults. A "black box"—the most serious type of warning that a prescription drug can have—has been added to the labels of antidepressant medications. These labels warn people that antidepressants may cause some people to have suicidal thoughts or make suicide attempts. Anyone taking antidepressants should be monitored closely, especially when they first start treatment with medications.

Some people do better with cognitive behavior therapy, while others do better with medication. Still others do best with a combination of the two. Talk with your doctor about the best treatment for you.

Panic Disorder

Causes

Panic disorder sometimes runs in families, but no one knows for sure why some people have it while others don't. Researchers have found that several parts of the brain are involved in fear and anxiety. By learning more about fear and anxiety in the brain, scientists may be able to create better treatments. Researchers are also looking for ways in which stress and environmental factors may play a role.

Signs and Symptoms

People with panic disorder may have:

- Sudden and repeated attacks of fear
- A feeling of being out of control during a panic attack
- An intense worry about when the next attack will happen
- A fear or avoidance of places where panic attacks have occurred in the past
- Physical symptoms during an attack, such as a pounding or racing heart, sweating, breathing problems, weakness or dizziness, feeling hot or a cold chill, tingly or numb hands, chest pain, or stomach pain.

Who Is at Risk?

Panic disorder affects about 6 million American adults and is twice as common in women as men. Panic attacks often begin in late adolescence or early adulthood, but not everyone who experiences panic attacks will develop panic disorder. Many people have just one attack and never have another. The tendency to develop panic attacks appears to be inherited.

Diagnosis

Panic attacks can occur at any time, even during sleep. An attack usually peaks within 10 minutes, but some symptoms may last much longer.

People who have full-blown, repeated panic attacks can become very disabled by their condition and should seek treatment before they start to avoid places or situations where panic attacks have occurred. For example, if a panic attack happened in an elevator, someone with panic disorder may develop a fear of elevators that could affect the choice of a job or an apartment, and restrict where that person can seek medical attention or enjoy entertainment.

Some people's lives become so restricted that they avoid normal activities, such as grocery shopping or driving. About one-third become housebound or are able to confront a feared situation only when accompanied by a spouse or other trusted person. When the condition progresses this far, it is called agoraphobia, or fear of open spaces.

Early treatment can often prevent agoraphobia, but people with panic disorder may sometimes go from doctor to doctor for years and visit the emergency room repeatedly before someone correctly diagnoses their condition. This is unfortunate, because panic disorder is one of the most treatable of all the anxiety disorders, responding in most cases to certain kinds of medication or certain kinds of cognitive psychotherapy, which help change thinking patterns that lead to fear and anxiety.

Panic disorder is often accompanied by other serious problems, such as depression, drug abuse, or alcoholism. These conditions need to be treated separately. Symptoms of depression include feelings of sadness or hopelessness, changes in appetite or sleep patterns, low energy, and difficulty concentrating. Most people with depression can be effectively treated with antidepressant medications, certain types of psychotherapy, or a combination of the two.

First, talk to your doctor about your symptoms. Your doctor should do an exam to make sure that another physical problem isn't causing the symptoms. The doctor may refer you to a mental health specialist.

Treatments

Panic disorder is generally treated with psychotherapy, medication, or both.

Psychotherapy. A type of psychotherapy called cognitive behavior therapy is especially useful for treating panic disorder. It teaches a person different ways of thinking, behaving, and reacting to situations that help him or her feel less anxious and fearful.

Medication. Doctors also may prescribe medication to help treat panic disorder. The most commonly prescribed medications for panic disorder are anti-anxiety medications and antidepressants. Anti-anxiety medications are powerful and there are different types. Many types begin working right away, but they generally should not be taken for long periods.

Antidepressants are used to treat depression, but they also are helpful for panic disorder. They may take several weeks to start working. Some of these medications may cause side effects such as headache, nausea, or difficulty sleeping. These side effects are usually not a problem for most people, especially if the dose starts off low and is increased slowly over time. **Talk to your doctor about any side effects you may have.**

It's important to know that although antidepressants can be safe and effective for many people, they may be risky for some, especially children, teens, and young adults. A "black box"—the most serious type of warning that a prescription drug can have—has been added to the labels of antidepressant medications. These labels warn people that antidepressants may cause some people to have suicidal thoughts or make suicide attempts. Anyone taking antidepressants should be monitored closely, especially when they first start treatment with medications.

Another type of medication called beta-blockers can help control some of the physical symptoms of panic disorder such as excessive sweating, a pounding heart, or dizziness. Although beta blockers are not commonly prescribed, they may be helpful in certain situations that bring on a panic attack.

Some people do better with cognitive behavior therapy, while others do better with medication. Still others do best with a combination of the two. Talk with your doctor about the best treatment for you.

Social Phobia

Causes

Social phobia sometimes runs in families, but no one knows for sure why some people have it while others don't. Researchers have found that several parts of the brain are involved in fear and anxiety. By learning more about fear and anxiety in the brain, scientists may be able to create better treatments. Researchers are also looking for ways in which stress and environmental factors may play a role.

Signs and Symptoms

People with social phobia tend to:

- Be very anxious about being with other people and have a hard time talking to them, even though they wish they could

- Be very self-conscious in front of other people and feel embarrassed

- Be very afraid that other people will judge them

- Worry for days or weeks before an event where other people will be

- Stay away from places where there are other people

- Have a hard time making friends and keeping friends

- Blush, sweat, or tremble around other people

- Feel nauseous or sick to their stomach when with other people.

Who Is at Risk?

Social phobia affects about 15 million American adults. Women and men are equally likely to develop the disorder, which usually begins in childhood or early adolescence. There is some evidence that genetic factors are involved. Social phobia is often accompanied by other anxiety disorders or depression. Substance abuse may develop if people try to self-medicate their anxiety.

Diagnosis

Social phobia usually starts during youth. A doctor can tell that a person has social phobia if the person has had symptoms for at least 6 months. Without treatment, social phobia can last for many years or a lifetime.

Social phobia can be limited to one situation (such as talking to people, eating or drinking, or writing on a blackboard in front of others) or may be so broad (such as in generalized social phobia) that the person experiences anxiety around almost anyone other than the family.

First, talk to your doctor about your symptoms. Your doctor should do an exam to make sure that another physical problem isn't causing the symptoms. The doctor may refer you to a mental health specialist.

Treatments

Social phobia is generally treated with psychotherapy, medication, or both.

Psychotherapy. A type of psychotherapy called cognitive behavior therapy (cbt) is especially useful for treating social phobia. It teaches a person different ways of thinking, behaving, and reacting to situations that help him or her feel less anxious and fearful. It can also help people learn and practice social skills.

Medication. Doctors also may prescribe medication to help treat social phobia. The most commonly prescribed medications for social phobia are anti-anxiety medications and antidepressants. Anti-anxiety medications are powerful and there are different types. Many types begin working right away, but they generally should not be taken for long periods.

Antidepressants are used to treat depression, but they are also helpful for social phobia. They are probably more commonly prescribed for social phobia than anti-anxiety medications. Antidepressants may take several weeks to start working. Some may cause side effects such as headache, nausea, or difficulty sleeping. These side effects are usually not a problem for most people, especially if the dose starts off low and is increased slowly over time. Talk to your doctor about any side effects you may have.

A type of antidepressant called monoamine oxidase inhibitors (MAOIs) are especially effective in treating social phobia. However, they are rarely used as a first line of treatment because when MAOIs are combined with certain foods or other medicines, dangerous side effects can occur.

It's important to know that although antidepressants can be safe and effective for many people, they may be risky for some, especially children, teens, and young adults. A "black box"—the most serious type of warning that a prescription drug can have—has been added to the labels of antidepressant medications. These labels warn people that antidepressants may cause some people to have suicidal thoughts or make suicide attempts.

Anyone taking antidepressants should be monitored closely, especially when they first start treatment with medications.

Another type of medication called beta-blockers can help control some of the physical symptoms of social phobia such as excessive sweating, shaking, or a racing heart. They are most commonly prescribed when the symptoms of social phobia occur in specific situations, such as "stage fright."

Some people do better with cognitive behavior therapy, while others do better with medication. Still others do best with a combination of the two. Talk with your doctor about the best treatment for you.

Chapter 23

Bipolar Disorder

Bipolar disorder, also known as manic-depression, is a treatable psychiatric disorder marked by extreme changes in mood, thoughts, behaviors, activity, and sleep. A person with bipolar disorder will experience intense emotional states or "mood episodes," shifting from mania to depression. The ups and downs experienced by someone with bipolar disorder are very different from the normal ups and downs that most people experience from time to time. These changes in mood can last for hours, days, weeks, or months. In between these extremes, the person's mood may be normal.

Families and society are affected by bipolar disorder as well. Symptoms of bipolar disorder may result in poor social functioning and poor job or school performance. Many people with bipolar disorder have difficulty holding a job or caring for themselves, so they rely on others for help. Sometimes symptoms may be so severe that an individual with bipolar disorder may need to be hospitalized for a period of time. There are treatments that help improve functioning and relieve many symptoms of bipolar disorder. Recovery is possible! A combination of helpful therapies, education in managing one's illness, and supports to provide assistance and encouragement can lead to experiencing fewer

Text in this chapter is excerpted from "What is Bipolar Disorder?" Mental Illness Research, Education and Clinical Centers (MIRECC) at the U.S. Department of Veteran Affairs (VA), July 2014.

symptoms, improving relationships with other people, and achieving meaningful and fulfilling life goals.

Prevalence

About one in every 160 people (0.6%) develop Bipolar I Disorder at some point in their life. Bipolar disorder affects men and women at equal rates, and it is found among all ages, races, ethnic groups, and social classes. It can affect multiple members within families. Individuals with a parent or sibling who has bipolar disorder are four to six times more likely to develop the illness compared to individuals who do not have a family history of bipolar disorder. The risk is highest for an identical twin of a person with bipolar disorder. The identical twin has a 40 to 70 percent chance of developing the disorder.

Diagnosis

Bipolar disorder is a psychiatric disorder that must be diagnosed by a trained mental health professional. Diagnostic interviews and medical evaluations are used to determine the diagnosis. There are currently no physical or lab tests that can diagnose bipolar disorder, but they can help rule out other conditions that sometimes have similar symptoms to bipolar disorder (e.g., thyroid dysfunction, brain tumor, and drug use). To make the diagnosis, a trained mental health professional will conduct a comprehensive interview and pay careful attention to the symptoms experienced, the severity of the symptoms, and how long they have lasted. Individuals with bipolar disorder can be misdiagnosed with major depression because people are more likely to seek treatment when feeling depressed than when feeling manic. A thorough interview is needed to prevent this misdiagnosis from occurring.

Course of Illness

Bipolar disorder usually begins in late teens or early adulthood. More than half of all cases start before age 25. However, some people may experience their first symptoms in childhood or later in life. Bipolar disorder is a treatable, chronic illness that requires careful management throughout a person's life. Symptoms vary over time in severity. More than 90% of individuals who have a single manic episode go on to have recurrent mood episodes, and approximately 60% of manic episodes occur immediately before a major depressive episode. Bipolar disorder can also negatively affect relationships, work, school, and the ability to perform day-to-day activities. However, in most cases, individuals with the disorder are able to function between mood episodes.

Causes

There is no simple answer to what causes bipolar disorder because several factors play a part in the onset of the disorder. These include: a family history of bipolar disorder, environmental stressors and stressful life events, and biological factors.

Research shows that the risk for bipolar disorder results from the influence of genes acting together with environmental factors. A family history of bipolar disorder does not necessarily mean children or other relatives will develop the disorder. However, studies have shown that bipolar disorder does run in families, and a family history of bipolar disorder is one of the strongest and most consistent risk factors for the disorder (see section on prevalence). Others believe the environment plays a key role in whether someone will develop bipolar disorder. For example, sleep deprivation, substance abuse, and stressful life events, such as family conflict and loss of a job or a loved one, increase the likelihood of the disorder.

An imbalance of the neurotransmitters norepinephrine and serotonin is also linked to bipolar disorder. Neurotransmitters are brain chemicals that communicate information throughout the brain and body. The exact role of these neurotransmitters in bipolar disorder is not yet understood.

Types of Bipolar Disorder

The main types of bipolar disorder are bipolar I disorder, bipolar II disorder, and cyclothymic disorder.

Bipolar I Disorder

Bipolar I disorder is characterized by the occurrence of one or more manic episodes. Although most people with the disorder also have a major depressive episode during the course of their lives, it is not a requirement for the diagnosis.

Bipolar II Disorder

Bipolar II disorder is characterized by the occurrence of at least one hypomanic episode and at least one major depressive episode.

Cyclothymic Disorder

Cyclothymic disorder is characterized by the occurrence of numerous periods of hypomanic and depressive symptoms over a two year span without ever meeting criteria for a manic, hypomanic, or depressive episode. These periods of mood disturbance must be present for at least half the time during the two year period, and the individual cannot be symptom-free for more than two months at a time.

Symptoms of Bipolar Disorder

Individuals with bipolar disorder may have symptoms of mania, hypomania, and depression.

What is a Manic Episode?

A manic episode is defined as a distinct period during which a person abnormally and persistently feels extremely happy or extremely irritable and has increased energy. This period of abnormal mood must occur most of the day, nearly every day, for *at least one week (less if hospitalized)*. During this period of time, the person must also experience at least 3 of the symptoms below (4 of the symptoms below if the mood is only irritable). The mood disturbance and accompanying symptoms must be severe enough to impair social or work functioning, require hospitalization, or include psychotic features [i.e., hallucinations (false perceptions, such as hearing voices) and delusions (false beliefs, such as paranoid delusions)].

- Inflated self-esteem or grandiosity (has a high opinion of self and may be unrealistic about his or her abilities)

- Decreased need for sleep (e.g., feels rested after only 3 hours of sleep)

- More talkative than usual or pressure to keep talking

- Flight of ideas or racing thoughts (has too many thoughts at the same time or rapid speech that jumps from topic to topic)

- Distractibility (attention is easily drawn to unimportant or irrelevant things)

- Increased goal-directed activities (e.g., social, sexual, or at work or school) or psychomotor agitation (purposeless nongoal-directed activity)

- Excessive involvement in activities with a high potential for painful consequences (e.g., shopping sprees, driving recklessly, and unsafe sex)

What is a Hypomanic Episode?

A hypomanic episode, like a manic episode, is defined as a distinct period during which a person abnormally and persistently feels extremely happy or extremely irritable and has increased energy. This period of abnormal mood must occur most of the day, nearly every day, *for at least 4 consecutive days*. During this period of time, the person must also experience at least 3 of the symptoms listed above (4 of the symptoms if the mood is only irritable). In contrast to a manic episode, symptoms of a hypomanic episode must *not* be severe enough to cause impairment in social or work functioning or to require hospitalization. Additionally, the individual must *not* have any psychotic symptoms.

What is a Depressive Episode?

A depressive episode is defined as a distinct period during which an individual abnormally and persistently feels depressed or loses interest or pleasure in most activities. This period of abnormal mood must occur most of the day, nearly every day, *for at least two weeks*. During this period of time, the person must also experience at least 4 of the symptoms below. The mood disturbance and accompanying symptoms must be severe enough to impair social, work, or other areas of functioning.

- Significant weight loss when not dieting, weight gain, or a decrease or increase in appetite

- Insomnia or hypersomnia (difficulty falling asleep or staying asleep, waking early in the morning and not being able to get back to sleep, or sleeping excessively)

- Psychomotor agitation (e.g., inability to sit still or pacing) or psychomotor retardation (e.g., slowed speech, thinking, and body movements)

- Fatigue or loss of energy

- Feelings of worthlessness or excessive or inappropriate guilt

- Diminished ability to think or concentrate or indecisiveness

- Recurrent thoughts of death (not just fear of dying), recurrent suicidal ideation without a specific plan, a specific plan for committing suicide, or a suicide attempt

Other Common Symptoms

There are other psychiatric symptoms that people with bipolar disorder may experience. Symptoms of anxiety are very common among people with the disorder. They might complain of bodily aches and pains rather than feelings of sadness. They may also experience psychotic symptoms, including hallucinations (false perceptions, such as hearing voices) and delusions (false beliefs, such as paranoid delusions). These psychotic symptoms usually disappear when the symptoms of bipolar disorder have been controlled. Individuals with bipolar disorder are also at great risk for suicide, particularly during a depressive episode.

Similar Psychiatric Disorders

The symptoms of bipolar disorder may overlap with symptoms of other psychiatric disorders.

People with bipolar disorder often seek treatment for their depressive symptoms rather than their manic symptoms. This can result in a misdiagnosis of major depression. Major depression can be distinguished from bipolar disorder by the absence of manic episodes. Bipolar disorder shares symptoms with other psychiatric disorders as well. Attention-deficit/hyperactivity disorder can mimic the manic symptoms in bipolar disorder because it is characterized by excessive energy, impulsive behavior, and poor judgment.

Some individuals have psychotic symptoms when manic (e.g., the belief that the person is Jesus Christ). These symptoms are similar to those seen in psychotic disorders, such as schizophrenia and schizoaffective disorder. The symptoms of these disorders, however, differ over time. Individuals with bipolar disorder usually do not experience psychotic symptoms when their mood is stable, while individuals with schizophrenia or schizoaffective disorder experience psychotic symptoms even during periods of stable mood. Bipolar disorder must also be distinguished from a mood disorder that is due to a general medical condition, where mood symptoms are judged to be the direct consequence of a general medical condition.

Additionally, bipolar disorder must be distinguished from a substance-induced mood disorder, in which mood symptoms are judged to be the direct consequence of alcohol/drug abuse, medication, or toxin exposure.

How Family Members Can Help

The family environment is important in the recovery of individuals with bipolar disorder. Even though the disorder can be a frustrating illness, family members can help the process of recovery in many ways.

Encourage Treatment and Rehabilitation

Medications and psychotherapy can help a person with bipolar disorder feel better, engage in meaningful activities, and improve their quality of life. The first step is to visit a doctor for a thorough evaluation. If possible, it is often helpful for family members to be present at the evaluation to offer support, help answer the doctor's questions, and learn about the illness. If medication is prescribed, family members can provide support in regularly taking those medications. Taking medication can be difficult - there will be times when an individual with bipolar disorder may not want to take it or may just forget to take it. Encouragement and reminders are helpful. Family members can help the person fit taking medication into their daily routine. An individual with bipolar disorder may also be referred to psychosocial treatment and rehabilitation. Family members can be very helpful in supporting therapy attendance. Some ways to encourage therapy attendance are giving reminders, offering support, and providing transportation to the clinic.

Provide Support

Family stress is a powerful predictor of relapse. Conversely, family support decreases the rate of relapse. Helping an individual with bipolar disorder pursue meaningful goals and activities can be very beneficial in the process of recovery. It is best if family members try to be understanding rather than critical, negative, or blaming. It may be difficult at times, but families often do best when they are patient and appreciate any progress that is being made, however slow it may be. If family members are having difficulty being supportive, it might be because of what they believe is causing the disorder. Studies show that family members try to make sense of bipolar disorder by determining its cause.

There is a tendency to think of the causes of the disorder as "moral" or "organic." Family members who believe the cause of bipolar disorder is "moral" believe it is caused by the individual's personality (i.e., the individual is weak, lazy, or lacking self-discipline). Family members who believe the cause of bipolar disorder is "organic" believe in the medical model of disease (i.e., it is a medical illness). The belief that the disorder is caused by moral weakness, laziness, or lack of self-discipline leads family members to believe that individuals with bipolar disorder are able to control their symptoms. The belief that people have control over, and as a result are responsible for their symptoms, can lead to feelings of anger and may prevent family members from being supportive of their ill relative.

In contrast, belief in the medical model of bipolar disorder may lead family members to believe that the symptoms are not controllable, and therefore individuals are not responsible for their symptoms. This leads to greater feelings of warmth and sympathy and a greater willingness to help. Research has shown that family members who hold a medical view of bipolar disorder are less critical of their relative than those who hold a moral view of the disorder. Family members' views on what causes bipolar disorder are important because critical and hostile attitudes have been shown to be predictive of relapse.

Take Care of Themselves

Family members often feel guilty about spending time away from their ill relative; however, it is important that they take good care of themselves. There are many ways to do this. Family members should not allow their ill relative to monopolize their time. Spending time alone or with other family members and friends is important for their own well-being. Family members may also consider joining a support or therapy group. Counseling can often help family and friends better cope with a loved one's illness. Finally, family members should not feel responsible for solving the problem themselves. They can't. They should get the help of a mental health professional if needed.

There are a variety of medications and therapies available to those suffering from bipolar disorder. Medications can help reduce symptoms and are recommended as the first-line treatment for bipolar disorder. Individuals with bipolar disorder can also learn to manage their symptoms and improve their functioning with psychosocial treatment and rehabilitation. Research has shown that the treatments listed here are effective for people with bipolar disorder. They are considered to be evidence-based practices.

Psychoeducation

Psychoeducation provides patients with an understanding of their illness and the most effective ways of treating symptoms and preventing relapse. Psychoeducation covers topics such as the nature and course of bipolar disorder, the importance of active involvement in treatment, the potential benefits and adverse effects of various treatment options, identification of early signs of relapse, and behavior changes that reduce the likelihood of relapse.

Cognitive Behavioral Therapy

Cognitive behavioral therapy (CBT) is a blend of two therapies: cognitive therapy and behavioral therapy. Cognitive therapy focuses on a person's thoughts and beliefs and how they influence a person's mood and actions. CBT aims to change a person's way of thinking to be more adaptive and healthy. Behavioral therapy focuses on a person's actions and aims to change unhealthy behavior patterns. CBT is used as an adjunct to medication treatment and includes psychoeducation about the disorder as well as problem-solving techniques. Individuals learn to identify what triggers episodes of the illness, which can reduce the chance of relapse. This can help individuals with bipolar disorder minimize the types of stress that can lead to a hospitalization.

CBT also helps individuals learn how to identify maladaptive thoughts, logically challenge them, and replace them with more adaptive thoughts. CBT further targets depressive symptoms by encouraging patients to schedule pleasurable activities. Individuals who receive both CBT and medication treatment have better outcomes than those who do not receive CBT as an adjunctive treatment. CBT may be done one-on-one or in a group setting.

Interpersonal and Social Rhythm Therapy

In Interpersonal and Social Rhythm Therapy (IPSRT), patients first learn to recognize the relationship between their circadian rhythms and daily routines, and their mental health symptoms. IPSRT then focuses on stabilizing sleep/wake cycles, maintaining regular patterns of daily activities (i.e., sleeping, eating, exercise, and other stimulating activities), and addressing potential problems that may disrupt these routines. This often involves resolving current interpersonal problems and developing strategies to prevent such problems from recurring in the future. When combined with medication, IPSRT can help individuals increase their targeted lifestyle routines and reduce both depressive and manic symptoms.

Family-Based Services

Mental illness affects the whole family. Family services teach families to work together towards recovery. In family-based services, the family and clinician meet to discuss problems the family is experiencing. Families then attend educational sessions where they will learn basic facts about mental illness, coping skills, communication skills, problem-solving skills, and ways to work with one another toward recovery. individuals with bipolar disorder who participate in family interventions along with taking medication have fewer relapses, longer time between relapses, better medication adherence, less severe mood symptoms, and increased positive communication between family members. There is a range of family programs available to fit the specific needs of each family.

Some families benefit from just a few sessions, while more intensive services are especially helpful for families that are experiencing high levels of stress and tension and for individuals with bipolar disorder who are chronically symptomatic or prone to relapse. Generally, these longer-term interventions last 6-9 months and can be conducted in single family or multi-family formats.

Social Skills Training

Many people with bipolar disorder have difficulties with social skills. social skills training (SST) aims to correct these deficits by teaching skills to help express emotion and communicate more effectively so individuals are more likely to achieve their goals, develop relationships, and live independently. Social skills are taught in a very systematic way using behavioral techniques, such as modeling, role playing, positive reinforcement, and shaping.

Illness Self-Management Components of illness self-management include psychoeducation, coping skills training, relapse prevention, and social skills training. Individuals learn about their psychiatric illness, their treatment choices, medication adherence strategies, and coping skills to deal with stress and symptoms. Relapse prevention involves recognizing situations that might trigger symptoms, tracking warning signs and symptoms of relapse, and developing a plan to cope with triggers and warning signs to prevent relapse. This treatment approach also teaches individuals social skills in order to improve the quality of their relationships with others.

Assertive Community Treatment

Assertive Community Treatment (ACT) is an approach that is most effective for individuals with the greatest service needs, such as those with a history of multiple hospitalizations or those who are homeless. In ACT, the person receives treatment from an interdisciplinary team of usually 10 to 12 professionals, including case managers, a psychiatrist, several nurses and social workers, vocational specialists, substance abuse treatment specialists, and peer specialists. The team provides coverage 24 hours a day, 7 days per week, and limits caseloads to ensure a high staff to client ratio, usually 1 staff member for every 10 clients. Services provided in ACT include: case management, comprehensive treatment planning, crisis intervention, medication management, individual supportive therapy, substance abuse treatment, rehabilitation services (e.g., supported employment), and peer support. The VA's version of this program is called Mental Health Intensive Case Management (MHICM).

Psychosocial Interventions for Alcohol and Substance Use Disorders

Many individuals with bipolar disorder also struggle with an alcohol or substance use disorder. Co-occurring disorders are best treated concurrently, meaning that treatment for bipolar disorder should be integrated with the treatment for the alcohol or drug problem. Integrated treatment includes motivational enhancement and cognitive-behavioral interventions. Integrated treatments are effective at reducing substance use, preventing relapse, and keeping individuals in treatment longer. These interventions can be delivered one-on-one or in a group format.

Supported Employment

Research shows that about 70% of adults with severe mental illness want to work and about 60% can be successfully employed through supported employment. Supported employment is a program designed to help people with severe mental illness find and keep competitive employment. The approach is characterized by a focus on competitive work, a rapid job search without prevocational training, and continued support once a job is obtained. Employment specialists work with individuals to identify their career goals and skills. Case managers and mental health providers work closely with employment specialist to provide support during the job seeking and keeping process.

Psychosocial Interventions for Weight Management

Weight gain is a significant and frustrating side effects of some medications used to treat the symptoms of bipolar disorder. Weight gain can lead to problems such as diabetes and hypertension, making it a serious health issue for many individuals. Resources to support weight loss are available. Weight programs generally last 3 months or longer and include education about nutrition and portion control. Participants learn skills to monitor their daily food intake and activity levels, have regular weigh-ins, and set realistic and attainable personal wellness goals. Participation in such a program can help prevent additional weight gain and lead to modest weight loss. The VA's version of this program is called MOVE! It is offered in a supportive group setting.

Mood Stabilizers: What You Should Know

- Bipolar disorder is regarded as a medical disorder (like diabetes). Mood stabilizers are usually the first choice to treat bipolar disorder. Except for lithium, many of these medications are anticonvulsants. Anticonvulsant medications are usually used to treat seizures, but they also help control mood.

- Research has found that mood stabilizers are effective for treating the symptoms of bipolar disorder, but it is not clear exactly how they work. Brain chemicals called neurotransmitters (chemical messengers) are believed to regulate mood. It is thought that lithium may affect the activity of two of these neurotransmitters, serotonin and dopamine. Anticonvulsants are believed to work by increasing the neurotransmitter, GABA, which has a calming effect on the brain. It is also believed that they decrease glutamate, which is an excitatory neurotransmitter.

- All mood stabilizing medications must be taken as prescribed. After achieving the desired, effective dose of a mood stabilizer, it may take an additional 1-2 weeks before you can expect to see improvement in manic symptoms. It may take up to 4 weeks for depressive symptoms to lessen. It is important that you don't stop taking your medication because you think it's not working. Give it time!

- You and your doctor have a lot of choices of medications, and it is hard to know which one may work best for you. Sometimes the mood stabilizing medication you first try may not lead to improvements in symptoms. This is because each person's brain chemistry is unique; what works well for one person may not do as well for another. Be open to trying a different medication or combination of medications in order to find a good fit. Let your doctor know if your symptoms have not improved or have worsened, and do not give up searching for the right medication!

- Once you have responded to medication treatment, it is important to continue taking your medication as prescribed. In general, it is necessary for individuals with bipolar disorder to continue taking mood stabilizing medications for extended periods of time (at least 2 years). Discontinuing treatment earlier may lead to a relapse of symptoms. If you have had a number of episodes of mania or depression, your doctor may recommend longer-term treatment. If episodes of mania or depression occur while on mood stabilizers, your doctor may add other medications to be taken for shorter periods of time. To prevent symptoms from returning or worsening, do not abruptly stop taking your medications, even if you are feeling better, as this may result in a relapse. You should only stop taking your medication under your doctor's supervision. If you want to stop taking your medication, talk to your doctor about how to correctly stop.

- Here is a safe rule of thumb if you miss a dose of your mood stabilizing medication: if it has been *3 hours or less* from the time you were supposed to take your medication, take your medication. If it has been *more than 3 hours* after the dose should have been taken, just skip the forgotten dose and resume taking your medication at the next regularly scheduled time. *Never double up on doses of your mood stabilizer to "catch up" on those you have forgotten.*

- Mood stabilizing medications can interact with other medications to create potentially serious health consequences. Be sure to tell your doctor about all the medications you are taking, including prescription medications, over-the-counter medications, herbal supplements, vitamins, and minerals.

- Like all medications, mood stabilizing medications can have side effects. In many cases, these side effects are mild and tend to diminish with time. Many people have few or no side effects, and the side effects people typically experience are tolerable and subside within a few days. Your doctor will discuss some common side effects with you. Check with your doctor if any of the common side effects persist or become bothersome. If you experience side effects, talk to your doctor before making any decisions about discontinuing treatment.

• In rare cases, these medications can cause severe side effects. Contact your doctor immediately if you experience one or more severe symptoms.

Mood Stabilizing Medications

Lithium (Eskalith or Lithobid)
Valproate/Valproic Acid/Divalproex Sodium (Depakote or Depakene)
Carbamazepine (Equetro or Tegretol)
Lamotrigine (Lamictal)
Oxcarbazepine (Trileptal)
Gabapentin (Fanatrex, Gabarone, Horizant, or Neurontin)
Topiramate (Topamax or Topiragen)
Oxcarbazepine (Trileptal)

Common side effects of lithium: acne; fine hand tremor; increased thirst; nausea; low thyroid hormone (associated with brittle hair, low energy, and sensitivity to cold temperatures); rash; weight gain.

Lithium toxicity is a serious condition caused by having too much lithium in your system. For this reason, your doctor will require you to do periodic blood tests to ensure that lithium is not impacting your kidney or thyroid functioning. In addition, use of certain pain medications (such as ibuprofen) or physical activity with significant sweating can cause your lithium level to increase. You should talk to your doctor about how to exercise safely. Some signs of lithium toxicity include new onset of nausea, vomiting, diarrhea, headache, loss of coordination, slurred speech, nystagmus (abnormal eye movements), dizziness, seizure, confusion, increased thirst, and worsening tremors. You should contact your doctor right away if you experience any of these symptoms.

Common side effects of anticonvulsants: appetite change; dizziness; double vision; headache; irritability; loss of balance/coordination; nausea; sedation; vomiting; weight gain or loss.

Lamotrigine and Carbamazepine may affect white blood cells, the liver, and other organs. Individuals prescribed these medications will need to have their blood checked periodically to make sure the medications are not impacting their organs in a negative way.

Lamotrigine and Carbamazepine can also cause a serious skin rash that should be reported to your doctor immediately. In some cases, this rash can cause permanent disability or be life threatening. The risk for getting this rash can be minimized by very slowly increasing your dose of Lamotrigine. This rash occurs to a lesser extent with Carbamazepine although the risk is higher for individuals of Asian ancestry, including South Asian Indians.

Anticonvulsant medications may increase suicidal thinking and behaviors. Close monitoring for new or worsening symptoms of depression, suicidal thoughts or behavior, or any unusual changes in mood or behavior is advised.

Antipsychotic Medications: What You Should Know

- Antipsychotic medications are sometimes used for treatment when individuals are in a manic episode or a depressive episode. They vary in their effectiveness for treating these episodes. Your doctor will help you choose the best one for you.

- All antipsychotic medications must be taken as prescribed. Their effects can sometimes be noticed within the same day of the first dose. However, the full benefit of the medication may not be realized until after a few weeks of treatment. It is important that you don't stop taking your medication because you think it's not working. Give it time!

- Like mood stabilizers, the antipsychotic medication you try first may not lead to improvements in symptoms. It may be necessary to try another medication or combination of medications. Talk to your doctor if your symptoms do not improve.

- Once you have responded to treatment, it is important to continue taking your medication as prescribed to prevent your symptoms from coming back or worsening. Do not abruptly stop taking your medications, even if you are feeling better as this may result in a relapse. Medication should only be stopped under your doctor's supervision. If you want to stop taking your medication, talk to your doctor about how to correctly stop.

- Most antipsychotics are prescribed once daily. If you forget to take your medication, do not double up the next day to "catch up" on the dose you missed. If your medication is prescribed to be taken twice a day, and you forget to take a dose, a rule of thumb is: if it has been *6 hours or less* from the time you were supposed to take your medication, go ahead and take your medication. If it is *more than 6 hours* after the missed dose should have been taken, just skip the forgotten dose and resume taking your medication at the next regularly scheduled time. *Never double up on doses of your antipsychotic to "catch up" on those you have forgotten.*

- Some antipsychotic medications are available as long-acting injectables. Use of injectable medications is one strategy that can be used for individuals who regularly forget to take their medication.

- Like all medications, antipsychotic medications can have side effects. In many cases they are mild and tend to diminish with time. Many people have few or no side effects, and the side effects people typically experience are tolerable and subside within a few days. Your doctor will discuss some common side effects with you. Check with your doctor if any of the common side effects persist or become bothersome. If you experience side effects, talk to your doctor before making any decisions about discontinuing treatment.

- In rare cases, these medications can cause severe side effects. Contact your doctor immediately if you experience one or more severe symptoms.

Antipsychotic Medications

These are sometimes referred to as conventional, typical or first-generation antipsychotic medications:

Chlorpromazine (Thorazine)
Fluphenazine (Prolixin)
Haloperidol (Haldol)
Loxapine (Loxitane or Loxapac)
Perphenazine (Trilafon)
Thiothixene (Navane)
Trifluoperazine (Stelazine)

These are sometimes referred to as atypical or second-generation antipsychotic medications:

Aripiprazole (Abilify)
Asenapine (Saphris)

Clozapine (Clozaril)
Iloperidone (Fanapt)
Lurasidone (Latuda)
Olanzapine (Zyprexa)
Paliperidone (Invega)
Quetiapine (Seroquel)
Risperidone (Risperdal)
Ziprasidone (Geodon)

Long-Acting Injectable Antipsychotic Medications

Certain antipsychotic medications are available as long-acting injectables. These medications are given every two to four weeks. Some patients find these more convenient because they don't have to take the medications daily. The side effects of these medications are similar to their oral counterparts.

Fluphenazine (Prolixin decanoate)
Haloperidol (Haldol decanoate)
Olanzapine (Zyprexa Relprevv)
Paliperidone (Sustenna)
Risperidone (Risperdal Consta)

Side Effects of Antipsychotic Medications

Some individuals experience side effects that mimic symptoms of Parkinson's disease, which are called parkinsonian or extrapyramidal symptoms. These include tremor, shuffling walk, and muscle stiffness. A related side effect is akathisia, which is a feeling of internal restlessness. Additionally, prolonged use of antipsychotics may cause tardive dyskinesia, a condition marked by involuntary muscle movements in the face and body. An uncommon, but serious side effect is called Neuroleptic Malignant Syndrome (NMS). These symptoms include high fever, muscle rigidity, and irregular heart rate or blood pressure. Contact your doctor immediately if any of these symptoms appear.

People taking antipsychotic medications can also experience a variety of other side effects including: unusual dreams; blank facial expression; blurred vision; breast enlargement or pain; breast milk production; constipation; decreased sexual performance in men; diarrhea; dizziness or fainting when you sit up or stand up; difficulty urinating; drowsiness; dry mouth; excessive saliva; missed menstrual periods; mood changes; nausea; nervousness; restlessness and sensitivity to the sun.

Weight gain, changes in blood sugar regulation, and changes in blood levels of lipids (cholesterol and triglycerides) are common with some antipsychotics. Therefore, your doctor will check your weight and blood chemistry on a regular basis. If you have a scale at home, it would be helpful to regularly check your own weight. Each of these medications differs in their risk of causing these side effects. If you start to gain weight, talk to your doctor. It may be recommended that you switch medications or begin a diet and exercise program.

Clozapine can cause agranulocytosis, which is a loss of the white blood cells that help a person fight off infection. Therefore, people with who take clozapine must get their white blood cell counts checked frequently. This very serious condition is reversible if clozapine is discontinued. Despite this serious side effect, clozapine remains the most effective antipsychotic available and can be used safely if monitoring occurs at the appropriate time intervals.

Antidepressant Medications: What You Should Know

- Antidepressant medications are sometimes used to treat symptoms of depression in bipolar disorder. Individuals who are prescribed antidepressants are usually required to take a mood-stabilizing medication at the same time to reduce the risk of switching from depression to mania or hypomania.

- Research has found that antidepressants are effective for treating depression, but it is not clear exactly how they work. Brain chemicals called neurotransmitters (chemical messengers) are believed to regulate mood. Antidepressant medications work to increase the following neurotransmitters: serotonin, norepinephrine, and/or dopamine.

- All antidepressants must be taken as prescribed for 3 to 4 weeks before you can expect to see positive changes in your symptoms. It is important that you don't stop taking your medication because you think it's not working. Give it time!

- Like mood stabilizers, the antidepressant you try first may not lead to improvements in mood. It may be necessary to try another medication or combination of medications. Talk to your doctor if your symptoms do not improve.

- Once you have responded to treatment, it is important to continue taking your medication to prevent your symptoms from coming back or worsening. Do not abruptly stop taking your medication, even if you are feeling better, as this may result in a relapse. Medication should only be stopped under your doctor's supervision. If you want to stop taking your medication, talk to your doctor about how to correctly stop.

- Here is a safe rule of thumb if you miss a dose of your antidepressant medication: if it has been *3 hours or less* from the time you were supposed to take your medication, take your medication. If it has been *more than 3 hours* after the dose should have been taken, just skip the forgotten dose and resume taking your medication at the next regularly scheduled time. *Never double up on doses of your antidepressant to "catch up" on those you have forgotten.*

- Like all medications, antidepressants can have side effects. In many cases, they are mild and tend to diminish with time. Many people have few or no side effects, and the side effects people typically experience are tolerable and subside within a few days. Your doctor will discuss some common side effects with you. Check with your doctor if any of the common side effects persist or become bothersome. If you experience side effects, talk to your doctor before making any decisions about discontinuing treatment. In rare cases, these medications can cause severe side effects. Contact your doctor immediately if you experience one or more severe symptoms.

- There are five different classes of antidepressant medications. This text lists antidepressant medications by class along with their common side effects.

Antidepressant Class #1: Selective Serotonin Reuptake Inhibitors (SSRI)

SSRIs are the most commonly prescribed class of antidepressants because they tend to have the fewest side effects. SSRIs increase the level of serotonin by inhibiting reuptake of the neurotransmitter.

Fluoxetine (Prozac)
Citalopram (Celexa)
Sertraline (Zoloft)
Paroxetine (Paxil)
Escitalopram (Lexapro)

Common side effects for SSRIs: Abnormal dreams; anxiety; blurred vision; constipation; decreased sexual desire or ability; diarrhea;

dizziness; drowsiness; dry mouth; flu-like symptoms (e.g., fever, chills, muscle aches); flushing; gas; increased sweating; increased urination; lightheadedness when you stand or sit up; loss of appetite; nausea; nervousness; runny nose; sore throat; stomach upset; stuffy nose; tiredness; trouble concentrating; trouble sleeping; yawning; vomiting; weight loss.

Antidepressant Class #2: Serotonin and Norepinephrine Reuptake Inhibitors (SNRI)

SNRIs are similar to SSRIs in that they increase levels of serotonin in the brain. They also increase norepinephrine in the brain to improve mood.

Venlafaxine (Effexor)
Duloxetine (Cymbalta)
Desvenlafaxine (Pristiq)

Common side effects for SNRIs: anxiety; blurred vision; changes in taste; constipation; decreased sexual desire or ability; diarrhea; dizziness; drowsiness; dry mouth; fatigue; flushing; headache; increased sweating; loss of appetite; nausea; nervousness; sore throat; stomach upset; trouble sleeping; vomiting; weakness; weight loss; yawning.

Antidepressant Class #3: Atypical Antidepressants

In addition to targeting serotonin and/or norepinephrine, atypical antidepressants may also target dopamine. They also tend to have fewer side effects than the older classes of medication listed below (antidepressant Classes 4 and 5). The common side effects differ for each of the medications in this class of antidepressants.

Bupropion (Wellbutrin)

Common side effects: Constipation; dizziness; drowsiness; dry mouth; headache; increased sweating; loss of appetite; nausea; nervousness; restlessness; taste changes; trouble sleeping; vomiting; weight changes.

Mirtazapine (Remeron)

Common side effects: Constipation; dizziness; dry mouth; fatigue; increased appetite; low blood pressure; sedation; weight gain.

Trazodone (Desyrel)

Common side effects: Blurred vision; constipation; decreased appetite; dizziness; drowsiness; dry mouth; general body discomfort;

headache; light-headedness; muscle aches/pains; nausea; nervousness; sleeplessness; stomach pain; stuffy nose; swelling of the skin; tiredness; tremors.

Nefazodone (Serzone)

Common side effects: Abnormal dreams; abnormal skin sensations; changes in taste; chills; confusion; constipation; decreased concentration; decreased sex drive; diarrhea; dizziness; drowsiness; dry mouth; fever; frequent urination; headache; incoordination; increased appetite; increased cough; indigestion; lightheadedness; memory loss; mental confusion; ringing in the ears; sleeplessness; sore throat; swelling of the hands and feet; tremor; urinary retention; urinary tract infection; vaginal infection; weakness.

Antidepressant Class #4: Tricyclics And Tetracyclics (TCA and TECA)

This is an older class of antidepressants that also work by increasing levels of serotonin and norepinephrine in the brain. These medications are good alternatives if the newer medications are ineffective.

Amitriptyline (Elavil or Endep)
Amoxapine (Asendin)
Clomipramine (Anafranil)
Desipramine (Norpramin or Pertofrane)
Doxepin (Sinequan or Adapin)
Imipramine (Tofranil)
Nortriptyline (Pamelor)
Protriptyline (Vivactil)
Trimipramine (Surmontil)
Maprotiline (Ludiomil)

Common side effects for the TCAs: Abnormal dreams; anxiety or nervousness; blurred vision; change in appetite or weight; changes in blood pressure; change in sexual desire or ability; clumsiness; confusion; constipation; decreased memory or concentration; dizziness; drowsiness; dry mouth; excess sweating; excitement; headache; heartburn; indigestion; nausea; nightmares; pounding in the chest; pupil dilation; restlessness; sleeplessness; stuffy nose; swelling; tiredness; tremors; trouble sleeping; upset stomach; urinary retention; vomiting; weakness.

Antidepressant Class #5: Monoamine Oxidase Inhibitors (MAOI)

MAOIs are an older class of antidepressants that are not frequently used because of the need to follow a special diet to avoid potential side effects. However, these medications can be very effective. These drugs work by blocking an enzyme called monoamine oxidase, which breaks down the brain chemicals serotonin, norepinephrine, and dopamine.

When taking MAOIs, it is important to follow a low "tyramine" diet, which avoids foods such as cheeses, pickles, and alcohol, and to avoid some over-the-counter cold medications. Most people can adopt to a low tyramine diet without much difficulty. Your doctor will provide a complete list of all food, drinks, and medications to avoid.

Phenelzine (Nardil)
Tranylcypromine (Parnate)
Selegiline (Emsam) patch

Common side effects for MAO/MAOIs: Blurred vision; changes in sexual function; diarrhea, gas, constipation, or upset stomach; difficulty swallowing or heartburn; dizziness, lightheadedness or fainting; drowsiness; dry mouth; headache; nausea, muscle pain or weakness; purple blotches on the skin; rash, redness, irritation, or sores in the mouth (if you are taking the orally disintegrating tablets); sleeping problems; stomach pain, tiredness; tremors; twitching; unusual muscle movements; vomiting, unusual dreams; upset stomach; weakness.

Chapter 24

Stress and Eating Disorders

Chapter Contents

Section 24.1

Eating Disorders

Text in this chapter is excerpted from "Eating Disorders—About
More Than Food," National Institute of Mental Health (NIMH), 2014;
and text from "Having eating disorders," Office on Women's Health
(OWH), January 7, 2015.

The eating disorders such as anorexia nervosa, bulimia nervosa,
and binge-eating disorder, and their variants, all feature serious
disturbances in eating behavior and weight regulation. They are
associated with a wide range of adverse psychological, physical,
and social consequences. A person with an eating disorder may
start out just eating smaller or larger amounts of food, but at some
point, their urge to eat less or more spirals out of control. Severe
distress or concern about body weight or shape, or extreme efforts
to manage weight or food intake, also may characterize an eating
disorder.

Eating disorders are real, treatable medical illnesses. They frequently coexist with other illnesses such as depression, substance
abuse, or anxiety disorders. Other symptoms can become life-threatening if a person does not receive treatment, which is reflected by
anorexia being associated with the highest mortality rate of any psychiatric disorder.

Eating disorders affect both genders, although rates among women
and girls are 2½ times greater than among men and boys. Eating
disorders frequently appear during the teen years or young adulthood
but also may develop during childhood or later in life.

What are the different types of eating disorders?

Anorexia nervosa

Many people with anorexia nervosa see themselves as overweight,
even when they are clearly underweight. Eating, food, and weight
control become obsessions. People with anorexia nervosa typically
weigh themselves repeatedly, portion food carefully, and eat very small

quantities of only certain foods. Some people with anorexia nervosa also may engage in binge eating followed by extreme dieting, excessive exercise, self-induced vomiting, or misuse of laxatives, diuretics, or enemas.

Symptoms of anorexia nervosa include:

- Extremely low body weight

- Severe food restriction

- Relentless pursuit of thinness and unwillingness to maintain a normal or healthy weight

- Intense fear of gaining weight

- Distorted body image and self-esteem that is heavily influenced by perceptions of body weight and shape, or a denial of the seriousness of low body weight

- Lack of menstruation among girls and women.

Some who have anorexia nervosa recover with treatment after only one episode. Others get well but have relapses. Still others have a more chronic, or long-lasting, form of anorexia nervosa, in which their health declines as they battle the illness.

Other symptoms and medical complications may develop over time, including:

- Thinning of the bones (osteopenia or osteoporosis)

- Brittle hair and nails

- Dry and yellowish skin

- Growth of fine hair all over the body (lanugo)

- Mild anemia, muscle wasting, and weakness

- Severe constipation

- Low blood pressure, or slowed breathing and pulse

- Damage to the structure and function of the heart

- Brain damage

- Multi-organ failure

- Drop in internal body temperature, causing a person to feel cold all the time

- Lethargy, sluggishness, or feeling tired all the time
- Infertility

Bulimia nervosa

People with bulimia nervosa have recurrent and frequent episodes of eating unusually large amounts of food and feel a lack of control over these episodes. This binge eating is followed by behavior that compensates for the overeating such as forced vomiting, excessive use of laxatives or diuretics, fasting, excessive exercise, or a combination of these behaviors.

Unlike anorexia nervosa, people with bulimia nervosa usually maintain what is considered a healthy or normal weight, while some are slightly overweight. But like people with anorexia nervosa, they often fear gaining weight, want desperately to lose weight, and are intensely unhappy with their body size and shape. Usually, bulimic behavior is done secretly because it is often accompanied by feelings of disgust or shame. The binge eating and purging cycle can happen anywhere from several times a week to many times a day.

Other symptoms include:

- Chronically inflamed and sore throat
- Swollen salivary glands in the neck and jaw area
- Worn tooth enamel, and increasingly sensitive and decaying teeth as a result of exposure to stomach acid
- Acid reflux disorder and other gastrointestinal problems
- Intestinal distress and irritation from laxative abuse
- Severe dehydration from purging of fluids
- Electrolyte imbalance—too low or too high levels of sodium, calcium, potassium, and other minerals that can lead to a heart attack or stroke

Binge-eating disorder

People with binge-eating disorder lose control over their eating. Unlike bulimia nervosa, periods of binge eating are not followed by compensatory behaviors like purging, excessive exercise, or fasting. As a result, people with binge-eating disorder often are overweight or obese. People with binge-eating disorder who are obese are at higher risk for developing cardiovascular disease and high blood pressure.

They also experience guilt, shame, and distress about their binge eating, which can lead to more binge eating.

How are eating disorders treated?

Typical treatment goals include restoring adequate nutrition, bringing weight to a healthy level, reducing excessive exercise, and stopping binging and purging behaviors. Specific forms of psychotherapy, or talk therapy—including a family-based therapy called the Maudsley approach and cognitive behavioral approaches—have been shown to be useful for treating specific eating disorders. Evidence also suggests that antidepressant medications approved by the U.S. Food and Drug Administration may help for bulimia nervosa and also may be effective for treating co-occurring anxiety or depression for other eating disorders.

Treatment plans often are tailored to individual needs and may include one or more of the following:

* Individual, group, or family psychotherapy

* Medical care and monitoring

* Nutritional counseling

* Medications (for example, antidepressants)

Some patients also may need to be hospitalized to treat problems caused by malnutrition or to ensure they eat enough if they are very underweight. Complete recovery is possible.

What is being done to better understand and treat eating disorders?

Researchers are finding that eating disorders are caused by a complex interaction of genetic, biological, psychological, and social factors. But many questions still need answers. Researchers are studying questions about behavior, genetics, and brain function to better understand risk factors, identify biological markers, and develop specific psychotherapies and medications that can target areas in the brain that control eating behavior. Brain imaging and genetic studies may provide clues for how each person may respond to specific treatments for these medical illnesses. Ongoing efforts also are aimed at developing and refining strategies for preventing and treating eating disorders among adolescents and adults.

How do I get help for eating disorders?

Eating disorders are real medical illnesses. They can lead to serious problems with your heart and other parts of your body. They even can lead to death.

Eating disorders are treatable. Girls with eating disorders can go on to lead full, happy lives.

Treatment for an eating disorder may include talk therapy, medicine, and nutrition counseling. Treatment depends on the type of disorder and the needs of the person who has it.

If you think you have an eating disorder, talk to your doctor or another trusted adult. You also can call or chat with a special eating disorders helpline. Sometimes, a person doesn't have an eating disorder, but has unhealthy dieting behaviors that can turn into an eating disorder. If that's you, get help before any problems get worse. You deserve to feel great!

If you have an eating disorder, you may feel really bad. Don't give up! You can feel better.

Section 24.2

Anorexia nervosa

Text in this section is excerpted from "Anorexia nervosa fact sheet,"
Office on Women's Health (OWH), July 16, 2012.

A person with anorexia nervosa, often called anorexia, has an intense fear of gaining weight. Someone with anorexia thinks about food a lot and limits the food she or he eats, even though she or he is too thin. Anorexia is more than just a problem with food. It's a way of using food or starving oneself to feel more in control of life and to ease tension, anger, and anxiety. Most people with anorexia are female. An anorexic:

- Has a low body weight for her or his height

- Resists keeping a normal body weight

- Has an intense fear of gaining weight

- Thinks she or he is fat even when very thin

- Misses 3 menstrual periods in a row (for girls/women who have started having their periods)

Who becomes anorexic?

While anorexia mostly affects girls and women (85–95 percent of anorexics are female), it can also affect boys and men. It was once thought that women of color were shielded from eating disorders by their cultures, which tend to be more accepting of different body sizes. It is not known for sure whether African American, Latina, Asian/ Pacific Islander, and American Indian and Alaska Native people develop eating disorders because American culture values thin people. People with different cultural backgrounds may develop eating disorders because it's hard to adapt to a new culture (a theory called "culture clash"). The stress of trying to live in two different cultures may cause some minorities to develop their eating disorders.

What causes anorexia?

There is no single known cause of anorexia. Eating disorders are real, treatable medical illnesses with causes in both the body and the mind. Some of these things may play a part:

- **Culture.** Women in the U.S. are under constant pressure to fit a certain ideal of beauty. Seeing images of flawless, thin females everywhere makes it hard for women to feel good about their bodies. More and more, women are also feeling pressure to have a perfect body.

- **Families.** If you have a mother or sister with anorexia, you are more likely to develop the disorder. Parents who think looks are important, diet themselves, or criticize their children's bodies are more likely to have a child with anorexia.

- **Life changes or stressful events.** Traumatic events (like rape) as well as stressful things (like starting a new job), can lead to the onset of anorexia.

- **Personality traits.** Someone with anorexia may not like her or himself, hate the way she or he looks, or feel hopeless. She or he often sets hard-to-reach goals for her or himself and tries to be perfect in every way.

- **Biology.** Genes, hormones, and chemicals in the brain may be factors in developing anorexia.

What are signs of anorexia?

Someone with anorexia may look very thin. She or he may use extreme measures to lose weight by:

- Making her or himself throw up
- Taking pills to urinate or have a bowel movement
- Taking diet pills
- Not eating or eating very little
- Exercising a lot, even in bad weather or when hurt or tired
- Weighing food and counting calories
- Eating very small amounts of only certain foods
- Moving food around the plate instead of eating it

Someone with anorexia may also have a distorted body image, shown by thinking she or he is fat, wearing baggy clothes, weighing her or himself many times a day, and fearing weight gain.

Anorexia can also cause someone to not act like her or himself. She or he may talk about weight and food all the time, not eat in front of others, be moody or sad, or not want to go out with friends. People with anorexia may also have other psychiatric and physical illnesses, including:

- Depression
- Anxiety
- Obsessive behavior
- Substance abuse
- Issues with the heart and/or brain
- Problems with physical development

What happens to your body with anorexia?

With anorexia, your body doesn't get the energy from foods that it needs, so it slows down. Look at the picture below to find out how anorexia affects your health.

240

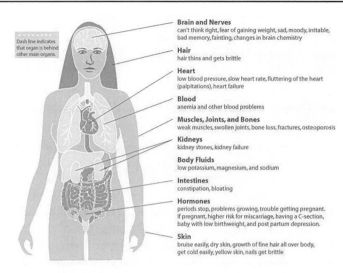

Dash line indicates that organ is behind other main organs.

Brain and Nerves
can't think right, fear of gaining weight, sad, moody, irritable, bad memory, fainting, changes in brain chemistry

Hair
hair thins and gets brittle

Heart
low blood pressure, slow heart rate, fluttering of the heart (palpitations), heart failure

Blood
anemia and other blood problems

Muscles, Joints, and Bones
weak muscles, swollen joints, bone loss, fractures, osteoporosis

Kidneys
kidney stones, kidney failure

Body Fluids
low potassium, magnesium, and sodium

Intestines
constipation, bloating

Hormones
periods stop, problems growing, trouble getting pregnant. If pregnant, higher risk for miscarriage, having a C-section, baby with low birthweight, and post partum depression.

Skin
bruise easily, dry skin, growth of fine hair all over body, get cold easily, yellow skin, nails get brittle

Figure 24.1. *Anorexia affecting various body parts*

Can someone with anorexia get better?

Yes. Someone with anorexia can get better. A health care team of doctors, nutritionists, and therapists will help the patient get better. They will:

- Help bring the person back to a normal weight

- Treat any psychological issues related to anorexia

- Help the person get rid of any actions or thoughts that cause the eating disorder

These three steps will prevent "relapse" (relapse means to get sick again, after feeling well for a while).

Is it safe for young people to take antidepressants for anorexia?

It may be safe for young people to be treated with antidepressants. However, drug companies who make antidepressants are required to post a "black box" warning label on the medication. A "black box" warning is the most serious type of warning on prescription drugs.

It may be possible that antidepressants make children, adolescents, and young adults more likely to think about suicide or commit suicide.

The latest information from the FDA—including what drugs are included in this warning and things to look for—can be found on their website at http://www.fda.gov.

Some research suggests that the use of medicines—such as antidepressants, antipsychotics, or mood stabilizers—may sometimes work for anorexic patients. It is thought that these medicines help the mood and anxiety symptoms that often co-exist with anorexia. Other recent studies, however, suggest that antidepressants may not stop some patients with anorexia from relapsing. Also, no medicine has shown to work 100 percent of the time during the important first step of restoring a patient to healthy weight. So, it is not clear if and how medications can help anorexic patients get better, but research is still happening.

Some forms of psychotherapy can help make the psychological reasons for anorexia better. Psychotherapy is sometimes known as "talk therapy." It uses different ways of communicating to change a patient's thoughts or behavior. This kind of therapy can be useful for treating eating disorders in young patients who have not had anorexia for a long time.

Individual counseling can help someone with anorexia. If the patient is young, counseling may involve the whole family. Support groups may also be a part of treatment. In support groups, patients, and families meet and share what they've been through.

Some researchers point out that prescribing medicines and using psychotherapy designed just for anorexic patients works better at treating anorexia than just psychotherapy alone. Whether or not a treatment works, though, depends on the person involved and his or her situation. Unfortunately, no one kind of psychotherapy always works for treating adults with anorexia.

What is outpatient care for anorexia treatment and how is it different from inpatient care?

With outpatient care, the patient receives treatment through visits with members of their health care team. Often this means going to a doctor's office. Outpatients usually live at home.

Some patients may need "partial hospitalization." This means that the person goes to the hospital during the day for treatment, but sleeps at home at night.

Sometimes, the patient goes to a hospital and stays there for treatment. This is called inpatient care. After leaving the hospital, the patient continues to get help from her health care team and becomes an outpatient.

Can women who had anorexia in the past still get pregnant?

It depends. When a woman has "active anorexia," meaning she currently has anorexia, she does not get her period and usually does not ovulate. This makes it hard to get pregnant. Women who have recovered from anorexia and are at a healthy weight have a better chance of getting pregnant. If you're having a hard time getting pregnant, see your doctor.

Can anorexia hurt a baby when the mother is pregnant?

Yes. Women who have anorexia while they are pregnant are more likely to lose the baby. If a woman with anorexia doesn't lose the baby, she is more likely to have the baby early, deliver by C-section, deliver a baby with a lower birthweight, and have depression after the baby is born.

What should I do if I think someone I know has anorexia?

If someone you know is showing signs of anorexia, you may be able to help.

1. **Set a time to talk.** Set aside a time to talk privately with your friend. Make sure you talk in a quiet place where you won't be distracted.

2. **Tell your friend about your concerns.** Be honest. Tell your friend about your worries about her or his not eating or over exercising. Tell your friend you are concerned and that you think these things may be a sign of a problem that needs professional help.

3. **Ask your friend to talk to a professional.** Your friend can talk to a counselor or doctor who knows about eating issues. Offer to help your friend find a counselor or doctor and make an appointment, and offer to go with her or him to the appointment.

4. **Avoid conflicts.** If your friend won't admit that she or he has a problem, don't push. Be sure to tell your friend you are always there to listen if she or he wants to talk.

5. **Don't place shame, blame, or guilt on your friend.** Don't say, "You just need to eat." Instead, say things like, "I'm concerned about you because you won't eat breakfast or lunch." Or, "It makes me afraid to hear you throwing up."

6. **Don't give simple solutions.** Don't say, "If you'd just stop, then things would be fine!"

7. **Let your friend know that you will always be there no matter what.**

Section 24.3

Bulimia nervosa

Text in this section is excerpted from "Bulimia nervosa fact sheet," Office on Women's Health (OWH), July 16, 2012.

Bulimia nervosa (buh-LEE-me-ah nur-VOH-suh), often called bulimia, is a type of eating disorder. A person with bulimia eats a lot of food in a short amount of time (binging) and then tries to prevent weight gain by getting rid of the food (purging). Purging might be done by:

• Making yourself throw up

• Taking laxatives (pills or liquids that speed up the movement of food through your body and lead to a bowel movement)

A person with bulimia feels he or she cannot control the amount of food eaten. Also, bulimics might exercise a lot, eat very little or not at all, or take pills to pass urine often to prevent weight gain.

Unlike anorexia, people with bulimia can fall within the normal range for their age and weight. But **like** people with anorexia, bulimics:

- Fear gaining weight

- Want desperately to lose weight

- Are very unhappy with their body size and shape

Who becomes bulimic?

Many people think that eating disorders affect only young, upper-class white females. It is true that most bulimics are women (around 85–90 percent). But bulimia affects people from all walks of life, including males, women of color, and even older women. It is not known for sure whether African American, Latina, Asian/Pacific Islander, and American Indian and Alaska Native people develop eating disorders because American culture values thin people. People with different cultural backgrounds may develop eating disorders because it's hard to adapt to a new culture (a theory called "culture clash"). The stress of trying to live in two different cultures may cause some minorities to develop their eating disorders.

What causes bulimia?

Bulimia is more than just a problem with food. A binge can be triggered by dieting, stress, or uncomfortable emotions, such as anger or sadness. Purging and other actions to prevent weight gain are ways for people with bulimia to feel more in control of their lives and ease stress and anxiety. There is no single known cause of bulimia, but there are some factors that may play a part.

- **Culture.** Women in the U.S. are under constant pressure to fit a certain ideal of beauty. Seeing images of flawless, thin females everywhere makes it hard for women to feel good about their bodies.

- **Families.** If you have a mother or sister with bulimia, you are more likely to also have bulimia. Parents who think looks are important, diet themselves, or criticize their children's bodies are more likely to have a child with bulimia.

- **Life changes or stressful events.** Traumatic events (like rape), as well as stressful things (like starting a new job), can lead to bulimia.

- **Personality traits.** A person with bulimia may not like herself, hate the way she looks, or feel hopeless. She may be very moody, have problems expressing anger, or have a hard time controlling impulsive behaviors.

- **Biology.** Genes, hormones, and chemicals in the brain may be factors in developing bulimia.

What are signs of bulimia?

A person with bulimia may be thin, overweight, or have a normal weight. Also, bulimic behavior, such as throwing up, is often done in private because the person with bulimia feels shame or disgust. This makes it hard to know if someone has bulimia. But there are warning signs to look out for. Someone with bulimia may use extreme measures to lose weight by:

- Using diet pills, or taking pills to urinate or have a bowel movement
- Going to the bathroom all the time after eating (to throw up)
- Exercising a lot, even in bad weather or when hurt or tired

Someone with bulimia may show signs of throwing up, such as:

- Swollen cheeks or jaw area
- Calluses or scrapes on the knuckles (if using fingers to induce vomiting)
- Teeth that look clear
- Broken blood vessels in the eyes

People with bulimia often have other mental health conditions, including:

- Depression
- Anxiety
- Substance abuse problems

Someone with bulimia may also have a distorted body image, shown by thinking she or he is fat, hating her or his body, and fearing weight gain.

Bulimia can also cause someone to not act like her or himself. She or he may be moody or sad, or may not want to go out with friends.

What happens to someone who has bulimia?

Bulimia can be very harmful to the body. Look at the picture to find out how bulimia affects your health.

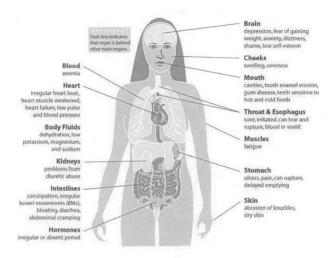

Figure 24.2. *Bulimia affecting body parts*

Can someone with bulimia get better?

Yes. Someone with bulimia can get better. A health care team of doctors, nutritionists, and therapists will help the patient recover. They will help the person learn healthy eating patterns and cope with their thoughts and feelings. Treatment for bulimia uses a combination of options. Whether or not the treatment works depends on the patient.

To stop a person from binging and purging, a doctor may recommend the patient:

- Receive nutritional advice and psychotherapy, especially cognitive behavioral therapy (CBT)

- Be prescribed medicine

CBT is a form of psychotherapy that focuses on the important role of thinking in how we feel and what we do. CBT that has been tailored to treat bulimia has shown to be effective in changing binging and purging behavior, and eating attitudes. Therapy for a person with bulimia may be one-on-one with a therapist or group-based.

Some antidepressants, such as fluoxetine (Prozac), which is the only medication approved by the U.S. Food and Drug Administration (FDA) for treating bulimia, may help patients who also have depression and/or anxiety. It also appears to help reduce binge-eating and purging behavior, reduces the chance of relapse, and improves eating attitudes. ("Relapse" means to get sick again, after feeling well for a while.)

Is it safe for young people to take antidepressants for bulimia?

It may be safe for young people to be treated with antidepressants. However, drug companies who make antidepressants are required to post a "black box" warning label on the medication. A "black box" warning is the most serious type of warning on prescription medicines.

It may be possible that antidepressants make children, adolescents, and young adults more likely to think about suicide or commit suicide.

The FDA offers the latest information, including which drugs are included in this warning and danger signs to look for, on their website at http://www.fda.gov.

Can women who had bulimia in the past still get pregnant?

Active bulimia can cause a woman to miss her period sometimes. Or, she may never get her period. If this happens, she usually does not ovulate. This makes it hard to get pregnant. Women who have recovered from bulimia have a better chance of getting pregnant once their monthly cycle is normal. If you're having a hard time getting pregnant, see your doctor.

How does bulimia affect pregnancy?

If a woman with active bulimia gets pregnant, these problems may result:

- Miscarriage
- High blood pressure in the mother
- Baby isn't born alive
- Baby tries to come out with feet or bottom first
- Birth by C-section
- Baby is born early
- Low birth weight
- Birth defects, such as blindness or mental retardation

- Problems breastfeeding

- Depression in the mother after the baby is born

- Diabetes in the mother during pregnancy

If a woman takes laxatives or diuretics during pregnancy, her baby could be harmed. These things take away nutrients and fluids from a woman before they are able to feed and nourish the baby. It is possible they may lead to birth defects as well, particularly if they are used regularly.

What should I do if I think someone I know has bulimia?

If someone you know is showing signs of bulimia, you may be able to help.

1. **Set a time to talk.** Set aside a time to talk privately with your friend. Make sure you talk in a quiet place where you won't be distracted.

2. **Tell your friend about your concerns.** Be honest. Tell your friend about your worries about his or her eating or exercising habits. Tell your friend you are concerned and that you think these things may be a sign of a problem that needs professional help.

3. **Ask your friend to talk to a professional.** Your friend can talk to a counselor or doctor who knows about eating issues. Offer to help your friend find a counselor or doctor and make an appointment, and offer to go with him or her to the appointment.

4. **Avoid conflicts.** If your friend won't admit that he or she has a problem, don't push. Be sure to tell your friend you are always there to listen if he or she wants to talk.

5. **Don't place shame, blame, or guilt on your friend.** Don't say, "You just need to eat." Instead, say things like, "I'm concerned about you because you won't eat breakfast or lunch." Or, "It makes me afraid to hear you throwing up."

6. **Don't give simple solutions.** Don't say, "If you'd just stop, then things would be fine!"

7. **Let your friend know that you will always be there no matter what.**

Section 24.4

Binge Eating

Text in this section is excerpted from "Chronic Stress Can Get Under Your Skin," United States Department of Agriculture (USDA), March 20, 2013.

Chronic Stress Can Get Under Your Skin

A certain level of stress is good. That burst of adrenaline you get when you have a big task ahead with a deadline, such as cleaning the house before family arrives, is beneficial and helps you rise to the challenge. It even promotes and improves memory to help your remember not to wait until the last minute next year.

The problems begin when we experience prolonged or repeated stress. Chronic stress over time leads to wear-and-tear on the body, and is strongly linked to chronic diseases such as heart disease.

Long-term stress affects the brain. It can cause anxiety, exhaustion, depression, and decreased coping skills. It leads to impaired memory and decision-making ability. It can affect eating, sleeping and activity habits. Studies show that under stress many women shift from normal meal foods (vegetables, fruits, meat) to sweets, high fat snacks, and or "comfort foods." Men, in contrast, tend to seek out extra meal-type foods.

Chronic stress promotes increased calorie intake and binge eating. These dietary responses are thought to be a form of self-medication. It may be that overeating can reduce the negative feelings associated with stress in the short term; but over the long-term, the practice can increase the amount and location of body fat. People who are highly stressed report more sleep difficulties than low stress people, and are less likely to exercise. Regular exercise, plenty of sleep, and a healthy diet are key factors to stress reduction, it can be very difficult to break out of the stress cycle and regain control of your life.

Scientists are just recently beginning to understand how stress gets "under the skin" and influences health, but it appears that stress affects most systems of the body. Stress causes fat stores to move from peripheral areas and deposit around your waist. Thus, it is associated with increased abdominal obesity in people of all weights, even very lean individuals.

Chronic stress also suppresses the immune system. Studies have shown that people reporting being highly stressed produce fewer antibodies after receiving a vaccination, and that high stress levels negatively affect the ability to resist cold and flu viruses. Chronic stress affects the cardiovascular system by increasing insulin resistance, elevating blood pressure, and promoting the generation of atherosclerotic plaques.

Recent research has also linked stress with other conditions. High stress levels are associated with poorer cognitive and physical functioning in older adults, and have been linked to accelerated cell aging. One study found that the cells of women caring for chronically ill children had aged the equivalent of an extra 10 years more than women with healthy children.

Major life events, including divorce, loss of a job or home, illness, or death of a family member are clearly stressful. Other significant stressors include social rejection such as being targeted for excessive criticism, bullying, or exclusion at work. Being "broken-up" with by a significant other, being shunned by a family member, and feeling "less" than others in the community also can lead to feelings of stress.

So, what can one do to lower long-term stress and improve mood and health? The feeling of having no control over a situation contributes to amount of stress experienced as a result. If you can't fix the problem—learning to "let go" can change for the better how that situation affects you. Learn to say "no" when you feel overwhelmed by daily life. Planning and taking a vacation can work wonders. Having a trip already planned to look forward to can improve your mood. Laugh. Smile at people even if you don't feel like it. Spend some time relaxing with those you care about, or make some new friends. Take care of yourself; eat healthy foods, be sure you get enough sleep, but not too much; and don't give up exercising just because the weather is cold and the days are short.

The new Choice Fitness Center in Grand Forks offers not only many exercise options in a pleasant environment, but also places to get some coffee, relax and have a quiet chat with friends–activities that are proven stress-busters.

Chapter 25

Obsessive-Compulsive Disorder

Do you feel the need to check and re-check things over and over? Do you have the same thoughts constantly? Do you feel a very strong need to perform certain rituals repeatedly and feel like you have no control over what you are doing?

If so, you may have a type of anxiety disorder called obsessive-compulsive disorder (OCD).

What is OCD?

Everyone double checks things sometimes. For example, you might double check to make sure the stove or iron is turned off before leaving the house. But people with OCD feel the need to check things repeatedly, or have certain thoughts or perform routines and rituals over and over. The thoughts and rituals associated with OCD cause distress and get in the way of daily life.

The frequent upsetting thoughts are called obsessions. To try to control them, a person will feel an overwhelming urge to repeat certain

---

Text in this chapter is excerpted from "Obsessive-Compulsive Disorder: When Unwanted Thoughts Take Over," National Institute of Mental Health (NIMH) at the National Institutes of Health (NIH), 2013.

rituals or behaviors called compulsions. People with OCD can't control these obsessions and compulsions.

For many people, OCD starts during childhood or the teen years. Most people are diagnosed by about age 19. Symptoms of OCD may come and go and be better or worse at different times.

What causes OCD?

OCD sometimes runs in families, but no one knows for sure why some people have it, while others don't. Researchers have found that several parts of the brain are involved in obsessive thoughts and compulsive behavior, as well as fears and anxiety associated with them. By learning more about fear and anxiety in the brain, scientists may be able to create better treatments. Researchers are also looking for ways in which stress and environmental factors may play a role.

What are the signs and symptoms of OCD?

People with OCD generally:

- Have repeated thoughts or images about many different things, such as fear of germs, dirt, or intruders; acts of violence; hurting loved ones; sexual acts; conflicts with religious beliefs; or being overly tidy

- Do the same rituals over and over such as washing hands, locking and unlocking doors, counting, keeping unneeded items, or repeating the same steps again and again

- Can't control the unwanted thoughts and behaviors

- Don't get pleasure when performing the behaviors or rituals, but get brief relief from the anxiety the thoughts cause

- Spend at least 1 hour a day on the thoughts and rituals, which cause distress and get in the way of daily life.

How is OCD treated?

First, talk to your doctor about your symptoms. Your doctor should do an exam to make sure that another physical problem isn't causing the symptoms. The doctor may refer you to a mental health specialist.

OCD is generally treated with psychotherapy, medication, or both.

Psychotherapy. A type of psychotherapy called cognitive behavioral therapy (CBT) is especially useful for treating OCD. It teaches a person different ways of thinking, behaving, and reacting to situations that help him or her better manage obsessive thoughts, reduce compulsive behavior, and feel less anxious. One specific form of CBT, exposure and response prevention, has been shown to be helpful in reducing the intrusive thoughts and behaviors associated with OCD.

Medication. Doctors may also prescribe medication to help treat OCD. The most commonly prescribed medications for OCD are antidepressants. Although antidepressants are used to treat depression, they are also particularly helpful for OCD. They may take several weeks—10 to 12 weeks for some—to start working. Some of these medications may cause side effects such as headache, nausea, or difficulty sleeping. These side effects are usually not severe for most people, especially if the dose starts off low and is increased slowly over time. Talk to your doctor about any side effects you may have.

It's important to know that although antidepressants can be safe and effective for many people, they may be risky for some, especially children, teens, and young adults. A "black box"—the most serious type of warning that a prescription drug can have—has been added to the labels of antidepressant medications. These labels warn people that antidepressants may cause some people to have suicidal thoughts or make suicide attempts. Anyone taking antidepressants should be monitored closely, especially when they first start treatment with medications.

In addition to prescribing antidepressants, doctors may prescribe other medications such as benzodiazepines to address the anxiety and distress that accompany OCD. Not all medications are effective for everyone. Talk to your doctor about the best treatment choice for you.

Combination. Some people with OCD do better with CBT, especially exposure and response prevention. Others do better with medication. Still others do best with a combination of the two. Many studies have shown that combining CBT with medication is the best approach for treating OCD, particularly in children and adolescents. Talk with your doctor about the best treatment for you.

What is it like having OCD?

"I couldn't do anything without rituals. They invaded every aspect of my life. Counting really bogged me down. I would wash my hair three times as opposed to once because three was a good luck number and one wasn't. It took me longer to read because I'd count the lines in a paragraph. When I set my alarm at night, I had to set it to a number that wouldn't add up to a 'bad' number."

"Getting dressed in the morning was tough, because I had a routine, and if I didn't follow the routine, I'd get anxious and would have to get dressed again. I always worried that if I didn't do something, my parents were going to die. I'd have these terrible thoughts of harming my parents. I knew that was completely irrational, but the thoughts triggered more anxiety and more senseless behavior. Because of the time I spent on rituals, I was unable to do a lot of things that were important to me."

"I knew the rituals didn't make sense, and I was deeply ashamed of them, but I couldn't seem to overcome them until I got treatment."

Chapter 26

Stress and Addiction

Chapter Contents

Section 26.1

Stress and Substance Abuse

Text in this section is excerpted from "PTSD and Substance Abuse
in Veterans," National Center for Posttraumatic Stress Disorder
(PTSD) at the U.S. Department of Veterans Affairs (VA), March
24, 2015; and text from "Link between Underage Substance Use
and Problems in Adulthood," Substance Abuse and Mental Health
Services Administration (SAMHSA), 2014.

Some people try to cope with their post-traumatic stress disorder
(PTSD) symptoms by drinking heavily, using drugs, or smoking too
much. People with PTSD have more problems with drugs and alcohol both before and after getting PTSD. Also, even if someone does
not have a problem with alcohol before a traumatic event, getting
PTSD increases the risk that he or she will develop a drinking or drug
problem.

Eventually, the overuse of these substances can develop into substance use disorder (SUD), and treatment should be given for both
PTSD and SUD to lead to successful recovery. The good news is that
treatment of co-occurring (happening at the same time) PTSD and
SUD works.

How common is co-occurring PTSD and SUD in Veterans?

Studies show that there is a strong relationship between PTSD
and SUD, in both civilian and military populations, as well as for both
men and women.

Specific to Veterans:

- More than 2 of 10 Veterans with PTSD also have SUD.

- War Veterans with PTSD and alcohol problems tend to be binge
  drinkers. Binges may be in response to bad memories of combat
  trauma.

- Almost 1 out of every 3 Veterans seeking treatment for SUD also has PTSD.

- The number of Veterans who smoke (nicotine) is almost double for those with PTSD (about 6 of 10) versus those without a PTSD diagnosis (3 of 10).

- In the wars in Iraq and Afghanistan, about 1 in 10 returning soldiers seen in VA have a problem with alcohol or other drugs.

How can co-occurring PTSD and SUD create problems?

If someone has both PTSD and SUD, it is likely that he or she also has other health problems (such as physical pain), relationship problems (with family and/or friends), or problems in functioning (like keeping a job or staying in school). Using drugs and/or alcohol can make PTSD symptoms worse.

For example:

- PTSD may create sleep problems (trouble falling asleep or waking up during the night). You might "medicate" yourself with alcohol or drugs because you think it helps your sleep, but drugs and alcohol change the quality of your sleep and make you feel less refreshed.

- PTSD makes you feel "numb," like being cut off from others, angry and irritable, or depressed. PTSD also makes you feel like you are always "on guard." All of these feelings can get worse when you use drugs and alcohol.

- Drug and alcohol use allows you to continue the cycle of "avoidance" found in PTSD. Avoiding bad memories and dreams or people and places can actually make PTSD last longer. You cannot make as much progress in treatment if you avoid your problems.

- You may drink or use drugs because it distracts you from your problems for a short time, but drugs and alcohol make it harder to concentrate, be productive, and enjoy all parts of your life.

VA has made it easier to get help. It is important to know that treatment can help and you are not alone.

What treatments are offered for co-occurring PTSD and SUD?

Evidence shows that in general people have improved PTSD and SUD symptoms when they are provided treatment that addresses both conditions. This can involve any of the following (alone or together):

- Individual or group cognitive behavioral treatments (CBT)

- Specific psychological treatments for PTSD, such as Cognitive Processing Therapy (CPT) or Prolonged Exposure (PE)

- Behavioral couples therapy with your spouse or significant other

- Medications that may help you manage the PTSD or SUD symptoms

Talk with your provider about treatment for specific symptoms like pain, anger, or sleep problems.

What should I do if I think I have co-occurring PTSD and SUD?

The first step is to talk to a health professional and ask for more information about treatment options. Each VA medical center has an SUD-PTSD Specialist trained in treating both conditions to reach the best health outcomes. If there are signals you are at risk for both disorders, you will be encouraged to talk with a provider about how to best support your recovery. There are treatment resources at every VA medical center. The VA wants you to have the best possible care for co-occurring PTSD and SUD.

- Find a VA PTSD Program
- Find a VA SUD Program

If you continue to be troubled or distracted by your experiences for more than three months or have questions about your drinking or drug use, learn more about treatment options. Life can be better! Talk to a VA or other health professional to discuss choices for getting started.

Link between Underage Substance Use and Problems in Adulthood

Children and adolescents who use alcohol and drugs at an early are more likely to face problems with substance use as adults, according to a new SAMHSA Treatment Episode Data Set (TEDS) Report.

Past studies have shown an association between consuming alcohol for the first time at an early age and misuse, abuse, or dependency later in life. Evidence now shows that early use of other substances – including marijuana, cocaine, and other psychostimulants and inhalants – pose similar long-term risks to the individual. These findings highlight the need to prevent and, importantly, delay drug initiation among adolescents and children for as long as possible. "Early to late adolescence is considered a critical risk period for the beginning of alcohol and drug use," said SAMHSA Administrator Pamela S. Hyde. "Knowing the age a person starts the use of a substance can inform treatment facilities so that they can better provide timely and appropriate prevention and treatment programs."

Adolescent years can be tumultuous. Teenagers' brains are still growing, and the instability of added emotional and physical changes means that they are particularly susceptible to risky behavior. Unfortunately, alcohol and drug use can seriously affect brain development, particularly in the realms of learning, memory, critical thinking, planning, impulse control, and regulating emotion. Many adolescents report feeling an intense pressure from their peer group to engage in drug use, leading them to unsafe behavior such as driving under the influence or engaging in risky sexual activity.

The SAMHSA Report found that 74 percent of adults participating in a substance abuse treatment program had initiated alcohol or drug use before the age of seventeen. Those who began at a very young age, 11 years old or younger, were more likely to have multiple substance dependencies when compared to those who waited until they were 25 years and older.

Though all adolescents are at risk, particular sensitivity and care should be taken with young people suffering from trauma. Many victims of Post-Traumatic Stress Disorder, for example, go on to develop substance abuse problems. At first, substance use may serve to help the individual cope with the emotional stress, but the depressive values of substances like alcohol can actually worsen depression. Progression from occasional usage to more serious abuse can be a slippery slope. In the long run, addressing the nature and impact of trauma can foster healing and growth, whereas using substances as a coping mechanism can lead to longer-term health issues.

SAMHSA recognizes the important role that parents play in prevention and intervention. The "Talk. They Hear You." campaign works to reduce underage drinking among youth by providing parents and caregivers with information and many resources they need to start addressing the issue of alcohol with their children early. SAMHSA's Too Smart To Start website also provides useful programs and strategies, downloadable materials, interactive games and exercises, and other resources to support youth, families, educators, and communities.

Substance use can interfere with health and academic performance and can negatively affect relationships with friends and family. Talking with young people early and often about the dangers of underage drinking and other substance usage can help. Youth need to understand and feel confident that they do not need to rely on illegal substances to fit in, have fun, or deal with the pressures of growing up.

Did you know?

SAMHSA manages several grant programs intended to prevent alcohol and drug use among youth. Among those are the Partnerships for Success grant program, which is designed to address two of the nation's top substance abuse prevention priorities: underage drinking among persons aged 12 to 20 and prescription drug misuse and abuse among persons aged 12 to 25. In partnership with the Office of National Drug Control Policy, SAMHSA also manages the Drug Free Communities Support Program, which works to reduce substance use among youth.

Section 26.2

Stress and Tobacco

Text in this section is excerpted from"Stress and Smoking," Centers
for Disease Control and Prevention (CDC), March 15, 2015; and text
from "Adult Smoking," Centers for Disease Control and Prevention
(CDC), February 5, 2013.

Stress can be caused by anything from major life events to daily hassles that add up over time. Even happy events, like holidays with family or a pregnancy, can be stressful. The causes of stress are different for each person. Knowing your specific stressors is an important step in finding ways to deal with them.

Stress-Smoking Link

Many people smoke when they feel stressed. Even though they know that smoking hurts them and the ones they love, some smokers find it hard to give up cigarettes as a way to cope with stress.

Stress is part of life, so a key part of quitting smoking for many people is finding ways to handle stress and take care of themselves without smoking. Spend some time thinking about and looking for ways to deal with the busy days that are so often a part of life.

Dealing with Stress

Here are some tips that may help reduce the stress in your life. Try them out. Come up with your own ideas. If something works for you, great! If not, no big deal. Simply try another one. Keep looking for ways to make your quit easier.

- Take a break. Even if it is just for a few minutes, take a breather from a stressful situation. This might mean doing something that you find relaxing, like playing a game or talking with a friend. It could also mean stepping away from the situation for a while by taking a walk or going to get a snack.

- Breathe deeply. Take a few slow, deep breaths. For an extra benefit, breathe in through your nose and out through your mouth. You will feel your body relax.

- Exercise. When your body is active, it sends out natural chemicals that improve your mood and reduce your stress. Walking is one of the easiest exercises for most people. Even a short walk every day will help you to reduce your stress and improve your health.

- Visualize. Close your eyes and imagine you are in a place where you feel safe, comfortable, and relaxed. It can be a real place or one you make up. Picture it as clearly as you can. Let yourself enjoy being there for a few minutes.

- Scan for tension. Our bodies hold on to stress and tension. Scan through your body and look for places where you are tight. These are areas you should target for stress relief. Some simple things you can do to reduce stress include stretching, exercise, or getting a massage. Even a few minutes of rubbing your shoulders, neck, and head can release lots of tension.

- Talk to someone. Talking with a friend or family member about your life is a great way to help reduce stress.

- Focus on the here and now. A lot of people get stressed out thinking about the future. Try focusing just on what is happening now' not on what you might have to deal with in the future.

- Take care of yourself. Especially right after quitting smoking, you should make extra efforts to take care of yourself. This includes basic things like:

- Eating a balanced diet

- Drinking lots of water

- Getting enough sleep

- Cut out caffeine. Caffeine helps keep you awake when you are tired, but it also can make you feel tense, jittery, worried, and stressed. If you are feeling stressed' drinking caffeinated coffee, tea, or soda can make it worse. This is especially true when you are quitting smoking. Cutting back or even eliminating caffeine can help reduce your stress.

- Face the problem. Stop and think about what makes you stressed. Is there something you could be doing to fix the problem? It can be helpful to talk with others about what is happening and see if there are ways to make it better.

Focusing on People with Mental Illness

Cigarette smoking is the leading preventable cause of disease, disability, and death in the U.S. Despite overall declines in smoking, more people with mental illness smoke than people without mental illness. Because many people with mental illness smoke, many of them will get sick and die early from smoking.

Recent research has shown that, like other smokers, adults with mental illness who smoke want to quit, can quit, and benefit from proven stop-smoking treatments. Some mental health providers and facilities have made progress in this area, while others are now beginning to address tobacco use. The 2006 Surgeon General's Report found that smoke-free policies reduce exposure to secondhand smoke and help smokers quit. Mental health facilities can benefit by making their campuses 100% smoke-free and by making stopping tobacco use part of an overall approach to treatment and wellness. It is critical that people with mental illness get the mental health services they need and are able to get help to quit smoking to improve their overall health and wellness.

Smoking is much more common in adults with mental illness than other adults

Smoking and mental illness

- Nicotine has mood-altering effects that put people with mental illness at higher risk for cigarette use and nicotine addiction.
- People with mental illness are more likely to have stressful living conditions, be low income, and lack access to health insurance, health care, and help quitting. All of these factors make it more challenging to quit.
- Evidence shows that there has been direct tobacco marketing to people with mental illness and other vulnerable groups of people.

Smokers who quit have immediate health benefits.

- Risk for a heart attack drops sharply just 1 year after quitting.
- After 2 to 5 years, the chance of stroke can fall to about the same as a nonsmoker's.
- Within 5 years of quitting, the chance of cancer of the mouth, throat, esophagus, and bladder is cut in half.
- Ten years after quitting smoking, the risk for dying from lung cancer drops by half.

Adults with mental illness who smoke want to and are able to quit.

- Like other smokers, smokers with mental illness are interested in quitting, are able to quit, and have a better chance of quitting successfully when they have access to proven stop-smoking treatments.

- With careful monitoring, quitting smoking does not interfere with treatments for mental illness and can be part of the treatment.

- People with mental illness face challenges in quitting smoking and may benefit from extra help to succeed in quitting. This can include more counseling as well as longer use or a combination of stop-smoking medicines.

More attention is needed to help people with mental illness quit smoking.

- Some mental health facilities still allow smoking.

- Some mental health facilities allow smoking as a reward for progress.

- Some mental health facilities now provide counseling and medicine to help smokers quit.

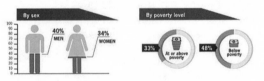

Figure 26.1. *Percent of Adults with Mental Illness Who Smoke*

By Sex: 40% Men, 35% Women.
By Poverty Level: 33% at or above poverty, 48% below poverty.

Smoking Statistics for U.S. Adults with Mental Illness

- **By Age**
- Ages 18: 24 – 42%
- Ages 25: 44 – 41%
- Ages 45: 64 – 34%
- Ages 65: – 13%
- **By Education**
- Less than high school: 47%

- High school graduate: 40%
- Some college: 38%
- College graduate: 19%

- **By Racial/Ethnic Groups**
- American Indian/Alaska Native (Non-Hispanic): 55%
- Other (Non-Hispanic): 40%
- White (Non-Hispanic): 38%
- Black (Non-Hispanic): 34%
- Hispanic: 32%
- Asian (Non-Hispanic): 21%

- **By Region**
- Midwest: 39%
- South: 38%
- Northeast: 35%
- West: 32%

Cigarette Use Among Adults with Any Mental Illness

- States that have less than 30%: Georgia and Utah
- States that have 30 to 34%: California, Colorado, Hawaii, Maryland, Massachusetts, Montana, New York, Rhode Island, Texas and Washington
- States that have 35 to 39%: Connecticut, Delaware, Florida, Kansas, Idaho, Illinois, Indiana, Maine, Missouri, Oregon, Nebraska, New Hampshire, New Jersey, New Mexico, Nevada, North Dakota, Ohio, Pennsylvania, Vermont, Virginia, Wisconsin, and Wyoming.
- States that have 40 to 44%: Arkansas, Arizona, Iowa, Kentucky, Michigan, Minnesota, Mississippi, North Carolina, South Carolina, and South Dakota
- States that have 45% or more: Alabama, Louisiana, Oklahoma, Tennessee, and West Virginia

What Can Be Done

Federal agencies and national partners are working to reduce tobacco use among people with mental illness.

This includes:

- Helping states develop action plans to reduce smoking by people with mental illness.
- Providing funding to promising state and local programs that make stop-smoking treatment part of mental health treatment and wellness.
- Making stop-smoking treatments more available to people who want to quit.
- Conducting research focused on the health and longevity of people with mental illness.
- Providing information to mental health treatment facilities on the benefits of tobacco-free campus policies (i.e., no use of any tobacco product inside the facility or anywhere on its grounds). Several states are already putting these policies in place.

More progress can be achieved:

By mental health professionals

- Asking their patients if they use tobacco; if they do, helping them quit.
- Offering proven quitting treatments, including tailored quit assistance, to patients who use tobacco.
- Referring patients interested in quitting to 1-800-QUIT-NOW, www.smokefree.gov, or other resources.
- Providing more counseling, support, and stop-smoking medicines.
- Making quitting tobacco part of an overall approach to treatment and wellness.
- Monitoring and adjusting mental health medicines as needed in people trying to quit using tobacco.

By mental health facilities

- Including quitting treatments as part of mental health treatment and wellness.

- Stopping practices that encourage tobacco use (such as not providing cigarettes to patients and not allowing staff to smoke with patients).

- Making their entire campus 100% smoke-free as noted in the 2006 Surgeon General's Report. Several states are already putting these recommendations in place.

By state and community leaders

- Helping mental health and tobacco control programs to work together to reduce tobacco use among people with mental illness.

- Encouraging state mental health and addiction agencies to put in place tobacco quitting programs and tobacco-free campuses.

- Supporting sustained, evidence-based tobacco control programs.

By people with mental illness

- Deciding to quit using tobacco right away. The sooner they stop, the sooner their bodies can begin to heal, and the less likely they are to get sick from tobacco use.

- Asking their doctors and mental health treatment providers for help to quit.

- Calling 1-800-QUIT-NOW for free help quitting and going to www.smokefree.gov for a step-by-step quit guide.

- Avoiding secondhand smoke; making their home and vehicles smoke-free.

- Supporting friends who are trying to quit.

Section 26.3

Stress and Alcohol

Text in this section is excerpted from "The Link Between Stress
and Alcohol," National Institute on Alcohol Abuse and Alcoholism
(NIAAA) at the National Institutes of Health (NIH), 2012.

Today, more and more servicemen and women are leaving active
duty and returning to civilian life. That transition can be difficult.
The stresses associated with military service are not easily shed. But
dealing with stress is not limited to recent Veterans. A new job, a death
in the family, moving across the country, a breakup, or getting married—all are situations that can result in psychological and physical
symptoms collectively known as "stress."

One way that people may choose to cope with stress is by turning
to alcohol. Drinking may lead to positive feelings and relaxation,
at least in the short term. Problems arise, however, when stress
is ongoing and people continue to try and deal with its effects by
drinking alcohol. Instead of "calming your nerves," long-term, heavy
drinking can actually work against you, leading to a host of medical and psychological problems and increasing the risk for alcohol
dependence.

This section explores the relationship between alcohol and stress,
including identifying some common sources of stress, examining how
the body responds to stressful situations, and the role that alcohol
plays—both in alleviating and perpetuating stress.

Common Types of Stress

Most causes of stress can be grouped into four categories: general-life stress, catastrophic events, childhood stress, and racial/eth-
nic minority stress (see Figure 26.2.). Each of these factors vary or
are influenced in a number of ways by severity, duration, whether
the stress is expected or not, the type of threat (emotional or physical), and the individual's mental health status (For example, does
the person suffer from anxiety, co-occurring mental health disorders,

General Life Stressors	Fateful/Catastrophic Events
• Divorce/break-up • Job loss • Changing jobs or moving • Problems at work or school • Trouble with a neighbor • Family member in poor health	• September 11, 2001 attacks • Other terrorist attacks • Fires, floods, earthquakes, hurricanes, and other natural disasters • Nuclear disasters
Childhood Maltreatment	**Minority Stress**
• Emotional abuse • Emotional neglect • Physical abuse • Physical neglect • Sexual abuse	• Racial/ethnic minority • Sexual minority • Female

Figure 26.2. *The four categories of stress.*

or alcoholism?). Examples of some of the most common stressors are provided below and summarized in Figure 29.2.

General-Life Stressors

General-life stressors include getting married or divorced, moving, or starting a new job. Problems at home or work, a death in the family, or an illness also can lead to stress. People with an alcohol use disorder (AUD) may be at particular risk for these types of stresses. For example, drinking may cause problems at work, in personal relationships, or trouble with police.

Catastrophic Events

Studies consistently show that alcohol consumption increases in the first year after a disaster, including both manmade and natural events. As time passes, that relationship is dampened. However, much of this research focuses on drinking only and not on the prevalence of AUDs. In the studies that looked specifically at the development of AUDs, the results are less consistent. In some cases, studies have found no increases in AUDs among survivors after events such as the Oklahoma City bombing, September 11, Hurricane Andrew, or jet crashes. However, other studies of September 11 survivors have found that AUDs increased. This trend was similar in studies of Hurricane Katrina, the Mount St. Helens volcano eruption, and other events. Most of these studies included only adults. Additional studies are needed to better understand how adolescents and young people respond to disasters and whether there is a link to alcohol use.

Childhood Stress

Maltreatment in childhood includes exposure to emotional, sexual, and/or physical abuse or neglect during the first 18 years of life. Although they occur during childhood, these stressors have long-lasting effects, accounting for a significant proportion of all adult psychopathology. Studies typically show that maltreatment in childhood increases the risk for both adolescent and adult alcohol consumption1 as well as increased adult AUDs. However, childhood maltreatment is more likely to occur among children of alcoholics, who often use poor parenting practices and who also pass along genes to their offspring that increase the risk of AUDs. Additional research is needed to learn exactly how the stresses of childhood neglect and abuse relate to alcohol use.

Racial and Ethnic Minority Stress

Stress also can arise as a result of a person's minority status, especially as it pertains to prejudice and discrimination. Such stress may range from mild (e.g., hassles such as being followed in a store) to severe (e.g., being the victim of a violent crime). The stress may be emotional (e.g., workplace harassment) or physical (e.g., hate crimes). The relationship of these stress factors to alcohol use is complicated by other risk factors as well, such as drinking patterns and individual differences in how the body breaks down (or metabolizes) alcohol.

Coping with Stress

The ability to cope with stress (known as resilience) reflects how well someone is able to adapt to the psychological and physiological responses involved in the stress response.

When challenged by stressful events, the body responds rapidly, shifting normal metabolic processes into high gear. To make this rapid response possible, the body relies on an intricate system—the hypothalamic–pituitary–adrenal (HPA) axis—that involves the brain and key changes in the levels of hormonal messengers in the body. The system targets specific organs, preparing the body either to fight the stress factor (stressor) or to flee from it (i.e., the fight-or-flight response).

The hormone cortisol has a key role in the body's response to stress. One of cortisol's primary effects is to increase available energy by increasing blood sugar (i.e., glucose) levels and mobilizing fat and protein metabolism to increase nutrient supplies to the muscles, preparing the body to respond quickly and efficiently. A healthy stress response is characterized by an initial spike in cortisol levels followed by a rapid fall in those levels as soon as the threat is over.

People are most resilient when they are able to respond quickly to stress, ramping up the HPA axis and then quickly shutting it down once the threat or stress has passed.

Personality, heredity, and lifestyle all can dictate how well someone handles stress. People who tend to focus on the positive, remain optimistic, and use problem solving and planning to cope with problems are more resilient to stress and its related disorders, including AUDs.

The personality characteristics of resilience are in sharp contrast to the ones associated with an increased risk for substance use disorders (e.g., impulsivity, novelty seeking, negative emotionality, and anxiety). A person with a history of alcoholism in his or her family may have more difficulty dealing with the stress factors that can lead to alcohol use problems. Likewise, having a mother who drank alcohol during pregnancy, experiencing childhood neglect or abuse, and the existence of other mental health issues such as depression can add to that risk.

Alcohol's Role in Stress

To better understand how alcohol interacts with stress, researchers looked at the number of stressors occurring in the past year in a group of men and women in the general population and how those stressors related to alcohol use. They found that both men and women who reported higher levels of stress tended to drink more. Moreover, men tended to turn to alcohol as a means for dealing with stress more often than did women. For example, for those who reported at least six stressful incidents, the percentage of men binge drinking was about 1.5 times that of women, and AUDs among men were 2.5 times higher than women.

Veterans who have been in active combat are especially likely to turn to alcohol as a means of relieving stress. Post-traumatic stress disorder (PTSD), which has been found in 14 to 22 percent of Veterans returning from recent wars in Afghanistan and Iraq has been linked to increased risk for alcohol abuse and dependence.

Stress and Alcoholism Recovery

The impact of stress does not cease once a patient stops drinking. Newly sober patients often relapse to drinking to alleviate the symptoms of withdrawal, such as alcohol craving, feelings of anxiety, and difficulty sleeping. Many of these symptoms of withdrawal can be traced to the HPA axis, the system at the core of the stress response.

Long-term, heavy drinking can actually alter the brain's chemistry, re-setting what is "normal." It causes the release of higher amounts of cortisol and adrenocorticotropic hormone. When this hormonal balance is shifted, it impacts the way the body perceives stress and how it responds to it. For example, a long-term heavy drinker may experience higher levels of anxiety when faced with a stressful situation than someone who never drank or who drank only moderately.

In addition to being associated with negative or unpleasant feelings, cortisol also interacts with the brain's reward or "pleasure" systems. Researchers believe this may contribute to alcohol's reinforcing effects, motivating the drinker to consume higher levels of alcohol in an effort to achieve the same effects.

Cortisol also has a role in cognition, including learning and memory. In particular, it has been found to promote habit-based learning, which fosters the development of habitual drinking and increases the risk of relapse. Cortisol also has been linked to the development of psychiatric disorders (such as depression) and metabolic disorders.

These findings have significant implications for clinical practice. By identifying those patients most at risk of alcohol relapse during early recovery from alcoholism, clinicians can help patients to better address how stress affects their motivation to drink.

Early screening also is vital. For example, Veterans who turn to alcohol to deal with military stress and who have a history of drinking prior to service are especially at risk for developing problems. Screening for a history of alcohol misuse before military personnel are exposed to military trauma may help identify those at risk for developing increasingly severe PTSD symptoms.

Interventions then can be designed to target both the symptoms of PTSD and alcohol dependence. Such interventions include cognitive–behavioral therapies, such as exposure-based therapies, in which the patient confronts the cues that cause feelings of stress but without the risk of danger. Patients then can learn to recognize those cues and to manage the resulting stress. Researchers recommend treating PTSD and alcohol use disorders simultaneously rather than waiting until after patients have been abstinent from alcohol or drugs for a sustained period (e.g., 3 months).

Medications also are currently being investigated for alcoholism that work to stabilize the body's response to stress. Some scientists believe that restoring balance to the stress-response system may help alleviate the problems associated with withdrawal and, in turn, aid in recovery. More work is needed to determine the effectiveness of these medications.

Conclusion

Although the link between stress and alcohol use has been recognized for some time, it has become particularly relevant in recent years as combat Veterans, many with PTSD, strive to return to civilian lifestyles. In doing so, some turn to alcohol as a way of coping.

Unfortunately, alcohol use itself exacts a psychological and physiological toll on the body and may actually compound the effects of stress. More research is needed to better understand how alcohol alters the brain and the various circuits involved with the HPA axis. Powerful genetic models and brain-imaging techniques, as well as an improved understanding of how to translate research using animals to the treatment of humans, should help researchers to further define the complex relationship between stress and alcohol.

Section 26.4

Stress and Drugs

Text in this section is excerpted from""DrugFacts: Understanding
Drug Abuse and Addiction," National Institute on Drug Abuse
(NIDA), November 2012; "How do adolescents become addicted to
drugs, and which factors increase risk?" is excerpted from
"Principles of Adolescent Substance Use Disorder Treatment: A
Research-Based Guide," National Institute on Drug Abuse (NIDA),
January 2014; and text from "Why do drug-addicted
persons keep using drugs?" is excerpted from
"Principles of Drug Addiction Treatment: A Research-Based
Guide (Third Edition)," National Institute on Drug Abuse
(NIDA), December 2012.

Many people do not understand why or how other people become
addicted to drugs. It is often mistakenly assumed that drug abusers
lack moral principles or willpower and that they could stop using drugs
simply by choosing to change their behavior. In reality, drug addiction
is a complex disease, and quitting takes more than good intentions
or a strong will. In fact, because drugs change the brain in ways that
foster compulsive drug abuse, quitting is difficult, even for those who
are ready to do so. Through scientific advances, we know more about
how drugs work in the brain than ever, and we also know that drug
addiction can be successfully treated to help people stop abusing drugs
and lead productive lives.

Drug abuse and addiction have negative consequences for individuals and for society. Estimates of the total overall costs of substance abuse in the United States, including productivity and health-
and crime-related costs, exceed $600 billion annually. This includes
approximately $193 billion for illicit drugs, $193 billion for tobacco,
and $235 billion for alcohol. As staggering as these numbers are,
they do not fully describe the breadth of destructive public health
and safety implications of drug abuse and addiction, such as family
disintegration, loss of employment, failure in school, domestic violence,
and child abuse.

What Is Drug Addiction?

Addiction is a chronic, often relapsing brain disease that causes compulsive drug seeking and use, despite harmful consequences to the addicted individual and to those around him or her. Although the initial decision to take drugs is voluntary for most people, the brain changes that occur over time challenge an addicted person's self-control and hamper his or her ability to resist intense impulses to take drugs.

Fortunately, treatments are available to help people counter addiction's powerful disruptive effects. Research shows that combining addiction treatment medications with behavioral therapy is the best way to ensure success for most patients. Treatment approaches that are tailored to each patient's drug abuse patterns and any co-occurring medical, psychiatric, and social problems can lead to sustained recovery and a life without drug abuse.

Similar to other chronic, relapsing diseases, such as diabetes, asthma, or heart disease, drug addiction can be managed successfully. And as with other chronic diseases, it is not uncommon for a person to relapse and begin abusing drugs again. Relapse, however, does not signal treatment failure—rather, it indicates that treatment should be reinstated or adjusted or that an alternative treatment is needed to help the individual regain control and recover.

What Happens to Your Brain When You Take Drugs?

Drugs contain chemicals that tap into the brain's communication system and disrupt the way nerve cells normally send, receive, and process information. There are at least two ways that drugs cause this disruption: (1) by imitating the brain's natural chemical messengers and (2) by overstimulating the "reward circuit" of the brain.

Some drugs (e.g., marijuana and heroin) have a similar structure to chemical messengers called neurotransmitters, which are naturally produced by the brain. This similarity allows the drugs to "fool" the brain's receptors and activate nerve cells to send abnormal messages.

Other drugs, such as cocaine or methamphetamine, can cause the nerve cells to release abnormally large amounts of natural neurotransmitters (mainly dopamine) or to prevent the normal recycling of these brain chemicals, which is needed to shut off the signaling between neurons. The result is a brain awash in dopamine, a neurotransmitter present in brain regions that control movement, emotion, motivation, and feelings of pleasure. The overstimulation of this reward system, which normally responds to natural behaviors linked to survival (eating, spending time with loved ones, etc.), produces euphoric effects in response to psychoactive drugs. This reaction sets in motion a reinforcing pattern that "teaches" people to repeat the rewarding behavior of abusing drugs.

As a person continues to abuse drugs, the brain adapts to the overwhelming surges in dopamine by producing less dopamine or by reducing the number of dopamine receptors in the reward circuit. The result is a lessening of dopamine's impact on the reward circuit, which reduces the abuser's ability to enjoy not only the drugs but also other events in life that previously brought pleasure. This decrease compels the addicted person to keep abusing drugs in an attempt to bring the dopamine function back to normal, but now larger amounts of the drug are required to achieve the same dopamine high—an effect known as tolerance.

Long-term abuse causes changes in other brain chemical systems and circuits as well. Glutamate is a neurotransmitter that influences the reward circuit and the ability to learn. When the optimal concentration of glutamate is altered by drug abuse, the brain attempts to compensate, which can impair cognitive function. Brain imaging studies of drug-addicted individuals show changes in areas of the brain that are critical to judgment, decision making, learning and memory, and behavior control. Together, these changes can drive an abuser to seek out and take drugs compulsively despite adverse, even devastating consequences—that is the nature of addiction.

Why Do Some People Become Addicted while Others Do Not?

No single factor can predict whether a person will become addicted to drugs. Risk for addiction is influenced by a combination of factors that include individual biology, social environment, and age or stage of development. The more risk factors an individual has, the greater the chance that taking drugs can lead to addiction. For example:

- **Biology.** The genes that people are born with—in combination with environmental influences—account for about half of their addiction vulnerability. Additionally, gender, ethnicity, and the presence of other mental disorders may influence risk for drug abuse and addiction.

- **Environment.** A person's environment includes many different influences, from family and friends to socioeconomic status and quality of life in general. Factors such as peer pressure, physical and sexual abuse, stress, and quality of parenting can greatly influence the occurrence of drug abuse and the escalation to addiction in a person's life.

- **Development.** Genetic and environmental factors interact with critical developmental stages in a person's life to affect addiction vulnerability. Although taking drugs at any age can lead to addiction, the earlier that drug use begins, the more likely it will progress to more serious abuse, which poses a special challenge to adolescents. Because areas in their brains that govern decision making, judgment, and self-control are still developing, adolescents may be especially prone to risk-taking behaviors, including trying drugs of abuse.

Prevention Is the Key

Drug addiction is a preventable disease. Results from NIDA-funded research have shown that prevention programs involving families, schools, communities, and the media are effective in reducing drug abuse. Although many events and cultural factors affect drug abuse trends, when youths perceive drug abuse as harmful, they reduce their drug taking. Thus, education and outreach are key in helping youth and the general public understand the risks of drug abuse. Teachers, parents, and medical and public health professionals must keep sending the message that drug addiction can be prevented if one never abuses drugs.

How do adolescents become addicted to drugs, and which factors increase risk?

Addiction occurs when repeated use of drugs changes how a person's brain functions over time. The transition from voluntary to compulsive drug use reflects changes in the brain's natural inhibition and reward centers that keep a person from exerting control over the impulse to use drugs even when there are negative consequences—the defining characteristic of addiction.

Some people are more vulnerable to this process than others, due to a range of possible risk factors. Stressful early life experiences such as being abused or suffering other forms of trauma are one important risk factor. Adolescents with a history of physical and/or sexual abuse are more likely to be diagnosed with substance use disorders. Many other risk factors, including genetic vulnerability, prenatal exposure to alcohol or other drugs, lack of parental

279

supervision or monitoring, and association with drug-using peers also play an important role.

At the same time, a wide range of genetic and environmental influences that promote strong psychosocial development and resilience may work to balance or counteract risk factors, making it ultimately hard to predict which individuals will develop substance use disorders and which won't.

Why do drug-addicted persons keep using drugs?

Nearly all addicted individuals believe at the outset that they can stop using drugs on their own, and most try to stop without treatment. Although some people are successful, many attempts result in failure to achieve long-term abstinence. Research has shown that long-term drug abuse results in changes in the brain that persist long after a person stops using drugs. These drug-induced changes in brain function can have many behavioral consequences, including an inability to exert control over the impulse to use drugs despite adverse consequences—the defining characteristic of addiction.

Understanding that addiction has such a fundamental biological component may help explain the difficulty of achieving and maintaining abstinence without treatment. Psychological stress from work, family problems, psychiatric illness, pain associated with medical problems, social cues (such as meeting individuals from one's drug-using past), or environmental cues (such as encountering streets, objects, or even smells associated with drug abuse) can trigger intense cravings without the individual even being consciously aware of the triggering event. Any one of these factors can hinder attainment of sustained abstinence and make relapse more likely. Nevertheless, research indicates that active participation in treatment is an essential component for good outcomes and can benefit even the most severely addicted individuals.

Chapter 27

Common Reactions after Trauma

After going through a trauma, survivors often say that their first feeling is relief to be alive. This may be followed by stress, fear, and anger. Trauma survivors may also find they are unable to stop thinking about what happened. Many survivors will show a high level of arousal, which causes them to react strongly to sounds and sights around them.

Most people have some kind of stress reaction after a trauma. Having such a reaction has nothing to do with personal weakness. Stress reactions may last for several days or even a few weeks. For most people, if symptoms occur, they will slowly decrease over time.

What are common reactions to trauma?

All kinds of trauma survivors commonly experience stress reactions. This is true for veterans, children, and disaster rescue or relief workers. If you understand what is happening when you or someone you know reacts to a traumatic event, you may be less fearful and better able to handle things.

Reactions to a trauma may include:

- Feeling hopeless about the future

- Feeling detached or unconcerned about others

Text in this chapter is excerpted from "Common Reactions After Trauma," U.S. Department of Veterans Affairs (VA), August 13, 2015.

- Having trouble concentrating or making decisions
- Feeling jumpy and getting startled easily at sudden noises
- Feeling on guard and constantly alert
- Having disturbing dreams and memories or flashbacks
- Having work or school problems

You may also experience more physical reactions such as:

- Stomach upset and trouble eating
- Trouble sleeping and feeling very tired
- Pounding heart, rapid breathing, feeling edgy
- Sweating
- Severe headache if thinking of the event
- Failure to engage in exercise, diet, safe sex, regular health care
- Excess smoking, alcohol, drugs, food
- Having your ongoing medical problems get worse

You may have more emotional troubles such as:

- Feeling nervous, helpless, fearful, sad
- Feeling shocked, numb, and not able to feel love or joy
- Avoiding people, places, and things related to the event
- Being irritable or having outbursts of anger
- Becoming easily upset or agitated
- Blaming yourself or having negative views of oneself or the world
- Distrust of others, getting into conflicts, being over-controlling
- Being withdrawn, feeling rejected, or abandoned
- Loss of intimacy or feeling detached

Recovery from stress reactions

Turn to your family and friends when you are ready to talk. They are your personal support system. Recovery is an ongoing gradual process. It doesn't happen through suddenly being "cured" and it doesn't mean that you will forget what happened. Most people will recover from trauma naturally. If your stress reactions are getting in the way of your relationships, work, or other important activities, you may want to talk to a counselor or your doctor. Good treatments are available.

Common problems that can occur after a trauma

Post-traumatic stress disorder (PTSD). PTSD is a condition that can develop after you have gone through a life-threatening event. If you have PTSD, you may have trouble keeping yourself from thinking over and over about what happened to you. You may try to avoid people and places that remind you of the trauma. You may feel numb. Lastly, if you have PTSD, you might find that you have trouble relaxing. You may startle easily and you may feel on guard most of the time.

Depression. Depression involves feeling down or sad more days than not. If you are depressed, you may lose interest in activities that used to be enjoyable or fun. You may feel low in energy and be overly tired. You may feel hopeless or in despair, and you may think that things will never get better. Depression is more likely when you have had losses such as the death of close friends. If you are depressed, at times you might think about hurting or killing yourself. For this reason, getting help for depression is very important.

Self-blame, guilt, and shame. Sometimes in trying to make sense of a traumatic event, you may blame yourself in some way. You may think you are responsible for bad things that happened, or for surviving when others didn't. You may feel guilty for what you did or did not do. Remember, we all tend to be our own worst critics. Most of the time, that guilt, shame, or self-blame is not justified.

Suicidal thoughts. Trauma and personal loss can lead a depressed person to think about hurting or killing themselves. If you think someone you know may be feeling suicidal, you should directly ask them. You will NOT put the idea in their head. If someone is thinking about killing themselves, call the Suicide Prevention Lifeline 1-800-273-TALK (8255). You can also call a counselor, doctor, or 911.

Anger or aggressive behavior. Trauma can be connected with anger in many ways. After a trauma, you might think that what happened to you was unfair or unjust. You might not understand why the event happened and why it happened to you. These thoughts can result

283

in intense anger. Although anger is a natural and healthy emotion, intense feelings of anger and aggressive behavior can cause problems with family, friends, or co-workers. If you become violent when angry, you just make the situation worse. Violence can lead to people being injured, and there may be legal consequences.

Alcohol/Drug abuse. Drinking or "self-medicating" with drugs is a common, and unhealthy, way of coping with upsetting events. You may drink too much or use drugs to numb yourself and to try to deal with difficult thoughts, feelings, and memories related to the trauma. While using alcohol or drugs may offer a quick solution, it can actually lead to more problems. If someone close begins to lose control of drinking or drug use, you should try to get them to see a health care provider about managing their drinking or drug use.

Summing it all up

Right after a trauma, almost every survivor will find himself or herself unable to stop thinking about what happened. Stress reactions, such as increased fear, nervousness, jumpiness, upsetting memories, and efforts to avoid reminders, will gradually decrease over time for most people.

Use your personal support systems, family and friends, when you are ready to talk. Recovery is an ongoing gradual process. It doesn't happen through suddenly being "cured" and it doesn't mean that you will forget what happened. Most people will recover from trauma naturally over time. If your emotional reactions are getting in the way of your relationships, work, or other important activities, you may want to talk to a counselor or your doctor. Good treatments are available.

Chapter 28

Types of Stress-Related Disorders That Develop after Trauma

Chapter Contents

Section 28.1

Dissociative Disorders

Dissociation is a psychological state that involves feeling disconnected from reality. A dissociative disorder is a mental health condition in which the affected person experiences a disconnection from their thoughts, feelings, memories, perceptions, consciousness, or identity.

For many people, dissociation is used as a defense mechanism to block out the memory of extremely stressful or traumatic life experiences, particularly from childhood. Dissociative disorders are often found in individuals who were exposed to physical, emotional, or sexual abuse as children, for instance, and in those who endured such traumatic events as natural disasters, wars, accidents, violent crimes, or the tragic loss of a loved one. Dissociative disorders often manifest themselves during stressful situations in adulthood, which can make it difficult for people affected to deal with the challenges of everyday life.

Research suggests that around 2 to 3 percent of people are affected by dissociative disorders. Some of the common symptoms include episodes of memory or sensory loss, feelings of emotional detachment, or a sense of watching oneself from the outside. Dissociative disorders often coincide with other mental health issues, such as mood swings, attention deficits, drug and alcohol dependence, anxiety, panic attacks, and suicidal tendencies.

According to the American Psychiatric Association's *Diagnostic and Statistical Manual,* dissociative disorders take three main forms: depersonalization/derealization disorder; dissociative amnesia; and dissociative identity disorder.

Depersonalization/Derealization Disorder

Depersonalization is a profound sense of detachment or alienation from one's own body, mind, or identity. People with depersonalization disorder may experience an "out of body" sensation, or feel as if they are looking at their own life from an external perspective, like watching a movie. Some people affected by this condition may not recognize their own face in a mirror.

Derealization is the sense that the world does not seem real. People with derealization disorder may report that their surroundings appear hazy, foggy, phony, or far away. Familiar places may seem unfamiliar, and close friends may seem like strangers. In some cases, situations take on a dreamlike quality, and the affected person may feel disoriented and have difficulty determining what is real and what is not.

Dissociative Amnesia

Dissociative amnesia is the inability to remember people, events, or personal information. This memory loss is too substantial to be considered normal forgetfulness, and it is not related to aging, disease, or a head injury. In most cases, people with dissociative amnesia forget a traumatic incident or an extremely stressful period of time. They may also experience smaller lapses in which they forget the content of a conversation or a talent or skill that they have learned.

Dissociative amnesia may be localized, selective, or generalized. In localized amnesia, the memory lapse is concerned with a particular event or span of time. In selective amnesia, the affected person forgets certain parts of a traumatic incident but may remember others. In generalized amnesia, the affected person is unable to remember anything about their own identity or life history. In rare cases dissociative amnesia may take the form of fugue, in which a person travels for hours or days without a sense of their own identity, then suddenly regains awareness and wonders how they got there.

Dissociative Identity Disorder

Dissociative identity disorder, formerly known as multiple personality disorder, is characterized by a deep uncertainty or confusion about one's identity. People affected by this disorder may feel the presence of other people or alternate identities (known as "alters") within themselves. Each of these alters may have their own name, history, voice, mannerisms, and worldview.

A child who has suffered a severe psychological trauma is more likely to develop a dissociative identity disorder. Since the child's mind lacks the coping mechanisms to process the stressful experience, the still-developing personality may find it easier to dissociate and pretend that it was happening to someone else.

Treatment for Dissociative Disorders

Before diagnosing a dissociative disorder, a doctor may perform tests to rule out physical conditions that may cause similar symptoms, such as a head injury, brain tumor, sleep deprivation, or drug addiction. If no physical cause is found, the patient may be referred to a mental health professional for further evaluation. The mental health specialist will likely inquire about childhood trauma and screen the patient for trauma-related conditions, such as anxiety, depression, post-traumatic stress disorder, and substance abuse. Although there is no medication to treat dissociation, antidepressants and anti-anxiety drugs may provide some relief from the symptoms of associated conditions.

Psychiatrists often treat dissociative disorders with counseling designed to help the patient cope with the underlying trauma. They view dissociation as a normal defense mechanism that the brain may use to adapt to a difficult situation in early life. Dissociation only becomes dysfunctional when it persists into adulthood and governs an individual's response to everyday challenges. In these cases, the patient may benefit from a course of psychotherapy to help them understand and process the traumatic event.

Eye movement desensitization and reprocessing (EMDR) is another technique that can help alleviate symptoms related to psychological trauma. In EMDR, the patient makes side-to-side eye motions, usually by following the movement of the therapist's finger, while recalling the traumatic incident. Although doctors are not sure how EMDR works, it appears to help the brain process distressing memories so that they have less impact on the patient's daily life.

References:

1. National Alliance on Mental Illness. "Dissociative Disorders," n.d.

2. NHS Choices. "Dissociative Disorders." Gov.UK, 2014.

3. International Society for the Study of Trauma and Dissociation. "Dissociation FAQs," 2014.

Section 28.2

Acute Stress Disorder

Text in this section is excerpted from "Acute Stress Disorder," U.S.
Department of Veterans Affairs, August 13, 2015.

Acute stress disorder (ASD) is a mental disorder that can occur in
the first month following a trauma. The symptoms that define ASD
overlap with those for PTSD. One difference, though, is that a PTSD
diagnosis cannot be given until symptoms have lasted for one month.
Also, compared to PTSD, ASD is more likely to involve feelings such as
not knowing where you are, or feeling as if you are outside of your body.

How common is ASD?

Studies of ASD vary in terms of the tools used and the rates of ASD
found. Overall, within one month of a trauma, survivors show rates of
ASD ranging from 6% to 33%. Rates differ for different types of trauma.
For example, survivors of accidents or disasters such as typhoons show
lower rates of ASD. Survivors of violence such as robbery, assaults,
and mass shootings show rates at the higher end of that range.

Who is at risk for ASD as a result of trauma?

Several factors can place you at higher risk for developing ASD
after a trauma:

* Having gone through other traumatic events
* Having had PTSD in the past
* Having had prior mental health problems
* Tending to have symptoms, such as not knowing who or where
  you are, when confronted with trauma

Does ASD predict PTSD?

If you have ASD, you are very likely to get PTSD. Research has
found that over 80% of people with ASD have PTSD six months later.
Not everyone with ASD will get PTSD, though.

Also, those who do not get ASD can still develop PTSD later on. Studies indicate that a small number (4% to 13%) of survivors who do not get ASD in the first month after a trauma will get PTSD in later months or years.

Are there effective treatments for ASD?

Yes, a type of treatment called cognitive behavioral therapy (CBT) has been shown to have positive results. Research shows that survivors who get CBT soon after going through a trauma are less likely to get PTSD symptoms later. A mental health care provider trained in treatment for trauma can judge whether CBT may be useful for a trauma survivor.

Another treatment called psychological debriefing (PD) has sometimes been used in the wake of a traumatic event. However, there is little research to back its use for effectively treating ASD or PTSD. It should also be noted that with more severe trauma or reactions such as PTSD, debriefing is not recommended.

Section 28.3

Post-Traumatic Stress Disorder (PTSD)

Text in this section is excerpted from "Post-Traumatic Stress Disorder (Easy-to-Read)," National Institute of Mental Health (NIMH), 2013.

It's natural to be afraid when you're in danger. It's natural to be upset when something bad happens to you or someone you know. But if you feel afraid and upset weeks or months later, it's time to talk with your doctor. You might have post-traumatic stress disorder.

What is post-traumatic stress disorder, or PTSD?

PTSD is a real illness. You can get PTSD after living through or seeing a dangerous event, such as a war, a hurricane, or a bad accident.

PTSD makes you feel stressed and afraid after the danger is over. It affects your life and the people around you.

If you have PTSD, you can get treatment and feel better.

Who gets PTSD?

PTSD can happen to anyone at any age. Children get PTSD, too.

You don't have to be physically hurt to get PTSD. You can get it after you see other people, such as a friend or family member, get hurt.

What causes PTSD?

Living through or seeing something that's upsetting and dangerous can cause PTSD. This can include:

- Death or serious illness of a loved one

- War or combat

- Car accidents and plane crashes

- Hurricanes, tornadoes, and fires

- Violent crimes, like a robbery or shooting

There are many other things that can cause PTSD. Talk to your doctor if you are troubled by something that happened to you or someone you care about.

How do I know if I have PTSD?

Your doctor can help you find out. Call your doctor if you have any of these problems for at least 1 month:

- Suffering from bad dreams

- Feeling like the scary event is happening again (flashbacks)

- Experiencing scary thoughts you can't control

- Staying away from places and things that remind you of what happened

- Feeling worried, guilty, or sad

- Sleeping too little or too much

- Feeling on edge

- Fighting with loved ones or frequent angry outbursts

- Thoughts of hurting yourself or others
- Feeling alone

Children who have PTSD may show other types of problems. These can include:

- Behaving like they did when they were younger
- Being unable to talk
- Complaining of stomach problems or headaches a lot
- Refusing to go places or play with friends

When does PTSD start?

PTSD starts at different times for different people. Signs of PTSD may start soon after a frightening event and then continue. Other people develop new or more severe signs months or even years later.

How can I get better?

PTSD can be treated. A doctor or mental health professional who has experience in treating people with PTSD can help you. Treatment may include "talk" therapy, medication, or both.

Treatment might take 6 to 12 weeks. For some people, it takes longer. Treatment is not the same for everyone. What works for you might not work for someone else.

Drinking alcohol or using other drugs will not help PTSD go away and may even make it worse.

How PTSD Can Happen: An Example

Janet was in a car crash last year. The crash was frightening, and a man in another car died. Janet thought she was lucky. She lived through it and she wasn't badly hurt.

Janet felt fine for a while, but things changed. She started to have nightmares every night. And when she was awake, she could see the crash happening over and over in her mind. She felt tense every time she rode in a car, and tried to avoid it as much as she could. Janet started yelling at her husband over little things. And sometimes she just felt numb inside.

Janet's husband asked her to see her doctor, who told her she might have PTSD. Janet's doctor put her in touch with a doctor trained to help people with PTSD. Soon Janet was being treated. It helped her to feel less tense and scared, and it helped her to sleep. It also helped her to share her feelings with the doctor. It wasn't easy, but after a couple of months Janet began to feel better.

Facts about PTSD

- PTSD can affect anyone at any age
- Millions of Americans get PTSD every year
- Many war veterans have had PTSD
- Women tend to get PTSD more often than men
- PTSD can be treated. You can feel better

Don't Hurt Yourself

You are not alone. Get help if you are thinking about hurting yourself.

- Call your doctor
- Call 911 if you need help right away
- Talk to a trained counselor at the National Suicide Prevention Lifeline at 1-800-273-TALK (8255); TTY: 1-800-799-4TTY (4889)

Chapter 29

Trauma and Relationship Problems

How does trauma affect relationships?

Trauma survivors with PTSD may have trouble with their close family relationships or friendships. The symptoms of PTSD can cause problems with trust, closeness, communication, and problem solving. These problems may affect the way the survivor acts with others. In turn, the way a loved one responds to him or her affects the trauma survivor. A circular pattern can develop that may sometimes harm relationships.

How might trauma survivors react?

In the first weeks and months following a trauma, survivors may feel angry, detached, tense or worried in their relationships. In time, most are able to resume their prior level of closeness in relationships. Yet the 5% to 10% of survivors who develop PTSD may have lasting relationship problems.

Survivors with PTSD may feel distant from others and feel numb. They may have less interest in social or sexual activities. Because survivors feel irritable, on guard, jumpy, worried, or nervous, they may not

---

Text in this chapter is excerpted from "Relationships and PTSD," U.S. Department of Veterans Affairs (VA), August 13, 2015.

be able to relax or be intimate. They may also feel an increased need to protect their loved ones. They may come across as tense or demanding.

The trauma survivor may often have trauma memories or flashbacks. He or she might go to great lengths to avoid such memories. Survivors may avoid any activity that could trigger a memory. If the survivor has trouble sleeping or has nightmares, both the survivor and partner may not be able to get enough rest. This may make sleeping together harder.

Survivors often struggle with intense anger and impulses. In order to suppress angry feelings and actions, they may avoid closeness. They may push away or find fault with loved ones and friends. Also, drinking and drug problems, which can be an attempt to cope with PTSD, can destroy intimacy and friendships. Verbal or physical violence can occur.

In other cases, survivors may depend too much on their partners, family members, and friends. This could also include support persons such as health care providers or therapists.

Dealing with these symptoms can take up a lot of the survivor's attention. He or she may not be able to focus on the partner. It may be hard to listen carefully and make decisions together with someone else. Partners may come to feel that talking together and working as a team are not possible.

How might loved ones react?

Partners, friends, or family members may feel hurt, cut off, or down because the survivor has not been able to get over the trauma. Loved ones may become angry or distant toward the survivor. They may feel pressured, tense, and controlled. The survivor's symptoms can make a loved one feel like he or she is living in a war zone or in constant threat of danger. Living with someone who has PTSD can sometimes lead the partner to have some of the same feelings of having been through trauma.

In sum, a person who goes through a trauma may have certain common reactions. These reactions affect the people around the survivor. Family, friends, and others then react to how the survivor is behaving. This in turn comes back to affect the person who went through the trauma.

Trauma types and relationships

Certain types of "man-made" traumas can have a more severe effect on relationships. These traumas include:

- Childhood sexual and physical abuse

- Rape
- Domestic violence
- Combat
- Terrorism
- Genocide
- Torture
- Kidnapping
- Prisoner of war

Survivors of man-made traumas often feel a lasting sense of terror, horror, endangerment, and betrayal. These feelings affect how they relate to others. They may feel like they are letting down their guard if they get close to someone else and trust them. This is not to say a survivor never feels a strong bond of love or friendship. However, a close relationship can also feel scary or dangerous to a trauma survivor.

Do all trauma survivors have relationship problems?

Many trauma survivors do not develop PTSD. Also, many people with PTSD do not have relationship problems. People with PTSD can create and maintain good relationships by:

- Building a personal support network to help cope with PTSD while working on family and friend relationships
- Sharing feelings honestly and openly, with respect and compassion
- Building skills at problem solving and connecting with others
- Including ways to play, be creative, relax, and enjoy others

What can be done to help someone who has PTSD?

Relations with others are very important for trauma survivors. Social support is one of the best things to protect against getting PTSD. Relationships can offset feelings of being alone. Relationships may also help the survivor's self-esteem. This may help reduce depression and guilt. A relationship can also give the survivor a way to help someone else. Helping others can reduce feelings of failure or feeling cut off from others. Lastly, relationships are a source of support when coping with stress.

297

If you need to seek professional help, try to find a therapist who has skills in treating PTSD as well as working with couples or families.

Many treatment approaches may be helpful for dealing with relationship issues. Options include:

- One-to-one and group therapy
- Anger and stress management
- Assertiveness training
- Couples counseling
- Family education classes
- Family therapy

Chapter 30

Trauma among Children and Teens

What events cause PTSD in children?

Children and teens could have PTSD if they have lived through an event that could have caused them or someone else to be killed or badly hurt. Such events include sexual or physical abuse or other violent crimes. Disasters such as floods, school shootings, car crashes, or fires might also cause PTSD. Other events that can cause PTSD are war, a friend's suicide, or seeing violence in the area they live.

Child protection services in the U.S. get around three million reports each year. This involves 5.5 million children. Of the reported cases, there is proof of abuse in about 30%. From these cases, we have an idea how often different types of abuse occur:

- 65% neglect

- 18% physical abuse

Text in this chapter is excerpted from "Helping Children and Adolescents Cope with Violence and Disasters: What Parents Can Do," National Institute of Mental Health (NIMH) at the National Institutes of Health (NIH), 2013.

- 10% sexual abuse

- 7% psychological (mental) abuse

Also, three to ten million children witness family violence each year. Around 40% to 60% of those cases involve child physical abuse. (Note: It is thought that two-thirds of child abuse cases are not reported.)

How many children get PTSD?

Studies show that about 15% to 43% of girls and 14% to 43% of boys go through at least one trauma. Of those children and teens who have had a trauma, 3% to 15% of girls and 1% to 6% of boys develop PTSD. Rates of PTSD are higher for certain types of trauma survivors.

What are the risk factors for PTSD?

Three factors have been shown to raise the chances that children will get PTSD. These factors are:

- How severe the trauma is

- How the parents react to the trauma

- How close or far away the child is from the trauma

Children and teens that go through the most severe traumas tend to have the highest levels of PTSD symptoms. The PTSD symptoms may be less severe if the child has more family support and if the parents are less upset by the trauma. Lastly, children and teens who are farther away from the event report less distress.

Other factors can also affect PTSD. Events that involve people hurting other people, such as rape and assault, are more likely to result in PTSD than other types of traumas. Also, the more traumas a child goes through, the higher the risk of getting PTSD. Girls are more likely than boys to get PTSD.

It is not clear whether a child's ethnic group may affect PTSD. Some research shows that minorities have higher levels of PTSD symptoms. Other research suggests this may be because minorities may go through more traumas.

Another question is whether a child's age at the time of the trauma has an effect on PTSD. Researchers think it may not be that the effects of trauma differ according to the child's age. Rather, it may be that PTSD looks different in children of different ages.

What does PTSD look like in children?

School-aged children (ages 5–12)

These children may not have flashbacks or problems remembering parts of the trauma, the way adults with PTSD often do. Children, though, might put the events of the trauma in the wrong order. They might also think there were signs that the trauma was going to happen. As a result, they think that they will see these signs again before another trauma happens. They think that if they pay attention, they can avoid future traumas.

Children of this age might also show signs of PTSD in their play. They might keep repeating a part of the trauma. These games do not make their worry and distress go away. For example, a child might always want to play shooting games after he sees a school shooting. Children may also fit parts of the trauma into their daily lives. For example, a child might carry a gun to school after seeing a school shooting.

Teens (ages 12–18)

Teens are in between children and adults. Some PTSD symptoms in teens begin to look like those of adults. One difference is that teens are more likely than younger children or adults to show impulsive and aggressive behaviors.

What are the other effects of trauma on children?

Besides PTSD, children and teens that have gone through trauma often have other types of problems. Much of what we know about the effects of trauma on children comes from the research on child sexual abuse. This research shows that sexually abused children often have problems with

- Fear, worry, sadness, anger, feeling alone and apart from others, feeling as if people are looking down on them, low self-worth, and not being able to trust others

- Behaviors such as aggression, out-of-place sexual behavior, self-harm, and abuse of drugs or alcohol

How is PTSD treated in children and teens?

For many children, PTSD symptoms go away on their own after a few months. Yet some children show symptoms for years if they do not get treatment. There are many treatment options, described below:

301

Cognitive-Behavioral Therapy (CBT)

CBT is the most effective approach for treating children. One type of CBT is called Trauma-Focused CBT (TF-CBT). In TF-CBT, the child may talk about his or her memory of the trauma. TF-CBT also includes techniques to help lower worry and stress. The child may learn how to assert himself or herself. The therapy may involve learning to change thoughts or beliefs about the trauma that are not correct or true. For example, after a trauma, a child may start thinking, "the world is totally unsafe."

Some may question whether children should be asked to think about and remember events that scared them. However, this type of treatment approach is useful when children are distressed by memories of the trauma. The child can be taught at his or her own pace to relax while they are thinking about the trauma. That way, they learn that they do not have to be afraid of their memories. Research shows that TF-CBT is safe and effective for children with PTSD.

CBT often uses training for parents and caregivers as well. It is important for caregivers to understand the effects of PTSD. Parents need to learn coping skills that will help them help their children.

Psychological first aid / crisis management

Psychological First Aid (PFA) has been used with school-aged children and teens that have been through violence where they live. PFA can be used in schools and traditional settings. It involves providing comfort and support, and letting children know their reactions are normal. PFA teaches calming and problem solving skills. PFA also helps caregivers deal with changes in the child's feelings and behavior. Children with more severe symptoms may be referred for added treatment.

Eye movement desensitization and reprocessing (EMDR)

EMDR combines cognitive therapy with directed eye movements. EMDR is effective in treating both children and adults with PTSD, yet studies indicate that the eye movements are not needed to make it work.

Play therapy

Play therapy can be used to treat young children with PTSD who are not able to deal with the trauma more directly. The therapist uses games, drawings, and other methods to help children process their traumatic memories.

Other treatments

Special treatments may be needed for children who show out-of-place sexual behaviors, extreme behavior problems, or problems with drugs or alcohol.

What can you do to help?

Learn about PTSD and pay attention to how your child is doing. Watch for signs such as sleep problems, anger, and avoidance of certain people or places. Also watch for changes in school performance and problems with friends.

You may need to get professional help for your child. Find a mental health provider who has treated PTSD in children. Ask how the therapist treats PTSD, and choose someone who makes you and your child feel at ease. You, as a parent, might also get help from talking to a therapist on your own.

Commonly experienced responses to trauma among children:

Children age 5 and under may react in a number of ways including:

- Showing signs of fear
- Clinging to parent or caregiver
- Crying or screaming
- Whimpering or trembling
- Moving aimlessly
- Becoming immobile
- Returning to behaviors common to being younger
- Thumbsucking
- Bedwetting
- Being afraid of the dark.

Children age 6 to 11 may react by:

- Isolating themselves
- Becoming quiet around friends, family, and teachers
- Having nightmares or other sleep problems
- Refusing to go to bed
- Becoming irritable or disruptive
- Having outbursts of anger
- Starting fights
- Being unable to concentrate
- Refusing to go to school
- Complaining of physical problems
- Developing unfounded fears
- Becoming depressed
- Expressing guilt over what happened
- Feeling numb emotionally
- Doing poorly with school and homework
- Losing interest in fun activities.

Adolescents age 12 to 17 may react by:

- Having flashbacks to the event (flashbacks are the mind reliving the event)
- Having nightmares or other sleep problems
- Avoiding reminders of the event
- Using or abusing drugs, alcohol, or tobacco
- Being disruptive, disrespectful, or behaving destructively
- Having physical complaints
- Feeling isolated or confused
- Being depressed
- Being angry
- Losing interest in fun activities
- Having suicidal thoughts.

Adolescents may feel guilty. They may feel guilt for not preventing injury or deaths. They also may have thoughts of revenge.

What can parents do to help?

After violence or disaster, parents and family members should identify and address their own feelings—this will allow them to help others. Explain to children what happened and let them know:

- You love them
- The event was not their fault
- You will do your best to take care of them
- It's okay for them to feel upset.

Do:

- Allow children to cry
- Allow sadness
- Let children talk about feelings
- Let them write about feelings
- Let them draw pictures about the event or their feelings.

Don't:

- Expect children to be brave or tough
- Make children discuss the event before they are ready
- Get angry if children show strong emotions
- Get upset if they begin bedwetting, acting out, or thumb-sucking.

Other tips:

- If children have trouble sleeping give them extra attention, let them sleep with a light on, or let them sleep in your room (for a short time).
- Try to keep normal routines, for example, reading bedtime stories, eating dinner together, watching TV together, read-

ing books, exercising, or playing games. If you can't keep normal routines, make new ones together.
• Help children feel in control when possible by letting them choose meals, pick out clothes, or make some decisions for themselves.

Chapter 31

PTSD among Military Personnel

Adjusting to Life at Home

It can be difficult to change to a "civilian" mindset once you are back at home with family, friends, co-workers, and U.S. civilians. However, many people have successfully made this transition—and you can, too. The purpose of this chapter is to help you shift gears and begin your next phase of life at home with your family.

For those of you who have deployed more than once, you might expect that with each deployment, the emotional cycle will become easier. But things may actually become more difficult. This is especially the case if you have unresolved problems from previous separations and reunions. Each deployment is also different from the last.

Reunion can also be a time of considerable stress for both you and your family. You may find that coming home is, in fact, harder than going to war. In order to get through homecoming as smoothly as possible, you need to know what kinds of issues you might face and make sure you have realistic expectations.

Text in this chapter is excerpted from "Returning from the War Zone—A Guide for Military Personnel," National Center for Posttraumatic Stress Disorder (PTSD) at the U.S. Department of Veterans Affairs (VA), January 2014.

By drawing your attention to potential challenges, we hope to help you and your family experience the smoothest possible readjustment.

You are not alone. Many troops wrestle with reintegration issues. Time spent in a war zone changes people. It also changes those back home who welcome them back into family life.

Almost all service members will have reactions after returning from a war zone. These behaviors are *normal*, especially during the first weeks at home. **Most service members will successfully readjust** with few major problems. It may take a few months, but you will feel better again.

You, your family, and friends need to be prepared for some common stress reactions. Such predictable reactions do not, by themselves, mean that you have a problem, such as post-traumatic stress disorder (PTSD), which requires professional help. Below are lists of common physical, mental/emotional, and behavioral reactions that you should expect.

Common Reactions to Trauma

Physical Reactions

- Trouble sleeping, overly tired
- Stomach upset, trouble eating
- Headaches and sweating when thinking of the war
- Rapid heartbeat or breathing
- Existing health problems become worse
- Experiencing shock, being numb, unable to feel happy

Mental and Emotional Reactions

- Bad dreams, nightmares
- Flashbacks or frequent unwanted memories
- Anger
- Feeling nervous, helpless, or fearful
- Feeling guilty, self-blame, shame
- Feeling sad, rejected, or abandoned

- Agitated, easily upset, irritated, or annoyed

- Feeling hopeless about the future

Insomnia can occur, and when you do sleep, you may have nightmares. Or you may have no trouble sleeping, but wake up feeling overly tired.

If any of your comrades died during the war, you may be thinking a lot about them. You may feel anger, resentment, or even guilt related to their deaths. Or, you might be in a state of shock, feeling emotionally numb or dazed.

During this time, you may find common family issues more irritating. You may feel anxious or "keyed up." Anger and aggression are common war zone stress reactions, but they may scare your partner, children, and you as well. Minor incidents can lead to severe over-reactions, such as yelling at your partner, kids, or others.

Behavioral Reactions

- Trouble concentrating

- Edgy, jumpy and easily startled

- Being on guard, always alert, concerned too much

- about safety and security

- Avoiding people or places related to the trauma

- Too much drinking, smoking, or drug use

- Lack of exercise, poor diet, or health care

- Problems doing regular tasks at work or school

- Aggressive driving habits

Some avoidance is normal. But if you are constantly avoiding everything that reminds you of your war zone experiences, this can create major difficulties at home. For instance, you may avoid seeing other people for fear that they might ask you about the war. If you are doing this, you can become isolated and withdrawn. Your family and friends will not be able to provide the social support you need, even if you don't know it.

Aggressive driving is also extremely common among service members returning from conflicts in the Middle East. Although you want to drive when you get back, you need to use extra caution. This is particularly true if you're feeling edgy or upset.

Back Home with Family

There is usually a "honeymoon" phase shortly after demobilization, but honeymoons come to an end. You and members of your family have had unique experiences and have changed. You'll need to get to know each other again and appreciate what each other went through. Very likely, you'll need to renegotiate some of your roles. You will need time to rebuild intimacy and learn how to rely on one another again for support.

In addition, your interests may have changed. You may need to re-examine future plans, dreams, and expectations. You and your family will also need to re-examine common goals.

When you return to life at home, you may:

- Feel pressured by requests for time and attention from family, friends, and others

- Be expected to perform home, work, and school responsibilities, or care for children before you are ready

- Find that your parents are trying to be too involved or treat you like a child again

- Face different relationships with children who now have new needs and behaviors

- Be confronted by the needs of partners who have had their own problems

Financial Concerns

You may have financial issues to handle when you return home.

- Be careful not to spend impulsively.

- Seek assistance if making ends meet is hard due to changes in income.

Work Challenges

Readjusting to work can take time.

- You may feel bored, or that you find no meaning in your former work.

- You may have trouble finding a job.

If You Have Children

Children react differently to deployment depending on their age. They can cry, act out, be clingy, withdraw or rebel. To help you can:

- Provide extra attention, care and physical closeness.

- Understand that they may be angry and perhaps rightly so.

- Discuss things. Let kids know they can talk about how they feel. Accept how they feel and don't tell them they should not feel that way.

- Tell kids their feelings are normal. Be prepared to tell them many times.

- Maintain routines and plan for upcoming events.

Common Reactions You May Have That Will Affect Family-and-Friend Relationships

At first, many service members feel disconnected or detached from their partner and/or family. You may be unable to tell your family about what happened. You may not want to scare them by speaking about the war. Or maybe you think that no one will understand. You also may find it's hard to express positive feelings. This can make loved ones feel like they did something wrong or are not wanted anymore. Sexual closeness may also be awkward for a while. Remember, it takes time to feel close again.

When reunited with family, you may also feel:

- Mistrusting: During your deployment you trusted only those closest to you, in your unit. It can be difficult to begin to confide in your family and friends again.

- Over-controlling or overprotective: You might find that you're constantly telling the kids "Don't do that!" or "Be careful, it's not safe!" Rigid discipline may be necessary during wartime, but families need to discuss rules and share in decisions.

- Short tempered: More conflicts with others may be due to poor communication and/or unreasonable expectations.

Resilience Training

Service members are well trained to go to war, but in the past they were not well prepared to come home. In the past few years, the military has made a greater effort to prepare troops for re-entry to civilian life. One way to prepare is to make troops aware that the same mindset that helps them survive in a combat zone can backfire when used in the "home zone." Postdeployment resilience training helps service members understand how a military mindset is useful at war but not at home. For example:

- Discipline, which is essential in the military, can cause problems if applied too strictly with family. Your 13-year-old daughter might not obey orders in the same way you are used to!

- While deployed, buddies are the only ones you talk with, but at home this can lead you to withdraw from family and friends. Take time to reconnect with loved ones.

Each branch of the military has their own training on how to build resilience.

What do families experience during deployment?

It's important to remember that those who were at home while you were away faced their own challenges and opportunities. While you were deployed, your family members probably:

- Experienced loneliness, concern, and worry

- Learned new skills

- Took on new responsibilities

- Had to deal with problems without your help

- Created new support systems and friendships

Family Concerns

The separation that occurs while you're deployed to a war zone will affect your family. Most family members are relieved that you've returned home safely, but you all are a little afraid about what to expect. When you're apart, it is harder to share common experiences. You miss one another. Your absence could have created insecurity, misunderstanding, and distance within your family. You may be concerned about:

- How much each of you has changed

- Whether you are still needed or loved

- Whether your loved ones understand what you've been through

Your loved ones may think you'll never understand how hard it was to manage things at home without you. Now, they may be having a hard time adjusting back to a two-adult household. For example, they may not want you to take on responsibilities that you had before deployment. They may also be afraid of your reaction to how the family has changed during your absence.

These concerns can be resolved once you return home. If you and family members talk about them, you will all gain an appreciation for what everyone has been through. This deeper understanding can bring you closer as a family.

Healthy Coping for Common Reactions to Trauma

With homecoming, you may need to re-learn how to feel safe, comfortable, and trusting with your family. You must get to know one another again. Good communication with your partner, children, parents, siblings, friends, coworkers, and others is the key. Give each other the chance to understand what you have been through. When talking as a family, be careful to listen to one another. Families work best when there is respect for one another, and a willingness to be open and consider alternatives.

Tips for Feeling Better

It's fine for you to spend some time alone. But, if you spend too much time alone or avoid social gatherings, you will be isolated from family and friends. You need the support of these people for a healthy adjustment. You can help yourself to feel better by:

- Getting back to regular patterns of sleep and exercise

- Pursuing hobbies and creative activities

- Planning sufficient R&R and intimate time

- Trying relaxation techniques (meditation, breathing exercises) to reduce stress

- Learning problems to watch out for and how to cope with them

- Striking a balance between staying connected with former war buddies and spending individual time with your partner, kids, other family members, and friends

- Communicating more than the "need-to-know" bare facts

- Talking about your war zone experiences at a time and pace that feels right to you

- Not drinking to excess, or when you're feeling depressed or to avoid disturbing memories. Drink responsibly, or don't drink

- Creating realistic workloads for home, school, and work

Steps to Assuming Normal Routines

Soon after your return, plan to have an open and honest discussion with your family about responsibilities. You all need to decide how they should be split up now that you're home. It's usually best to take on a few tasks at first and then more as you grow accustomed to being home. Be willing to compromise so that both you and your family members feel your needs are understood and respected.

Try to re-establish a normal sleep routine as quickly as possible. Go to bed and get up at the same time every day. Do not drink to help yourself sleep. You might try learning some relaxation techniques, such as deep breathing, yoga, or meditation.

Steps to Controlling Anger

Recognize and try to control your angry feelings. Returning service members don't always realize how angry they are. In fact, you may only recognize your emotion when someone close to you points it out. You can help control your anger by:

- Counting to 10 or 20 before reacting

- Figuring out the cues or situations that trigger your anger so you can be better prepared

- Learning relaxation techniques (breathing, yoga, meditation)

- Learning ways to deal with irritation and frustration and how not to be provoked into aggressive behavior

- Walking away

- Thinking about the ultimate consequences of your responses

- Writing things down

- Learn tips to controlling anger

Important Points to Remember

- Readjusting to civilian life takes time—don't worry that you're experiencing some challenges. Find solutions to these problems. Don't avoid.

- Take your time adding responsibilities and activities back into your life.

- Reconnect with your social supports. This may be the last thing you feel like doing, but do it anyway. Social support is critical to successful reintegration.

- Review Resilience Training to understand where some of your automatic behaviors come from.

- Remind your loved ones that you love them.

- Realize that you need to talk about the experiences you had during deployment. If you can't talk to family or friends, be sure to talk to a chaplain or counselor.

Red Flags

You now know the reactions that are normal following deployment to war. But sometimes the behaviors that kept you alive in the war zone get on the wrong track. You may not be able to shut them down after you've returned home safely.

Some problems may need outside assistance to solve. Even serious post-deployment psychological problems can be treated successfully and cured.

Admitting you have a problem can be tough:

- You might think you should cope on your own.
- You think others can't help you.
- You believe the problem(s) will go away on their own.
- You are embarrassed to talk to someone about it.

Confront Mental Health "Stigma"

Mental health problems are not a sign of weakness. The reality is that injuries, including psychological injuries, affect the strong and the brave just like everyone else. Some of the most successful officers and enlisted personnel have experienced these problems.

But stigma about mental health issues can be a huge barrier for people who need help. Finding the solution to your problem is a sign of strength and maturity. Getting assistance from others is sometimes the only way to solve something. For example, if you cannot scale a wall on your own and need a comrade to do so, you use them! Knowing when and how to get help is actually part of military training.

If your reactions are causing significant distress or interfering with how you function, you will need outside assistance. Things to watch for include:

- Relationship troubles—frequent and intense conflicts, poor communication, inability to meet responsibilities

- Work, school, or other community functioning—frequent absences, conflicts, inability to meet deadlines or concentrate, poor performance

- Thoughts of hurting someone, or yourself

If you get assistance early, you can prevent more serious problems from developing. If you delay seeking help because of avoidance or stigma, your problems may actually cause you to lose your job, your relationships, and your happiness. **Mental and emotional problems can be managed or treated, and early detection is essential.**

Many of the common reactions to experience in a war zone are also symptoms of more serious problems such as PTSD. In PTSD, however, they're much more intense and troubling, and they don't go away. If these symptoms don't decrease over a few months, or if they continue to cause significant problems in your daily life, it's time to seek treatment from a professional.

PTSD Screening Test

In your life, have you ever had any experience that was so frightening, horrible, or upsetting that, in the past month, you:

- Have had nightmares about it or thought about it when you did not want to?
- Tried hard not to think about it or went out of your way to avoid situations that reminded you of it?

- Were constantly on guard, watchful, or easily startled?
- Felt numb or detached from others, activities, or your surroundings?

Current research recommends that if you answered "yes" to any three items you should seek more information from a mental health care provider. *A positive screen does not mean that you have PTSD. Only a qualified mental health-care practitioner, such as a clinician or psychologist, can diagnose you with PTSD.*

Symptoms of PTSD

Re-experiencing

Bad memories of a traumatic event can come back at any time. You may feel the same terror and horror you did when the event took place. Sometimes there's a trigger: a sound, sight, or smell that causes you to relive the event.

Avoidance

People with PTSD often go to great lengths to avoid things that might remind them of the traumatic event they endured.

Negative changes in beliefs and feelings

The way you think about yourself and others changes because of the trauma. You may have trouble experiencing your emotions, think no one can be trusted, or feel guilt or shame.

Hypervigilance or Increased Arousal

Those suffering from PTSD may operate on "high-alert" at all times, often have very short fuses, and tend to startle easily.

How likely are you to get PTSD?

It depends on many factors, such as:

- How severe the trauma was
- If you were injured

- The intensity of your reaction to the trauma
- Whether someone you were close to died or was injured
- How much your own life was in danger
- How much you felt you could not control things
- How much help and support you got following the event

Effects of PTSD on the family

- Trauma and PTSD can lead to low satisfaction with family relationships.
- Veterans with PTSD are more likely to be violent with partners and children.
- Family functioning also influences the person with PTSD. It is a two way street.

How common is PTSD in OEF/OIF military personnel?

About 7% of U.S. civilians have PTSD in their lifetime. According to research following the early years of the current conflicts in Afghanistan and Iraq, 11-20% of veterans developed PTSD.

Steps to solving the problem and getting help

PTSD is a treatable condition. If you think you have PTSD, or just some of its reactions or symptoms (such as nightmares or racing thoughts), it's important to let your doctor or even a chaplain know. These people can help you set up other appointments as needed.

There are several steps to addressing PTSD:

- Assessment: Having a professional evaluate you with a full interview
- Educating yourself and your family about PTSD, its symptoms, and how it can affect your life
- Some antidepressants can relieve symptoms of PTSD. These medications do not treat the underlying cause, yet do provide some symptom relief.

- Cognitive behavioral therapy (CBT) generally seeks to balance your thinking and help you express and cope with your emotions about the traumatic experience.

There are different types of therapy but in most you will learn:

- How the problem affects you and others

- Goal setting about ways to improve your life

- New coping skills

- How to accept your thoughts and feelings, and strategies to deal with them

We encourage you to meet with several therapists before choosing one. Finding a therapist involves learning:

- What kinds of treatment each therapist offers

- What you can expect from the treatment and the therapist

- What the therapist expects of you

Other Treatable Mental Health Problems

PTSD is not the only serious problem that can occur after deployment. Watch out for signs of these other conditions in yourself and your comrades.

Depression: We all experience sadness or feel down from time to time. That's a normal part of being human. Depression, however, is different. It lasts longer and is more serious than normal sadness or grief. Common symptoms include:

- Feeling down or sad more days than not

- Losing interest in hobbies or activities that you used to find enjoyable or fun

- Being excessively low in energy and/or overly tired

- Feeling that things are never going to get better

Suicidal Thoughts and Suicide: War experiences and war zone stress reactions, especially those caused by personal loss, can lead a depressed person to think about hurting or killing him- or herself. If you or someone you know is feeling this way, take it seriously, and get help. Suicide Hotline: 1-800-273-TALK (8255) and?press 1 for veterans.

Violence and Abuse: Anger can sometimes turn into violence or physical abuse. It can also result in emotional and/or verbal abuse that can damage relationships. Abuse can take the form of threats, swearing, criticism, throwing things, conflict, pushing, grabbing, and hitting. If you were abused as a child, you are more at risk for abusing your partner or family members.

Here are a few warning signs that may lead to domestic violence:

- Controlling behaviors or jealousy

- Blaming others for problems or conflict

- Radical mood changes

- Verbal abuse such as humiliating, manipulating, confusing

- Self-destructive or overly risky actions; heated arguments

Substance Abuse: It's common for troops to "self-medicate." They drink or abuse drugs to numb out the difficult thoughts, feelings, and memories related to war zone experiences. While alcohol or drugs may seem to offer a quick solution, they actually lead to more problems. At the same time, a vast majority of people in our society drink. Sometimes it can be difficult to know if your drinking is actually a problem. Warning signs of an alcohol problem include:

- Frequent excessive drinking

- Having thoughts that you should cut down

- Feeling guilty or bad about your drinking

- Others becoming annoyed with you or criticizing how much you drink

- Drinking in the morning to calm your nerves

- Problems with work, family, school, or other regular activities caused by drinking

Concussions or Mild Traumatic Brain Injury (mTBI): Explosions that produce dangerous blast waves of high pressure rattle your brain inside your skull and can cause mTBI. Helmets cannot protect against this type of impact. In fact, 60 to 80 percent of service members who have injuries from some form of blast may have TBI.

Symptoms associated with mild TBI (or concussion) can parallel those of PTSD but also include:

- Headaches or dizziness

- Vision problems
- Emotional problems, such as impatience or impulsiveness
- Trouble concentrating, making decisions, or thinking logically
- Trouble remembering things, amnesia
- Lower tolerance for lights and noise

Know that PTSD is often associated with these other conditions. However, there are effective treatments for all of these problems.

Chapter 32

Recent Research on PTSD

Exposure therapy has best evidence

The review found that exposure therapy had the strongest evidence for reducing PTSD symptoms. Exposure therapy had a large impact on symptom reduction and moderate impact on PTSD remission. Other psychological therapies that improved PTSD symptoms include cognitive processing therapy, cognitive therapy, cognitive behavioral therapy-mixed therapies, eye movement desensitization and reprocessing, and narrative exposure therapy.

"In contrast, the amount of benefit found in drug studies is generally small or medium." This is how clinical psychologist and report author Catherine Forneris, Ph.D., M.D., A.B.P.P., professor in the Professor in the Department of Psychiatry at the University of North Carolina (UNC), Chapel Hill, explains exposure therapy. "Exposure therapy is used to

---

This chapter is excerpted from "Certain therapies and medications improve outcomes of adults with post-traumatic stress disorder," Agency for Healthcare Research and Quality (AHRQ), July 2013; text from "Military Researchers Advance Treatment Studies for PTSD, Depression" from "Military Researchers Advance Treatment Studies for PTSD, Depression," Health.mil at Military Health System (MHS), September 16, 2013; text from "Complex Take-home Message for Public Housing Policy" from "Girls Thrive Emotionally, Boys Falter After Move to Better Neighborhood," National Institute of Mental Health (NIMH), March 11, 2014; and text from "Attention-Control Video Game Curbs Combat Vets' PTSD Symptoms," National Institute of Mental Health (NIMH), July 24, 2015.

treat a variety of anxiety disorders. In exposure therapy, you place your-self in the feared situation or a situation that comes close to the feared situation, and you allow yourself to get physiologically and emotionally aroused. You continue to 'expose' yourself to the feared situation until the arousal goes down and you are able to retrain your body and mind that this situation is not as dangerous as you perceived it to be."

For example, if the trauma was a motor vehicle accident, the expo-sure would be sitting in the car, then driving on the road, then driving on the highway under conditions similar to the accident. That is *in vivo* exposure therapy. Therapists also use imaginal exposure ther-apy when it's too dangerous or impossible to recreate the situation, explains Forneris.

"This is when the person just thinks about the situation, for exam-ple, someone who has been in combat or experienced sexual assault. We focus on the images or aspects of the trauma frightening to them, talk about it out loud, or they may make an audio recording of their trauma narrative and then listen to it. That can be as powerful in some instances for generating the anxiety responses." The goal is to enable the person to eventually manage or extinguish the anxiety related to the trauma.

Cognitive therapy helps

Cognitive therapy is a type of psychotherapy based on the concept that the way we think about things affects how we feel and act. Says Forneris, "It's having patients recognize when and how their thinking is inaccurate or distorted, teaching them to hit the pause button, take a step back, and ask themselves what evidence they have that supports this thought as true or if it has been distorted in their mind because of the emotion associated with it."

She gives the example of a rape victim who takes blame for her assault because of what she was wearing at the time. Thereafter, she is reluctant to dress in a feminine way when going out with friends to a club. "We address the thought that she is somehow responsible for the attack, pointing out that she has dressed nicely hundreds of times before and she didn't get attacked," says Forneris. "Eventually she can reason that 'Just because I dress nicely is not an invitation for someone to hurt me. I'm going out with my friends who will support me if I feel uncom-fortable.' It's helping her refocus on the reality, not what she thinks is reality based on her distorted thought and emotional response."

The review also found eye movement desensitization and repro-cessing (EMDR) to be effective, which has an exposure aspect to it.

Individuals imagine some aspect of the trauma until they get physiologically aroused. At that point, the practitioner uses a finger or wand and asks them to track something on a screen so that their eyes are moving very rapidly left to right.

Military Researchers Advance Treatment Studies for PTSD

What if a single needle prick cured post-traumatic stress? Or an ancient remedy stopped suicidal thoughts? Or virtual reality replaced traditional therapy?

What may seem like far-fetched ideas now could become viable treatment options not too far into the future.

These are just a few of the cutting edge approaches military researchers are exploring to better treat post-traumatic stress and suicidal ideation that Robert McLay, research director for the Naval Medical Center, San Diego, shared during the 2013 Warrior Resilience Conference. The virtual conference was held in August.

McLay cautions that current evidence-based treatments such as cognitive processing therapy, prolonged exposure therapy and selective serotonin reuptake inhibitors should be tried first.

Here are a few of the latest research endeavors happening at the Naval Medical Center, San Diego:

Stellate ganglion block. This procedure involves injecting a local anesthetic into the stellate ganglion, which is a ball of nerves in the neck where the "flight or fight" signals from the brain go out to the body. Stellate ganglion block has been used for a long time to ease pain, but now researchers are learning that it also seems to reduce post-traumatic stress. In a pilot study by the center, patients experienced significant drops in post-traumatic symptoms, however, effects faded with time. Research on dosage amounts continues.

Transcranial magnetic stimulation. Brain scans show changes in brains with PTSD. The brain is a neurochemical circuit and post-traumatic stress disturbs this circuit, resulting in changes based on the electrical charge of the brain. Transcranial magnetic stimulation is a new technology that can change the brain's charge. It already has been approved for use in treating depression. Early studies by the center showed a significant drop in post-traumatic stress symptoms in half of the patients in the study. The improvements gained from the noninvasive method wear off, but they are not completely reversed. Research into this technology continues.

Attention retraining. This computer-based method focuses on how patients look at and respond to different stimuli. The goal is to train patients not to focus on anxiety-inducing or negative thoughts, events or situations. This method is used to treat other anxiety conditions and may be effective for PTSD. The center showed in a recent study that although patients improved with attention retraining, they often did not continue the treatment as directed, and the gains were lost.

Virtual reality assisted exposure therapy. This intervention builds upon exposure therapy, which is considered currently to be the most effective treatment for PTSD. This therapy creates a realistic, anxiety-provoking simulation that teaches patients to overcome their fears by facing them and talking about them. It aims to make exposure therapy more engaging and effective by using virtual reality as an alternative to traditional methods. Clinical trials at the Virtual Reality Medical Center in San Diego showed that 50 to 75 percent of patients got better and stayed better with this therapy.

Caring letters project. This suicide prevention program sends brief, caring emails and reminders of available treatments to service members following psychiatric hospitalization. Previous studies suggest that repeated, caring communication helps reduce suicide in high-risk patients. The center is conducting a two-year, multisite study of 4,730 patients to study the effect the caring letters project has on suicide rates.

Ketamine. This ancient remedy has been used in developing countries as an anesthetic for years. It also has been touted as a miraculous, short-term antidepressant. The center's researchers have shown that ketamine may be able to help people who are at their very lowest feel better, resulting in reduced suicide and improved long-term outcomes. They studied the use of ketamine with patients with suicide ideation in emergency rooms. Research results so far have shown that most patients who received ketamine felt better almost immediately and that these improvements lasted at least two weeks. These patients experienced reduced feelings of hopelessness, depression and suicidality. The center is conducting more ketamine clinical trials.

Complex Take-Home Message for Public Housing Policy

Girls in public housing benefited emotionally from a move to a better neighborhood while boys fared worse than if they'd stayed in the poor neighborhood, a study partly funded by NIMH has found. Rates of depression and conduct disorder markedly increased in boys and decreased in girls. Boys also experienced significantly increased rates of post-traumatic stress disorder (PTSD).

"Better understanding of interactions among individual, family, and neighborhood risk factors is needed to guide future public housing policy changes in light of these sex differences," concluded the research team, which was headed by Ronald Kessler, Ph.D., of Harvard University, Jens Ludwig, Ph.D., of the University of Chicago, and Jeffrey Kling, Ph.D., of the National Bureau of Economic Research. Although not addressed by the study, they suggested that girls might have had better social skills to take advantage of opportunities offered by the better neighborhoods and presumably had different experiences there than boys.

The researchers reported their results March 4, 2014 in the *Journal of the American Medical Association.*

The findings are the latest to emerge from a public housing experiment in five major cities during the mid-to-late 1990s, in which randomly selected families with young children were offered the opportunity to move out of impoverished neighborhoods. They were offered either restricted vouchers to move to lower poverty neighborhoods or unrestricted vouchers to move to any neighborhood of their choice. The primary goals were to increase educational achievement and economic self-sufficiency, but by far the most common reason for moving that families gave was to get away from gangs and drugs. After a year, families that accepted either type of vouchers were living in neighborhoods with poverty rates averaging 34 percent, compared to 50 percent for control group families.

Mental illness is more prevalent among youth in impoverished neighborhoods, suggesting that an upscale move might be beneficial. Among adult family members, health and well-being had improved when surveyed a decade later. Yet among their offspring, there were hints by middle childhood that girls were doing better and boys were doing worse psychologically. The researchers followed-up with a more formal evaluation of the children's mental health in 2008–2010, when they were in their mid-to-late teens – 1407 boys and 1465 girls from 2134 families.

The one-year prevalence of depression was 7.1 percent among boys whose families had received the restricted vouchers and moved into low poverty neighborhoods, compared to 3.5 percent among boys in control group families who did not receive vouchers. Rates of conduct disorder among low poverty group boys were 6.4 percent, compared to 2.1 percent in the control group. Rates of PTSD were 6.2 percent in the low poverty group, compared to 3.5 percent among boys in the control group, and 4.9 percent in families with unrestricted vouchers. This effect of neighborhood is comparable to the impact of combat exposure on PTSD rates in the military, the researchers noted.

Girls showed a contrasting trend, with 6.5 percent in families receiving unrestricted vouchers developing depression, compared to 10.9 percent among control group families. Rates of conduct disorder among unrestricted voucher group girls were 0.3 percent, compared to 2.9 percent in control group families. The protective effect of neighborhood on depression in girls was comparable to the inverse effect of sexual assault on depression rates in young women, according to Kessler and colleagues.

Given the complexities posed by these results, the researchers suggest that a challenge for future research may be to "develop nuanced decision rules for matching public housing families with neighborhoods to maximize the health and well-being of all family members."

Part Four

Treating Stress-Related Disorders

Chapter 33

Finding and Choosing a Therapist

Here are some suggestions for finding a therapist, counselor, or mental health care provider who can help your recovery.

Things to consider

- Make sure the provider has experience treating people who have experienced a trauma.

- Try to find a provider who specializes in evidence-based medications for PTSD or effective psychotherapy for PTSD (e.g., cognitive behavioral therapy (CBT); Cognitive Processing Therapy (CPT); prolonged exposure therapy (PE); or eye movement desensitization and reprocessing (EMDR)).

- Find out what type(s) of insurance the provider accepts and what you will have to pay (out-of-pocket costs) for care.

- You may find more than one therapist.

This chapter includes excerpts from "Finding a Therapist," National Center for Posttraumatic Stress Disorder (PTSD) at the U.S. Department of Veterans Affairs (VA), October 2, 2015.

First steps

- Contact your family doctor to ask for a recommendation. You can also ask friends and family if they can recommend someone.

- If you have health insurance, call to find out which mental health providers your insurance company will pay for. Your insurance company may require that you choose a provider from among a list they maintain.

Finding a provider using the internet

These resources can help you locate a therapist, counselor, or mental health provider who is right for you. Note: These resources can be used by anyone, but if you are a Veteran, also see the "Help for Veterans" section below.

- Sidran Institute Help Desk will help you find therapists who specialize in trauma treatment. Email or call the Help Desk at (410) 825-8888.

- Anxiety and Depression Association of America offers a therapist search by location and mental health disorder. Call (240) 485-1011 or email.

- Association for Behavioral and Cognitive Therapies offers a search of licensed therapists who offer cognitive or behavioral therapies.

- EMDR International Association has a locator listing professionals who provide EMDR.

- ISTSS Clinician Directory is a service provided by the International Society for Traumatic Stress Studies (ISTSS) that lets you consider many factors in searching for a clinician, counselor, or mental health professional.

- American Psychological Association has a Psychologist Locator that allows you to search by location, specialty, insurance accepted, and gender of provider.

- Psychology Today, offers a therapist directory by location. You can also find treatment centers here.

- Substance Abuse and Mental Health Services Administration (SAMHSA) offers a Mental Health Services Locator by location and type of facility (inpatient, outpatient, residential). Call for assistance 24 hours a day 1-800-662-HELP (4357).

Finding a provider by phone

In addition to the numbers listed above, you can also find a therapist, counselor, or mental health provider in the following ways:

- Some mental health services are listed in the phone book. In the Government pages, look in the "County Government Offices" section, and find "Health Services (Dept. of)" or "Department of Health Services." "Mental Health" will be listed.

- In the yellow pages, mental health providers are listed under "counseling," "psychologists," "social workers," "psychotherapists," "social and human services," or "mental health."

- You can also call the psychology department of a local college or university.

Help for Veterans

- All VA Medical Centers and many VA clinics provide PTSD care.

- Some VA centers have specialty programs for PTSD. Use the VA PTSD Program Locator to find a VA PTSD program.

- Vet Centers provide readjustment counseling to Veterans and their families after war. Find a Vet Center near you.

- VA Medical Centers and Vet Centers are also listed in the phone book. In the Government pages, look under "United States Government Offices." Then look for "Veterans Affairs, Dept of." In that section, look under "Medical Care" and "Vet Centers - Counseling and Guidance."

Choosing a Therapist

There are a many things to consider when choosing a therapist. Some practical issues are location, cost, and what insurance the therapist accepts. Other issues include the therapist's background, training, and the way he or she works with people.

Your therapist should explain the therapy, how long treatment is expected to last, and how to tell if it is working. The information below can help you choose a therapist who is right for you.

Questions to ask before therapy

Here is a list of questions you may want to ask a possible therapist:

- What is your education? Are you licensed? How many years have you been practicing?

- What are your special areas of practice?

- Have you ever worked with people who have been through trauma? Do you have any special training in PTSD treatment?

- What kinds of PTSD treatments do you use? Have they been proven effective for dealing with my kind of problem or issue? How much therapy would you recommend?

- Do you prescribe medications?

- What are your fees? (Fees are usually based on a 45-minute to 50-minute session.) Do you have any discounted fees?

- What types of insurance do you accept? Do you file insurance claims? Do you contract with any managed care organizations? Do you accept Medicare or Medicaid insurance?

These questions are just guidelines. In the end, your choice of a therapist will be based on many factors. Think about your comfort with the person as well as his or her qualifications and experience treating PTSD. And keep in mind the importance of evidence-based, trauma-focused treatments like Cognitive Processing Therapy (CPT), Prolonged Exposure (PE), and Eye Movement Desensitization and Reprocessing (EMDR).

Paying for therapy

If you have health insurance, check to see what mental health services are covered. Medicare, Medicaid, and most major health plans typically cover a certain number of mental health counseling sessions per year. Note that you may have a small additional amount you will have to pay, called a co-payment (or co-pay). Call your insurance company to see what they cover so you won't be surprised by a big bill.

If you don't have health insurance that will cover your therapy, you may still be able to get counseling, even if you can't afford to pay full price. Many community mental health centers have sliding scales that base your fee on what you are able to pay.

Making your therapy a good "fit"

In PTSD treatment, or any mental health therapy, you work together with your therapist to get better. A good "fit" between a therapist and a patient can make a difference. You will want to choose a therapist you are comfortable with so that you can get better. This means you should feel like you can ask questions that help you understand treatment and your progress in therapy.

The most effective PTSD treatments are time-limited, usually lasting 10-12 weeks. If you are not getting better or if you feel your therapist is not a good fit for you, look for someone else to work with. Sometimes it takes a few tries to find just the right therapist. This is not unusual and your therapist should be understanding. If you are getting treatment at the VA, a patient advocate can help you if this issue arises.

Chapter 34

Psychotherapies for Stress-Related Disorders

Several types of psychotherapy – or "talk therapy" – can help people with depression. Some treatments are short-term, lasting 10 to 20 weeks, and others are longer, depending on the person's needs.

Effective Talk Therapies

Two main types of psychotherapies – cognitive-behavioral therapy (CBT) and interpersonal therapy (IPT) – have been shown to be effective in treating depression.

There are various cognitive-behavioral therapies that can be effective in treating depression in older adults. These include cognitive therapy, problem-solving therapy, and behavioral activation treatment, among others. By teaching new ways of thinking and behaving, CBT (cognitive-behavioral therapy) helps people change negative habits that may contribute to their depression. IPT (interpersonal

---

This chapter includes excerpts from "Depression," NIHSeniorHealth at the National Institute of Health (NIH), July 2013; text from "Anxiety Disorders," National Institute of Mental Health (NIMH), May 2015; text from "Dialectical Behavior Therapy," National Registry of Evidence-based Programs and Practices (NREPP), June 25, 2012; and text from "Interpersonal Psychotherapy for Depressed Adolescents (IPT-A)," National Registry of Evidence-based Programs and Practices (NREPP), January 28, 2014.

therapy) helps people understand and work through troubled personal relationships or events that may cause their depression or make it worse.

Sometimes Psychotherapy Is Not Enough

For mild to moderate depression, psychotherapy may be the best treatment option. However, sometimes psychotherapy alone is not enough. A study examining depression treatment among older adults found that patients who got better with medication and IPT were less likely to have the depression return if they continued their combination treatment for at least two years.

Cognitive Behavioral Therapy (CBT)

CBT can be useful in treating anxiety disorders. It can help people change the thinking patterns that support their fears and change the way they react to anxiety-provoking situations.

For example, CBT can help people with panic disorder learn that their panic attacks are not really heart attacks and help people with social phobia learn how to overcome the belief that others are always watching and judging them. When people are ready to confront their fears, they are shown how to use exposure techniques to desensitize themselves to situations that trigger their anxieties.

Exposure-based treatment has been used for many years to treat specific phobias. The person gradually encounters the object or situation that is feared, perhaps at first only through pictures or tapes, then later face-to-face. Sometimes the therapist will accompany the person to a feared situation to provide support and guidance. Exposure exercises are undertaken once the patient decides he is ready for it and with his cooperation.

To be effective, therapy must be directed at the person's specific anxieties and must be tailored to his or her needs. A typical "side effect" is temporary discomfort involved with thinking about confronting feared situations.

CBT may be conducted individually or with a group of people who have similar problems. Group therapy is particularly effective for social phobia. Often "homework" is assigned for participants to complete between sessions. If a disorder recurs at a later date, the same therapy can be used to treat it successfully a second time.

Medication can be combined with psychotherapy for specific anxiety disorders, and combination treatment has been found to be the best approach for many people.

Some people with anxiety disorders might benefit from joining a self-help or support group and sharing their problems and achievements with others. Internet chat rooms might also be useful in this regard, but any advice received over the Internet should be used with caution, as Internet acquaintances have usually never seen each other and false identities are common. Talking with a trusted friend or member of the clergy can also provide support, but it is not necessarily a sufficient alternative to care from an expert clinician.

Stress management techniques and meditation can help people with anxiety disorders calm themselves and may enhance the effects of therapy. There is preliminary evidence that aerobic exercise may have a calming effect. Since caffeine, certain illicit drugs, and even some over-the-counter cold medications can aggravate the symptoms of anxiety disorders, avoiding them should be considered. Check with your physician or pharmacist before taking any additional medications.

The family can be important in the recovery of a person with an anxiety disorder. Ideally, the family should be supportive but not help perpetuate their loved one's symptoms. Family members should not trivialize the disorder or demand improvement without treatment.

Dialectical Behavior Therapy (DBT)

Dialectical Behavior Therapy (DBT) is a cognitive-behavioral treatment program developed by Marsha Linehan, Ph.D., in the early 1980s. Originally developed to treat chronically suicidal patients, DBT evolved into a treatment for suicidal individuals with borderline personality disorder (BPD). It has since been adapted for individuals with a wide range of psychiatric and substance use disorders. The term dialectical conveys the multiple tensions patients experience during therapy and the importance of enhancing dialectical thinking patterns to replace rigid thinking. DBT requires the therapist to balance strategies to maintain therapeutic progress for patients who at various moments may fluctuate between a suicidal crisis, rigid refusal to collaborate, rapid emotional escalation—or the beginning of successful collaboration.

Practice

The central dialectic in this therapeutic approach is the balance between acceptance and change, while working toward the client's goals. The DBT therapist balances change techniques (e.g., problem solving) with acceptance strategies (e.g., validation). Acceptance procedures also include mindfulness and maintaining a nonjudgmental stance. The DBT approach includes five core strategies in its application:

- Dialectics
- Problem solving (e.g., behavior therapy)
- Acceptance (e.g., validation)
- Case management strategies
- Communication strategies

Standard outpatient DBT treatment consists of modes:

- Individual therapy
- Skills training group
- Telephone consultation
- Clinical treatment team meeting

Core Components and Understanding the DBT Approach

DBT is a comprehensive treatment with four standard components in an outpatient setting: (1) individual therapy; (2) skills training; (3) clinician-client telephone consultation between sessions; and (4) weekly meetings for the clinical team to provide support for one another to decrease staff burnout, process therapeutic challenges, and promote adherence to the treatment model.

The five functions of treatment determine the modalities of treatment delivery:

1. Enhancing and maintaining client motivation (individual therapy, skills training, coaching)

2. Increasing client capabilities (skills training, individual therapy, coaching)

3. Ensuring generalization to the natural environment (telephone or in-person consultation)

4. Structuring the environment (telephone consultation, case management strategies)

5. Enhancing the motivation and capabilities of treatment providers (DBT team meetings)

Goals of Individual Therapy

DBT individual therapy aims to help the client progress through four main treatment stages, each with defined goals and targets. This organization assists in first addressing issues that are life threatening, prevent effective treatment, or prevent a reasonable quality of life.

Table 34.1. Four Stages of DBT Individual Therapy

Stage I: Moving From Being Out of Control of One's Behavior to Being in Control	Stage II: Moving From Being Emotionally Shut Down to Experiencing Emotions Fully	Stage III: Building an Ordinary Life, Solving Ordinary Life Problems	Stage IV: Moving From Incompleteness to Completeness/ Connection
• Goal: Keep client alive, improve functioning • Targets: Address life-threatening behaviors and those that interfere with effective treatment and may destroy quality of life • Increase behavioral skills	• Goal: Help client experience emotions • Target: Increase emotional experiencing; decrease emotional suffering	• Goal: Help client deal with problems of everyday living • Target: Focus on management of aspects of daily living (e.g., marital conflict, job dissatisfaction)	• Goal: Help client move toward a life that involves an ongoing capacity for experiences of joy and freedom • Target: Focus on helping client reach a sense of connectedness to a greater whole

Interpersonal Psychotherapy for Depressed Adolescents (IPT-A)

Interpersonal Psychotherapy for Depressed Adolescents (IPT-A) is a short-term, manual-driven outpatient treatment intervention that focuses on the current interpersonal problems of adolescents (aged

12-18 years) with mild to moderate depression severity. Adapted from the original IPT program developed for adults, IPT-A addresses the developmental and interpersonal needs of adolescents and their families.

IPT-A attempts to improve the adolescents' communication and social problem-solving skills to increase their personal effectiveness and satisfaction with current relationships, ultimately resulting in the relief of depression symptoms. IPT-A links the onset and perpetuation of depression symptoms to problems or conflicts in interpersonal relationships while acknowledging the contributions of genetic, biological, and personality factors to increased vulnerability for depression episodes. IPT-A helps adolescents understand the effects of interpersonal events and situations on their mood, and each adolescent chooses the focus of treatment by identifying one of four interpersonal problem areas—grief, role disputes, role transitions, or interpersonal deficits—temporally associated with the onset or continuation of the current depression episode. IPT-A also addresses items commonly contributing to developmental problems (e.g., separation from parents, the exploration of authority in relationship to parents, development of dyadic relationships, death of a relative or friend, peer pressure, single-parent families). IPT-A is not intended for adolescents who are acutely suicidal or homicidal, psychotic, bipolar, or intellectually disabled or for those who are actively abusing substances.

IPT-A is delivered by a therapist in hospital-based, school-based, and community outpatient clinics over 12 weeks through weekly 35- to 50-minute treatment sessions. Parental involvement is strongly encouraged (but not mandatory) at three phases of IPT-A:

1. During the first IPT-A session. At least one parent helps confirm the diagnosis of depression and level of interpersonal functioning and receives education from the therapist on the nature, course, and treatment options available for depression.

2. During the middle phase of treatment (typically after the adolescent participates in four one-on-one sessions with the therapist). If the adolescent's identified problem area involves a parent, then the possibility of a parent-adolescent session is offered to the adolescent as an opportunity to practice problem-solving skills and new communication techniques with the parent in a safe and supportive therapeutic environment.

3. At the end of treatment. Ideally, the adolescent's overall progress, interpersonal skills and strategies learned, and warning

signs of possible relapse are discussed at a final dyadic session. Changes in family interactions and functioning during treatment are highlighted with discussion around their maintenance after treatment. If the adolescent has not fully recovered from depression or has an additional mental disorder, then continued treatment options are discussed.

If necessary, treatment with IPT-A can be extended to 16 weeks through additional sessions. However, because the focus of IPT-A is on short-term treatment for current interpersonal problems associated with mild to moderate depression severity, continuation of treatment beyond 16 weeks is not recommended.

Chapter 35

Medications for Stress-Related Disorders

What medications are used to treat depression?

Depression is commonly treated with antidepressant medications. Antidepressants work to balance some of the natural chemicals in our brains. These chemicals are called neurotransmitters, and they affect our mood and emotional responses. Antidepressants work on neurotransmitters such as serotonin, norepinephrine, and dopamine.

The most popular types of antidepressants are called selective serotonin reuptake inhibitors (SSRIs). These include:

- Fluoxetine
- Citalopram
- Sertraline
- Paroxetine
- Escitalopram

Other types of antidepressants are serotonin and norepinephrine reuptake inhibitors (SNRIs). SNRIs are similar to SSRIs and include

---

Text in this chapter is excerpted from "Mental Health Medications," National Institute of Mental Health (NIMH) at the National Institutes of Health (NIH), April 2015.

venlafaxine and duloxetine. Another antidepressant that is commonly used is bupropion. Bupropion, which works on the neurotransmitter dopamine, is unique in that it does not fit into any specific drug type.

SSRIs and SNRIs are popular because they do not cause as many side effects as older classes of antidepressants. Older antidepressant medications include tricyclics, tetracyclics, and monoamine oxidase inhibitors (MAOIs). For some people, tricyclics, tetracyclics, or MAOIs may be the best medications.

What are the side effects?

Antidepressants may cause mild side effects that usually do not last long. **Any unusual reactions or side effects should be reported to a doctor immediately.**

The most common side effects associated with SSRIs and SNRIs include:

- Headache, which usually goes away within a few days.

- Nausea (feeling sick to your stomach), which usually goes away within a few days.

- Sleeplessness or drowsiness, which may happen during the first few weeks but then goes away. Sometimes the medication dose needs to be reduced or the time of day it is taken needs to be adjusted to help lessen these side effects.

- Agitation (feeling jittery).

- Sexual problems, which can affect both men and women and may include reduced sex drive, and problems having and enjoying sex.

Tricyclic antidepressants can cause side effects, including:

- Dry mouth.

- Constipation.

- Bladder problems. It may be hard to empty the bladder, or the urine stream may not be as strong as usual. Older men with enlarged prostate conditions may be more affected.

- Sexual problems, which can affect both men and women and may include reduced sex drive, and problems having and enjoying sex.

- Blurred vision, which usually goes away quickly.

- Drowsiness. Usually, antidepressants that make you drowsy are taken at bedtime.

People taking MAOIs need to be careful about the foods they eat and the medicines they take. Foods and medicines that contain high levels of a chemical called tyramine are dangerous for people taking MAOIs. Tyramine is found in some cheeses, wines, and pickles. The chemical is also in some medications, including decongestants and over-the-counter cold medicine.

Mixing MAOIs and tyramine can cause a sharp increase in blood pressure, which can lead to stroke. People taking MAOIs should ask their doctors for a complete list of foods, medicines, and other substances to avoid. An MAOI skin patch has recently been developed and may help reduce some of these risks. A doctor can help a person figure out if a patch or a pill will work for him or her.

How should antidepressants be taken?

People taking antidepressants need to follow their doctors' directions. The medication should be taken in the right dose for the right amount of time. It can take three or four weeks until the medicine takes effect. Some people take the medications for a short time, and some people take them for much longer periods. People with long-term or severe depression may need to take medication for a long time.

Once a person is taking antidepressants, it is important not to stop taking them without the help of a doctor. Sometimes people taking antidepressants feel better and stop taking the medication too soon, and the depression may return. When it is time to stop the medication, the doctor will help the person slowly and safely decrease the dose. It's important to give the body time to adjust to the change. People don't get addicted, or "hooked," on the medications, but stopping them abruptly can cause withdrawal symptoms.

If a medication does not work, it is helpful to be open to trying another one. A study funded by NIMH found that if a person with difficult-to-treat depression did not get better with a first medication, chances of getting better increased when the person tried a new one or added a second medication to his or her treatment. The study was called STAR*D (Sequenced Treatment Alternatives to Relieve Depression).

Are herbal medicines used to treat depression?

The herbal medicine St. John's wort has been used for centuries in many folk and herbal remedies. Today in Europe, it is used widely to treat mild-to-moderate depression. In the United States, it is one of the top-selling botanical products. However, FDA has not approved its use as an over-the-counter or prescription medicine for depression. and there are serious concerns about its safety and effectiveness.

Research has shown that St. John's wort can dangerously interact with other prescription medications, including those used to control HIV. On February 10, 2000, the FDA issued a Public Health Advisory letter stating that the herb appears to interfere with certain medications used to treat heart disease, depression, seizures, certain cancers, and organ transplant rejection. Also, St. John's wort may interfere with oral contraceptives.

Because St. John's wort may not mix well with other medications, people should always talk with their doctors before taking it or any herbal supplement.

FDA warning on antidepressants

Antidepressants are safe and popular, but some studies have suggested that they may have unintentional effects, especially in young people. In 2004, the FDA looked at published and unpublished data on trials of antidepressants that involved nearly 4,400 children and adolescents. They found that 4 percent of those taking antidepressants thought about or tried suicide (although no suicides occurred), compared to 2 percent of those receiving placebos (sugar pill).

The FDA adopted a "black box" warning label—the most serious type of warning—on all antidepressant medications. The warning says there is an increased risk of suicidal thinking or attempts in children, adolescents, and young adults up through age 24.

The warning also says that patients of all ages taking antidepressants should be watched closely, especially during the first few weeks of treatment. Possible side effects to look for are depression that gets worse, suicidal thinking or behavior, or any unusual changes in behavior such as trouble sleeping, agitation, or withdrawal from normal social situations. Families and caregivers should report any changes to the doctor.

Results of a comprehensive review of pediatric trials conducted between 1988 and 2006 suggested that the benefits of antidepressant medications likely outweigh their risks to children and adolescents with major depression and anxiety disorders. The study was funded in part by NIMH.

Finally, the FDA has warned that combining the newer SSRI or SNRI antidepressants with one of the commonly-used "triptan" medications used to treat migraine headaches could cause a life-threatening illness called "serotonin syndrome." A person with serotonin syndrome may be agitated, have hallucinations (see or hear things that are not real), have a high temperature, or have unusual blood pressure changes. Serotonin syndrome is usually associated with the older antidepressants called MAOIs, but it can happen with the newer antidepressants as well, if they are mixed with the wrong medications.

What medications are used to treat bipolar disorder?

Bipolar disorder, also called manic-depressive illness, is commonly treated with mood stabilizers. Sometimes, antipsychotics and antidepressants are used along with a mood stabilizer.

Mood stabilizers

People with bipolar disorder usually try mood stabilizers first. In general, people continue treatment with mood stabilizers for years. Lithium is a very effective mood stabilizer. It was the first mood stabilizer approved by the FDA in the 1970's for treating both manic and depressive episodes.

Anticonvulsant medications also are used as mood stabilizers. They were originally developed to treat seizures, but they were found to help control moods as well. One anticonvulsant commonly used as a mood stabilizer is valproic acid, also called divalproex sodium. For some people, it may work better than lithium. Other anticonvulsants used as mood stabilizers are carbamazepine, lamotrigine and oxcarbazepine.

Atypical antipsychotics

Atypical antipsychotic medications are sometimes used to treat symptoms of bipolar disorder. Often, antipsychotics are used along with other medications.

Antipsychotics used to treat people with bipolar disorder include:

- Olanzapine, which helps people with severe or psychotic depression, which often is accompanied by a break with reality, hallucinations, or delusions

- Aripiprazole, which can be taken as a pill or as a shot

- Risperidone

- Ziprasidone

- Clozapine, which is often used for people who do not respond to lithium or anticonvulsants.

- Lurasidone

Antidepressants

Antidepressants are sometimes used to treat symptoms of depression in bipolar disorder. Fluoxetine, paroxetine, or sertraline are a few that are used. However, people with bipolar disorder should not take an antidepressant on its own. Doing so can cause the person to rapidly switch from depression to mania, which can be dangerous. To prevent this problem, doctors give patients a mood stabilizer or an antipsychotic along with an antidepressant.

Research on whether antidepressants help people with bipolar depression is mixed. An NIMH-funded study found that antidepressants were no more effective than a placebo to help treat depression in people with bipolar disorder. The people were taking mood stabilizers along with the antidepressants.

What are the side effects?

Treatments for bipolar disorder have improved over the last 10 years. But everyone responds differently to medications. If you have any side effects, tell your doctor right away. He or she may change the dose or prescribe a different medication.

Different medications for treating bipolar disorder may cause different side effects. Some medications used for treating bipolar disorder have been linked to unique and serious symptoms, which are described below.

Lithium can cause several side effects, and some of them may become serious. They include:

- Loss of coordination

- Excessive thirst

- Frequent urination

- Blackouts

- Seizures

- Slurred speech

- Fast, slow, irregular, or pounding heartbeat

- Hallucinations (seeing things or hearing voices that do not exist)

- Changes in vision

- Itching, rash

- Swelling of the eyes, face, lips, tongue, throat, hands, feet, ankles, or lower legs

If a person with bipolar disorder is being treated with lithium, he or she should visit the doctor regularly to check the levels of lithium in the blood, and make sure the kidneys and the thyroid are working normally.

Some possible side effects linked with valproic acid/divalproex sodium include:

- Changes in weight

- Nausea

- Stomach pain

- Vomiting

- Anorexia

- Loss of appetite

Valproic acid may cause damage to the liver or pancreas, so people taking it should see their doctors regularly.

Valproic acid may affect young girls and women in unique ways. Sometimes, valproic acid may increase testosterone (a male hormone) levels in teenage girls and lead to a condition called polycystic ovarian syndrome (PCOS). PCOS is a disease that can affect fertility and make the menstrual cycle become irregular, but symptoms tend to go away after valproic acid is stopped. It also may cause birth defects in women who are pregnant.

Lamotrigine can cause a rare but serious skin rash that needs to be treated in a hospital. In some cases, this rash can cause permanent disability or be life-threatening.

In addition, valproic acid, lamotrigine, carbamazepine, oxcarbazepine and other anticonvulsant medications have an FDA warning. The warning states that their use may increase the risk of suicidal thoughts and behaviors. People taking anticonvulsant medications for bipolar or other illnesses should be closely monitored for new or worsening symptoms of depression, suicidal thoughts or behavior, or any unusual changes in mood or behavior. People taking these medications should not make any changes without talking to their health care professional.

Other medications for bipolar disorder may also be linked with rare but serious side effects. Always talk with the doctor or pharmacist about any potential side effects before taking the medication.

How should medications for bipolar disorder be taken?

Medications should be taken as directed by a doctor. Sometimes a person's treatment plan needs to be changed. When changes in medicine are needed, the doctor will guide the change. **A person should never stop taking a medication without asking a doctor for help.**

There is no cure for bipolar disorder, but treatment works for many people. Treatment works best when it is continuous, rather than on and off. However, mood changes can happen even when there are no breaks in treatment. Patients should be open with their doctors about treatment. Talking about how treatment is working can help it be more effective.

It may be helpful for people or their family members to keep a daily chart of mood symptoms, treatments, sleep patterns, and life events. This chart can help patients and doctors track the illness. Doctors can use the chart to treat the illness most effectively.

Because medications for bipolar disorder can have serious side effects, it is important for anyone taking them to see the doctor regularly to check for possibly dangerous changes in the body.

What medications are used to treat anxiety disorders?

Antidepressants, anti-anxiety medications, and beta-blockers are the most common medications used for anxiety disorders.

Anxiety disorders include:

- Generalized anxiety disorder (GAD)

- Panic disorder

- Social anxiety disorder.

Antidepressants

Antidepressants were developed to treat depression, but they also help people with anxiety disorders. SSRIs such as fluoxetine, sertraline, escitalopram, paroxetine, and citalopram are commonly prescribed for panic disorder, OCD, PTSD, and social anxiety disorder. The SNRI venlafaxine is commonly used to treat GAD. The antidepressant bupropion is also sometimes used. When treating anxiety disorders, antidepressants generally are started at low doses and increased over time.

Some tricyclic antidepressants work well for anxiety. For example, imipramine is prescribed for panic disorder and GAD. Clomipramine is used to treat OCD. Tricyclics are also started at low doses and increased over time.

MAOIs are also used for anxiety disorders. Doctors sometimes prescribe phenelzine, tranylcypromine, and isocarboxazid. People who take MAOIs must avoid certain food and medicines that can interact with their medicine and cause dangerous increases in blood pressure.

Benzodiazepines (Anti-anxiety medications)

The anti-anxiety medications called benzodiazepines can start working more quickly than antidepressants. The ones used to treat anxiety disorders include:

- Clonazepam, which is used for social phobia and GAD

- Lorazepam, which is used for panic disorder

- Alprazolam, which is used for panic disorder and GAD.

People can build a tolerance to benzodiazepines if they are taken over a long period of time and may need higher and higher doses to get the same effect. Some people may become dependent on them. To avoid these problems, doctors usually prescribe the medication for short periods, a practice that is especially helpful for people who have substance abuse problems or who become dependent on medication easily. If people suddenly stop taking benzodiazepines, they may get withdrawal symptoms, or their anxiety may return. Therefore, they should be tapered off slowly.

Buspirone is an anti-anxiety medication used to treat GAD. Unlike benzodiazepines, however, it takes at least two weeks for buspirone to begin working.

Clonazepam, listed above, is an anticonvulsant medication. See FDA warning on anticonvulsants under the bipolar disorder section.

Beta-blockers

Beta-blockers control some of the physical symptoms of anxiety, such as trembling and sweating. Propranolol is a beta-blocker usually used to treat heart conditions and high blood pressure. The medicine also helps people who have physical problems related to anxiety. For example, when a person with social phobia must face a stressful situation, such as giving a speech, or attending an important meeting, a doctor may prescribe a beta-blocker. Taking the medicine for a short period of time can help the person keep physical symptoms under control.

What are the side effects?

The most common side effects for benzodiazepines are drowsiness and dizziness. Other possible side effects include:

- Upset stomach
- Blurred vision
- Headache
- Confusion
- Grogginess
- Nightmares

As noted above, long-term use of benzodiazepines can lead to tolerance (needing more of the medication to get the same effect) and dependence. To avoid these problems, doctors usually prescribe the medication for short periods. Recent research has found that benzodiazepines are prescribed especially frequently for older people.

Possible side effects from buspirone include:

- Dizziness
- Headaches
- Nausea
- Nervousness
- Lightheadedness
- Excitement
- Trouble sleeping

Common side effects from beta-blockers include:

- Fatigue
- Cold hands

- Dizziness

- Weakness

In addition, beta-blockers generally are not recommended for people with asthma or diabetes because they may worsen symptoms.

Like benzodiazepines, buspirone and beta-blockers are usually taken on a short-term basis for anxiety. Both should be tapered off slowly. Talk to the doctor before stopping any anti-anxiety medication.

Chapter 36

Complementary and Alternative Medicine (CAM) Therapies for Stress-Related Disorders

Chapter Contents

Section 36.1

Overview of Stress Management Strategies

This section is excerpted from "Advance Research on Mind and Body Interventions, Practices, and Disciplines," National Center for Complementary and Integrative Health (NCCIH), January 4, 2012; and text from "Complementary, Alternative, or Integrative Health: What's In a Name?" National Center for Complementary and Integrative Health (NCCIH), July 8, 2015.

The term complementary and alternative medicine (CAM) includes a large and diverse group of interventions, practices, and disciplines that are based in physical procedures or techniques administered or taught to others by a trained practitioner or teacher. They are used to improve health and well-being and in the treatment of illness or symptoms such as chronic pain or stress.

These interventions, practices, and disciplines are grouped together in this plan as mind and body approaches because, from a research perspective, they all share a set of characteristics that create similar challenges in designing rigorous and definitive clinical investigations of their benefit and safety. For example, (1) it is generally difficult or impossible to mask practitioners and/or participants involved in clinical research, (2) claims about benefit often relate to subjective clinical outcomes, (3) in practice, the interventions are often individualized, or they are complicated procedures that are difficult to systematize or characterize fully, and (4) means to objectively measure the impact of the interventions on important biological processes are frequently lacking, particularly those that purport to act through processes not understood or well characterized by modern science.

The public's interest in at least some of these approaches is growing. For example, NHIS data show a significant increase between 2002 and 2007 in the use of mind and body approaches such as controlled breathing practices, meditation, massage therapy, and yoga. There is also great interest across many health care disciplines regarding the potential application of some mind and body approaches to a variety of challenging health problems and to health promotion. In large part this interest is based on emerging evidence from research carried out over the past decade. For example, a large body of clinical research evidence now suggests that practices such as meditation and yoga can enhance quality of life, reduce psychological stress, and improve some mental health outcomes. At the same time, a growing body of basic research evidence suggests that mindfulness and other meditation practices engage neurobiological mechanisms known to be involved in cognition, emotion regulation, and behavior. In addition, mainstream clinical practice guidelines include evidence-based recommendations that spinal manipulation, acupuncture, and massage be considered for some patients with chronic back pain.

Complementary versus Alternative

Many Americans—more than 30 percent of adults and about 12 percent of children—use health care approaches developed outside of mainstream Western, or conventional, medicine. When describing these approaches, people often use "alternative" and "complementary" interchangeably, but the two terms refer to different concepts:

If a non-mainstream practice is used together with conventional medicine, it's considered "complementary."

- If a non-mainstream practice is used in place of conventional medicine, it's considered "alternative."

- True alternative medicine is uncommon. Most people who use non-mainstream approaches use them along with conventional treatments.

Integrative Medicine

There are many definitions of "integrative" health care, but all involve bringing conventional and complementary approaches together in a coordinated way. The use of integrative approaches to health and wellness has grown within care settings across the United States. Researchers are currently exploring the potential benefits of integrative health in a variety of situations, including pain management for military personnel and veterans, relief of symptoms in cancer patients and survivors, and programs to promote healthy behaviors.

Integrative Approaches for Pain Management for Military Personnel and Veterans

Chronic pain is a common problem among active-duty military personnel and veterans. NCCIH, the U.S. Department of Veterans Affairs, and other agencies are sponsoring research to see whether integrative approaches can help. For example, NCCIH-funded studies are testing the effects of adding mindfulness meditation, self-hypnosis, or other complementary approaches to pain management programs for veterans. The goal is to help patients feel and function better and reduce their need for pain medicines that can have serious side effects.

Integrative Approaches for Symptom Management in Cancer Patients and Survivors

Cancer treatment centers with integrative health care programs may offer services such as acupuncture and meditation to help manage symptoms and side effects for patients who are receiving conventional cancer treatment. Although research on the potential value of these integrative programs is in its early stages, some studies have had promising results. For example, NCCIH-funded research has suggested that:

Cancer patients who receive integrative therapies while in the hospital have less pain and anxiety.

Massage therapy may lead to short-term improvements in pain and mood in patients with advanced cancer.

Yoga may relieve the persistent fatigue that some women experience after breast cancer treatment.

Integrative Approaches and Health-Related Behaviors

Healthy behaviors, such as eating right, getting enough physical activity, and not smoking, can reduce people's risks of developing serious diseases. Can integrative approaches promote these types of behaviors? Researchers are working to answer this question. Preliminary research suggests that yoga and meditation-based therapies may help smokers quit, and NCCIH-funded studies are testing whether adding mindfulness-based approaches to weight control programs will help people lose weight more successfully.

Terms NCCIH Uses

NCCIH generally uses the term "complementary health approaches" when we discuss practices and products of non-mainstream origin. We use "integrative health" when we talk about incorporating complementary approaches into mainstream health care.

Types of Complementary Health Approaches

Most complementary health approaches fall into one of two subgroups—natural products or mind and body practices.

Natural Products

This group includes a variety of products, such as **herbs** (also known as botanicals), **vitamins and minerals**, and **probiotics**. They are widely marketed, readily available to consumers, and often sold as dietary supplements.

According to the 2012 National Health Interview Survey (NHIS), which included a comprehensive survey on the use of complementary health approaches by Americans, 17.7 percent of American adults had used a dietary supplement other than vitamins and minerals in the past year. These products were the most popular complementary health approach in the survey. The most commonly used natural product was fish oil.

Researchers have done large, rigorous studies on a few natural products, but the results often showed that the products didn't work. Research on others is in progress. While there are indications that some may be helpful, more needs to be learned about the effects of these products in the human body and about their safety and potential interactions with medicines and other natural products.

Mind and Body Practices

Mind and body practices include a large and diverse group of procedures or techniques administered or taught by a trained practitioner or teacher. The 2012 NHIS showed that **yoga, chiropractic and osteopathic manipulation**, **meditation**, and **massage therapy** are among the most popular mind and body practices used by adults. The popularity of yoga has grown dramatically in recent years, with almost twice as many U.S. adults practicing yoga in 2012 as in 2002.

Other mind and body practices include **acupuncture, relaxation techniques** (such as breathing exercises, guided imagery, and progressive muscle relaxation), **tai chi, gi qong, healing touch, hypnotherapy**, and **movement therapies** (such as Feldenkrais method, Alexander technique, Pilates, Rolfing Structural Integration, and Trager psychophysical integration).

The amount of research on mind and body approaches varies widely depending on the practice. For example, researchers have done many studies on acupuncture, yoga, spinal manipulation, and meditation, but there have been fewer studies on some other practices.

Other Complementary Health Approaches

The two broad areas discussed above—natural products and mind and body practices—capture most complementary health approaches. However, some approaches may not neatly fit into either of these groups—for example, the practices of traditional healers, Ayurvedic medicine, traditional Chinese medicine, homeopathy, and naturopathy.

Section 36.2

Acupuncture

This section includes excerpts from "Acupuncture," National Center for Complementary and Integrative Health (NCCIH), March 4, 2015; text from "Acupuncture: What You Need To Know," National Center for Complementary and Integrative Health (NCCIH), July 8, 2015; and text from "Acupuncture May Help Symptoms of Posttraumatic Stress Disorder," National Center for Complementary and Integrative Health (NCCIH), September 3, 2014.

The term "acupuncture" describes a family of procedures involving the stimulation of points on the body using a variety of techniques. The acupuncture technique that has been most often studied scientifically involves penetrating the skin with thin, solid, metallic needles that are manipulated by the hands or by electrical stimulation. Practiced in China and other Asian countries for thousands of years, acupuncture is one of the key components of traditional Chinese medicine.

Although millions of Americans use acupuncture each year, often for chronic pain, there has been considerable controversy surrounding its value as a therapy and whether it is anything more than placebo. Research exploring a number of possible mechanisms for acupuncture's pain-relieving effects is ongoing.

What's the Bottom Line?

How much do we know about acupuncture?

There have been extensive studies conducted on acupuncture, especially for back and neck pain, osteoarthritis/knee pain, and headache. However, researchers are only beginning to understand whether acupuncture can be helpful for various health conditions.

What do we know about the effectiveness of acupuncture?

Research suggests that acupuncture can help manage certain pain conditions, but evidence about its value for other health issues is uncertain.

What do we know about the safety of acupuncture?

Acupuncture is generally considered safe when performed by an experienced, well-trained practitioner using sterile needles. Improperly performed acupuncture can cause serious side effects.

What the Science Says about the Effectiveness of Acupuncture

Results from a number of studies suggest that acupuncture may help ease types of pain that are often chronic such as low-back pain, neck pain, and osteoarthritis/knee pain. It also may help reduce the frequency of tension headaches and prevent migraine headaches. Therefore, acupuncture appears to be a reasonable option for people with chronic pain to consider. However, clinical practice guidelines are inconsistent in recommendations about acupuncture.

The effects of acupuncture on the brain and body and how best to measure them are only beginning to be understood. Current evidence suggests that many factors—like expectation and belief—that are unrelated to acupuncture needling may play important roles in the beneficial effects of acupuncture on pain.

Read more about acupuncture for these pain conditions and others:

For Low-Back Pain

- A 2012 analysis of data on participants in acupuncture studies looked at back and neck pain together and found that actual acupuncture was more helpful than either no acupuncture or simulated acupuncture.

- A 2010 review by the Agency for Healthcare Research and Quality found that acupuncture relieved low-back pain immediately after treatment but not over longer periods of time.

- A 2008 systematic review of studies on acupuncture for low-back pain found strong evidence that combining acupuncture with usual care helps more than usual care alone. The same review also found strong evidence that there is no difference between the effects of actual and simulated acupuncture in people with low-back pain.

- Clinical practice guidelines issued by the American Pain Society and the American College of Physicians in 2007 recommend acupuncture as one of several nondrug approaches physicians should consider when patients with chronic low-back pain do not respond to self-care (practices that people can do by themselves, such as remaining active, applying heat, and taking pain-relieving medications).

For Neck Pain

- A 2014 Australian clinical study involving 282 men and women showed that needle and laser acupuncture were modestly better at relieving knee pain from osteoarthritis than no treatment, but not better than simulated (sham) laser acupuncture. Participants received 8 to 12 actual and simulated acupuncture treatments over 12 weeks. These results are generally consistent with previous studies, which showed that acupuncture is consistently better than no treatment but not necessarily better than simulated acupuncture at relieving osteoarthritis pain.

- A 2009 analysis found that actual acupuncture was more helpful for neck pain than simulated acupuncture, but the analysis was based on a small amount of evidence (only three studies with small study populations).

- A large German study with more than 14,000 participants evaluated adding acupuncture to usual care for neck pain. The researchers found that participants reported greater pain relief than those who didn't receive it; the researchers didn't test actual acupuncture against simulated acupuncture.

For Osteoarthritis / Knee Pain

- A 2014 Australian clinical study involving 282 men and women showed that needle and laser acupuncture were modestly better at relieving knee pain from osteoarthritis than no treatment, but not better than simulated (sham) laser acupuncture. Participants received 8 to 12 actual and simulated acupuncture treatments over 12 weeks. These results are generally consistent with previous studies, which showed that acupuncture is consistently better than no treatment but not necessarily better than simulated acupuncture at relieving osteoarthritis pain.

- A major 2012 analysis of data on participants in acupuncture studies found that actual acupuncture was more helpful for osteoarthritis pain than simulated acupuncture or no acupuncture.

- A 2010 systematic review of studies of acupuncture for knee or hip osteoarthritis concluded that actual acupuncture was more helpful for osteoarthritis pain than either simulated acupuncture or no acupuncture. However, the difference between actual and simulated acupuncture was very small, while the difference between acupuncture and no acupuncture was large.

For Headache

- A 2012 analysis of data on individual participants in acupuncture studies looked at migraine and tension headaches. The analysis showed that actual acupuncture was more effective than either no acupuncture or simulated acupuncture in reducing headache frequency or severity.

- A 2009 systematic review of studies concluded that actual acupuncture, compared with simulated acupuncture or pain-relieving drugs, helped people with tension-type headaches. A 2008 systematic review of studies suggested that actual acupuncture has a very slight advantage over simulated acupuncture in reducing tension-type headache intensity and the number of headache days per month.

- A 2009 systematic review found that adding acupuncture to basic care for migraines helped to reduce migraine frequency. However, in studies that compared actual acupuncture with simulated acupuncture, researchers found that the differences between the two treatments may have been due to chance.

For Other Conditions

- Results of a systematic review that combined data from 11 clinical trials with more than 1,200 participants suggested that acupuncture (and acupuncture point stimulation) may help with certain symptoms associated with cancer treatments.

- There is not enough evidence to determine if acupuncture can help people with depression.

- Acupuncture has been promoted as a smoking cessation treatment since the 1970s, but research has not shown that it helps people quit the habit.

Read more about the challenges of studying acupuncture:

- Studying acupuncture is challenging because:

- Clinical trials often differ in terms of technique, the number of acupuncture points, the number of sessions, and the duration of those sessions.

- Results of an acupuncture session may be associated with a person's beliefs and expectations about their treatment or from their relationship with the therapist, rather than from acupuncture treatment itself.

What Is Simulated Acupuncture?

In some clinical trials, researchers test a product or practice against an inactive product or technique (called a placebo) to see if the response is due to the test protocol or to something else. Many acupuncture trials rely on a technique called simulated acupuncture, which may use blunt-tipped retractable needles that touch the skin but do not penetrate (in real acupuncture, needles penetrate the skin). Researchers also may simulate acupuncture in other ways. However, in some instances, researchers have observed that simulated acupuncture resulted in some degree of pain relief.

What the Science Says about Safety and Side Effects of Acupuncture

- Relatively few complications from using acupuncture have been reported. Still, complications have resulted from use of nonsterile needles and improper delivery of treatments.

- When not delivered properly, acupuncture can cause serious adverse effects, including infections, punctured organs, collapsed lungs, and injury to the central nervous system.

Read more about what the science says about safety and side effects of acupuncture:

The U.S. Food and Drug Administration (FDA) regulates acupuncture needles as medical devices for use by licensed practitioners and requires that needles be manufactured and labeled according to certain standards. For example, the FDA requires that needles be sterile, nontoxic, and labeled for single use by qualified practitioners only.

NCCIH-Funded Research

NCCIH funds research to evaluate acupuncture's effectiveness for various kinds of pain and other conditions, and to further understand how the body responds to acupuncture and how acupuncture might work. Some recent NCCIH-supported studies are looking at:

If acupuncture can reduce the frequency of hot flashes associated with menopause

Whether acupuncture can reduce pain and discomfort that may accompany chemotherapy

Objectively determining if actual acupuncture is more effective than simulated acupuncture or usual care for pain relief, and (if so) by how much.

More to Consider

- Don't use acupuncture to postpone seeing a health care provider about a health problem.

- If you decide to visit an acupuncturist, check his or her credentials. Most states require a license, certification, or registration to practice acupuncture; however, education and training standards and requirements for obtaining these vary from state to state. Although a license does not ensure quality of care, it does indicate that the practitioner meets certain standards regarding the knowledge and use of acupuncture. Most states require a diploma from the National Certification Commission for Acupuncture and Oriental Medicine for licensing.

- Some conventional medical practitioners—including physicians and dentists—practice acupuncture. In addition, national acupuncture organizations (which can be found through libraries or by searching the Internet) may provide referrals to acupuncturists. When considering practitioners, ask about their training and experience.

- Ask the practitioner about the estimated number of treatments needed and how much each treatment will cost. Some insurance companies may cover the costs of acupuncture, while others may not.

Help your health care providers give you better coordinated and safe care by telling them about all the health approaches you use. Give them a full picture of what you do to manage your health.

Acupuncture May Help Symptoms of Post-traumatic Stress Disorder

A pilot study shows that acupuncture may help people with post-traumatic stress disorder. Post-traumatic stress disorder (PTSD) is an anxiety disorder that can develop after exposure to a terrifying event or ordeal in which grave physical harm occurred or was threatened. Traumatic events that may trigger PTSD include violent personal assaults, natural or human-caused disasters, accidents, or military combat.

Michael Hollifield, M.D., and colleagues conducted a clinical trial examining the effect of acupuncture on the symptoms of PTSD. The researchers analyzed depression, anxiety, and impairment in 73 people with a diagnosis of PTSD. The participants were assigned to receive either acupuncture or group cognitive-behavioral therapy over 12 weeks, or were assigned to a wait-list as part of the control group. The people in the control group were offered treatment or referral for treatment at the end of their participation.

The researchers found that acupuncture provided treatment effects similar to group cognitive-behavioral therapy; both interventions were superior to the control group. Additionally, treatment effects of both the acupuncture and the group therapy were maintained for 3 months after the end of treatment.

The limitations of the study are consistent with preliminary research. For example, this study had a small group of participants that lacked diversity, and the results do not account for outside factors that may have affected the treatments' results.

Section 36.3

Herbal Supplements May Improve Stress Symptoms

This section is excerpted from "Kava," National Center for Complementary and Integrative Health (NCCIH) at the National Institutes of Health (NIH), January 27, 2015; and text from "Valerian," Office of Dietary Supplements (ODS) at the National Institutes of Health (NIH), March 15, 2013.

Kava

Kava is native to the islands of the South Pacific and is a member of the pepper family. Kava has been used as a ceremonial beverage in the South Pacific for centuries.

Historically, kava was used to help people fall asleep and fight fatigue, as well as to treat asthma and urinary tract infections. It also had a topical use as a numbing agent. More recent folk or traditional uses include anxiety, insomnia, and menopausal symptoms.

The root and rhizome (underground stem) of kava are used to prepare beverages, extracts, capsules, tablets, and topical solutions.

What the Science Says

- Although scientific studies provide some evidence that kava may be beneficial for the management of anxiety, the U.S. Food and Drug Administration (FDA) has issued a warning that using kava supplements has been linked to a risk of severe liver damage.

- Kava is not a proven therapy for other uses.

- NCCIH-funded studies on kava were suspended after the FDA issued its warning.

Side Effects and Cautions

- Kava has been reported to cause liver damage, including hepatitis and liver failure (which can cause death).

- Kava has been associated with several cases of dystonia (abnormal muscle spasm or involuntary muscle movements). Kava may interact with several drugs, including drugs used for Parkinson's disease.

- Long-term and/or heavy use of kava may result in scaly, yellowed skin.

- Avoid driving and operating heavy machinery while taking kava because the herb has been reported to cause drowsiness.

Tell all your health care providers about any complementary health approaches you use. Give them a full picture of what you do to manage your health. This will help ensure coordinated and safe care.

Valerian

- Valerian is an herb sold as a dietary supplement in the United States.

- Valerian is a common ingredient in products promoted as mild sedatives and sleep aids for nervous tension and insomnia.

- Evidence from clinical studies of the efficacy of valerian in treating sleep disorders such as insomnia is inconclusive.

- Constituents of valerian have been shown to have sedative effects in animals, but there is no scientific agreement on valerian's mechanisms of action.

- Although few adverse events have been reported, long-term safety data are not available.

What is valerian?

Valerian (*Valeriana officinalis*), a member of the Valerianaceae family, is a perennial plant native to Europe and Asia and naturalized in North America. It has a distinctive odor that many find unpleasant. Other names include setwall (English), *Valerianae radix* (Latin), *Baldrianwurzel* (German), and *phu* (Greek). The genus *Valerian* includes over 250 species, but *V. officinalis* is the species most often used in the United States and Europe and is the only species discussed in this text.

What are common valerian preparations?

Preparations of valerian marketed as dietary supplements are made from its roots, rhizomes (underground stems), and stolons (horizontal stems). Dried roots are prepared as teas or tinctures, and dried plant materials and extracts are put into capsules or incorporated into tablets.

There is no scientific agreement as to the active constituents of valerian, and its activity may result from interactions among multiple constituents rather than any one compound or class of compounds. The content of volatile oils, including valerenic acids; the less volatile sesquiterpenes; or the valepotriates (esters of short-chain fatty acids) is sometimes used to standardize valerian extracts. As with most herbal preparations, many other compounds are also present.

Valerian is sometimes combined with other botanicals. Because this text focuses on valerian as a single ingredient, only clinical studies evaluating valerian as a single agent are included.

What are the historical uses of valerian?

Valerian has been used as a medicinal herb since at least the time of ancient Greece and Rome. Its therapeutic uses were described by Hippocrates, and in the 2nd century, Galen prescribed valerian for insomnia. In the 16th century, it was used to treat nervousness, trembling, headaches, and heart palpitations. In the mid-19th century, valerian was considered a stimulant that caused some of the same complaints it is thought to treat and was generally held in low esteem as a medicinal herb. During World War II, it was used in England to relieve the stress of air raids.

In addition to sleep disorders, valerian has been used for gastrointestinal spasms and distress, epileptic seizures, and attention deficit hyperactivity disorder. However, scientific evidence is not sufficient to support the use of valerian for these conditions.

What clinical studies have been done on valerian and sleep disorders?

Although the results of some studies suggest that valerian may be useful for insomnia and other sleep disorders, results of other studies do not. Interpretation of these studies is complicated by the fact the studies had small sample sizes, used different amounts and sources of valerian, measured different outcomes, or did not consider potential bias resulting from high participant withdrawal rates. Overall, the evidence from these trials for the sleep-promoting effects of valerian is inconclusive.

How does valerian work?

Many chemical constituents of valerian have been identified, but it is not known which may be responsible for its sleep-promoting effects in animals and in in vitro studies. It is likely that there is no single active compound and that valerian's effects result from multiple constituents acting independently or synergistically.

Two categories of constituents have been proposed as the major source of valerian's sedative effects. The first category comprises the major constituents of its volatile oil including valerenic acid and its derivatives, which have demonstrated sedative properties in animal studies. However, valerian extracts with very little of these components also have sedative properties, making it probable that other components are responsible for these effects or that multiple constituents contribute to them. The second category comprises the iridoids, which include the valepotriates. Valepotriates and their derivatives are active as sedatives in vivo but are unstable and break down during storage or in an aqueous environment, making their activity difficult to assess.

A possible mechanism by which a valerian extract may cause sedation is by increasing the amount of gamma aminobutyric acid (GABA, an inhibitory neurotransmitter) available in the synaptic cleft. Results from an in vitro study using synaptosomes suggest that a valerian extract may cause GABA to be released from brain nerve endings and then block GABA from being taken back into nerve cells. In addition, valerenic acid inhibits an enzyme that destroys GABA. Valerian extracts contain GABA in quantities sufficient to cause a sedative effect, but whether GABA can cross the blood-brain barrier to contribute to valerian's sedative effects is not known. Glutamine is present in aqueous but not in alcohol extracts and may cross the blood-brain barrier and be converted to GABA. Levels of these constituents vary significantly among plants depending on when the plants are harvested, resulting in marked variability in the amounts found in valerian preparations.

What is the regulatory status of valerian in the United States?

In the United States, valerian is sold as a dietary supplement, and dietary supplements are regulated as foods, not drugs. Therefore, premarket evaluation and approval by the Food and Drug Administration are not required unless claims are made for specific disease prevention or treatment. Because dietary supplements are not always tested for manufacturing consistency, the composition may vary considerably between manufacturing lots.

Can valerian be harmful?

Few adverse events attributable to valerian have been reported for clinical study participants. Headaches, dizziness, pruritus, and gastrointestinal disturbances are the most common effects reported in clinical trials but similar effects were also reported for the placebo. In one study an increase in sleepiness was noted the morning after 900 mg of valerian was taken. Investigators from another study concluded that 600 mg of valerian (LI 156) did not have a clinically significant effect on reaction time, alertness, and concentration the morning after ingestion. Several case reports described adverse effects, but in one case where suicide was attempted with a massive overdose it is not possible to clearly attribute the symptoms to valerian.

Valepotriates, which are a component of valerian but are not necessarily present in commercial preparations, had cytotoxic activity in vitro but were not carcinogenic in animal studies.

Who should not take valerian?

- Women who are pregnant or nursing should not take valerian without medical advice because the possible risks to the fetus or infant have not been evaluated.

- Children younger than 3 years old should not take valerian because the possible risks to children of this age have not been evaluated.

- Individuals taking valerian should be aware of the theoretical possibility of additive sedative effects from alcohol or sedative drugs, such as barbiturates and benzodiazepines.

Does valerian interact with any drugs or supplements or affect laboratory tests?

Valerian might have additive therapeutic and adverse effects if taken with sedatives, other medications, or certain herbs and dietary supplements with sedative properties. These include the following:

- Benzodiazepines such as Xanax, Valium, Ativan, and Halcion.

- Barbiturates or central nervous system (CNS) depressants such as phenobarbital (Luminal), morphine, and propofol (Diprivan).

- Dietary supplements such as St. John's wort, kava, and melatonin.

Individuals taking these medications or supplements should discuss the use of valerian with their healthcare providers.

Although valerian has not been reported to influence laboratory tests, this has not been rigorously studied.

Section 36.4

Massage Therapy

This section is excerpted from "Massage Therapy for Health Purposes: What You Need To Know," National Center for Complementary and Integrative Health (NCCIH) at the National Institutes of Health (NIH), September 3, 2015; and text from "Massage Therapy What You Knead to Know," News in Health at the National Institutes of Health (NIH), July 2012.

What's the Bottom Line?

How much do we know about massage?

A lot of research on the effects of massage therapy has been carried out.

What do we know about the effectiveness of massage?

While often preliminary or conflicting, there is scientific evidence that massage may help with back pain and may improve quality of life for people with depression, cancer, and HIV/AIDS.

What do we know about the safety of massage?

Massage therapy appears to have few risks if it is used appropriately and provided by a trained massage professional.

What Is Massage Therapy?

The term "massage therapy" includes many techniques, and the type of massage given usually depends on your needs and physical condition.

For More Information

- Massage therapy dates back thousands of years. References to massage appear in ancient writings from China, Japan, India, and Egypt.

- In general, massage therapists work on muscle and other soft tissue to help you feel better.

- In Swedish massage, the therapist uses long strokes, kneading, deep circular movements, vibration, and tapping.

- Sports massage combines techniques of Swedish massage and deep tissue massage to release chronic muscle tension. It is adapted to the needs of athletes.

- Myofascial trigger point therapy focuses on trigger points— areas that are painful when pressed and are associated with pain elsewhere in the body.

- Massage therapy is sometimes done using essential oils as a form of aromatherapy.

What the Science Says about the Effectiveness of Massage

A lot of the scientific research on massage therapy is preliminary or conflicting, but much of the evidence points toward beneficial effects on pain and other symptoms associated with a number of different conditions. Much of the evidence suggests that these effects are short term and that people need to keep getting massages for the benefits to continue.

Researchers have studied the effects of massage for many conditions. Some that they have studied more extensively are the following

Pain

- A 2008 systematic review and 2011 NCCIH-funded clinical trial concluded that massage may be useful for chronic low-back pain.

- Massage may help with chronic neck pain, a 2009 NCCIH-funded clinical trial reported.

- Massage may help with pain due to osteoarthritis of the knee, according to a 2012 NCCIH-funded study.

- Studies suggest that for women in labor, massage provided some pain relief and increased their satisfaction with other forms of pain relief, but the evidence is not strong, a 2012 review concluded.

Cancer

Numerous systematic reviews and clinical studies have suggested that at least for the short term, massage therapy for cancer patients may reduce pain, promote relaxation, and boost mood. However, the National Cancer Institute urges massage therapists to take specific precautions with cancer patients and avoid massaging:

- Open wounds, bruises, or areas with skin breakdown

- Directly over the tumor site

- Areas with a blood clot in a vein

- Sensitive areas following radiation therapy.

Mental Health

- A 2010 meta-analysis of 17 clinical trials concluded that massage therapy may help to reduce depression.

- Brief, twice-weekly yoga and massage sessions for 12 weeks were associated with a decrease in depression, anxiety, and back and leg pain in pregnant women with depression, a 2012 NCCIH-funded randomized controlled trial showed. Also, the women's babies weighed more than babies born to women who didn't receive the therapy.

- However, a 2013 research review concluded that there is not enough evidence to determine if massage helps pregnant mothers with depression.

- A 2010 review concluded that massage may help older people relax.

- For generalized anxiety disorder, massage therapy was no better at reducing symptoms than providing a relaxing environment and deep breathing lessons, according to a small, 2010 NCCIH-supported clinical trial.

Fibromyalgia

A 2010 review concluded that massage therapy may help temporarily reduce pain, fatigue, and other symptoms associated with fibromyalgia, but the evidence is not definitive. The authors noted that it is important that the massage therapist not cause pain.

Headaches

Clinical trials on the effects of massage for headaches are preliminary and only somewhat promising.

HIV/AIDS

Massage therapy may help improve the quality of life for people with HIV or AIDS, a 2010 systematic review of four small clinical trials concluded.

Infant Care

Massaging preterm infants using moderate pressure may improve weight gain, a 2010 review suggested. We don't have enough evidence to know if massage benefits healthy infants who are developing normally, a 2013 review determined.

Other Conditions

Researchers have studied massage for the following but it's still unclear if it helps:

• Behavior of children with autism or autism spectrum disorders

• Immune function in women with breast cancer

• Anxiety and pain in patients following heart surgery

• Quality of life and glucose levels in people with diabetes

• Lung function in children with asthma.

What the Science Says about the Safety and Side Effects of Massage Therapy

Massage therapy appears to have few risks when performed by a trained practitioner. However, massage therapists should take some precautions in people with certain health conditions.

For More Information

- In some cases, pregnant women should avoid massage therapy. Talk with your health care provider before getting a massage if you are pregnant.

- People with some conditions such as bleeding disorders or low blood platelet counts should avoid having forceful and deep tissue massage. People who take anticoagulants (also known as blood thinners) also should avoid them. Massage should not be done in any potentially weak area of the skin, such as wounds.

- Deep or intense pressure should not be used over an area where the patient has a tumor or cancer, unless approved by the patient's health care provider.

NCCIH-Funded Research

NCCIH-sponsored studies have investigated the effects of massage on a variety of conditions including

For More Information

- The effects of an 8-week course of Swedish massage compared to usual care on pain and function in adults with osteoarthritis of the knee

- Whether massage helps with generalized anxiety disorder

- The effect of massage therapy on cancer-related fatigue

- How massage therapy and progressive muscle relaxation compare for reducing chronic low-back pain in patients referred from primary care practices

- The frequency and length of massages needed to address neck pain.

Training, Licensing, and Certification

In the United States, 44 states and the District of Columbia regulate massage therapists. Cities, counties, or other local governments also may regulate massage. Training standards and requirements for massage therapists vary greatly by state and locality.

For More Information

Most states that regulate massage therapists require them to have a minimum of 500 hours of training from an accredited training program. The National Certification Board for Therapeutic Massage and Bodywork certifies practitioners who pass a national examination and fulfill other requirements.

More to Consider

- Do not use massage therapy to replace conventional care or to postpone seeing a health care provider about a medical problem.

- If you have a medical condition and are unsure whether massage therapy would be appropriate for you, discuss your concerns with your health care provider, who may also be able to help you select a massage therapist.

- Ask about the training, experience, and credentials of the massage therapist you are considering. Also ask about the number of treatments that might be needed, the cost, and insurance coverage.

Tell all your health care providers about any complementary and integrative health approaches you use. Give them a full picture of what you do to manage your health. This will ensure coordinated and safe care.

Massage Therapy

Many people associate massage with vacations or spas and consider them something of a luxury. But research is beginning to suggest this ancient form of hands-on healing may be more than an indulgence—may help improve your health.

Massage therapists use their fingers, hands, forearms and elbows to manipulate the muscles and other soft tissues of the body. Variations in focus and technique lead to different types of massage, including Swedish, deep tissue and sports massage.

In Swedish massage, the focus is general and the therapist may use long strokes, kneading, deep circular movements, vibration and tapping. With a deep tissue massage, the focus is more targeted, as therapists work on specific areas of concern or pain. These areas may have muscle "knots" or places of tissue restriction.

Some common reasons for getting a massage are to relieve pain, heal sports injuries, reduce stress, relax, ease anxiety or depression, and aid general wellness. Unfortunately, scientific evidence on massage therapy is limited. Researchers are actively trying to understand exactly how massage works, how much is best, and how it might help with specific health conditions. Some positive benefits have been reported.

"Massage therapy has been noted to relax the nervous system by slowing heart rate and blood pressure. Stress and pain hormones are also decreased by massage, reducing pain and enhancing immune function," says Dr. Tiffany Field, who heads a touch research institute at the University of Miami Medical School. Much of her NIH-funded research focuses on the importance of massage for pregnant women and infants. Some of her studies suggest that massage may improve weight gain and immune system function in preterm infants.

A study published earlier this year looked at how massage affects muscles at the molecular level. The findings suggest that kneading eases sore muscles after exercise by turning off genes associated with inflammation and turning on genes that help muscles heal.

A recent NIH-supported study found that an hour-long "dose" of Swedish massage therapy once a week was optimal for knee pain from osteoarthritis, especially when practical matters like time, labor and convenience were considered. Other research suggests that massage therapy is effective in reducing and managing chronic low-back pain, which affects millions of Americans.

If you're considering massage therapy for a specific medical condition, talk with your health care provider. Never use massage to replace your regular medical care or as a reason to postpone seeing a health care professional.

Every therapist and every massage is unique. If you decide to try massage therapy, work with different therapists until you find one that meets your needs. One of the best ways to get a great massage is to communicate with your therapist. Most will check in with you during your session for feedback, but—if not—speak up!

Section 36.5

Meditation

Text in this section is excerpted from "Meditation Programs for Psychological Stress and Well-Being," Agency for Healthcare Research and Quality (AHRQ), January 6, 2014.

The National Center for Complementary and Alternative Medicine defines meditation as a "mind-body" method. This category of complementary and alternative medicine includes interventions that employ a variety of techniques that facilitate the mind's capacity to affect bodily function and symptoms. In meditation, a person learns to focus attention. Some forms of meditation instruct the student to become mindful of thoughts, feelings, and sensations, and to observe them in a nonjudgmental way. Many believe this practice evokes a state of greater calmness, physical relaxation, and psychological balance.

Current Practice and Prevalence of Use

Many people use meditation to treat stress and stress-related conditions, as well as to promote general health. A national survey in 2008 found that the number of people meditating is increasing, with approximately 10 percent of the population having some experience with meditation. A number of hospitals and programs offer courses in meditation to patients seeking alternative or additional methods to relieve symptoms or to promote health.

Forms of Meditation

Meditation training programs vary in several ways, including the emphasis on religion or spirituality, the type of mental activity promoted, the nature and amount of training, the use of an instructor, and the qualifications of an instructor, which may all affect the level and nature of the meditative skills learned. Some meditative techniques are integrated into a broader alternative approach that includes dietary and/or movement therapies (e.g., Ayurveda or yoga).

381

Researchers have categorized meditative techniques as emphasizing "mindfulness," "concentration," and "automatic self-transcendence." Popular techniques such as transcendental meditation (TM) emphasize the use of a mantra in such a way that one "transcends" to an effortless state where there is no focused attention. Other popular techniques, such as mindfulness-based stress reduction (MBSR), are classified as "mindfulness" and emphasize training in present-focused awareness. Uncertainty remains about the extent to which these distinctions actually influence psychosocial stress outcomes.

Psychological Stress and Well-Being

Researchers have postulated that meditation programs may affect a range of outcomes related to psychological stress and well-being. The research ranges from the rare examination of positive outcomes, such as increased well-being, to the more common approach of examining reductions in negative outcomes, such as anxiety or sleep disturbance. Some studies address symptoms related to the primary condition (e.g., pain in patients with low back pain or anxiety in patients with social phobia), whereas others address similar emotional symptoms in clinical groups of people who may or may not have clinically significant symptoms (e.g., anxiety or depression in individuals with cancer).

Evidence to Date

Reviews to date have demonstrated that both "mindfulness" and "mantra" meditation techniques reduce emotional symptoms (e.g., anxiety and depression, stress) and improve physical symptoms (e.g., pain) from a small to moderate degree. These reviews have largely included uncontrolled studies or studies that used control groups that did not receive additional treatment (i.e., usual care or wait list). In wait-list controlled studies, the control group receives usual care while "waiting" to receive the intervention at some time in the future, providing a usual-care control for the purposes of the study. Thus, it is unclear whether the apparently beneficial effects of meditation training are a result of the expectations for improvement that participants naturally form when obtaining this type of treatment. Additionally, many programs involve lengthy and sustained efforts on the part of participants and trainers, possibly yielding beneficial effects from the added attention, group participation, and support participants receive, as well as the suggestion that symptoms will likely improve with these increased efforts.

The meditation literature has significant limitations related to inadequate control comparisons. An informative analogy is the use of placebos in pharmaceutical trials. The placebo is typically designed to match the "active intervention" in order to elicit the same expectations of benefit on the part of both provider and patient, but not contain the "active" ingredient. Additionally, placebo treatment includes all components of care received by the active group, including office visits and patient-provider interactions. These nonspecific factors are particularly important to control when the evaluation of outcome relies on patient reporting. In this situation, in which double-blinding has not been feasible, the challenge to execute studies that are not biased by these nonspecific factors is more pressing. Thus, there is a clear need to examine the specific effects of meditation in randomized controlled trials (RCTs) in which expectations for outcome and attentional support are controlled.

Section 36.6

Spirituality May Alleviate Distress

Text in this section is excerpted from "Spirituality in Cancer Care (PDQ®)," National Cancer Institute (NCI), May 18, 2015.

Religious and spiritual values are important to patients coping with cancer.

Studies have shown that religious and spiritual values are important to Americans. Most American adults say that they believe in God and that their religious beliefs affect how they live their lives. However, people have different ideas about life after death, belief in miracles, and other religious beliefs. Such beliefs may be based on gender, education, and ethnic background.

Many patients with cancer rely on spiritual or religious beliefs and practices to help them cope with their disease. This is called spiritual coping. Many caregivers also rely on spiritual coping. Each person may have different spiritual needs, depending on cultural and religious traditions. For some seriously ill patients, spiritual well-being may affect how much anxiety they feel about death. For others, it may affect what they decide about end-of-life treatments. Some patients and their family caregivers may want doctors to talk about spiritual concerns, but may feel unsure about how to bring up the subject.

Some studies show that doctors' support of spiritual well-being in very ill patients helps improve their quality of life. Health care providers who treat patients coping with cancer are looking at new ways to help them with religious and spiritual concerns. Doctors may ask patients which spiritual issues are important to them during treatment as well as near the end of life. When patients with advanced cancer receive spiritual support from the medical team, they may be more likely to choose hospice care and less aggressive treatment at the end of life.

Spirituality and religion may have different meanings.

The terms spirituality and religion are often used in place of each other, but for many people they have different meanings. Religion may be defined as a specific set of beliefs and practices, usually within an organized group. Spirituality may be defined as an individual's sense of peace, purpose, and connection to others, and beliefs about the meaning of life. Spirituality may be found and expressed through an organized religion or in other ways. Patients may think of themselves as spiritual or religious or both.

Serious illness, such as cancer, may cause spiritual distress.

Serious illnesses like cancer may cause patients or family caregivers to have doubts about their beliefs or religious values and cause much spiritual distress. Some studies show that patients with cancer may feel that they are being punished by God or may have a loss of faith after being diagnosed. Other patients may have mild feelings of spiritual distress when coping with cancer.

Spirituality and Quality of Life

Spiritual and religious well-being may help improve quality of life.

It is not known for sure how spirituality and religion are related to health. Some studies show that spiritual or religious beliefs and practices create a positive mental attitude that may help a patient feel better and improve the well-being of family caregivers. Spiritual and religious well-being may help improve health and quality of life in the following ways:

- Decrease anxiety, depression, anger, and discomfort.
- Decrease the sense of isolation (feeling alone) and the risk of suicide.
- Decrease alcohol and drug abuse.
- Lower blood pressure and the risk of heart disease.
- Help the patient adjust to the effects of cancer and its treatment.
- Increase the ability to enjoy life during cancer treatment.
- Give a feeling of personal growth as a result of living with cancer.
- Increase positive feelings, including:
- Hope and optimism.
- Freedom from regret.
- Satisfaction with life.
- A sense of inner peace.
- Spiritual and religious well-being may also help a patient live longer.

Spiritual distress may also affect health.

Spiritual distress may make it harder for patients to cope with cancer and cancer treatment. Health care providers may encourage patients to meet with experienced spiritual or religious leaders to help deal with their spiritual issues. This may improve their health, quality of life, and ability to cope.

Section 36.7

Yoga

Text in this section is excerpted from "Yoga for Health," National
Center for Complementary and Integrative Health (NCCIH) at the
National Institutes of Health (NIH), September 1, 2015.

Yoga for Health

Yoga is a mind and body practice with historical origins in ancient
Indian philosophy. Like other meditative movement practices used for
health purposes, various styles of yoga typically combine physical postures, breathing techniques, and meditation or relaxation. This section
provides basic information about yoga, summarizes scientific research on
effectiveness and safety, and suggests sources for additional information.

Key Facts

- Recent studies in people with chronic low-back pain suggest that
  a carefully adapted set of yoga poses may help reduce pain and
  improve function (the ability to walk and move). Studies also suggest that practicing yoga (as well as other forms of regular exercise) might have other health benefits such as reducing heart rate
  and blood pressure, and may also help relieve anxiety and depression. Other research suggests yoga is not helpful for asthma, and
  studies looking at yoga and arthritis have had mixed results.

- People with high blood pressure, glaucoma, or sciatica, and
  women who are pregnant should modify or avoid some yoga poses.

- Ask a trusted source (such as a health care provider or local
  hospital) to recommend a yoga practitioner. Contact professional
  organizations for the names of practitioners who have completed
  an acceptable training program.

Tell all your health care providers about any complementary health
approaches you use. Give them a full picture of what you do to manage
your health. This will help ensure coordinated and safe care.

About Yoga

Yoga in its full form combines physical postures, breathing exercises, meditation, and a distinct philosophy. There are numerous styles of yoga. Hatha yoga, commonly practiced in the United States and Europe, emphasizes postures, breathing exercises, and meditation. Hatha yoga styles include Ananda, Anusara, Ashtanga, Bikram, Iyengar, Kripalu, Kundalini, Viniyoga, and others.

Side Effects and Risks

- Yoga is generally low-impact and safe for healthy people **when practiced appropriately under the guidance of a well-trained instructor.**

- Overall, those who practice yoga have a low rate of side effects, and the risk of serious injury from yoga is quite low. However, certain types of stroke as well as pain from nerve damage are among the rare possible side effects of practicing yoga.

- Women who are pregnant and people with certain medical conditions, such as high blood pressure, glaucoma (a condition in which fluid pressure within the eye slowly increases and may damage the eye's optic nerve), and sciatica (pain, weakness, numbing, or tingling that may extend from the lower back to the calf, foot, or even the toes), should modify or avoid some yoga poses.

Use of Yoga for Health in the United States

According to the 2007 National Health Interview Survey (NHIS), which included a comprehensive survey on the use of complementary health approaches by Americans, yoga is the sixth most commonly used complementary health practice among adults. More than 13 million adults practiced yoga in the previous year, and between the 2002 and 2007 NHIS, use of yoga among adults increased by 1 percent (or approximately 3 million people). The 2007 survey also found that more than 1.5 million children practiced yoga in the previous year.

Many people who practice yoga do so to maintain their health and well-being, improve physical fitness, relieve stress, and enhance quality of life. In addition, they may be addressing specific health conditions, such as back pain, neck pain, arthritis, and anxiety.

What the Science Says about Yoga

Current research suggests that a carefully adapted set of yoga poses may reduce low-back pain and improve function. Other studies also suggest that practicing yoga (as well as other forms of regular exercise) might improve quality of life; reduce stress; lower heart rate and blood pressure; help relieve anxiety, depression, and insomnia; and improve overall physical fitness, strength, and flexibility. But some research suggests yoga may not improve asthma, and studies looking at yoga and arthritis have had mixed results.

- One NCCIH-funded study of 90 people with chronic low-back pain found that participants who practiced Iyengar yoga had significantly less disability, pain, and depression after 6 months.

- In a 2011 study, also funded by NCCIH, researchers compared yoga with conventional stretching exercises or a self-care book in 228 adults with chronic low-back pain. The results showed that both yoga and stretching were more effective than a self-care book for improving function and reducing symptoms due to chronic low-back pain.

- Conclusions from another 2011 study of 313 adults with chronic or recurring low-back pain suggested that 12 weekly yoga classes resulted in better function than usual medical care.

However, studies show that certain health conditions may not benefit from yoga.

- A 2011 systematic review of clinical studies suggests that there is no sound evidence that yoga improves asthma.

- A 2011 review of the literature reports that few published studies have looked at yoga and arthritis, and of those that have, results are inconclusive. The two main types of arthritis—osteoarthritis and rheumatoid arthritis—are different conditions, and the effects of yoga may not be the same for each. In addition, the reviewers suggested that even if a study showed that yoga helped osteoarthritic finger joints, it may not help osteoarthritic knee joints.

Training, Licensing, and Certification

There are many training programs for yoga teachers throughout the country. These programs range from a few days to more than 2 years. Standards for teacher training and certification differ depending on the style of yoga.

There are organizations that register yoga teachers and training programs that have complied with a certain curriculum and educational standards. For example, one nonprofit group (the Yoga Alliance) requires at least 200 hours of training, with a specified number of hours in areas including techniques, teaching methodology, anatomy, physiology, and philosophy. Most yoga therapist training programs involve 500 hours or more. The International Association of Yoga Therapists is developing standards for yoga therapy training.

If You Are Considering Practicing Yoga

- Do not use yoga to replace conventional medical care or to postpone seeing a health care provider about pain or any other medical condition.

- If you have a medical condition, talk to your health care provider before starting yoga.

- Ask a trusted source (such as your health care provider or a nearby hospital) to recommend a yoga practitioner. Find out about the training and experience of any practitioner you are considering.

- Everyone's body is different, and yoga postures should be modified based on individual abilities. Carefully selecting an instructor who is experienced with and attentive to your needs is an important step toward helping you practice yoga safely. Ask about the physical demands of the type of yoga in which you are interested and inform your yoga instructor about any medical issues you have.

- Carefully think about the type of yoga you are interested in. For example, hot yoga (such as Bikram yoga) may involve standing and moving in humid environments with temperatures as high as 105°F. Because such settings may be physically stressful, people who practice hot yoga should take certain precautions. These include drinking water before, during, and after a hot yoga practice and wearing suitable clothing. People with conditions that may be affected by excessive heat, such as heart disease, lung disease, and a prior history of heatstroke may want to avoid this form of yoga. Women who are pregnant may want to check with their health care providers before starting hot yoga.

Tell all your health care providers about any complementary health approaches you use. Give them a full picture of what you do to manage your health. This will help ensure coordinated and safe care.

NCCIH-Funded Research

This section has discussed research on yoga for conditions such as low-back pain, depression, stress, blood pressure, and insomnia. NCCIH is currently supporting research on how practicing yoga may affect:

- Diabetes risk

- HIV

- Immune function

- Forms of arthritis

- Menopausal symptoms

- Multiple sclerosis

- Post-traumatic stress disorder (PTSD)

- Smoking cessation.

Section 36.8

Relaxation Techniques

Text in this section is excerpted from "Relaxation Techniques for Health: An Introduction," National Center for Complementary and Integrative Health (NCCIH) at the National Institute of Health (NIH), February 2013.

Relaxation Techniques for Health: An Introduction

Relaxation techniques include a number of practices such as progressive relaxation, guided imagery, biofeedback, self-hypnosis, and deep breathing exercises. The goal is similar in all: to consciously produce the body's natural relaxation response, characterized by slower breathing, lower blood pressure, and a feeling of calm and well-being.

Relaxation techniques (also called relaxation response techniques) may be used by some to release tension and to counteract the ill effects of stress. Relaxation techniques are also used to induce sleep, reduce pain, and calm emotions. This section provides basic information about relaxation techniques, and summarizes scientific research on effectiveness and safety.

Key Points

- Relaxation techniques may be an effective part of an overall treatment plan for anxiety, depression, and some types of pain. Some research also suggests that these techniques may help with other conditions, such as ringing in the ears and overactive bladder. However, their ability to improve conditions such as high blood pressure and asthma is unclear.

- Relaxation techniques are generally safe.

- Do not use relaxation techniques to replace scientifically proven treatments or to postpone seeing a health care provider about a medical problem.

Tell all your health care providers about any complementary health approaches you use. Give them a full picture of what you do to manage your health. This will help ensure coordinated and safe care.

About Relaxation Techniques

Relaxation is more than a state of mind; it physically changes the way your body functions. When your body is relaxed breathing slows, blood pressure and oxygen consumption decrease, and some people report an increased sense of well-being. This is called the "relaxation response." Being able to produce the relaxation response using relaxation techniques may counteract the effects of long- term stress, which may contribute to or worsen a range of health problems including depression, digestive disorders, headaches, high blood pressure, and insomnia.

Relaxation techniques often combine breathing and focused attention to calm the mind and the body. Most methods require only brief instruction from a book or experienced practitioner before they can be done without assistance. These techniques may be most effective when practiced regularly and combined with good nutrition, regular exercise, and a strong social support system.

The relaxation response techniques covered in this section include:

- **Autogenic training.** When using this method, you focus on the physical sensation of your own breathing or heartbeat and picture your body as warm, heavy, and/or relaxed.

- **Biofeedback.** Biofeedback-assisted relaxation uses electronic devices to teach you how to consciously produce the relaxation response.

- **Deep breathing or breathing exercises.** To relax using this method, you consciously slow your breathing and focus on taking regular and deep breaths.

- **Guided imagery.** For this technique, you focus on pleasant images to replace negative or stressful feelings and relax. Guided imagery may be directed by you or a practitioner through storytelling or descriptions designed to suggest mental images (also called visualization).

- **Progressive relaxation** (also called Jacobson's progressive relaxation or progressive muscle relaxation). For this relaxation method, you focus on tightening and relaxing each muscle group. Progressive relaxation is often combined with guided imagery and breathing exercises.

- **Self-Hypnosis.** In self-hypnosis you produce the relaxation response with a phrase or nonverbal cue (called a "suggestion").

Mind and body practices, such as meditation and yoga are also sometimes considered relaxation techniques.

Use of Relaxation Techniques for Health in the U.S.

People may use relaxation techniques as part of a comprehensive plan to treat, prevent, or reduce symptoms of a variety of conditions including stress, high blood pressure, chronic pain, insomnia, depression, labor pain, headache, cardiovascular disease, anxiety, chemotherapy side effects, and others.

According to the 2007 National Health Interview Survey, which included a comprehensive survey on the use of complementary health approaches by Americans, 12.7 percent of adults used deep-breathing exercises, 2.9 percent used progressive relaxation, and 2.2 percent used guided imagery for health purposes. Most of those people reported using a book to learn the techniques rather than seeing a practitioner.

How Relaxation Techniques May Work

To understand how consciously producing the relaxation response may affect your health, it is helpful to understand how your body responds to the opposite of relaxation—stress.

When you're under stress, your body releases hormones that produce the "fight-or-flight response." Heart rate and breathing rate go up and blood vessels narrow (restricting the flow of blood). This response allows energy to flow to parts of your body that need to take action, for example the muscles and the heart. However useful this response may be in the short term, there is evidence that when your body remains in a stress state for a long time, emotional or physical damage can occur. Long-term or chronic stress (lasting months or years) may reduce your body's ability to fight off illness and lead to or worsen certain health conditions. Chronic stress may play a role in developing high blood pressure, headaches, and stomach ache. Stress may worsen certain conditions, such as asthma. Stress also has been linked to depression, anxiety, and other mental illnesses.

In contrast to the stress response, the relaxation response slows the heart rate, lowers blood pressure, and decreases oxygen consumption and levels of stress hormones. Because relaxation is the opposite of stress, the theory is that voluntarily creating the relaxation response through regular use of relaxation techniques could counteract the negative effects of stress.

Status of Research on Relaxation Techniques

In the past 30 years, there has been considerable interest in the relaxation response and how inducing this state may benefit health. Research has focused primarily on illness and conditions in which stress may play a role either as the cause of the condition or as a factor that can make the condition worse.

Currently, research has examined relaxation techniques for:

- **Anxiety.** Studies have suggested that relaxation may assist in the conventional treatment of phobias or panic disorder. Relaxation techniques have also been used to relieve anxiety for people in stressful situations, such as when undergoing a medical procedure.

- **Asthma.** Several reviews of the literature have suggested that relaxation techniques, including guided imagery, may temporarily help improve lung function and quality of life and relieve anxiety in people with asthma. A more recent randomized clinical trial of asthma found that relaxation techniques may help improve immune function.

- **Depression.** In 2008, a major review of the evidence that looked at relaxation for depression found that relaxation techniques were more effective than no treatment for depression, but not as effective as cognitive-behavioral therapy.

- **Fibromyalgia.** Some preliminary studies report that using relaxation or guided imagery techniques may sometimes improve pain and reduce fatigue from fibromyalgia.

- **Headache.** There is some evidence that biofeedback and other relaxation techniques may help relieve tension or migraine headaches. In some cases, these mind and body techniques were more effective than medications for reducing the frequency, intensity, and severity of headaches.

- **Heart disease and heart symptoms.** Researchers have looked at relaxation techniques for angina and for preventing heart disease. When a cardiac rehabilitation program was combined with relaxation response training in a clinic, participants experienced significant reductions in blood pressure, decreases in lipid levels, and increases in psychological functioning when compared to participants' status before the program. Some studies have shown that relaxation techniques combined with other lifestyle changes and standard medical care may reduce the risk of recurrent heart attack.

- **High blood pressure.** A 2008 review of evidence for relaxation for high blood pressure found some evidence that progressive muscle relaxation lowered blood pressure a small amount. However, the review found no evidence that this effect was enough to reduce the risk of heart disease, stroke, or other health issues due to high blood pressure. In a recent randomized controlled trial, 8 weeks of relaxation response/ stress management was shown to reduce systolic blood pressure in hypertensive older adults, and some patients were able to reduce hypertension medication without an increase in blood pressure.

- **Hot flashes.** Relaxation exercises involving slow, controlled deep breathing may help relieve hot flashes associated with menopause.

- **Insomnia.** There is some evidence that relaxation techniques can help chronic insomnia.

- **Irritable bowel syndrome.** Some studies have indicated that relaxation techniques may prevent or relieve symptoms of irritable bowel syndrome (IBS) in some participants. One review of the research found some evidence that self-hypnosis may be useful for IBS.

- **Nausea.** Relaxation techniques may help relieve nausea caused by chemotherapy.

- **Nightmares.** Relaxation exercises may be an effective approach for nightmares of unknown cause and those associated with post-traumatic stress disorder (PTSD).

- **Overactive bladder.** Bladder re-training combined with relaxation and other exercises may help control urinary urgency.

- **Pain.** Some studies have shown that relaxation techniques may help reduce abdominal and surgery pain.

- **Ringing in the ears.** Use of relaxation exercises may help patients cope with the condition.

- **Smoking cessation.** Relaxation exercises may help reduce the desire to smoke.

- **Temporomandibular disorder** (pain and loss of motion in the jaw joints). A review of the literature found that relaxation techniques and biofeedback were more effective than placebo in decreasing pain and increasing jaw function.

Researchers have found no significant change in outcomes from relaxation techniques used during cardiac catheterization. However, patients experienced less distress prior to the procedure. Future research may investigate whether this has any long-term effect on outlook and recovery.

Many of the studies of relaxation therapy and health have followed a small number of patients for weeks or months. Longer studies involving more participants may reveal more about the cumulative effects of using relaxation techniques regularly.

NCCAM-Funded Research

NCCAM-supported studies have been investigating:

- Progressive relaxation and massage therapy for relieving low-back pain

- The effect of the relaxation response on blood pressure, stress hormones, and psychological well-being in older adults with hypertension

- Acupuncture and relaxation training for relieving stomach symptoms for people taking HIV medications.

Side Effects and Risks

- Relaxation techniques are generally considered safe for healthy people. There have been rare reports that certain relaxation techniques might cause or worsen symptoms in people with epilepsy or certain psychiatric conditions, or with a history of abuse or trauma. People with heart disease should talk to their health care provider before doing progressive muscle relaxation.

- Relaxation techniques are often used as part of a treatment plan and not as the only approach for potentially serious health conditions.

Training, Licensing, and Certification

There is no formal credential or license required for practicing or teaching most relaxation techniques. However, the techniques may be used or taught by licensed professionals, including physicians, recreational therapists, and psychologists.

If You Are Thinking about Using Relaxation Techniques for Health

- Do not use relaxation techniques to replace conventional care or to postpone seeing a health care provider about a medical problem.

- Ask about the training and experience of the practitioner or instructor you are considering for any complementary health approach.

- Look for published research studies on relaxation for the health condition in which you are interested. Remember that some claims for using relaxation therapies may exceed the available scientific evidence.

Tell all your health care providers about any complementary health approaches you use. Give them a full picture of what you do to manage your health. This will help ensure coordinated and safe care.

Chapter 37

Coping with Traumatic Stress Reactions

When trauma survivors take direct action to cope with their stress reactions, they put themselves in a position of power. Active coping with the trauma makes you begin to feel less helpless.

- Active coping means accepting the impact of trauma on your life and taking direct action to improve things.

- Active coping occurs even when there is no crisis. Active coping is a way of responding to everyday life. It is a habit that must be made stronger.

Know that recovery is a process

Following exposure to a trauma most people experience stress reactions. Understand that recovering from the trauma is a process and takes time. Knowing this will help you feel more in control.

- Having an ongoing response to the trauma is normal.

- Recovery is an ongoing, daily process. It happens little by little. It is not a matter of being cured all of a sudden.

- Healing doesn't mean forgetting traumatic events. It doesn't mean you will have no pain or bad feelings when thinking about them.

Text in this chapter is excerpted from "Coping with Traumatic Stress Reactions," U.S. Department of Veterans Affairs (VA), August 14, 2015.

- Healing may mean fewer symptoms and symptoms that bother you less.

- Healing means more confidence that you will be able to cope with your memories and symptoms. You will be better able to manage your feelings.

Positive coping actions

Certain actions can help to reduce your distressing symptoms and make things better. Plus, these actions can result in changes that last into the future. Here are some positive coping methods:

Learn about trauma and PTSD

It is useful for trauma survivors to learn more about common reactions to trauma and about PTSD. Find out what is normal. Find out what the signs are that you may need assistance from others. When you learn that the symptoms of PTSD are common, you realize that you are not alone, weak, or crazy. It helps to know your problems are shared by hundreds of thousands of others. When you seek treatment and begin to understand your response to trauma, you will be better able to cope with the symptoms of PTSD.

Talk to others for support

When survivors talk about their problems with others, something helpful often results. It is important not to isolate yourself. Instead make efforts to be with others. Of course, you must choose your support people with care. You must also ask them clearly for what you need. With support from others, you may feel less alone and more understood. You may also get concrete help with a problem you have.

Practice relaxation methods

Try some different ways to relax, including:
- Muscle relaxation exercises
- Breathing exercises
- Meditation
- Swimming, stretching, yoga
- Prayer

- Listening to quiet music

- Spending time in nature

While relaxation techniques can be helpful, in a few people they can sometimes increase distress at first. This can happen when you focus attention on disturbing physical sensations and you reduce contact with the outside world. Most often, continuing with relaxation in small amounts that you can handle will help reduce negative reactions. You may want to try mixing relaxation in with music, walking, or other activities.

Distract yourself with positive activities

Pleasant recreational or work activities help distract a person from his or her memories and reactions. For example, art has been a way for many trauma survivors to express their feelings in a positive, creative way. Pleasant activities can improve your mood, limit the harm caused by PTSD, and help you rebuild your life.

Talking to your doctor or a counselor about trauma and PTSD

Part of taking care of yourself means using the helping resources around you. If efforts at coping don't seem to work, you may become fearful or depressed. If your PTSD symptoms don't begin to go away or get worse over time, it is important to reach out and call a counselor who can help turn things around. Your family doctor can also refer you to a specialist who can treat PTSD. Talk to your doctor about your trauma and your PTSD symptoms. That way, he or she can take care of your health better.

Many with PTSD have found treatment with medicines to be helpful for some symptoms. By taking medicines, some survivors of trauma are able to improve their sleep, anxiety, irritability, and anger. It can also reduce urges to drink or use drugs.

Chapter 38

Treatment of PTSD

Nowadays, there are good treatments available for PTSD. When you have PTSD, dealing with the past can be hard. Instead of telling others how you feel, you may keep your feelings bottled up. But talking with a therapist can help you get better.

Cognitive behavioral therapy (CBT) is one type of counseling. Research shows it is the most effective type of counseling for PTSD. The VA is providing two forms of cognitive behavioral therapy to Veterans with PTSD: Cognitive Processing Therapy (CPT) and Prolonged Exposure (PE) therapy.

There is a similar kind of therapy called Eye Movement Desensitization and Reprocessing (EMDR) that is used for PTSD. Also, medications have been shown to be effective. A type of drug known as a selective serotonin reuptake inhibitor (SSRI), which is also used for depression, is effective for PTSD.

Types of cognitive behavioral therapy

What is cognitive therapy?

In cognitive therapy, your therapist helps you understand and change how you think about your trauma and its aftermath. Your goal is to understand how certain thoughts about your trauma cause you stress and make your symptoms worse.

Text in this chapter is excerpted from "Treatment of PTSD," U.S. Department of Veterans Affairs (VA), August 14, 2015.

You will learn to identify thoughts about the world and yourself that are making you feel afraid or upset. With the help of your therapist, you will learn to replace these thoughts with more accurate and less distressing thoughts. You will also learn ways to cope with feelings such as anger, guilt, and fear.

After a traumatic event, you might blame yourself for things you couldn't have changed. For example, a soldier may feel guilty about decisions he or she had to make during war. Cognitive therapy, a type of CBT, helps you understand that the traumatic event you lived through was not your fault.

What is exposure therapy?

In exposure therapy your goal is to have less fear about your memories. It is based on the idea that people learn to fear thoughts, feelings, and situations that remind them of a past traumatic event.

By talking about your trauma repeatedly with a therapist, you'll learn to get control of your thoughts and feelings about the trauma. You'll learn that you do not have to be afraid of your memories. This may be hard at first. It might seem strange to think about stressful things on purpose. But over time, you'll feel less overwhelmed.

With the help of your therapist, you can change how you react to the stressful memories. Talking in a place where you feel secure makes this easier.

You may focus on memories that are less upsetting before talking about worse ones. This is called "desensitization," and it allows you to deal with bad memories a little bit at a time. Your therapist also may ask you to remember a lot of bad memories at once. This is called "flooding," and it helps you learn not to feel overwhelmed.

You also may practice different ways to relax when you're having a stressful memory. Breathing exercises are sometimes used for this.

What is eye movement desensitization and reprocessing (EMDR)

Eye movement desensitization and reprocessing (EMDR) is another type of therapy for PTSD. Like other kinds of counseling, it can help change how you react to memories of your trauma.

While thinking of or talking about your memories, you'll focus on other stimuli like eye movements, hand taps, and sounds. For example, your therapist will move his or her hand, and you'll follow this movement with your eyes.

Experts are still learning how EMDR works, and there is disagreement about whether eye movements are a necessary part of the treatment.

Medication

Selective serotonin reuptake inhibitors (SSRIs) are a type of antidepressant medicine. These can help you feel less sad and worried. They appear to be helpful, and for some people they are very effective. SSRIs include citalopram (Celexa), fluoxetine (such as Prozac), paroxetine (Paxil), and sertraline (Zoloft).

Chemicals in your brain affect the way you feel. For example, when you have depression you may not have enough of a chemical called serotonin. SSRIs raise the level of serotonin in your brain.

There are other medications that have been used with some success. Talk to your doctor about which medications are right for you.

Other types of treatment

Some other kinds of counseling may be helpful in your recovery. However, more evidence is needed to support these types of treatment for PTSD.

Group therapy

Many people want to talk about their trauma with others who have had similar experiences.

In group therapy, you talk with a group of people who also have been through a trauma and who have PTSD. Sharing your story with others may help you feel more comfortable talking about your trauma. This can help you cope with your symptoms, memories, and other parts of your life.

Group therapy helps you build relationships with others who understand what you've been through. You learn to deal with emotions such as shame, guilt, anger, rage, and fear. Sharing with the group also can help you build self-confidence and trust. You'll learn to focus on your present life, rather than feeling overwhelmed by the past.

Brief psychodynamic psychotherapy

In this type of therapy, you learn ways of dealing with emotional conflicts caused by your trauma. This therapy helps you understand how your past affects the way you feel now.

Your therapist can help you:

- Identify what triggers your stressful memories and other symptoms

- Find ways to cope with intense feelings about the past

- Become more aware of your thoughts and feelings, so you can change your reactions to them

- Raise your self-esteem

Family therapy

PTSD can affect your whole family. Your kids or your partner may not understand why you get angry sometimes, or why you're under so much stress. They may feel scared, guilty, or even angry about your condition.

Family therapy is a type of counseling that involves your whole family. A therapist helps you and your family to communicate, maintain good relationships, and cope with tough emotions. Your family can learn more about PTSD and how it is treated.

In family therapy, each person can express his or her fears and concerns. It's important to be honest about your feelings and to listen to others. You can talk about your PTSD symptoms and what triggers them. You also can discuss the important parts of your treatment and recovery. By doing this, your family will be better prepared to help you.

You may consider having individual therapy for your PTSD symptoms and family therapy to help you with your relationships.

How long does treatment last?

CBT treatment for PTSD often lasts for three to six months. Other types of treatment for PTSD can last longer. If you have other mental health problems as well as PTSD, treatment may last for one to two years or longer.

What if someone has PTSD and another disorder? Is the treatment different?

It is very common to have PTSD at that same time as another mental health problem. Depression, alcohol or drug abuse problems, panic disorder, and anxiety disorders often occur along with PTSD. In many cases, the PTSD treatments described above will also help with the other disorders. The best treatment results occur when both

PTSD and the other problems are treated together rather than one after the other.

What will we work on in therapy?

When you begin therapy, you and your therapist should decide together what goals you hope to reach in therapy. Not every person with PTSD will have the same treatment goals. For instance, you might focus on:

- Reducing your PTSD symptoms

- Learning the best way to live with your symptoms

- Learning how to cope with other problems associated with PTSD, like feeling less guilt or sadness, improving relationships at work, or communicating with friends and family

Your therapist should help you decide which of these goals seems most important to you, and he or she should discuss with you which goals might take a long time to achieve.

What can I expect from my therapist?

Your therapist should help you decide which of these goals seems most important to you, and he or she should discuss with you which goals might take a long time to achieve.

The two of you should agree at the beginning that this plan makes sense for you. You should also agree on what you will do if it does not seem to be working. If you have any questions about the treatment, your therapist should be able to answer them.

You should feel comfortable with your therapist and feel you are working as a team to tackle your problems. It can be difficult to talk about painful situations in your life, or about traumatic experiences that you've had. Feelings that emerge during therapy can be scary and challenging. Talking with your therapist about the process of therapy, and about your hopes and fears in regards to therapy, will help make therapy successful.

If you do not like your therapist or feel that the therapist is not helping you, it might be helpful to talk with another professional. In most cases, you should tell your therapist that you are seeking a second opinion.

Chapter 39

Suicide Prevention

Suicide is a major public health concern. Over 41,000 people die by suicide each year in the United States. More than twice as many people die by suicide each year than by homicide. Suicide is tragic. But it is often preventable. Knowing the risk factors for suicide and who is at risk can help reduce the suicide rate.

Who is at risk for suicide?

Suicide does not discriminate. People of all genders, ages, and ethnicities can be at risk for suicide. But people most at risk tend to share certain characteristics. The main risk factors for suicide are:

- Depression, other mental disorders, or substance abuse disorder
- A prior suicide attempt
- Family history of a mental disorder or substance abuse
- Family history of suicide
- Family violence, including physical or sexual abuse
- Having guns or other firearms in the home
- Incarceration, being in prison or jail

Text in this chapter is excerpted from "Suicide Prevention," National Institute of Mental Health (NIMH), April 2015.

- Being exposed to others' suicidal behavior, such as that of family members, peers, or media figures.

The risk for suicidal behavior is complex. Research suggests that people who attempt suicide differ from others in many aspects of how they think, react to events, and make decisions. There are differences in aspects of memory, attention, planning, and emotion, for example. These differences often occur along with disorders like depression, substance use, anxiety, and psychosis. Sometimes suicidal behavior is triggered by events such as personal loss or violence.

In order to be able to detect those at risk and prevent suicide, it is crucial that we understand the role of both long-term factors—such as experiences in childhood—and more immediate factors like mental health and recent life events. Researchers are also looking at how genes can either increase risk or make someone more resilient to loss and hardships.

Many people have some of these risk factors but do not attempt suicide. Suicide is not a normal response to stress. **It is however, a sign of extreme distress, not a harmless bid for attention.**

What about gender?

Men are more likely to die by suicide than women, but women are more likely to attempt suicide. Men are more likely to use deadlier methods, such as firearms or suffocation. Women are more likely than men to attempt suicide by poisoning.

What about children?

Children and young people are at risk for suicide. Suicide is the second leading cause of death for young people ages 15 to 34.

What about older adults?

Older adults are at risk for suicide, too. While older adults were the demographic group with the highest suicide rates for decades, suicide rates for middle aged adults have increased to comparable levels (ages 24-62). Among those age 65+, white males comprise over 80% of all late life suicides.

What about different racial/ethnic groups?

Among racial and ethnic groups, American Indians and Alaska Natives tend to have the highest rate of suicides, followed by non-Hispanic Whites. Hispanics tend to have the lowest rate of suicides, while African Americans tend to have the second lowest rate.

How can suicide be prevented?

Effective suicide prevention is based on sound research. Programs that work take into account people's risk factors and promote interventions that are appropriate to specific groups of people. For example, research has shown that mental and substance abuse disorders are risk factors for suicide. Therefore, many programs focus on treating these disorders in addition to addressing suicide risk specifically.

Psychotherapy, or "talk therapy," can effectively reduce suicide risk. One type is called cognitive behavioral therapy (CBT). CBT can help people learn new ways of dealing with stressful experiences by training them to consider alternative actions when thoughts of suicide arise.

Another type of psychotherapy called dialectical behavior therapy (DBT) has been shown to reduce the rate of suicide among people with borderline personality disorder, a serious mental illness characterized by unstable moods, relationships, self-image, and behavior. A therapist trained in DBT helps a person recognize when his or her feelings or actions are disruptive or unhealthy, and teaches the skills needed to deal better with upsetting situations.

Medications may also help; promising medications and psychosocial treatments for suicidal people are being tested.

Still other research has found that many older adults and women who die by suicide saw their primary care providers in the year before death. Training doctors to recognize signs that a person may be considering suicide may help prevent even more suicides.

What should I do if someone I know is considering suicide?

If you know someone who may be considering suicide, do not leave him or her alone. Try to get your loved one to seek immediate help from a doctor or the nearest hospital emergency room, or call 911. Remove access to firearms or other potential tools for suicide, including medications.

If you are in crisis

Call the toll-free National Suicide Prevention Lifeline at 1-800-273-TALK (8255), available 24 hours a day, 7 days a week. The service is available to anyone. All calls are confidential.

Part Five

Stress Management

Chapter 40

The Basics of Preventing and Managing Stress

Not all stress is bad. But chronic (ongoing) stress can lead to health problems.

Preventing and managing chronic stress can help lower your risk for serious conditions like heart disease, obesity, high blood pressure, and depression.

You can prevent or reduce stress by:

- Planning ahead

- Deciding which tasks need to be done first

- Preparing for stressful events

Some stress is hard to avoid. You can find ways to manage stress by:

- Noticing when you feel stressed

- Taking time to relax

- Getting active and eating healthy

- Talking to friends and family

This chapter includes excerpts from "Manage Stress," Office of Disease Prevention and Health Promotion (ODPHP), July 30, 2015; and text from "Manage Stress workbook," United States Department of Veterans Affairs (VA), June 2014.

What are the signs of stress?

When people are under stress, they may feel:

- Worried
- Angry
- Irritable
- Depressed
- Unable to focus

Stress also affects the body. Physical signs of stress include:

- Headaches
- Back pain
- Problems sleeping
- Upset stomach
- Weight gain or loss
- Tense muscles
- Frequent or more serious colds

Stress is different for everyone.

What causes stress?

Change is often a cause of stress. Even positive changes, like having a baby or getting a job promotion, can be stressful.
Stress can be short-term or long-term.

Common causes of short-term stress:

- Needing to do a lot in a short amount of time
- Experiencing many small problems in the same day, like a traffic jam or running late
- Getting lost
- Having an argument

Common causes of long-term stress:

- Death of a loved one
- Chronic (ongoing) illness

- Caring for someone with a serious illness
- Problems at work or at home
- Money problems

What are the benefits of managing stress?

Over time, chronic stress can lead to health problems. Managing stress can help you:

- Sleep better
- Control your weight
- Get sick less often and feel better faster when you are sick
- Have less neck and back pain
- Be in a better mood
- Get along better with family and friends

Take Action!

Being prepared and feeling in control of your situation will help lower your stress. Follow these 9 tips for preventing and managing stress.

1. Plan your time.

Think ahead about how you are going to use your time. Write a to-do list and figure out what's most important – then do that thing first. Be realistic about how long each task will take.

2. Prepare yourself.

Prepare ahead of time for stressful events like a job interview or a hard conversation with a loved one.

- Picture the event in your mind.
- Stay positive.
- Imagine what the room will look like and what you will say.
- Have a back-up plan.

3. Relax with deep breathing or meditation.

Deep breathing and meditation are two ways to relax your muscles and clear your mind.

4. Relax your muscles.

Stress causes tension in your muscles. Try stretching or taking a hot shower to help you relax.

5. Get active.

Regular physical activity can help prevent and manage stress. It can also help relax your muscles and improve your mood.

- Aim for 2 hours and 30 minutes a week of physical activity. Try going for a bike ride or taking a walk.

- Be sure to exercise for at least 10 minutes at a time.

- Do strengthening activities – like crunches or lifting weights – at least 2 days a week.

6. Eat healthy.

Give your body plenty of energy by eating healthy foods – including vegetables, fruits, and lean sources of protein.

7. Drink alcohol only in moderation.

Avoid using alcohol and drugs to manage your stress. If you choose to drink, drink only in moderation. This means no more than 1 drink a day for women and no more than 2 drinks a day for men.

8. Talk to friends and family.

Tell your friends and family if you are feeling stressed. They may be able to help.

9. Get help if you need it.

Stress is a normal part of life. But if your stress doesn't go away or keeps getting worse, you may need help. Over time, stress can lead to serious problems like depression, anxiety, or PTSD (post-traumatic stress disorder).

- If you are feeling down or hopeless, talk to a doctor about depression.

- If you are feeling anxious, find out how to get help for anxiety.

- If you have lived through a dangerous event, find out about treatment for PTSD.

A mental health professional (like a psychologist or social worker) can help treat these conditions with talk therapy (called psychotherapy) or medicines.

Lots of people need help dealing with stress – it's nothing to be ashamed of!

Other Factors for Managing Stress

Aligning Your Core Values

Losing track of your core values can contribute to unhealthy stress levels. Think about what really matters to you in your life. Spending time doing what is important to you can reduce stress and give you energy. Filling out a Personal Health Inventory can help you explore all areas of your life.

Problem Solving

Mindfulness practice helps you to slow down and become more aware of options. Mindfulness fosters flexibility, which can be essential for problem solving. Mindfulness also can help you assess how you feel about the various options and make an educated decision about the next best step.

When you face a difficult problem, begin by grounding yourself with mindful breathing. Next, visualize the problem without getting attached to finding solutions; just breathe and be aware of the issue. Allow solutions to come and go — jot down any that seem useful — and then come back to the meditation. As solutions emerge, take a moment to see how each one feels, noticing if one seems more right than another.

Developing Resilience

Resilience refers to a person's ability to withstand and bounce back from difficult situations. Mindfulness helps you reduce stress, which in turn increases your resilience. Mindfulness enables you to be better able to step back and assess situations from a calm place and ultimately to adapt to the present moment.

Positive coping involves doing things that keep your body and mind healthy and strong. Coping in healthy ways builds your resilience. Mindfulness is one form of healthy coping that builds your resilience. Getting enough rest and sleep, planning your days, staying physically active, eating healthy foods, and having supportive people in your life also build your resilience. Building your resilience helps you cope with stress in a healthier way. Positive coping, or dealing with stress well, leads to making better decisions, figuring out safe ways to solve problems, and lowering your chances of developing health problems like high blood pressure and depression. Positive coping even helps you deal better with physical and emotional pain, manage your weight, sleep better, and be calmer when in stressful situations, such as driving or being in crowded places.

Eating Wisely When Stressed

When we feel stressed, we tend to make poor food choices such as skipping meals and choosing less healthy, convenient options like fast food and processed foods. Such choices are partly due to high levels of stress hormones, which cause us to crave fat and sugar.

Unfortunately, eating lots of junk food and sugar and skipping meals actually creates physical stress for our bodies that adds to our overall stress load. When we choose healthier foods that are high in nutrients, our ability to handle stress improves because we've removed one source of physical stress from our lives. Ask your primary care team about a healthy eating plan and mindful eating, which have been shown to help reduce overeating and improve weight loss results.

Changing Unhelpful Thoughts

Habitual, negative thoughts can contribute to stress as well as perpetuate negative behaviors. Mindfulness can help you be more aware of your unhelpful thought patterns so you can replace them with thoughts that support your goals. Mindfulness helps you to get into the present to make the necessary changes.

Getting Social Support

Having social support is an important component for stress management. It is important to have the support of other Veterans and people who know what it has been like.

Increasing Self-Compassion

Self-compassion is the ability to be forgiving of yourself. Low self-compassion can increase stress levels and stress hormone levels while lowering self-esteem. You can improve self-compassion by working on unhelpful thoughts and by practicing compassion meditation.

Managing Interpersonal Stress

You can lower stress by practicing mindful communication. This includes saying what you really mean as well as mindful listening.

It will increase your awareness of unhelpful communication patterns and improve communication with difficult people.

Working with Chronic Pain

Being mindful can help you manage chronic pain, whether it is physical or emotional. Many people physically tighten up in response to pain or otherwise resist it. Resisting your feelings of pain creates another layer of distress and makes the suffering worse. You can lessen your suffering, possibly even get rid of it altogether, by eliminating your resistance to pain. Because pain is both real and inevitable, it's important to accept it.

If you are experiencing unusually severe pain, you should talk to your healthcare team about it.

You should contact your healthcare team or the VA Crisis Hotline at 1-800-273-8255 (Press 1) if your stress seems to be getting out of control or you are having thoughts of harming yourself or others.

You can always reach out to your primary care / Patient Aligned Care Team (PACT) for help.

Pleasant Activities Tip Sheet

Research has shown that ratings of mood improve if you add some pleasant activities to your routine. Here is a strategy to use pleasant activities to manage stress and add some fun to your life.

- Plan for at least one pleasant activity per day, even if just a few minutes long.
- The activity should not be for someone else — it should be designed to give you joy.
- If you can't do something you used to enjoy, think about a good replacement. For example, you may not be able to go deep sea fishing, but you might enjoy visiting the boat show or just walking on a pier.
- Aim for gentle pleasures, like taking a walk in a favorite place, walking the dog, or taking time to read the comic strips.
- Mix it up! Variety is the spice of life.
- Simplify — look for simple pleasures that don't require a lot of preparation or money.
- If you have trouble coming up with activities, think about what you enjoyed in the past.

Here are some examples of pleasant activities that some have chosen, but remember to focus on what you enjoy:

- Stop at a park on the way home from work to go for a walk by the lake.

- Go for a bike ride.

- Cut some flowers to put in a vase in your home.

- If you like boating, doing something like waxing your boat, visiting a marina, or fixing a part may be enjoyable.

- Go fishing.

- Park your car for a few minutes at a place with a nice view.

- Sit outside and watch for birds or wildlife.

- Check the rankings of your favorite sports team.

- Take a warm bath.

- Call an old friend.

Chapter 41

Developing Resilience: The Most Important Defense Against Stress

Can we learn to be more resilient? Could sensitive or less resilient individuals become hardier? In this modern age of hypersensitivity, when even the simplest of issues becomes major or easy tasks become insurmountable, people have learned to give up instead of plowing on through the problem.

The answer to the first question is a resounding yes. Remember your years in school? You probably had physical training or played sports, and the coach would push you past your comfort level to achieve greater results. As you found, you could endure. Or, do you recall, perhaps, growing up with just the basic necessities, playing outside, having no fast food or television, walking to and from school, and working in your yard because you were told to do so? This was the beginning of resilience.

Granted, when a person faces a problem, it often seems big to them at that moment. For some of us looking at the same issue, we cannot imagine why the individual sees it as so large. And, there's the rub—we differ in how we cope with stressful situations. Resilience comes from understanding yourself and how you react to your environment. It can change how you handle setbacks. Being more resilient can affect

Text in this chapter is excerpted from "Becoming More Resilient," Federal Bureau of Investigation (FBI), October 2012.

how enthusiastically you approach challenges. It can improve how you think during conflicts or stressful periods. Resilience can help you learn from past difficulties and derive knowledge and meaning from those setbacks and failures. Responding effectively to adversity, overcoming obstacles, getting through normal daily hassles, and dealing with life-altering events form the cornerstone of resilience.

Proactive use of resilience allows you the ability to seek out new experiences that will enrich your life. With this said, you need to understand yourself first. How? Introspection is the first step in understanding what you can or cannot do and your level of endurance at a mental, personal, and emotional level.

Areas of Focus

Emotional Intelligence

Emotional intelligence is a form of social intelligence that employs the skill of awareness, or being "clued in," to monitor one's own and others' emotions, discriminate among them, and, in the end, use the information to guide one's own thinking and actions. Several subcategories relating to both intrapersonal and interpersonal skills are important in understanding how it works.

Self-awareness involves observing yourself and recognizing a feeling as it happens. Self-regulation entails handling feelings appropriately; realizing what is behind a feeling; and finding ways to address fear, anxiety, anger, and sadness. Motivation includes channeling emotions in the service of a goal, controlling emotions, delaying gratification, and stifling impulses. Empathy involves remaining sensitive to others' feelings and concerns, taking their perspective, and appreciating the differences in how people feel about things. Social skills include managing emotions in others, embodying social competence, and handling relationships.

Self-Awareness

- Emotional awareness: recognizing emotions and their effects
- Accurate self-assessment: knowing personal strengths and limits
- Self-confidence: having a strong sense of self-worth and capabilities, a basic belief in the ability to do what is needed to produce a desired outcome

422

Self-Regulation

- Self-control: keeping disruptive emotions and impulses in check
- Trustworthiness: maintaining standards of honesty and integrity
- Conscientiousness: taking responsibility for personal performance
- Adaptability: learning to be flexible in handling change
- Innovation: being comfortable with novel ideas, approaches, and new information

Motivation

- Achievement drive: striving to improve or meet a standard of excellence
- Commitment: aligning with the goals of the group or organization
- Initiative: becoming ready to act on opportunities
- Optimism: maintaining persistence in pursuing goals despite obstacles and setbacks and aligning with hope—a predictor of success (e.g., I am able to motivate myself to try and try again in the face of setbacks. I like to push the limits of my ability. Under pressure, I rarely feel helpless. I easily can set negative feelings aside when called on to perform.)

Empathy

- Understanding others: sensing other people's feelings and perspectives and taking an active interest in their concerns
- Developing others: detecting other individuals' development needs and bolstering their abilities
- Leveraging diversity: cultivating opportunities through different kinds of people
- Maintaining political awareness: reading a group's emotional currents and power relationships (e.g., I am effective at listening to other people's problems. I rarely get angry at people who come around and bother me with foolish questions. I am adept at reading people's feelings by their facial expressions. I easily can "put myself into other people's shoes.")

Social Skills

- Influence: wielding effective tactics for persuasion
- Communication: listening openly and sending convincing messages
- Leadership: inspiring and guiding individuals and groups
- Change catalyst: initiating or managing change
- Building bonds: nurturing instrumental relationships
- Collaboration and cooperation: working with others toward shared goals
- Team capabilities: creating group synergy in pursuing collective goals

Your emotional resilience can improve and strengthen through understanding yourself better and improving your emotional intelligence. We all are born with different coping mechanisms; in fact, some of us have none. Emotional intelligence gives us the ability to, finally, become a more resilient person.

Visualization

Think about becoming mentally and emotionally tougher. Look to other people for examples of mental and emotional toughness. For instance, when I was a boy, I admired John Wayne and wanted to emulate his confidence, strength, and fortitude. Although he was an actor, the character traits he exuded made me want to be strong like him. The point? Seeing is believing; start acting like a more resilient person, and, eventually, you also will start to believe it. According to one expert, "It's not that less resilient people are lacking some kind of 'coping gene' or anything like that. Indeed, they have the power within to become just as resilient as their more intuitively resilient counterparts simply by training their minds to think more positively and then learning how to change their behaviors to reflect their new, more positive attitudes." You need to make a personal paradigm shift from being hopeless, hapless, and helpless to becoming stronger, tougher, and hardier.

Positive Psychology

Your mental outlook or mood affects how you behave and interact with the world. Start seeing the good in things, the brighter side of

424

life and the little enjoyments along the way that cheer you up. To this end, *positive psychology*—the study of the human condition and how people live and interact with their environment—focuses on cultivating personality strengths and honing an optimistic approach to life, rather than on cataloging human frailty and disease, which has served too long as the focus of psychology. Traditional psychology focused on atypical or dysfunctional people with mental illness, emotional problems, personality disorders, or other psychological issues and, in the end, how to treat them. By contrast, positive psychology, a relatively new field, examines how ordinary people can become happier and more fulfilled.

Cognitive Restructuring

Another way to become a more resilient person is through a process called *cognitive restructuring*—in short, changing a perception from a negative interpretation to a neutral or positive one and, in turn, making it less stressful. Cognitive restructuring also is known as reappraisal, relabeling, and reframing. Individuals acquire irrational or illogical cognitive interpretations or beliefs about themselves or their environment. The extent to which these beliefs are irrational is important and equals the amount of emotional distress experienced by the person.

From a visual model, cognitive restructuring entails 1) an activating adverse event or stressor (e.g., traffic jam) that triggers negative feelings; 2) beliefs, distortions, and inner dialogue about the problem (e.g., increased adrenalin, feelings of anxiety); and 3) behavioral and emotional consequences (e.g., stress of target organs, increase of heart rate and blood pressure). You can avoid all of this if, for instance, you tell yourself that you cannot do anything about the traffic, sit back and enjoy music, bide your time, and recognize that you, eventually, will get through it.

Another facet of cognitive restructuring is known as *cognitive distortions*. This encompasses behaviors that prove troublesome for persons who react (expressive) first and think (cognitive) second.

- All-or-nothing (dichotomous) thinking: "It's my way or the highway"-type thinking that leads to extreme actions, like leaving a partnership, quitting a job, or acting in other impulsive ways; mood swings; and interpersonal problems

- Overgeneralizing: making an inaccurate blanket statement (e.g., All people from the South are less intelligent than the rest of the country.)

- Labeling: defining or describing someone in terms of their appearance or behavior (e.g., identifying an overweight individual as lazy)

- Filtering: distorting what someone says into something different from what was communicated, perhaps, to fit one's own preconceptions or ideas

- Disqualifying the positive: continually downplaying positive experiences for useless reasons, often reveling in the negative

- Jumping to conclusions: Drawing inferences (usually negative) from little (if any) evidence

- Telescoping: perceiving recent events as distant and distant events as recent

- Emotional reasoning: assuming that reality is in line with one's current emotions (e.g., I am sad; therefore, everything around me is melancholy.)

- Making a habit of "should" statements: having patterns of thought that imply the way things "ought" to be, rather than embracing the actual situation or having rigid rules that "always apply" regardless of the circumstances

- Personalizing events: taking personal responsibility for something that you had no control over

Pursuit of Hope

Try to find the good in a bad situation, shift your focus to problem solving, keep the stressor in perspective, control your inner dialogue, stop negative self-talk, and, most important, avoid the blame game. How do you control these irrational beliefs? First, identify the irrational belief that you need to control. Believe it or not, some people cannot even identify what is bothering them. Second, can this perception be rationally supported? Third, what evidence exists for its falseness? Fourth, does any evidence exist for its truthfulness? Fifth, what is the worst thing that *actually* can happen? Sixth, what good can you derive from this experience?

In the end, everyone needs guidance, instruction, or a learning tool to go by from time to time. Having some beacon of light to guide you when everything seems dark, foreboding, and ominous just might make all the difference. That could come from reading an article or book, hearing an inspirational message, commiserating with friends, receiving a compliment, appreciating the laughter in children, or enjoying the warmth of a pet. Make a list of things you want or need to complete. A list is a great way of getting organized and feeling a sense of accomplishment.

Conclusion

Only you know what makes you tick or which methods work for you to become more resilient or hardy. Whatever allows you to deal with adversity, harness and use it, and always remember that no problem will last forever. Look back to a perceived problem you had 1, 5, or 10 years ago, and you probably will think, Wow, I was concerned about that! So, remember that same insight works going forward if you think of it in that context. Just live every day and make it to that future moment, and all will be different from today.

Chapter 42

Healthy Habits to Combat Stress

Chapter Contents

Section 42.1

Your Guide to Healthy Sleep

Text in this section is excerpted from "Get Enough Sleep," Office of Disease Prevention and Health Promotion (ODPHP), July 15, 2015.

Everyone needs to get enough sleep. Sleep helps keep your mind and body healthy.

How much sleep do I need?

Most adults need 7 to 8 hours of good quality sleep on a regular schedule each night. Make changes to your routine if you can't find enough time to sleep.

Getting enough sleep isn't only about total hours of sleep. It's also important to:

• Go to sleep at about the same time every day

• Get good quality sleep so you feel rested when you wake up

If you often have trouble sleeping – or if you don't feel well rested after sleeping – talk with your doctor.

How much sleep to children need?

Kids need even more sleep than adults.

• Teens need at least 9 hours of sleep each night.

• School-aged children need at least 10 hours of sleep each night.

• Preschoolers need to sleep between 11 and 12 hours a day.

• Newborns need to sleep between 16 and 18 hours a day.

Why is getting enough sleep important?

Getting enough sleep has many benefits. It can help you:

• Get sick less often

- Stay at a healthy weight

- Lower your risk of high blood pressure and diabetes

- Reduce stress and improve your mood

- Think more clearly and do better in school and at work

- Get along better with people

- Make good decisions and avoid injuries (For example, sleepy drivers cause thousands of car crashes every year.)

Does it matter when I sleep?

Yes. Your body sets your "biological clock" according to the pattern of daylight where you live. This helps you naturally get sleepy at night and stay alert during the day.

When people have to work at night and sleep during the day, they can have trouble getting enough sleep. When people travel to a different time zone, they can also have trouble sleeping.

Get sleep tips to help you:

- Work the night shift

- Deal with jet lag (trouble sleeping in a new time zone)

Why can't I fall asleep?

Many things can make it harder for you to sleep, including:

- Stress

- Pain

- Certain health conditions

- Some medicines

- Caffeine (usually from coffee, tea, and soda)

- Alcohol and other drugs

- Untreated sleep disorders, like sleep apnea or insomnia

If you are having trouble sleeping, make changes to your routine to get the sleep you need. For example, try to:

- Follow a regular sleep schedule

- Stay away from caffeine in the afternoon

- Take a hot bath before bed to relax

How can I tell if I have a sleep disorder?

Signs of a sleep disorder can include:

- Difficulty falling asleep

- Trouble staying asleep

- Sleepiness during the day that makes it difficult to do tasks like driving a car

- Frequent loud snoring

- Pauses in breathing or gasping while sleeping

- Pain or itchy feelings in your legs or arms at night that feel better when you move or massage the area

If you have any of these signs, talk to a doctor or nurse. You may need to be tested or treated for a sleep disorder.

Take Action!

Making small changes to your daily routine can help you get the sleep you need.

Change what you do during the day.

- Exercise earlier in the day, not right before you go to bed.

- Stay away from caffeine (including coffee, tea, and soda) late in the day.

- If you have trouble sleeping at night, limit daytime naps to 20 minutes or less.

- If you drink alcohol, drink only in moderation. This means no more than 1 drink a day for women and no more than 2 drinks a day for men. Alcohol can keep you from sleeping soundly.

- Don't eat a big meal close to bedtime.

- Quit smoking. The nicotine in cigarettes can make it harder for you to sleep.

Create a good sleep environment.

- Make sure your bedroom is dark. If there are street lights near your window, try putting up light-blocking curtains.

- Keep your bedroom quiet.
- Consider keeping electronic devices like TVs and computers out of the bedroom.

Set a bedtime routine.

- Go to bed at the same time every night.
- Get the same amount of sleep each night.
- Avoid eating, talking on the phone, reading, or watching TV in bed.
- Try not to lie in bed worrying about things. Check out these tips to help manage stress.

If you are still awake after staying in bed for more than 20 minutes, get up. Do something relaxing until you feel sleepy.

If you are concerned about your sleep, see a doctor.

Talk with a doctor or nurse if you have any of the following signs of a sleep disorder:

- Frequent, loud snoring
- Pauses in breathing during sleep
- Trouble waking up in the morning
- Pain or itchy feelings in your legs or arms at night that feel better when you move or massage the area
- Trouble staying awake during the day

Even if you aren't aware of problems like these, talk with a doctor if you feel like you often have trouble sleeping.

Keep a sleep diary for a week and share it with your doctor. A doctor can suggest different sleep routines or medicines to treat sleep disorders. Talk with a doctor before trying over-the-counter sleep medicine.

Section 42.2

Exercise Can Help Control Stress

Text in this section is excerpted from "Exercise: Benefits of Exercise,"
NIHSeniorHealth at the National Institute of Health (NIH),
January 2015.

One of the Healthiest Things You Can Do

Like most people, you've probably heard that physical activity and exercise are good for you. In fact, being physically active on a regular basis is one of the healthiest things you can do for yourself. Studies have shown that exercise provides many health benefits and that older adults can gain a lot by staying physically active. Even moderate exercise and physical activity can improve the health of people who are frail or who have diseases that accompany aging.

Being physically active can also help you stay strong and fit enough to keep doing the things you like to do as you get older. Making exercise and physical activity a regular part of your life can improve your health and help you maintain your independence as you age.

Be as Active as Possible

Regular physical activity and exercise are important to the physical and mental health of almost everyone, including older adults. Staying physically active and exercising regularly can produce long-term health benefits and even improve health for some older people who already have diseases and disabilities. That's why health experts say that older adults should aim to be as active as possible.

Being Inactive Can Be Risky

Although exercise and physical activity are among the healthiest things you can do for yourself, some older adults are reluctant to exercise. Some are afraid that exercise will be too hard or that physical activity will harm them. Others might think they have to join a gym or have special equipment. Yet, studies show that "taking it easy" is risky. For the most part, when older people lose their ability to do things on their own, it doesn't happen just because they've aged. It's usually because they're not active. Lack of physical activity also can lead to more visits to the doctor, more hospitalizations, and more use of medicines for a variety of illnesses.

Prevent or Delay Disease

Scientists have found that staying physically active and exercising regularly can help prevent or delay many diseases and disabilities. In some cases, exercise is an effective treatment for many chronic conditions. For example, studies show that people with arthritis, heart disease, or diabetes benefit from regular exercise. Exercise also helps people with high blood pressure, balance problems, or difficulty walking.

Manage Stress, Improve mood

Regular, moderate physical activity can help manage stress and improve your mood. And, being active on a regular basis may help reduce feelings of depression. Studies also suggest that exercise can improve or maintain some aspects of cognitive function, such as your ability to shift quickly between tasks, plan an activity, and ignore irrelevant information.

For more on cognitive function and exercise, see "Do Exercise and Physical Activity Protect the Brain?" from Go4Life, the exercise and physical activity campaign from the National Institute on Aging.

Some people may wonder what the difference is between physical activity and exercise. Physical activities are activities that get your body moving such as gardening, walking the dog and taking the stairs instead of the elevator. Exercise is a form of physical activity that is specifically planned, structured, and repetitive such as weight training, tai chi, or an aerobics class. Including both in your life will provide you with health benefits that can help you feel better and enjoy life more as you age.

Section 42.3

Mindful Eating

Text in this section is excerpted from "Manage Stress workbook," U.S. Department of Veterans Affairs (VA), June 2014; and text from "Does how much you eat affect how long you live?," National Institute on Aging (NIA), January 22, 2015.

Mindful eating is an ongoing practice, but it starts with three simple steps.

1.   Become aware of the physical characteristics of food. Make each bite a mindful bite. Think of your mouth as being a magnifying glass, able to zoom in. Imagine magnifying each bite 100%. Pay close attention to your senses. Use your tongue to feel the texture of your food and to gauge the temperature. Take a whiff of the aroma. Ask yourself, *"How does it really taste? What does it feel like in my mouth? Is this something I really want? Does it satisfy my taste buds? Is my mind truly present when I take a bite so that I experience it fully?"*

2.   Become aware of repetitive habits and the process of eating. Notice how you eat. Fast? Slow? Do you put your fork down between bites? Are you stuck in any mindless habits, such as eating a snack at the same time each day, multi-tasking while you eat, or eating the same foods over and over again? Ask yourself the following questions: *"Do I have any ingrained habits concerning how I snack? When I pick up my fork, what stands in the way of eating wisely?"*

3.   Become aware of mindless eating triggers. Look for specific cues that prompt you to start and stop eating. Is your kitchen a hot spot for snacking? Do feelings such as stress, discomfort, or boredom lead to a food binge? Do judgmental thoughts like "I'm an idiot!" trigger mindless eating?

Become an expert on the emotional buttons that trigger you to eat when you aren't physically hungry. When you know your triggers, you can anticipate and respond to them.

Ask yourself, *"What am I feeling right before I mindlessly snack? Is my environment, emotional state, or dining companion helping or hurting my efforts to eat wisely?"*

Does how much you eat affect how long you live?

Your body needs food to survive. However, the very process of extracting energy from food—metabolizing food—creates stress on your body. Overeating creates even more stress on the body. That's part of the reason why it can lead to a shorter lifespan and serious health problems common among older people, including cardiovascular disease and type 2 diabetes.

Calorie restriction, an approach primarily (but not exclusively) used in a research setting, is more tightly controlled than normal healthy eating or dieting. It is commonly defined by at least a 30 percent decrease in calorie consumption from the normal diet with a balanced amount of protein, fat, vitamins, and minerals. In the 1930s, investigators found that laboratory rats and mice lived up to 40 percent longer when fed a calorie-restricted diet, compared to mice fed a normal diet. Since that time, scientists observed that calorie restriction increased the lifespan of many other animal models, including yeast, worms, flies, some (but not all) strains of mice, and maybe even nonhuman primates. In addition, when started at an early age or as a young adult, calorie restriction was found to increase the health span of many animal models by delaying onset of age-related disease and delaying normal age-related decline.

Two studies of calorie restriction in non-human primates (the animals most closely related to humans) have had intriguing results. In a study conducted at NIA, monkeys fed a calorie-restricted diet had a notably decreased and/or delayed onset of age-related diseases, compared to the control group of "normal" eaters. In a University of Wisconsin study supported by NIA, calorie-restricted rhesus monkeys had three times fewer age-related diseases compared to the control group. The Wisconsin study also found that rhesus monkeys on a restricted diet had fewer age-related deaths compared to their normal fed controls. In 2007, when the findings from the study conducted at NIA were published, it was too early to determine whether calorie restriction had any effects on lifespan. Research in primates continues.

Despite its apparent widespread acceptance, calorie restriction does not increase lifespan in all animals. In studies of non-laboratory (wild) mice, researchers found that on average, calorie restriction did not have any effect on lifespan. Some of the calorie-restricted mice actually lived shorter than average lives. This may be due to differences in the genetics of the wild mice. A 2010 NIA-funded study provides further evidence that genetics may play a role in whether or not calorie restriction will have a positive effect on longevity. Looking at 42 closely related strains of laboratory mice, researchers found that only about a third of the strains on a calorie-restricted diet had an increase in longevity. One-third of the strains of mice on a calorie-restricted diet had a shortened lifespan, and the other third had no significant difference in lifespan compared to mice on a normal diet.

While animal studies are ongoing, researchers are also exploring calorie restriction in humans to test its safety and practicality, as well as to see if it will have positive effects on health. Participants in a 2002 pilot of the Comprehensive Assessment of Long-term Effects of Reducing Intake of Energy (CALERIE) study had, after 1 year, lowered their fasting glucose, total cholesterol, core body temperature, body weight, and fat. At the cellular level, they had better functioning mitochondria and reduced DNA damage. However, in terms of practicality, scientists observed that adapting and adhering to the regimen could be difficult. A longer-term trial is underway.

Given that ample studies have demonstrated mostly positive effects of calorie restriction in many organisms, today's scientific studies focus on finding the mechanisms and pathways by which calorie restriction works. Researchers are also studying compounds that might act the same way in the body, mimicking the benefits of calorie restriction.

A wide range of possible mechanisms for calorie restriction are being investigated. Some scientists are exploring the possibility that metabolizing fewer calories results in less oxidative damage to the cells. Other scientists are looking at how the relative scarcity of nutrients caused by calorie restriction might induce heat shock proteins and other defense mechanisms that allow the body to better withstand other stresses and health problems. Some researchers wonder if the effects of calorie restriction are controlled by the brain and nervous system. In one NIA-conducted study, calorie restriction increased the production of brain-derived neurotrophic factor, or BDNF, a protein that protects the brain from dysfunction and degeneration, and supports increased regulation of blood sugar and heart function in animal models. Still other studies indicate calorie restriction may influence hormonal balance, cell senescence, or gene expression. It is likely that calorie restriction works through a combination of these mechanisms, and others yet to be identified.

There is an intriguing overlap between the pathways that control normal aging and those that scientists think may be pertinent to calorie restriction. The most relevant are the sirtuins and mTOR (mammalian target of rapamycin) pathways discussed in "Pathways of Longevity Genes." In several, but not all cases, disrupting these pathways means the organism no longer responds positively to calorie restriction. These two pathways have been important for identifying at least two compounds that may mimic the effects of calorie restriction: resveratrol and rapamycin.

Resveratrol, found naturally in grapes, wine, and nuts, activates the sirtuin pathway. It has been shown to increase the lifespan of yeast, flies, worms, and fish. In 2006, NIA researchers, in collaboration with university scientists funded by NIA, reported on a study comparing mice fed a standard diet, a high fat-and-calorie diet, or a high fat-and-calorie diet supplemented with resveratrol beginning at middle age. Resveratrol appeared to lessen the negative effects of the high fat-and-calorie diet, both in terms of lifespan and disease. In a 2008 follow-up study, investigators found that resveratrol improved the health of aging mice fed a standard diet. It prevented age- and obesity-related decline in heart function. Mice on resveratrol had better bone health, reduced cataract formation, and enhanced balance and motor coordination compared to non-treated mice. In addition, resveratrol was found to partially mimic the effects of calorie restriction on gene expression profiles of liver, skeletal muscle, and adipose (fatty) tissue in the mice. However, the compound did not have an impact on the mice's overall survival or maximum lifespan. These findings suggest that resveratrol does not affect all aspects of the basic aging process and that there may be different mechanisms for health versus lifespan. Research on resveratrol continues in mice, along with studies in nonhuman primates and people.

Rapamycin, another possible calorie restriction mimetic, acts on the mTOR pathway. This compound's main clinical use is to help suppress the immune system of people who have had an organ transplant so that the transplant can succeed. A study by NIA's Interventions Testing Program, as discussed in "Living long and well: Can we do both? Are they the same?", reported in 2009 that rapamycin extended the median and maximum lifespan of mice, likely by inhibiting the mTOR pathway. Rapamycin had these positive effects even when fed to the mice beginning at early-old age (20 months), suggesting that an intervention started later in life may still be able to increase longevity.

Researchers are now looking at rapamycin's effects on health span and if there are other compounds that may have similar effects as rapamycin on the mTOR pathway.

Scientists do not yet know how resveratrol, rapamycin, and other compounds that demonstrate effects similar to calorie restriction will influence human aging. Learning more about these calorie restriction mimetics, and the mechanisms and pathways underlying calorie restriction, may point the way to future healthy aging therapies.

Chapter 43

Stressful Situations: Tips for Coping

Chapter Contents

Section 43.1

Work Stress

Text in this section is excerpted from "STRESS...At Work," Centers
for Disease Control and Prevention (CDC), June 6, 2014.

Preventing Job Stress – Getting Started

No standardized approaches or simple "how to" manuals exist for
developing a stress prevention program. Program design and appropriate solutions will be influenced by several factors-the size and complex-
ity of the organization, available resources, and especially the unique
types of stress problems faced by the organization.

Although it is not possible to give a universal prescription for preventing stress at work, it is possible to offer guidelines on the process
of stress prevention in organizations. In all situations, the process
for stress prevention programs involves three distinct steps: problem
identification, intervention, and evaluation. For this process to succeed,
organizations need to be adequately prepared. At a minimum, preparation for a stress prevention program should include the following:

- Building general awareness about job stress (causes, costs, and
  control)

- Securing top management commitment and support for the
  program

- Incorporating employee input and involvement in all phases of
  the program

- Establishing the technical capacity to conduct the program
  (e.g., specialized training for in-house staff or use of job stress
  consultants)

Bringing workers or workers and managers together in a committee
or problem-solving group may be an especially useful approach for
developing a stress prevention program. Research has shown these
participatory efforts to be effective in dealing with ergonomic problems
in the workplace, partly because they capitalize on workers' first-
hand knowledge of hazards encountered in their jobs. However, when

442

forming such working groups, care must be taken to be sure that they are in compliance with current labor laws.

Steps toward Prevention

Low morale, health and job complaints, and employee turnover often provide the first signs of job stress. But sometimes there are no clues, especially if employees are fearful of losing their jobs. Lack of obvious or widespread signs is not a good reason to dismiss concerns about job stress or minimize the importance of a prevention program.

Step 1—Identify the Problem. The best method to explore the scope and source of a suspected stress problem in an organization depends partly on the size of the organization and the available resources. Group discussions among managers, labor representatives, and employees can provide rich sources of information. Such discussions may be all that is needed to track down and remedy stress problems in a small company. In a larger organization, such discussions can be used to help design formal surveys for gathering input about stressful job conditions from large numbers of employees.

Regardless of the method used to collect data, information should be obtained about employee perceptions of their job conditions and perceived levels of stress, health, and satisfaction.

* Hold group discussions with employees.

* Design an employee survey.

* Measure employee perceptions of job conditions, stress, health, and satisfaction.

* Collect objective data.

* Analyze data to identify problem locations and stressful job conditions.

he list of job conditions that may lead to stress and the warning signs and effects of stress provide good starting points for deciding what information to collect.

Regardless of the method used to collect data, information should be obtained about employee perceptions of their job conditions and perceived levels of stress, health, and satisfaction. The list of job conditions that may lead to stress and the warning signs and effects of stress provide good starting points for deciding what information to collect.

Objective measures such as absenteeism, illness and turnover rates, or performance problems can also be examined to gauge the presence and scope of job stress. However, these measures are only rough indicators of job stress-at best.

Data from discussions, surveys, and other sources should be summarized and analyzed to answer questions about the location of a stress problem and job conditions that may be responsible-for example, are problems present throughout the organization or confined to single departments or specific jobs?

Survey design, data analysis, and other aspects of a stress prevention program may require the help of experts from a local university or consulting firm. However, overall authority for the prevention program should remain in the organization.

Step 2—Design and Implement Interventions. Once the sources of stress at work have been identified and the scope of the problem is understood, the stage is set for design and implementation of an intervention strategy.

In small organizations, the informal discussions that helped identify stress problems may also produce fruitful ideas for prevention. In large organizations, a more formal process may be needed. Frequently, a team is asked to develop recommendations based on analysis of data from Step 1 and consultation with outside experts.

- Target source of stress for change.

- Propose and prioritize intervention strategies.

- Communicate planned interventions to employees.

- Implement Interventions.

Certain problems, such as a hostile work environment, may be pervasive in the organization and require company-wide interventions. Other problems such as excessive workload may exist only in some departments and thus require more narrow solutions such as redesign of the way a job is performed. Still other problems may be specific to certain employees and resistant to any kind of organizational change, calling instead for stress management or employee assistance interventions. Some interventions might be implemented rapidly (e.g., improved communication, stress management training), but others may require additional time to put into place (e.g., redesign of a manufacturing process).

Step 3—Evaluate the Interventions. Evaluation is an essential step in the intervention process. Evaluation is necessary to determine whether the intervention is producing desired effects and whether changes in direction are needed.

444

Time frames for evaluating interventions should be established.

- Conduct both short- and long-term evaluations.
- Measure employee perceptions of job conditions, stress, health, and satisfaction.
- Include objective measures.
- Refine the intervention strategy and return to Step 1.

Interventions involving organizational change should receive both short- and long-term scrutiny. Short-term evaluations might be done quarterly to provide an early indication of program effectiveness or possible need for redirection. Many interventions produce initial effects that do not persist. Long-term evaluations are often conducted annually and are necessary to determine whether interventions produce lasting effects.

Evaluations should focus on the same types of information collected during the problem identification phase of the intervention, including information from employees about working conditions, levels of perceived stress, health problems, and satisfaction. Employee perceptions are usually the most sensitive measure of stressful working conditions and often provide the first indication of intervention effectiveness. Adding objective measures such as absenteeism and health care costs may also be useful. However, the effects of job stress interventions on such measures tend to be less clear-cut and can take a long time to appear.

The job stress prevention process does not end with evaluation. Rather, job stress prevention should be seen as a continuous process that uses evaluation data to refine or redirect the intervention strategy.

Section 43.2

Economic Hardship

This section includes excerpts from "Financial wellness at work,"
Consumer Financial Protection Bureau (CFPB), August 2014;
text from "Financial well-being: The goal of financial education,"
Consumer Financial Protection Bureau (CFPB), January 2015;
and text from "Your Money, Your Goals A financial empowerment
toolkit for workers," Consumer Financial Protection Bureau (CFPB),
April 2015.

Seven out of ten American workers say financial stress is their
most common cause of stress, and almost half (48%) say they find
dealing with their financial situation stressful. If an emergency
strikes, American workers and their families also have few resources
to fall back on. According to the 2012 FINRA Investor Education
Foundation's National Financial Capability Study, the percentage of
people with an emergency fund of at least three months of savings
increased five points between 2009 and 2012.That is good news, but
the challenge remains that 60% of households still have less than
three months of savings on hand. The Great Recession may have
elevated readings of financial stress, but the problem is not new.
Even when the economy was booming, financial stress was sapping
the productivity and hurting the health of millions of American
workers.

What financial well-being is

What emerged in the course of research is that financial well-being
describes a continuum— ranging from severe financial stress to being
highly satisfied with one's financial situation—not strictly aligned with
income level. For example, some people seem to have, and feel they
have, a high level of financial well-being, even though they may be
far from affluent. On the other hand, some people with much higher
incomes do not appear to have or feel they have a high level of financial
well-being at all. Moreover, through learning and effort, and given

reasonable opportunity and supports, it appears that people can move along the continuum to greater financial well-being.

> In summary, financial well-being can be defined as a state of being wherein a person can fully meet current and ongoing financial obligations, can feel secure in their financial future, and is able to make choices that allow enjoyment of life.

The definition of financial well-being is based on the consumer perspective and flows from the open-ended interviews conducted with a broadly diverse set of consumers across the United States, reinforced by interviews with financial practitioners. The specific individual goals and vision of a satisfying life differed greatly among respondents, yet there were two common themes that arose consistently: security and freedom of choice, in the present and in the future.

More specifically, analysis of the interview transcripts and discussion with the panel of experts suggests that the concept of financial well-being has four central elements:

- Having control over day-to-day, month-to-month finances;

- Having the capacity to absorb a financial shock;

- Being on track to meet your financial goals; and

- Having the financial freedom to make the choices that allow you to enjoy life.

These elements of financial well-being have strong time-frame dimensions: the first and fourth pertain mainly to one's present situation, and the second and third elements pertain to securing the future, as discussed below.

	Present	Future
Security	Control over your day-to-day, month-to-month finances	Capacity to absorb a financial shock
Freedom of choice	Financial freedom to make choices to enjoy life	On track to meet your financial goals

Figure 43.1. *Four Elements of Financial Well-being*

Having control over day-to-day, month-to-month finances

Individuals who have a relatively high level of financial well-being feel in control of their day-to-day financial lives. These individuals manage their finances; their finances do not manage them. Such individuals are able to cover expenses and pay bills on time, and do not worry about having enough money to get by. This is the aspect of financial well-being that was mentioned most frequently during the qualitative interviews.

Having the capacity to absorb a financial shock

Individuals who have a relatively high level of financial well-being also have the capacity to absorb a financial shock. Because of a combination of factors such as having a support system of family and friends, owning personal savings, and holding insurance of various types, their lives would not be up-ended if their car or home needed an emergency repair or if they were laid off temporarily from their job. They are able to cope with the financial challenges of unforeseen life events.

Being on track to meet your financial goals

Individuals experiencing financial well-being also say they are on track to meet their financial goals. They have a formal or informal financial plan, and they are actively working toward goals such as saving to buy a car or home, paying off student loans, or saving for retirement.

Having the financial freedom to make choices that allow you to enjoy life

Finally, individuals experiencing financial well-being perceive that they are able to make choices that allow them to enjoy life. They can splurge once in a while. They can afford "wants," such as being able to go out to dinner or take a vacation, in addition to meeting their "needs," and they are able to make choices such as to be generous toward their friends, family and community. This fourth element came through strongly in the interviews, and was not able in the variety of ways it was expressed. For example, financial freedom might mean being able to be generous with family, friends and community; or having the ability to go back to school or leave one job to look for a better one; or to go out to dinner or on vacation; or to work less to spend time with family. Because individuals value such different things, traditional measures such as income or net worth, while important, do not fully capture this aspect of the concept of financial well-being. It is these deeply personal preferences and aspirations that give meaning and purpose to the often challenging day-to-day financial decisions and tradeoffs we all must make to achieve it.

Financial empowerment can build economic stability

Sharing financial empowerment information and tools may feel like it's completely different than the work you normally do—one more thing you're being asked to add to your workload. But, once you become familiar with the tools, we believe it can become natural to integrate its information and tools into the work you do.

Paying bills and other expenses

It's a rule of thumb that to stay financially healthy you should spend less than you earn. But for some people, that rule of thumb may not feel helpful because they don't have enough income and financial resources to pay all their bills and living expenses. For others, balancing their personal priorities and their cultural expectations can create a challenge. And if your work is seasonal or irregular, you may be able to cover everything when you're working, but struggle to cover expenses in months or weeks when you're not.

Where does the money go?

No matter what your situation, it is important to start by understanding the differences among needs, obligations, and wants.

Needs are the things you must have to live. These include shelter and utilities, food, clothing, and transportation. The difficulty with needs, however, is that there is a wide range of options for shelter and utilities, food, clothing, and transportation. Determining what you can afford to get and maintain or sustain may be a challenge when it comes to needs.

Obligations are the things you must pay because you owe money or have been ordered to pay someone money. Debts are examples of obligations. Child support and alimony as well as judgments are also examples of obligations.

Wants are the things you can survive without. For example, while a reliable car to get to work is a need, a new car with expensive features is both a need and a want.

But, it's not always so clear-cut. One person may view something as a want, and another person may see it as a need.

Financial empowerment is about understanding your options and making choices that work for you. Being able to separate needs, obligations, and wants for yourself empowers you to set priorities and cut back on the things you decide are optional.

Many people who track their spending for a week or a month discover that they're spending money in small ways that add up and sometimes don't match their priorities. Once they track their spending, they're better able to make decisions about which bills and expenses can be reduced. To get a clear picture of how you use your money and resources now, use the spending tracker in *Tool 1* to get started.

Tool 1: Spending tracker

Whether they have a lot of money to spend or are struggling to make ends meet, most people can't tell you exactly how they spend their money during a month.

Before deciding on changes to your spending, it is a good idea to understand how you use your money now. This takes three steps and commitment:

- **Keep track of everything you spend money on for a week, two weeks, or one month**. A month is best, because all of your income and your bills will be included. But, keeping up with the tracking for a whole month can be a challenge.

- **Analyze your spending.** See how much you spend in each category. Notice trends. Identify areas you want to eliminate or cut back on.

- **Use this as information to figure out where you can make changes.**

It takes commitment, because this is a lot of work. But, it's important work. Many people are actually able to find money to save for emergencies, unexpected expenses, and goals by doing this work. Others are able to make their budgets balance.

Get a simple plastic case or envelope. Every time you spend money, get a receipt and put it into the case or envelope. If the receipt doesn't include what you purchased, take a few seconds and write this on the receipt. If you don't get a receipt, write one out on scrap paper.

Analyze your spending. Go through your receipts. Enter the total you spent and the date in the column that makes most sense to you. See how much you spend in each category and add the weekly amounts. Once you have these totals, add them together to get a total spending for the week. You can track your spending for one week, two weeks, or an entire month.

Create a worksheet as mentioned below and enter each amount from your receipts into its matching category column. Take care to make sure the entry also matches the correct date. Add each column. Add the total of all of the columns to get total spending for the week. Print and complete multiple copies of this sheet to analyze spending over the period of a month or longer.

Notice trends. Circle those items that are the same every month (for example, rent, car payment, cell phone payment). These are often

Table 43.1. Sample Worksheet: Week _____ for the Month of

Date of month	-	-	-	-	-	-	-	Total
Savings								
Debt payments								
Housing and Utilities								
Tools of the Trade / Job-Related Expenses								
Household supplies and expenses								
Groceries								
Eating out								
Pets								
Transportation								
Health care								
Personal care								
Childcare & school								
Entertainment								
Court-ordered obligations								
Gifts, donations, other								
Total								

your needs and obligations. This will make creating your budget easier. Identify areas you can eliminate or cut back on—these will generally be wants.

Here is a list of the categories used in the spending tracker:

Review your spending for the week or month. Which items *cannot* be cut or reduced? List these in the chart below. When you make your cash flow budget, you will just fill these in.

Table 43.2. Spending that cannot be cut

Spending that cannot be cut	Reason

Are there items that can be completely eliminated? If yes, the money you spend on these items can be used on other things like saving for emergencies or goals or paying down debt.

Table 43.3. Spending that can be eliminated

Spending that can be eliminated	Steps to eliminate

Once you have tracked your spending, be sure to add it into your budget or cash flow budget.

If you are trying to make ends meet or find money to save you may also want to cut back on the money and financial resources going to bills and living expenses. When this is the case, the key is to identify which bills and expenses can be cut.

Planning for and paying bills

Many people have recurring obligations like rent, utilities, car payments, child support payments, and insurance payments. Most of these obligations have a fixed due date, and if you are late, even by just a few days, you will likely pay an extra fee and risk a negative entry in your credit history. It can help you avoid late fees and other consequences of late or nonpayment if you can:

- Write down the regular bills you have

- Set up a bill paying calendar so you can visually see when payments are due

If you use a smartphone, text messaging, or e-mail, you might prefer to explore bill reminder services and apps. These services can send you reminders when it's time to pay your bills.

Another part of bill payment is *how* bills are paid. In general, you can pay your bills using:

- Cash

- Money orders

- Checks

- Credit cards

- Automatic debit

- Online bill payment

If you prefer to pay your bills in cash, you'll have to travel to a payment location – which costs you time and money for gas. If you have a checking account and have set up automatic bill payment, you'll save time, but you'll need to ensure that you have money in the account on the day the automatic payment is made. Otherwise, you'll probably have to pay an overdraft fee.

Unexpected expenses

Managing unexpected and periodic expenses can put a strain on your budget. Here are some examples of **unexpected expenses**:

- Fees for a school field trip for one of your children

- Tools of the trade you did not anticipate needing to buy

- The funeral of a friend or family member in another state

- Car or home repairs

- Health-care related expenses resulting from illness or injury.

Periodic expenses are different. These are expenses that happen occasionally. They are often predictable, but they can be hard to manage if you do not plan for them. Common periodic expenses include:

- Car insurance payments

- Life insurance payments

- Renter's insurance

- Income taxes (if you owe money)

- Property taxes

- Holiday-related expenses

- Health-care related co-payments (not related to illness or injury)

Bill calendar

Bills are a fact of life and—while they are not fun to pay—most are at least predictable.

Figuring out which bills you expect throughout the month can be helpful in a couple of ways. It helps you to plan to have enough money or other financial resources on hand to pay them. Thinking about the amounts and timing of your bills might also help you think of ways to reduce your expenses over the course of the month. Finally, some people find that thinking ahead about their bills helps reduce the stress of being surprised when they arrive in the mail.

Create a bill calendar using the following tool:

- Print the bill calendar and fill in the name of the month and year.

- Add numbers to represent the days of the month. Start with this week as the first week.

- Gather all of the bills you pay in one month OR use the information from your spending tracker.

- Write the due dates for these bills. Since due dates are when bills must arrive, write the date bills must be sent:

- If paying by mail, mark the due date at least 7 days before it is due.

- For in-person or automatic bill payment, mark one or two days before the due date to ensure you are not late.

- Fill in the calendar with the business or person you owe the money to, the date the money must be sent to arrive on time, and the amount that is due.

Put this calendar somewhere you will see it every day to ensure you are not forgetting about important bills.

Here is a sample week to show you how the tool works:

Once you become comfortable with this tool, you may want to explore online bill reminder services or apps that help keep you on track for paying your bills on time.

Table 43.5. Sample Bill Calendar for a Week

Sun.	Mon.	Tue.	Wed.	Thu.	Fri.	Sat.	End of Week
1	2	3	4	5	6	7	
Bills:	Bills: Phone Bill, $60 Rent $500	Bills:	Bills:	Bills:	Bills: Car Payment: $180	Bills:	Total Bills for Week: $740

How much debt is too much?

One way to know if you have too much debt is based on how much stress your debt causes you. If you are worried about your debt, you may have too much.

A more objective way to measure debt is the debt-to-income ratio. The debt-to-income ratio compares the amount of money you pay out each month for debt payments to your income before taxes and other deductions. The resulting number, a percentage, shows you how much of your income is dedicated to debt—your debt load. The higher the percentage, the less financially secure you may be, because you have less left over to cover everything else. Everything else is all of the other needs, wants, and obligations you pay each month that are not debt.

Debt-to-income ratio

The debt-to-income ratio is a simple calculation:

Total of your monthly debt payments ÷ Monthly gross income (income before taxes).

The result is a percentage that tells you how much of your income is going toward covering your debt. For example, if you have a debt-to-income ratio of 36%, you have 64 cents out of every dollar you earn to pay for everything else, including all of your living expenses and taxes.

Medical debt

For many Americans, medical debt comprises a large amount of the money they owe. Forty one percent of working age adults in America reported having trouble paying for medical bills in 2012.

Medical debt has increasingly been a major factor in decline in credit scores for some individuals. And medical debt is becoming a greater factor in the reason people file for bankruptcy—they could make ends meet were it not for their medical debts. The majority of individuals who filed for bankruptcy due to medical debt had health insurance.

Finally, once people have medical debt, they are much less likely to seek medical care—whether preventative or prescriptive. This can increase the amount they have to spend on treatment, because by the time they get medical care, the situation has become more acute and, therefore, more expensive to address.

What are the factors that can lead to medical debt?

Medical debt is almost always the result of an unplanned event—someone becoming ill or injured. Even with health insurance, co-pays and deductibles can add up. This is one reason that emergency savings is important for building financial stability.

Secondly, the costs of the care are almost never fully known upfront. Unlike the cost of a house or car, where you should know what you will pay when you sign the loan agreement, when you accept responsibility for payment of your treatment at a hospital or other medical provider, you generally have no idea how much the treatment will cost. You may also not know your share of the cost.

Invoices and bills may be confusing. Rather than one itemized bill, you may receive several bills over a period of weeks or months with hospital stays or situations that involved multiple health care services providers. Because of this confusion, people may be more likely to not recognize the information contained on the invoice or hesitate or delay paying a medical bill.

They may have questions about whether the amount was already paid by insurance, whether the correct amount was billed, or whether they actually received the billed treatment.

And without knowing how much the total cost should be, how much the insurer will cover, and how much of the cost will be passed on to you, it becomes difficult to determine whether you are being charged the right amount. That leaves consumers in a position where they need to review each medical bill carefully and contact providers or insurers when they have questions.

Uninsured individuals are generally charged more for services. Insurance companies negotiate discounts for services. This means that if you are uninsured, your bill will likely be higher than the bill that someone who has insurance receives for the same procedures and care.

So what can you do to avoid medical debt?

While there are no easy answers, there are specific things you may be able to do to lessen the impact of medical debt:

- **Get cost estimates up front**—then you can decide whether to proceed or delay elective procedures.

- **Find out whether there is a prompt payment discount**, which can be substantial. This may mean cutting back in other areas for a few months in order to pay the bill and secure the discount.

- **Ask for a discount on the treatment.**

- **Ask about "charity care"** from the hospital and government before or immediately following treatment.

- **If you are asked to put a hospital bill on a credit card, watch out.** Many hospitals have some obligation to provide for charity care for those who can't afford treatment. Once you put your hospital bill on a credit card, you won't be considered for a later write-down of your bill under the charity care program. Some medical providers even offer a credit card for you to use at the provider's office. Healthcare credit cards can have tricky terms, so make sure you know what you're getting into. For tips on healthcare credit cards see: http://www.consumerfinance.gov/blog/whats-the-deal-with-health-care-credit-cards-four-things-you-should-know/.

- If you can't afford to pay for the care even after charity care and discounts have been applied, **take steps to work with the provider to set up a reasonablerepayment plan.** As you negotiate, ensure that as long as you pay as agreed, reports made to credit reporting agencies will reflect that you are making payments as required by the plan. Be sure to get your repayment plan agreement in writing. Ask that the account will not be sent to collections as long as you are paying as agreed. Also, consider asking for the following terms:

- No interest on the debt

- Monthly statements showing the amount paid and the outstanding balance

- Request that the debt *not* be turned over to a third party collection agency – that the debt servicing stays in-house

- Be sure you do not sign an agreement that states you will make full payment of the debt if you are late or miss a payment on your plan.

- **Check your credit report** to make sure resolved bills are reported accurately or any errors are removed from your credit history. If the credit reporting agency doesn't respond, contact you state's consumer protection agency, attorney general, or the Consumer Financial Protection Bureau.

- If you do get sued by a medical service provider or hospital, *respond*. Get legal assistance from the legal aid organization in your community or a lawyer.

Be sure you do not jeopardize your ability to earn income or pay for your shelter or food because you have paid more income than you can afford to cover a medical debt.

Section 43.3

Caregiver Stress

Text in this section is excerpted from "Get Support If You Are a Caregiver," Office of Disease Prevention and Health Promotion (ODPHP), July 15, 2015.

When you are taking care of a loved one, make time to care for yourself, too. The emotional and physical stress of caregiving can cause health problems.

What is a caregiver?

A caregiver is someone who helps a family member, friend, or neighbor who is sick or has a disability. An informal or family caregiver often helps a loved one with basic daily tasks.

You may be a caregiver if you regularly help someone with:

- Grocery shopping
- Housework
- Getting dressed
- Taking and keeping track of medicine
- Using medical equipment
- Cooking food
- Transportation, like car rides to appointments
- Managing services, like talking to doctors

About 1 in 4 Americans is a caregiver. Most caregivers have other jobs and spend at least 20 hours a week caring for a loved one.

The stress of caregiving can hurt your health.

When you are caring for a loved one, it can be hard to take care of your own health. Caregivers are more at risk for colds and the flu. They are also more likely to have long-term health problems, like arthritis, diabetes, or depression.

Here are some signs you may have caregiver stress:

- Feeling angry or sad
- Feeling like it's more than you can handle
- Feeling like you don't have time to care for yourself
- Sleeping too much or too little
- Having trouble eating, or eating too much
- Losing interest in things you used to enjoy

The good news is that you can lower your risk for health problems if you take care of yourself and get support.

Take Action!

Take these steps to lower the stress of caregiving.

Take care of yourself.

Caregiving can be stressful. Stress can lead to problems like back pain and trouble sleeping. Taking care of yourself will give you the energy and strength to handle the demands of caregiving.

Take care of your body.

- Eat healthy to keep your body strong. Making smart food choices will help protect you from heart disease, bone loss, and high blood pressure.

- Get active to help you make it through the day. Aim for 2 hours and 30 minutes a week of moderate aerobic activity, like walking fast or dancing.

- Take steps to prevent back pain, like keeping your back straight and bending your knees when you lift something heavy.

- Make sure you get enough sleep. Most adults need 7 to 8 hours of sleep each night.

Take care of your mental health.

- Find ways to manage stress. Start by taking a few slow, deep breaths.

- Do something for yourself. Set aside time each day to do something you enjoy. Try reading, listening to music, or talking to a friend.

- Ask a neighbor to visit with your loved one while you take a walk.

- Get support from others to help you cope with the emotional stress of caregiving.

Ask for help.

You don't need to do it all yourself. Ask family members, friends, and neighbors to share caregiving tasks.

It's also a good idea to find out about professional and volunteer services that can help. If you are feeling overwhelmed, talk with a doctor about depression.

Section 43.4

Holiday Stress

Text in this section is excerpted from "Seven Ways to Manage Stress during the Holidays," U.S. Department of Veterans Affairs (VA), May 11, 2015.

Family, friends, fun, and food: holidays can be the best of times. But they're also stressful times, full of demands and deadlines.

"Stress during any time of year can become a problem and affect your health when it goes on for too long or feels overwhelming," says Dr. Peg Dundon. Dundon is the National Program Manager for Health Behavior at VA's National Center for Health Promotion and Disease Prevention (NCP).

Use these seven tips to de-stress during the holidays and year-round:

1. Get physical—Take a brisk walk or be physically active in another way. Regular activity is best. Even a 10-minute chunk of active time can help!

2. Be part of the solution—Learn problem-solving skills. They can improve your ability to cope. Your VA medical center may offer a class or information session. A web-based problem-solving program called "Moving Forward" is also available at www.veterantraining.va.gov.

3. Learn to relax—Discover relaxation and mindfulness skills. They can help you manage stress and even protect you from it.

4. Express yourself—Keeping your thoughts bottled up can increase stress. So speak up in respectful ways. Sharing thoughts and feelings in a polite yet firm manner can help reduce stress.

5. Manage Your Time—List what needs to get done, make plans for addressing issues, and stick to the plan as best you can.

6. Use positive power—Stress often is associated with negative, self-critical thinking. Focus your attention on positive thoughts about yourself and others.

7. Enjoy Yourself—Despite extra pressures from busy schedules, it's important to take time for yourself. Plan something you enjoy.

Section 43.5

Survivors of a Disaster or Other Traumatic Event

Text in this section is excerpted from "Tips for Survivors of a Disaster or Other Traumatic Event," Substance Abuse and Mental Health Administration (SAMHSA), September 18, 2013.

If you were involved in a disaster such as a hurricane, flood, or even terrorism, or another traumatic event like a car crash, you may be affected personally regardless of whether you were hurt or lost a loved one. You can be affected just by witnessing a disaster or other traumatic event. It is common to show signs of stress after exposure to a disaster or other traumatic event, and it is important to monitor your physical and emotional health.

Possible Reactions to a Disaster or Other Traumatic Event

Try to identify your early warning signs of stress. Stress usually shows up in the four areas shown below, but everyone should check for ANY unusual stress responses after a disaster or other traumatic event. Below are some of the most common reactions.

After the Event

Managing Your Tasks

If you've been involved in a disaster or other traumatic event, a number of tasks likely require your attention fairly urgently. First, make sure you are not injured, as sometimes survivors don't realize they've been physically hurt until many hours later. If you realize

You May

Feel Emotionally:	Have Behavioral Reactions, Such as:
• Anxious or fearful • Overwhelmed by sadness • Angry, especially if the event involved violence • Guilty, even when you had no control over the traumatic event • Heroic, like you can do anything • Like you have too much energy or no energy at all • Disconnected, not caring about anything or anyone • Numb, unable to feel either joy or sadness	• Having trouble falling asleep, staying asleep, sleeping too much, or trouble relaxing • Noticing an increase or decrease in your energy and activity levels • Feeling sad or crying frequently • Using alcohol, tobacco, illegal drugs or even prescription medication in an attempt to reduce distressing feelings or to forget • Having outbursts of anger, feeling really irritated and blaming other people for everything • Having difficulty accepting help or helping others • Wanting to be alone most of the time and isolating yourself
Have Physical Reactions, Such as:	Experience Problems in Your Thinking, Such as:
• Having stomachaches or diarrhea • Having headaches or other physical pains for no clear reason • Eating too much or too little • Sweating or having chills • Getting tremors (shaking) or muscle twitches • Being jumpy or easily startled	• Having trouble remembering things • Having trouble thinking clearly and concentrating • Feeling confused • Worrying a lot • Having difficulty making decisions • Having difficulty talking about what happened or listening to others

Figure 43.2. *Most Common Reactions to Disaster or Traumatic Event*

you've been injured, seek medical treatment before you do anything else. If you need to find a safe place to stay, work on that task next. Make sure to let a family member or friend know where you are and how to reach you. Secure your identification and any other papers you may need, such as insurance, bank, property, and medical records. Completing one task at a time may help you feel like you are gaining back some control, so make a list of the most important things you need to do. Remember to be patient with yourself. Take deep breaths or gently stretch to calm yourself before you tackle each task. Plan to do something relaxing after working for a while.

Practical Tips for Relieving Stress

These stress management activities seem to work well for most people. Use the ones that work for you.

Talk with others who understand and accept how you feel. Reach out to a trusted friend, family member, or faith-based leader to explore what meaning the event may have for you. Connect with other survivors of the disaster or other traumatic events and share your experience.

Body movement helps to get rid of the buildup of extra stress hormones. Exercise once daily or in smaller amounts throughout the day. Be careful not to lift heavy weights. You can damage your muscles if you have too much adrenaline in your system. If you don't like exercise, do something simple, like taking a walk, gently stretching, or meditating.

463

Take deep breaths. Most people can benefit from taking several deep breaths often throughout the day. Deep breathing can move stress out of your body and help you to calm yourself. It can even help stop a panic attack.

Listen to music. Music is a way to help your body relax naturally. Play music timed to the breath or to your heartbeat. Create a relaxing playlist for yourself and listen to it often.

Pay attention to your physical self. Make sure to get enough sleep and rest each day. Don't leave resting for the weekend. Eat healthy meals and snacks and make sure to drink plenty of water. Avoid caffeine, tobacco, and alcohol, especially in large amounts. Their effects are multiplied under stress and can be harmful, just making things worse.

Use known coping skills. How did you handle past traumatic events like a car crash or the death of a loved one? What helped then (e.g., spent time with family, went to a support group meeting)? Try using those coping skills now.

When Your Stress Is Getting the Best of You

Know that distressing feelings about a disaster or traumatic event usually fade over time (2–4 weeks after the event) as you get back to routines—and especially if you have engaged in some ways to help yourself. Try to use some of these tips several times a week.

If you or someone you care about continues to show signs of stress and you are becoming concerned about him or her, you may want to reach out for some extra help.

Chapter 44

Other Stress Management Strategies

Chapter Contents

Section 44.1

Abdominal Breathing

Text in this section is excerpted from "Abdominal Breathing,"
Mental Illness Research, Education and Clinical Centers (MIRECC),
July 2013.

What is Abdominal Breathing?

The goal of breath-focused relaxation is to shift from quick, shallow chest breathing to deeper, more relaxed abdominal breathing. During times of stress, our natural tendency is to either hold our breath, or to breathe in a shallow, rapid manner. When we are relaxed our breathing is naturally slower and deeper. When stress is chronic, we may habitually breathe shallowly, never really discharging the stale air from our lungs. Holding in your stomach for reasons of vanity also restricts breathing. In order to take a full deep breath, we must allow our diaphragm (the muscle separating our chest cavity from the abdominal cavity below the lungs) to drop down and our abdomen to expand. If we keep our stomach muscles held in tight when we breathe, we restrict the expansion of our lungs and rob our bodies of optimal oxygen. This puts our bodies in a state of alarm that creates the sensation of anxiety. Taking a few slow, deep breaths sends the signal to our body to relax. Deep breathing is also referred to as abdominal breathing, diaphragmatic breathing, or belly breathing. Abdominal breathing is a form of relaxation that you can use any time to help you to calm yourself physically and mentally and in turn, decrease stress.

Instructions for Learning Abdominal Breathing

1. Place one hand, palm side down, on your chest. Place the other hand, palm side down, on your stomach.

2. Breathe in through your nose to a slow count of 3 or 4 (one ... two ...three... four...). Notice the motion of each hand. When you breathe in, does the hand on your chest move? If so, which way does it move (out/up or in/down) and how much does it

move? Does the hand on your stomach move? If so, which way (out or in) and how much?

3. Now exhale through your nose, again to a slow count of 3 or 4. Notice again how each of your hands moves.

For the most relaxing breath, the hand on your chest should move very little while the hand on your stomach pushes out significantly on the inhale (in breath) and goes back in on the exhale (out breath). A common problem is for the chest to inflate on the in breath while the stomach stays still or even sucks in. When this happens, only the upper part of the lungs (the part behind the upper chest) is being used. When a full deep breath is properly taken, the diaphragm muscle drops down into the abdominal cavity to make room for the lungs to expand. As the diaphragm muscle drops down, it pushes the organs in the abdomen forward to make more room for the lungs. That is why the stomach goes out when you take the most relaxing type of breath.

Learning to take abdominal breaths versus chest breathing is a challenge for some people. The following tips can make it easier.

- Imagine yourself filling a medium-sized balloon in your stomach each time you inhale and releasing the air in the balloon when you exhale.

- Breathe in the same amount of air you breathe out.

- It is sometimes easier to first learn abdominal breathing while lying on your back with your hand on your stomach. It is easier to feel the stomach motion in this position versus sitting or standing.

- It is best to only practice a few deep breaths at a time at first. This is because deep breathing can make you feel light headed if you aren't used to it. If you begin to feel light headed, it is just your body's signal that it has had enough practice for now. Return to your normal breathing and practice again later. With practice, you will be able to take a greater number of deep breaths without becoming light headed.

- Start practicing this deep breathing technique when you are calm so you have mastered it and are ready to use it when you are stressed.

Key Points

- Abdominal breathing can help you achieve a state of relaxation because it has both meditative (mentally calming) and sedating (physically calming) qualities.

- Try not to get frustrated by "Worry" or "To-Do" thoughts that enter your head while you're relaxing. Gently let these thoughts pass and return to the task at hand. Focusing on your deep breathing will help you. Sometimes, it also helps to "place" busy thoughts on an imaginary conveyor belt like those found at the airport – eventually your thought luggage will come back round where you can pick it up after your relaxation trip. Or, mentally set your concerns on a shelf until you are ready to address them.

- Practice this type of breathing for about 5 minutes, one or more times a day, most days of the week.

- Learning to focus on one of the most calming processes in the body, namely your breathing, is one of the most reliable ways to achieve a relaxed state!

- This is a great relaxation exercise to learn because you can do it anywhere, anytime you want to take the edge off your anxiety stress level.

- It is normal for this new method of breathing to feel awkward at first. With practice it will feel more natural.

Longer Relaxation Exercises

Deep breathing can be expanded into a longer relaxation exercise as well. Two examples are given below:

Three-Part Rhythmic Breathing

Inhale … hold the breath … and then exhale … with the inhale, hold, and exhale each being of equal length. Inhale and exhale completely using the entire length of the lungs. Keep your shoulders and face relaxed while you hold your breath. Use a count that is comfortable for you. Repeat five times.

Breathing with Imagery

For about 30 seconds, simply relax with your eyes closed. Then start to pay attention to your breathing. Let your breathing become slow and relaxed, like a person sleeping. Feel the air entering thorough your nose with each inhalation, and feel your breath leave as you exhale. Imagine the tension is leaving your body with each out breath.

Now imagine that, as you breathe in, the air comes into your nose and caresses your face like a gentle breeze. As you breathe out, the exhalation carries away the tension from your face. As you breathe slowly in and out, tension gradually leaves your body and you become more and more relaxed.

Now imagine that, as you breathe in, the gentle air enters your nose and spreads relaxation up over the top of your head. As you exhale, imagine the tension leaving this area and passing out of our body. Then imagine the next breath carrying relaxation over your face, your scalp, and both sides of your head. As you exhale, let any tension flow out easily.

If other thoughts come to mind, simply return to paying attention to your breathing. Your breathing is slow and easy, with no effort at all. Let your body relax.

Now let your breath carry relaxation to your neck. As you exhale, tension passes out of your neck and out of your body with the exhaled air. Feel a breath carry relaxation into your shoulders. As you exhale, any tension leaves your shoulders and passes out of your body.

Now one breath at a time, focus your attention on each part of your body from the top down: your upper arms, forearms, hands, chest, back, stomach, hips, thighs, knees, calves, ankles, and feet. Imagine each breath of air carrying relaxation into each part of your body. As you breathe out, let any tension pass out through your nostrils.

This exercise takes several minutes. Do it at your own pace. When you have finished, sit quietly for a minute or two more.

Section 44.2

Pet Ownership Reduces Stress

Text in this section is excerpted from "Health Benefits of Pets,"
Centers for Disease Control and Prevention (CDC), April 30, 2014;
and text from "Dogs and PTSD," U.S. Department of Veterans
Affairs, August 14, 2015.

Most households in the United States have at least one pet. Why do people have pets? There are many reasons. Some of the health benefits of pets are listed below.

Pets can decrease your:

- Blood pressure

- Cholesterol levels

- Triglyceride levels

- Feelings of loneliness

Pets can increase your:

- Opportunities for exercise and outdoor activities

- Opportunities for socialization

- Many groups support the health benefits of pet ownership.

Dogs

Many studies show the health benefits of dog ownership. Dogs not only provide comfort and companionship, but several studies have found that dogs decrease stress and promote relaxation. Dogs have positive impacts on nearly all life stages. They influence social, emotional, and cognitive development in children, promote an active lifestyle, and have even been able to detect oncoming epileptic seizures or the presence of certain cancers.

Dogs and PTSD

Owning a dog can lift your mood or help you feel less stressed. Dogs can help people feel better by providing companionship. All dog owners, including those who have post-traumatic stress disorder (PTSD) can experience these benefits.

Clinically, there is not enough research yet to know if dogs actually help treat PTSD and its symptoms. Evidence-based therapies and medications for PTSD are supported by research. We encourage you to learn more about these treatments because it is difficult to draw strong conclusions from the few studies on dogs and PTSD that have been done.

What are the emotional benefits of having a dog?

Dogs can make great pets. Having a dog as a pet can benefit anyone who likes dogs, including people with PTSD. For example, dogs:

- Help bring out feelings of love.

- Are good companions.

- Take orders well when trained. This can be very comfortable for a Servicemember or Veteran who was used to giving orders in the military.

- Are fun and can help reduce stress.

- Are a good reason to get out of the house, spend time outdoors, and meet new people.

Recovering from PTSD

Recovering from PTSD is a process. Evidence-based treatments for PTSD help people do things they have been avoiding because of their PTSD, such as standing close to a stranger or going into a building without scanning it for danger first. Evidence-based treatments can also help people feel better. Dogs can help you deal with some parts of living with PTSD, but they are not a substitute for effective PTSD treatment.

Although people with PTSD who have a service dog for a physical disability or emotional support dog may feel comforted by the animal, there is some chance they may continue to believe that they cannot do certain things on their own. For example, if the dog keeps strangers from coming too close, the owner will not have a chance to learn that they can handle this situation without the dog. Becoming dependent on a dog can get in the way of the recovery process for PTSD. Based on what we know from research, evidence-based treatment provides the best chance of recovery from PTSD.

Section 44.3

Mindfulness Practice in the Treatment of Traumatic Stress

Text in this section is excerpted from "Mastering Mindfulness,"
NOAA Workforce Management Office (WFMO), April 2015.

Mindfulness is the practice of becoming fully aware of your surroundings and engaging yourself in the present. Doing so can often open your eyes to a new perspective.

Additionally, mindfulness heightens consciousness of your thoughts and feelings without labeling or judging them. Let's explore some of the main tenets of being mindful.

Deliberately paying attention

First, mindfulness involves purposefully being aware of yourself and your behaviors. Attaching purpose to what you experience helps you sharpen your mind and avoid thoughtlessly going through the motions.

Awareness of the present moment

As your mind wanders throughout the day, you typically think about the past or future—not the present. Distancing yourself from thoughts concerning the past or the future allows you to embrace the present moment as you experience it fully.

Avoiding judgment

Mindlessly judging others can become a habit. By removing judgment of whether experiences—or people—are good or bad can help you appreciate how and why people behave the way they do. Being mindful involves observing and accepting whatever happens without attachment or an emotional reaction.

The Benefits of Being Mindful

Practicing mindfulness can produce various benefits for your physical and emotional health, along with your relationships with others. Here are a few advantages of establishing a more mindful state:

Greater appreciation of the present

Savoring life's simple pleasures is easier when you're living in the moment. Mindfulness allows you to be more engaged in your everyday activities—and better equipped to handle adversity. So, enjoy the present and learn to worry less about the future or the past.

Stress reduction

Practicing mindful behaviors, including meditation and yoga, can bolster your positive disposition while lowering anxiety and stress. Mindfulness can help you focus on becoming aware of life's stressors and observing your responses.

Improved memory and concentration

Mindfulness may strengthen your memory and focus, too. A 2013 study by University of California, Santa Barbara, found students who took a mindfulness-training course prior to taking the Graduate Record Examinations (GRE) had improved working memory capacities, heightened focus, and better reading comprehension scores than their peers.

Strengthened relationships

Being skilled at handling stress in life can also help you respond to disturbances in your relationships. Mindfulness can keep you from becoming reactive and judgmental toward your partner or coworker, for example.

Mind Exercises Made Easy

It takes almost no time to implement mindfulness into your daily life, but the impact can be profound. Try the following exercises to conveniently work mindfulness into your routine.

Mindful meditation: Find a place free from distractions, clear your mind, and bring yourself to a relaxed posture. Then, slowly exhale, leaving a slight pause before inhaling. Inhale and pause again as you finish before exhaling. Continue this cycle. As you breathe, visualize an inspiring image and let all other thoughts float away. Be sure to take your time transitioning back to your regular day.

Deep breathing: If you don't have time to meditate, simply focus on your breath. Breathe in through your nose and out through your mouth. Inhale deeply into your belly—not just your chest. Concentrating on deep breathing can have a soothing effect and keep you cognizant of the present moment.

Still stressed?

If you'd like more help managing the stress in your life, seek support from your Employee Assistance Program (EAP) for a FREE expert consultation. Contact a program specialist 24/7 for assistance in improving your emotional health so you can feel more balanced and centered.

For more information on how you can become more mindful, or for help improving your emotional well-being or reducing stress, call your EAP today and speak to a specialist.

Live in the Moment

Life's short. Why not make the most of it? As you have likely experienced, sometimes life gets hectic— even chaotic. Learning to step back and be fully present in the here and now can have an overwhelmingly positive impact. From less stress, to better memory and focus, to savoring life's simple joys, mindfulness can serve your mind, body, and soul.

The Employee Assistance Program (EAP) can help you find your inner balance and improve your sense of well-being through:

In-person, short-term counseling from licensed EAP counselors. (1-800-222-0364)

Online information and interactive tools on topics such as: coping with stress and anxiety, self-improvement, emotional concerns, and other useful topics.

Section 44.4

Social Support: Who Can Give It and How to Get It

Text in this section is excerpted from "Peer Support Groups," U.S. Department of Veterans Affairs, August 14, 2015; and text from "Social Connections and Healthy Aging," Federal Occupational Health (FOH), 2014.

Peer support groups are a place where you can discuss day-to-day problems with other people who have been through trauma. Support groups have not been shown to reduce PTSD symptoms, but they can help you feel better in other ways. Because they can give you a sense of connection to other people, a peer support group could be a great addition to your treatment, or something you do after you finish an evidence-based treatment (PDF) for PTSD. Support groups can also help family members or friends who are caring for someone with PTSD.

Remember, if you are suffering from PTSD, is it important that you get treatment for PTSD as well. An evidence-based treatment provides the best chance of recovery from PTSD.

What are peer support groups like?

Peer support groups are led by someone like you who has been through a trauma. Groups often meet in person, but many groups also provide online (Internet) support.

Sharing your story with others may help you feel more comfortable talking about your trauma. Or it may help to listen to other people talk about their experiences with a similar trauma. Peer support groups can help you cope with memories of the trauma or other parts of your life that you are having trouble dealing with as a result of the event. You may learn to deal with emotions such as anger, shame, guilt, and fear if you open up to others who understand.

When you connect with other people it can help you feel better. You can work together with others to get better at talking about your PTSD or learning how to ask for help when you need it. You might even share some of the materials from this website to help others.

What are the benefits of joining a peer support group?

Joining a peer support group can help you to feel better in any number of ways, such as:

- Knowing that others are going through something similar
- Learning tips on how to handle day-to-day challenges
- Meeting new friends or connecting to others who understand you
- Learning how to talk about things that bother you or how to ask for help
- Learning to trust other people
- Hearing about helpful new perspectives from others

Peer support groups can be an important part of dealing with PTSD, but they are not a substitute for effective treatment for PTSD. If you have problems after a trauma that last more than a short time, you should get professional help.

How can I find a peer support group?

Here are some ideas to help you find a peer support group that can help you deal with PTSD or a traumatic experience:

- Do an online search for "PTSD support groups" or for a group that relates to the specific trauma you experienced, like "disaster support groups."
- Anxiety and Depression Association of America offers a list of support groups across the country for a number of different mental health conditions, including PTSD.
- Sidran Institute Help Desk locates support groups for people who have experienced trauma. Sidran does not offer clinical care or counseling services, but can help you locate care or support.
- National Alliance for Mental Illness (NAMI) Information Help-Line provides support, referral and information on mental illness care. You may also find family support groups in a NAMI state or local affiliate online or by calling 1-800-950-NAMI (6264).

Are there resources specific to Veterans and their families?

If you are a Veteran, or are a caregiver or family member of a Veteran, there are resources to help you deal with specific concerns:

- If you feel that you or your Veteran is in crisis, contact the Veterans Crisis Line: 1-800-273-8255 and press "1." You can also use the online chat, email, or texting service of the Veterans Crisis Line for immediate needs.

- Call the 24/7 Veteran Combat Call Center 1-877-WAR-VETS (1-877-927-8387) to talk to another combat Veteran, or visit the Vet Center homepage to ask about local support groups.

- The VA Caregiver Support Line provides services and support to family members who are taking care of a Veteran. Call 1-855-260-3274 or visit VA Caregiver Support.

- If you are a Veteran who wants to share your knowledge and experience with other Veterans dealing with mental health conditions, learn about VA's Peer Specialist and Peer Support Apprentice positions.

- Defense Centers of Excellence (DCoE) Outreach Center provides 24/7 information on psychological health and traumatic brain injury. Consultants can help you locate community resources by phone (1-866-966-1020) or email.

- For children with parents who have deployed, the Department of Defense created MilitaryKidsConnect (MKC), an online resource for kids to find information and support.

Keeping up with friends, family, and other social connections—and making new ones—can be important to your overall quality of life and feelings of well-being, especially as you age.

While social networks may get smaller as you grow older, it's important that you maintain and seek out, when possible, connections with those who can help you feel cared for and valued.

Social connections and health

More and more studies are finding the importance of social engagement for good health as we age. For example, recent research has found a connection between the psychological stress caused by depression and an increased risk for death and disability. Positive social interaction has been shown to be an antidote for this type of stress. A link has also been found between the distress of being socially isolated and poor health. In addition, research on adults 60 years and older has found a connection between feeling lonely and a declining ability to perform activities of daily living, as well an increased risk of death.

Stay connected

Relationships and social support are a key part of healthy aging. In fact, staying connected and socially involved can help to protect you from feelings of isolation, loneliness, and depression. Being socially engaged may also ward off poor health and ultimately help you maintain your overall well-being. Various studies have shown that older adults who participate in activities they find meaningful often report feeling healthier and happier.

Here are some activities that can help you stay connected to others:

- Phone a friend or loved one
- Join a walking or exercise group
- Participate in activities at your local community center
- Visit friends and family
- Go dancing
- Sign up for a class
- Join a senior center
- Form or join a book club
- Get involved with your local place of worship
- Play cards and other games with friends
- Go to a theater, movie, or sporting event
- Take short trips with an organized group

Go outside yourself

Consider volunteering at a hospital, library, or other organization. Volunteering with friends or loved ones can add to the benefit. This can give you a chance to do something meaningful for your community while bonding with someone close to you. Volunteering is a simple act of serving that allows you to give of yourself—and go outside yourself.

Being socially connected can make a difference in your life and your health.

Chapter 45

Stress Management for Children, Teens, and Families

Chapter Contents

Section 45.1

Childhood Traumatic Stress Management

This section includes excerpts from "Recognizing and Treating Child Traumatic Stress," Substance Abuse and Mental Health Services Administration (SAMHSA), June 8, 2015; text from "Coping with Disaster," Federal Emergency Management Agency (FEMA), January 31, 2015; and text from "Don't Leave Childhood Depression Untreated," U.S. Food and Drug Administration (FDA), September 10, 2014.

Types of Traumatic Events

Childhood traumatic stress occurs when violent or dangerous events overwhelm a child's or adolescent's ability to cope.

Traumatic events may include:

- Neglect and psychological, physical, or sexual abuse

- Natural disasters, terrorism, and community and school violence

- Witnessing or experiencing intimate partner violence

- Commercial sexual exploitation

- Serious accidents, life-threatening illness, or sudden or violent loss of a loved one

- Refugee and war experiences

- Military family-related stressors, such as parental deployment, loss, or injury

In one nationally representative sample of young people ages 12 to 17:

- 8% reported a lifetime prevalence of sexual assault

- 17% reported physical assault

- 39% reported witnessing violence

Also, many reported experiencing multiple and repeated traumatic events.

482

It is important to learn how traumatic events affect children. The more you know, the more you will understand the reasons for certain behaviors and emotions and be better prepared to help children and their families cope.

Signs of Child Traumatic Stress

The signs of traumatic stress are different in each child. Young children react differently than older children.

Preschool Children

- Fearing separation from parents or caregivers
- Crying and/or screaming a lot
- Eating poorly and losing weight
- Having nightmares

Elementary School Children

- Becoming anxious or fearful
- Feeling guilt or shame
- Having a hard time concentrating
- Having difficulty sleeping

Middle and High School Children

- Feeling depressed or alone
- Developing eating disorders and self-harming behaviors
- Beginning to abuse alcohol or drugs
- Becoming sexually active

For some children, these reactions can interfere with daily life and their ability to function and interact with others.

Impact of Child Traumatic Stress

The impact of child traumatic stress can last well beyond childhood. In fact, research shows that child trauma survivors are more likely to have:

- Learning problems, including lower grades and more suspensions and expulsions

- Increased use of health services, including mental health services

- Increased involvement with the child welfare and juvenile justice systems

- Long term health problems, such as diabetes and heart disease

Trauma is a risk factor for nearly all behavioral health and substance use disorders.

What Families and Caregivers Can Do to Help

Not all children experience child traumatic stress after experiencing a traumatic event, but those who do can recover. With proper support, many children are able to adapt to and overcome such experiences.

As a family member or other caring adult, you can play an important role. Remember to:

- Assure the child that he or she is safe. Talk about the measures you are taking to get the child help and keep him or her safe at home and school.

- Explain to the child that he or she is not responsible for what happened. Children often blame themselves for events, even those events that are completely out of their control.

- Be patient. There is no correct timetable for healing. Some children will recover quickly. Others recover more slowly. Try to be supportive and reassure the child that he or she does not need to feel guilty or bad about any feelings or thoughts.

Treatment for Child Traumatic Stress

Even with the support of family members and others, some children do not recover on their own. When needed, a mental health professional trained in evidence-based trauma treatment can help children and families cope with the impact of traumatic events and move toward recovery.

Effective treatments like trauma-focused cognitive behavioral therapies are available. There are a number of evidence-based and promising practices to address child traumatic stress.

Each child's treatment depends on the nature, timing, and amount of exposure to a trauma. Families and caregivers should ask their pediatrician, family physician, school counselor, or clergy member for a referral to a mental health professional and discuss available treatment options.

Helping Kids Cope with Disaster

Disasters can leave children feeling frightened, confused, and insecure. Whether a child has personally experienced trauma, has merely seen the event on television or has heard it discussed by adults, it is important for parents and teachers to be informed and ready to help if reactions to stress begin to occur.

Children may respond to disaster by demonstrating fears, sadness or behavioral problems. Younger children may return to earlier behavior patterns, such as bedwetting, sleep problems and separation anxiety. Older children may also display anger, aggression, school problems or withdrawal. Some children who have only indirect contact with the disaster but witness it on television may develop distress.

Recognize Risk Factors

For many children, reactions to disasters are brief and represent normal reactions to "abnormal events." A smaller number of children can be at risk for more enduring psychological distress as a function of three major risk factors:

- Direct exposure to the disaster, such as being evacuated, observing injuries or death of others, or experiencing injury along with fearing one's life is in danger.

- Loss/grief: This relates to the death or serious injury of family or friends.

- On-going stress from the secondary effects of disaster, such as temporarily living elsewhere, loss of friends and social networks, loss of personal property, parental unemployment, and costs incurred during recovery to return the family to pre-disaster life and living conditions.

Vulnerabilities in Children

In most cases, depending on the risk factors above, distressing responses are temporary. In the absence of severe threat to life, injury, loss of loved ones, or secondary problems such as loss of home, moves, etc., symptoms usually diminish over time. For those that were directly exposed to the disaster, reminders of the disaster such as high winds, smoke, cloudy skies, sirens, or other reminders of the disaster may cause upsetting feelings to return. Having a prior history of some type of traumatic event or severe stress may contribute to these feelings.

Children's coping with disaster or emergencies is often tied to the way parents cope. They can detect adults' fears and sadness. Parents and adults can make disasters less traumatic for children by taking steps to manage their own feelings and plans for coping. Parents are almost always the best source of support for children in disasters. One way to establish a sense of control and to build confidence in children before a disaster is to engage and involve them in preparing a family disaster plan. After a disaster, children can contribute to a family recovery plan.

Meeting the Child's Emotional Needs

Children's reactions are influenced by the behavior, thoughts, and feelings of adults. Adults should encourage children and adolescents to share their thoughts and feelings about the incident. Clarify misunderstandings about risk and danger by listening to children's concerns and answering questions. Maintain a sense of calm by validating children's concerns and perceptions and with discussion of concrete plans for safety.

Listen to what the child is saying. If a young child is asking questions about the event, answer them simply without the elaboration needed for an older child or adult. Some children are comforted by knowing more or less information than others; decide what level of information your particular child needs. If a child has difficulty expressing feelings, allow the child to draw a picture or tell a story of what happened.

Try to understand what is causing anxieties and fears. Be aware that following a disaster, children are most afraid that:

- The event will happen again.

- Someone close to them will be killed or injured.

- They will be left alone or separated from the family.

Reassuring Children after a Disaster

Suggestions to help reassure children include the following:

- Personal contact is reassuring. Hug and touch your children.

- Calmly provide factual information about the recent disaster and current plans for insuring their safety along with recovery plans.

- Encourage your children to talk about their feelings.

- Spend extra time with your children such as at bedtime.

- Re-establish your daily routine for work, school, play, meals, and rest.

- Involve your children by giving them specific chores to help them feel they are helping to restore family and community life.

- Praise and recognize responsible behavior.

- Understand that your children will have a range of reactions to disasters.

- Encourage your children to help update your a family disaster plan.

If you have tried to create a reassuring environment by following the steps above, but your child continues to exhibit stress, if the reactions worsen over time, or if they cause interference with daily behavior at school, at home, or with other relationships, it may be appropriate to talk to a professional. You can get professional help from the child's primary care physician, a mental health provider specializing in children's needs, or a member of the clergy.

Monitor and Limit Exposure to the Media

News coverage related to a disaster may elicit fear and confusion and arouse anxiety in children. This is particularly true for large-scale disasters or a terrorist event where significant property damage and loss of life has occurred. Particularly for younger children, repeated images of an event may cause them to believe the event is recurring over and over.

If parents allow children to watch television or use the Internet where images or news about the disaster are shown, parents should be with them to encourage communication and provide explanations. This may also include parent's monitoring and appropriately limiting their own exposure to anxiety-provoking information.

Use Support Networks

Parents help their children when they take steps to understand and manage their own feelings and ways of coping. They can do this by building and using social support systems of family, friends, community organizations and agencies, faith-based institutions, or other resources that work for that family. Parents can build their own unique social support systems so that in an emergency situation or when a disaster strikes, they can be supported and helped to manage their reactions. As a result, parents will be more available to their children and better able to support them. Parents are almost always the best source of support for children in difficult times. But to support their children, parents need to attend to their own needs and have a plan for their own support.

Preparing for disaster helps everyone in the family accept the fact that disasters do happen, and provides an opportunity to identify and collect the resources needed to meet basic needs after disaster. Preparation helps; when people feel prepared, they cope better and so do children.

Don't Leave Childhood Depression Untreated

Every psychological disorder, including depression, has some behavioral components.

Depressed children often lack energy and enthusiasm. They become withdrawn, irritable and sulky. They may feel sad, anxious and restless. They may have problems in school, and frequently lose interest in activities they once enjoyed.

Some parents might think that medication is the solution for depression-related problem behaviors. In fact, that's not the case. The Food and Drug Administration hasn't approved any drugs solely for the treatment of "behavior problems." When FDA approves a drug for depression—whether for adults or children—it's to treat the illness, not the behavior associated with it.

"There are multiple parts to mental illness, and the symptoms are usually what drug companies study and what parents worry about. But it's rare for us at FDA to target just one part of the illness," says Mitchell Mathis, M.D., a psychiatrist who is the Director of FDA's Division of Psychiatry Products.

Depression Is Treatable

The first step to treating depression is to get a professional diagnosis; most children who are moody, grouchy or feel that they are misunderstood are not depressed and don't need any drugs.

Only about 11 percent of adolescents have a depressive disorder by age 18, according to the National Institute of Mental Health (NIMH). Before puberty, girls and boys have the same incidence of depression. After adolescence, girls are twice as likely to have depression as boys. The trend continues until after menopause. "That's a clue that depression might be hormonal, but so far, scientists haven't found out exactly how hormones affect the brain," says child and adolescent psychiatrist Tiffany R. Farchione, M.D., the Acting Deputy Director of FDA's Division of Psychiatry Products.

It's hard to tell if a child is depressed or going through a difficult time because the signs and symptoms of depression change as children grow and their brains develop. Also, it can take time to get a correct diagnosis because doctors might be getting just a snapshot of what's going on with the young patient.

"In psychiatry, it's easier to take care of adults because you have a lifetime of patient experience to draw from, and patterns are more obvious" says Mathis. "With kids, you don't have that information. Because we don't like to label kids with lifelong disorders, we first look for any other reason for those symptoms. And if we diagnose depression, we assess the severity before treating the patient with medications."

Getting the Proper Care

The second step is to decide on a treatment course, which depends on the severity of the illness and its impact on the child's life. Treatments for depression often include psychotherapy and medication. FDA has approved two drugs—fluoxetine (Prozac) and escitalopram (Lexapro)—to treat depression in children. Prozac is approved for ages 8 and older; Lexapro for kids 12 and older.

"We need more pediatric studies because many antidepressants approved for adults have not been proven to work in kids," Farchione says. "When we find a treatment that has been shown to work in kids, we're encouraged because that drug can have a big impact on a child who doesn't have many medication treatment options."

FDA requires that all antidepressants include a boxed warning about the increased risks of suicidal thinking and behavior in children, adolescents and young adults up to age 24. "All of these medicines work in the brain and the central nervous system, so there are risks. Patients and their doctors have to weigh those risks against the benefits," Mathis says.

Depression can lead to suicide. Children who take antidepressants might have more suicidal thoughts, which is why the labeling includes a boxed warning on all antidepressants. But the boxed warning does not say not to treat children, just to be aware of, and to monitor them for, signs of suicidality.

"A lot of kids respond very well to drugs. Oftentimes, young people can stop taking the medication after a period of stability, because some of these illnesses are not a chronic disorder like a major depression,"

Mathis adds. "There are many things that help young psychiatric patients get better, and drugs are just one of them."

It's important that patients and their doctors work together to taper off the medications. Abruptly stopping a treatment without gradually reducing the dose might lead to problems, such as mood disturbance, agitation and irritability.

Depression in children shouldn't be left untreated. Untreated acute depression may get better on its own, but it relapses and the patient is not cured. Real improvement can take six months or more, and may not be complete without treatment. And the earlier the treatment starts, the better the outcome.

"Kids just don't have time to leave their depression untreated," Farchione says. "The social and educational consequences of a lengthy recovery are huge. They could fail a grade. They could lose all of their friends."

Medications help patients recover sooner and more completely.

Section 45.2

Nature Helps Kids Deal with Stress

Text in this section is excerpted from "Why Take Your Kids Outside," United States Fish and Wildlife Service (FWS), December 12, 2013.

1. It makes kids happier.

Nature turns frowns upside down. Studies indicate that children who play and explore outdoors are less stressed and may further benefit by learning confidence and social skills. In nature, kids and families get a chance to move at life's natural pace, where time disappears, no one is bored, and exploration turns into fun adventure. Key to nature play is the chance for kids to explore on their own terms and with their own choices, so they can discover themselves what is interesting and fun (this builds confidence too!). Choosing to climb a tree, hanging onto a rope swing, jumping over a log, skipping stones —all of these are examples of experiences in which children learn more about themselves, their decisions, and what to do in new settings.

2. It makes kids healthier.

Get out with the bugs to prevent getting a bug. Keeping kids active helps keep kids healthy. And nothing keeps kids active more than giving them fun and interesting things to explore and do. Studies indicate that even as little as 30 minutes of activity a day will keep you healthy. It can be as simple as a bike ride around the neighborhood or a hike in a local park. There are so many options when you're in nature—running, jumping, climbing, building and more. Research suggests that the most important thing for kids to make a habit of an active life is being introduced to their activities by a parent. And of course it's good for the parents too! Try it, you and your kids will like it.

3. It makes kids smarter.

Better focus without any hokus pokus! Nature has all sorts of patterns and parts. And all the parts somehow fit together. When children get to play in the outdoors from the earliest age, they learn - what is what, how things fit together, what they do. Opportunities for regular play in the outdoors — especially in gardens, woods, and creeks -- are especially beneficial.

In nature, kids see, hear, smell and touch things all at the same time, getting them to observe, ask questions and figure out things that have a lot of parts to them. The richness in the outdoors is far more stimulating—and gets the mind working more—than only watching television or playing electronic games. There is a place for that stuff but they are no substitute for what experience in nature brings to kids' development. In fact, children who play and learn on a regular basis in the outdoors take these enhanced skills with them to school—and tend to have higher school achievement and test scores too!

4. It's free!

Free is always a great price. Most activities you can do outside don't cost a single penny. The outdoors can offer you your very own economic stimulus package. You want to make your dollar go the extra mile. What could be better than having a great time for free? There are more things you can do in and around your home and nearby that will fill your family's days with great adventures. Families are event planning their summer "trips" with backyard campouts or hikes in local parks. And another great thing is that you can get all your favorite friends and families together too. It's not far away, you don't need a plane ticket or big entrance ticket. All you have to do is go explore!

5. It's fun for the entire family.

Unplug, relax and explore, together. Want to do something for the family that is easy and fun for you too? Activities in nature are something the whole family can enjoy. Whether the whole family, a grandparent and a grandchild, a dad or mother and a son or daughter, or others spend time outdoors, they may be changed in positive ways for ever.

With nature games, family activities, or camping, everyone can participate – letting go of the stresses of the day – relaxing and having some creative time to just be. And that time offers the kids a real chance to really benefit from a parents advice, knowledge and support in a way many other activities don't offer. This is that special time to share, explore, build memories – and through that build real family togetherness. Research indicates that children feel respected and cared for when adults they respect spend time with them outdoors. Kids, in turn, learn how to behave with the family and adults. They also tend to talk and communicate more, engage in conversation. Beyond family, a sense of connection to community and place is nourished. Everyone benefits—from individuals, to families, to whole communities.

Section 45.3

Combating Parental Stress

Text in this section is excerpted from "Preventing Child
Maltreatment and Promoting Well-Being: A Network for Action,"
U.S. Department of Health and Human Services (HHS), 2013.

Knowledge of Parenting and Child Development

Parents who understand the usual course of child development are more likely to be able to provide their children with respectful communication, consistent rules and expectations, and opportunities that promote independence. But no parent can be an expert on all aspects of infant, child, and teenage development or on the most effective ways to support a child at each stage. When parents are not aware of normal developmental milestones, interpret their child's behaviors in a negative way, or do not know how to respond to and effectively manage a child's behavior, they can become frustrated and may resort to harsh discipline.

As children grow and mature, parents need to continue to learn and change how they respond to their children's needs. Information about child development and parenting may come from many sources, including extended families, cultural practices, media, formal parent education classes, and a parent's own experiences. Interacting with other children of similar ages helps parents better understand their own child. Observing other caregivers who use positive techniques for managing children's behavior also provides an opportunity for parents to learn healthy alternatives.

Parenting styles need to be adjusted for each child's unique temperament and circumstances. Parents of children with special needs may benefit from additional coaching and support to reduce frustration and help them become the parents their children need.

Parental Resilience

Parents who can cope with the stresses of everyday life as well as an occasional crisis have resilience—the flexibility and inner strength to bounce back when things are not going well. Parents with resilience also know how to seek help in times of trouble. Their ability to deal with life's ups and downs serves as a model of coping behavior for their children.

Multiple life stressors, such as a family history of abuse or neglect, physical and mental health problems, marital conflict, substance abuse, and domestic or community violence—and financial stressors such as unemployment, financial insecurity, and homelessness—can reduce a parent's capacity to cope effectively with the typical day-to-day stresses of raising children.

All parents have inner strengths or resources that can serve as a foundation for building their resilience. These may include faith, flexibility, humor, communication skills, problem-solving skills, mutually supportive caring relationships, or the ability to identify and access outside resources and services when needed. All of these qualities strengthen their capacity to parent effectively, and they can be nurtured and developed through concrete skill-building activities or through supportive interactions with others.

Social Connections

Parents with a network of emotionally supportive friends, family, and neighbors often find that it is easier to care for their children and themselves. Most parents need people they can call on once in a while when they need a sympathetic listener, advice, or concrete support such as transportation or occasional child care. A parent's supportive relationships also model positive social interactions for children, while giving children access to other supportive adults. On the other hand, research has shown that parents who are isolated and have few social connections are at higher risk for child abuse and neglect.

Being new to a community, recently divorced, or a first-time parent makes a support network even more important. It may require extra effort for these families to build the new relationships they need. Some parents may need to develop self-confidence and social skills to expand their social networks. Helping parents identify resources and/ or providing opportunities for them to make connections within their neighborhoods or communities may encourage isolated parents to reach out. Often, opportunities exist within faith-based organizations, schools, hospitals, community centers, and other places where support groups or social groups meet.

Concrete Supports for Parents

Families whose basic needs (for food, clothing, housing, and transportation) are met have more time and energy to devote to their children's safety and well-being. When parents do not have steady financial resources, lack health insurance, or face a family crisis (such as a natural disaster or the incarceration of a parent), their ability to support their children's healthy development may be at risk. Some families also may need assistance connecting to social service supports such as alcohol and drug treatment, domestic violence counseling, or public benefits.

Partnering with parents to identify and access resources in the community may help prevent the stress that sometimes precipitates child maltreatment.

Offering concrete supports also may help prevent the unintended neglect that sometimes occurs when parents are unable to provide for their children.

When needed services do not exist in your community, work with parent-advocates and community leaders to help establish them. Parents who go public with their need usually find that they are not alone. The fact that a parent is willing to publicize a cause may mobilize the community. Parents who are new to advocacy may need help connecting with the media, businesses, funding, and other parts of the community to have their needs heard and identify solutions.

Part Six

Additional Help and Information

Chapter 46

Glossary of Terms Related to Stress and Stress-Related Disorders

abdominal migraine: A type of migraine that mostly affects young children and involves moderate to severe abdominal pain, with little or no headache.

acupuncture: The term "acupuncture" describes a family of procedures involving the stimulation of points on the body using a variety of techniques. The acupuncture technique that has been most often studied scientifically involves penetrating the skin with thin, solid, metallic needles that are manipulated by the hands or by electrical stimulation.

acne: Acne is a disorder resulting from the action of hormones and other substances on the skin's oil glands (sebaceous glands) and hair follicles.

acute: Refers to a disease or condition that has a rapid onset, marked intensity, and short duration.

acute stress disorder (ASD): A mental disorder that can occur in the first month following a trauma. ASD may involve feelings such as not knowing where you are, or feeling as if you are outside of your body.

This glossary contains terms excerpted from documents produced by several sources deemed reliable.

addiction: A chronic, relapsing disease characterized by compulsive drug seeking and use and by long-lasting changes in the brain.

anorexia nervosa: An eating disorder caused by a person having a distorted body image and not consuming the appropriate calorie intake resulting in severe weight loss.

anticonvulsant: A drug or other substance used to prevent or stop seizures or convulsions. Also called antiepileptic.

antidepressant: A medication used to treat depression.

anxiety disorder: Any of a group of illnesses that fill people's lives with overwhelming anxieties and fears that are chronic and unremitting. Anxiety disorders include panic disorder, obsessive-compulsive disorder, post-traumatic stress disorder, phobias, and generalized anxiety disorder.

anxiety: An abnormal sense of fear, nervousness, and apprehension about something that might happen in the future.

arousal: A traumatic reaction that makes a person feel nervous and on edge. The trauma memory might be so intense that it is hard to sleep or focus the mind. Some people become more jumpy or quick to anger. Others feel like they have to be more on guard.

aura: A warning of a migraine headache. Usually visual, it may appear as flashing lights, zigzag lines, or a temporary loss of vision, along with numbness or trouble speaking.

avoidance: One of the symptoms of post-traumatic stress disorder (PTSD). Those with PTSD avoid situations and reminders of their trauma.

biofeedback: A method of learning to voluntarily control certain body functions such as heartbeat, blood pressure, and muscle tension with the help of a special machine. This method can help control pain.

binge eating disorder: An eating disorder caused by a person being unable to control the need to overeat.

bipolar disorder: A depressive disorder in which a person alternates between episodes of major depression and mania (periods of abnormally and persistently elevated mood). Also referred to as manic depression.

body image: How a person feels about how she or he looks.

body mass index: A measure of body fat based on a person's height and weight.

borderline personality disorder: Borderline personality disorder (BPD) is a serious mental illness marked by unstable moods, behavior, and relationships.

broken heart syndrome: Broken heart syndrome is a condition in which extreme stress can lead to heart muscle failure. The failure is severe, but often short-term.

bulimia nervosa: An eating disorder caused by a person consuming an extreme amount of food all at once followed by self-induced vomiting or other purging.

caregiver: A caregiver is anyone who provides help to another person in need. Usually, the person receiving care has a condition such as dementia, cancer, or brain injury and needs help with basic daily tasks.

chronic: Refers to a disease or condition that persists over a long period of time.

cluster headache: Sudden, extremely painful headaches that occur in a closely grouped pattern several times a day and at the same times over a period of weeks.

cognition: Conscious mental activity that informs a person about his or her environment. Cognitive actions include perceiving, thinking, reasoning, judging, problem solving, and remembering.

cognitive behavioral therapy (CBT): A blend of two therapies— cognitive therapy (CT) and behavioral therapy. CT focuses on a person's thoughts and beliefs, how they influence a person's mood and actions, and aims to change a person's thinking to be more adaptive and healthy. Behavioral therapy focuses on a person's actions and aims to change unhealthy behavior patterns.

complementary and alternative medicine: Complementary and alternative medicine (CAM) is the term for medical products and practices that are not part of standard medical care.

coronary heart disease: Coronary heart disease (CHD) is a disease in which a waxy substance called plaque builds up inside the coronary arteries. These arteries supply oxygen-rich blood to your heart muscle.

cortisol: A hormone made by the adrenal cortex (the outer layer of the adrenal gland). It helps the body use glucose (a sugar), protein, and fats. Cortisol made in the laboratory is called hydrocortisone. It is used to treat many conditions, including inflammation, allergies, and some cancers. Cortisol is a type of glucocorticoid hormone.

counselor: A person who usually has a master's degree in counseling and has completed a supervised internship.

depression (depressive disorders): A group of diseases including major depressive disorder (commonly referred to as depression), dysthymia, and bipolar disorder.

dialectical behavior therapy: Dialectical behavior therapy (DBT) is a form of cognitive behavioral therapy used to treat people with suicidal thoughts and actions and borderline personality disorder (BPD). The term "dialectical" refers to a philosophic exercise in which two opposing views are discussed until a logical blending or balance of the two extremes—the middle way—is found.

disorder: An abnormality in mental or physical health.

dissociative disorder: A complex mental process known as dissociation allows children and adults to cope with a traumatic experience. "Dissociation" can take many forms, such as "blocking out" a painful experience from memory or feeling detached or "not in" one's own body.

dopamine: A brain chemical, classified as a neurotransmitter, found in regions of the brain that regulate movement, emotion, motivation, and pleasure.

dysthymia: A depressive disorder that is less severe than major depressive disorder but is more persistent.

eating disorders: Eating disorders, such as anorexia nervosa, bulimia nervosa, and binge-eating disorder, involve serious problems with eating. This could include an extreme decrease of food or severe overeating, as well as feelings of distress and concern about body shape or weight.

electroconvulsive therapy (ECT): A treatment for severe depression that is usually used only when people do not respond to medications and psychotherapy. ECT involves passing a low-voltage electric current through the brain. The person is under anesthesia at the time of treatment.

employee assistance programs: Employee Assistance Programs (EAPs) are worksite-based programs and/or resources designed to benefit both employers and employees. EAPs help businesses and organizations address productivity issues by helping employees identify and resolve personal concerns that affect job performance.

epinephrine: A hormone and neurotransmitter. Also called adrenaline.

fatigue: A condition marked by extreme tiredness and inability to function due lack of energy. Fatigue may be acute or chronic.

fibromyalgia syndrome: Fibromyalgia syndrome is a common and chronic disorder characterized by widespread pain, diffuse tenderness, and a number of other symptoms. The word "fibromyalgia" comes from the Latin term for fibrous tissue (*fibro*) and the Greek ones for muscle (*myo*) and pain (*algia*).

frostbite: Frostbite is an injury to the body that is caused by freezing. Frostbite causes a loss of feeling and color in affected areas. It most often affects the nose, ears, cheeks, chin, fingers, or toes.

gastritis: Gastritis is a condition in which the stomachlining—known as the mucosa—is inflamed, or swollen.

heat shock proteins: One of a group of proteins that help protect cells from stresses such as heat, cold, and low amounts of oxygen or glucose (sugar). Heat-shock proteins help other proteins function in normal cells and may be present at high levels in cancer cells. Blocking the activity of a heat-shock protein called HSP90 is being studied in the treatment of cancer. Other heat-shock proteins including HSP70 and gp96 are being studied in vaccines to treat cancer. Also called HSP and stress protein.

hormone: Substance produced by one tissue and conveyed by the bloodstream to another to effect a function of the body, such as growth or metabolism.

hypertension: Also called high blood pressure, it is having blood pressure greater than 0 over 90 mmHg (millimeters of mercury). Long-term high blood pressure can damage blood vessels and organs, including the heart, kidneys, eyes, and brain.

insomnia: Not being able to sleep

interpersonal therapy (IPT): Most often used on a one-on-one basis to treat depression or dysthymia (a more persistent but less severe form of depression).

ischemia: Lack of blood supply to a part of the body. Ischemia may cause tissue damage due to the lack of oxygen and nutrients.

isotretinoin: Isotretinoin is a drug approved for the treatment of severe acne that does not respond to other forms of treatment. If the drug is improperly used, it can cause severe side effects, including birth defects. Serious mental health problems have also been reported with isotretinoin use.

ketamine: Ketamine is a dissociative anesthetic that has some hallucinogenic effects. It distorts perceptions of sight and sound and makes the user feel disconnected and not in control. It is an injectable, short-acting anesthetic for use in humans and animals. It is referred to as a "dissociative anesthetic" because it makes patients feel detached from their pain and environment.

magnetic resonance imaging (MRI): An imaging technique that uses magnetic fields to take pictures of the structure of the brain.

mania: Feelings of intense mental and physical hyperactivity, elevated mood, and agitation.

massage therapy: Massage therapy encompasses many different techniques. In general, therapists press, rub, and otherwise manipulate the muscles and other soft tissues of the body. They most often use their hands and fingers, but may use their forearms, elbows, or feet.

meditation: Meditation is a mind and body practice. There are many types of meditation, most of which originated in ancient religious and spiritual traditions. Some forms of meditation instruct the practitioner to become mindful of thoughts, feelings, and sensations and to observe them in a nonjudgmental way.

mental illness: A health condition that changes a person's thinking, feelings, or behavior (or all three) and that causes the person distress and difficulty in functioning.

migraine: A medical condition that usually involves a very painful headache, usually felt on one side of the head. Besides intense pain, migraine also can cause nausea and vomiting and sensitivity to light and sound. Some people also may see spots or flashing lights or have a temporary loss of vision.

neurotransmitters: A chemical produced by neurons to carry messages from one nerve cell to another.

obsessive-compulsive disorder (OCD): An anxiety disorder in which a person suffers from obsessive thoughts and compulsive actions, such as cleaning, checking, counting, or hoarding. The person becomes trapped in a pattern of repetitive thoughts and behaviors that are senseless and distressing but very hard to stop.

osteoarthritis: Osteoarthritis (OA) is a painful, degenerative joint disease that often involves the hips, knees, neck, lower back, or small joints of the hands.

over-the-counter medicine: Over-the-counter medicine is also known as OTC or nonprescription medicine. All these terms refer to medicine that you can buy without a prescription. They are safe and effective when you follow the directions on the label and as directed by your health care professional.

parasympathetic nervous system: The part of the nervous system that slows the heart, dilates blood vessels, decreases pupil size, increases digestive juices, and relaxes muscles in the gastrointestinal tract.

panic disorder: An anxiety disorder in which a person suffers from sudden attacks of fear and panic. The attacks may occur without a known reason, but many times they are triggered by events or thoughts that produce fear in the person, such as taking an elevator or driving. Symptoms of the attacks include rapid heartbeat, chest sensations, shortness of breath, dizziness, tingling, and feeling anxious.

phobia: An intense fear of something that poses little or no actual danger. Examples of phobias include fear of closed-in places, heights, escalators, tunnels, highway driving, water, flying, dogs, and injuries involving blood.

postpartum depression: Postpartum depression is when a new mother has a major depressive episode within one month after delivery.

post-traumatic stress disorder (PTSD): A disorder that develops after exposure to a highly stressful event (e.g., wartime combat, physical violence, or natural disaster). Symptoms include sleeping difficulties, hypervigilance, avoiding reminders of the event, and re-experiencing the trauma through flashbacks or recurrent nightmares.

psoriasis: Psoriasis is a chronic autoimmune skin disease that speeds up the growth cycle of skin cells.

psychiatrist: A medical doctor (MD) who specializes in treating mental diseases. A psychiatrist evaluates a person's mental health along with his or her physical health and can prescribe medications.

psychiatry: The branch of medicine that deals with identifying, studying, and treating mental, emotional, and behavioral disorders.

psychologist: A mental health professional who has received specialized training in the study of the mind and emotions. A psychologist usually has an advanced degree such as a PhD.

psychotherapy: A treatment method for mental illness in which a mental health professional (psychiatrist, psychologist, counselor) and a patient discuss problems and feelings to find solutions. Psychotherapy can help individuals change their thought or behavior patterns or understand how past experiences affect current behaviors.

re-experiencing: A repeat of the feelings, bodily responses, and thoughts that occurred at the time of the traumatic event.

resilience: Resilience refers to the ability to successfully adapt to stressors, maintaining psychological well-being in the face of adversity. It's the ability to "bounce back" from difficult experiences.

schizophrenia: A chronic, severe, and disabling brain disease. People with schizophrenia often suffer terrifying symptoms such as hearing internal voices or believing that other people are reading their minds, controlling their thoughts, or plotting to harm them. These symptoms may leave them fearful and withdrawn. Their speech and behavior can be so disorganized that they may be incomprehensible or frightening to others.

selective serotonin reuptake inhibitors (SSRIs): A group of medications used to treat depression. These medications cause an increase in the amount of the neurotransmitter serotonin in the brain.

serotonin: A neurotransmitter that regulates many functions, including mood, appetite, and sensory perception.

social phobia: Social phobia is a strong fear of being judged by others and of being embarrassed. This fear can be so strong that it gets in the way of going to work or school or doing other everyday things.

stigma: A negative stereotype about a group of people.

stress response: When a threat to life or safety triggers a primal physical response from the body, leaving a person breathless, heart pounding, and mind racing. From deep within the brain, a chemical signal speeds stress hormones through the bloodstream, priming the body to be alert and ready to escape danger. Concentration becomes more focused, reaction time faster, and strength and agility increase. When the stressful situation ends, hormonal signals switch off the stress response and the body returns to normal.

sympathetic nervous system: The part of the body that increases heart rate, blood pressure, breathing rate, and pupil size. It also causes blood vessels to narrow and decreases digestive juices.

syndrome: A group of symptoms or signs that are characteristic of a disease.

tension-type headache: A primary headache that is band-like or squeezing and does not worsen with routine activity. It may be brought on by stress.

trauma: A life-threatening event, such as military combat, natural disasters, terrorist incidents, serious accidents, or physical or sexual assault in adult or childhood.

yoga: Yoga is a mind and body practice with origins in ancient Indian philosophy. The various styles of yoga typically combine physical postures, breathing techniques, and meditation or relaxation.

Chapter 47

Directory of Organizations for People with Stress-Related Disorders

Government Agencies That Provide Information about Stress-Related Disorders

Centers for Disease Control and Prevention (CDC)
1600 Clifton Rd.
Atlanta, GA 30333
Toll-Free: 800-CDC-INFO
(232-4636)
Phone: 404-639-3311
Website: www.cdc.gov
E-mail: cdcinfo@cdc.gov

Federal Emergency Management Agency (FEMA)
U.S. Department of Homeland Security
500 C St. S.W.
Washington, DC 20472
Toll-Free: 800-621-FEMA
(621-3362)
Phone: 202-646-2500
Website: www.fema.gov

Resources in this chapter were compiled from several sources deemed reliable; all contact information was verified and updated in September 2015.

Healthfinder®
National Health Information Center
P.O. Box 1133
Washington, DC 20013-1133
Fax: 301-984-4256
Website: www.healthfinder.gov
E-mail: healthfinder@nhic.org

National Cancer Institute (NCI)
NCI Office of Communications and Education, Public Inquiries Office,
6116 Executive Blvd.
Ste. 300
Bethesda, MD 20892-8322
Toll-Free: 800-4-CANCER (422-6237)
Website: www.cancer.gov
E-mail: cancergovstaff@mail.nih.gov

National Center for Posttraumatic Stress Disorder (NCPTSD)
VA Medical Center (116D)
215 N. Main St.
White River Junction, VT 05009
Phone: 802-296-6300
Fax: 802-296-5135
Website: www.ptsd.va.gov
E-mail: ncptsd@va.gov

National Heart, Lung, and Blood Institute (NHLBI)
P.O. Box 30105
Bethesda, MD 20824-0105
Phone: 301-592-8573
Fax: 301-592-8563
Website: www.nhlbi.nih.gov
E-mail: nhlbiinfo@nhlbi.nih.gov

National Institute of Allergy and Infectious Diseases (NIAID)
6610 Rockledge Dr.
MSC 6612
Bethesda, MD 20892-6612
Toll-Free: 866-284-4107
Fax: 301-402-3573
Website: www.niaid.nih.gov
E-mail: ocpostoffice@niaid.nih.gov

National Institute of Arthritis and Musculoskeletal and Skin Diseases (NIAMS)
Information Clearinghouse, National Institutes of Health
1 AMS Cir.
Bethesda, MD 20892-3675
Toll Free: 877-22-NIAMS (226-4267)
Phone: 301-495-4484
Fax: 301-718-6366
Website: www.niams.nih.gov
E-mail: niamsinfo@mail.nih.gov

*National Institute of
Neurological Disorders and
Stroke (NINDS)*
NIH Neurological Institute
P.O. Box 5801
Bethesda, MD 20824
Toll-Free: 800-352-9424
Phone: 301-496-5751
Website: www.ninds.nih.gov
E-mail: braininfo@ninds.nih.gov

*National Institute on Aging
(NIA)*
Bldg. 31, Rm. 5C27, 31 Center Dr.
MSC 2292
Bethesda, MD 20892
Phone: 301-496-1752
Fax: 301-496-1072
Website: www.nia.nih.gov

*National Institute on Alcohol
Abuse and Alcoholism
(NIAAA)*
5635 Fishers Ln.
MSC 9304
Bethesda, MD 20892-9304
Phone: 301-443-3860
Website: www.niaaa.nih.gov
E-mail: niaaaweb-r@exchange.
nih.gov

*National Institute on Drug
Abuse (NIDA)*
6001 Executive Blvd.
Rm. 5213
Bethesda, MD 20892-9561
Phone: 301-443-1124
Website: www.drugabuse.gov
E-mail: information@nida.nih.gov

*National Institute on Mental
Health (NIMH)*
*Science Writing, Press, and
Dissemination Branch*
6001 Executive Blvd.
Rm. 8184, MSC 9663
Bethesda, MD 20892-9663
Toll-Free: 866-615-6464
Phone: 301-443-4513
Fax: 301-443-4279
Website: www.nimh.nih.gov
E-mail: nimhinfo@nih.gov

*National Institutes of Health
(NIH)*
9000 Rockville Pike
Bethesda, MD 20892
Phone: 301-496-4000
Website: www.nih.gov
E-mail: NIHinfo@od.nih.gov

*National Women's Health
Information Center
(N.W.HIC)*
Office on Women's Health
200 Independence Ave.
S.W. Rm. 712E
Washington, DC 22031, 20201
Toll-Free: 800-994-9662
Website: www.womenshealth.gov

*Substance Abuse and
Mental Health Services
Administration (SAMHSA)*
1 Choke Cherry Rd.
Rockville, MD 20857
Toll-Free: 877-SAMHSA-7
(726-4727)
Fax: 240-221-4292
Website: www.samhsa.gov
Email: samhsainfo@samhsa.hhs.
gov

U.S. Food and Drug Administration (FDA)
10903 New Hampshire Ave.
Silver Spring, MD 20993
Toll-Free: 888-INFO-FDA (463-6332)
Website: www.fda.gov

U.S. National Library of Medicine (NLM)
8600 Rockville Pike
Bethesda, MD 20894
Toll-Free: 888-FIND-NLM (346-3656)
Phone: 301-594-5983
Fax: 301-402-1384
Website: www.nlm.nih.gov
Email: custserv@nlm.nih.gov

Private Agencies That Provide Information about Stress-Related Disorders

American Academy of Child and Adolescent Psychiatry
3615 Wisconsin Ave., N.W.
Washington, DC 20016-3007
Phone: 202-966-7300
Fax: 202-966-2891
Website: www.aacap.org

American Academy of Experts in Traumatic Stress
203 Deer Rd.
Ronkonkoma, NY 11749
Phone: 631-543-2217
Fax: 631-543-6977
Website: www.aaets.org
E-mail: info@aaets.org

American Academy of Family Physicians
P.O. Box 11210
Shawnee Mission, KS 66207-1210
Toll-Free: 800-274-2237
Phone: 913-906-6000
Fax: 913-906-6075
Website: www.aafp.org

American Association of Suicidology
5221 Wisconsin Ave., N.W.
Washington, DC 20015
Phone: 202-237-2280
Fax: 202-237-2282
Website: www.suicidology.org

American Foundation for Suicide Prevention
120 Wall St.
22nd Fl.
New York, NY 10005
Toll-Free: 888-333-AFSP (333-2377)
Phone: 212-363-3500
Fax: 212-363-6237
Website: www.afsp.org
E-mail: inquiry@afsp.org

American Heart Association National Center
7272 Greenville Ave.
Dallas, TX 75231
Toll-Free: 800-AHA-USA-1 (242-8721)
Website: www.heart.org

American Institute for Cognitive Therapy
136 East 57th St.
Ste. 1101
New York, NY 10022
Phone: 212-308-2440
Website: www.cognitivetherapynyc.com
E-mail: editor@cognitivetherapynyc.com

American Institute of Stress
Website: www.stress.org

American Massage Therapy Association
500 Davis St.
Ste. 900
Evanston, IL 60201-4695
Toll-Free: 877-905-0577
Phone: 847-864-0123
Fax: 847-864-5196
Website: www.amtamassage.org
E-mail: info@amtamassage.org

American Medical Association
515 North State St.
Chicago, IL 60654
Toll-Free: 800-621-8335
Website: www.ama-assn.org

American Music Therapy Association
8455 Colesville Rd.
Ste. 1000
Silver Spring, MD 20910
Phone: 301-589-3300
Fax: 301-589-5175
Website: www.musictherapy.org
E-mail: info@musictherapy.org

American Psychological Association
750 First St. NE
Washington, DC 20002-4242
Toll-Free: 800-374-2721
Phone: 202-336-5500
Website: www.apa.org

Anxiety Disorders Association of America
8730 Georgia Ave.
Silver Spring, MD 20910
Phone: 240-485-1001
Fax: 240-485-1035
Website: www.adaa.org

Anxiety Disorders Association of Canada
P.O. Box 117, Stn Cote St-Luc
Montreal
Quebec H4V 2Y3
Toll-Free: 888-223-2252
Phone: 514-484-0504
Fax: 514-484-7892
Website: www.anxietycanada.ca
E-mail: contactus@anxietycanada.ca

Association for Behavioral and Cognitive Therapies
305 7th Ave.
16th Fl.
New York, NY 10001
Phone: 212-647-1890
Fax: 212-647-1865
Website: www.abct.org
E-mail: mjeimer@abct.org

Association of Traumatic Stress Specialists
c/o MHANJ, 88 Pompton Ave.
Verona, NJ 07044
Phone: 973-559-9200
Website: www.atss.info
E-mail: admin@atss.info

Biofeedback Certification International Alliance
10200 W 44th Ave.
Wheat Ridge, CO 80033-2840
Phone: 303-420-2902
Fax: 303-422-8894
Website: www.bcia.org
E-mail: info@bcia.org

Cleveland Clinic
9500 Euclid Ave.
Cleveland, OH 44195
Toll-Free: 800-223-2273
Website: my.clevelandclinic.org

Depression and Bipolar Support Alliance
730 North Franklin St.
Ste. 501
Chicago, IL 60654-7225
Toll-Free: 800-826-3632
Fax: 312-642-7243
Website: www.dbsalliance.org

Family Caregiver Alliance
180 Montgomery St.
Ste. 900
San Francisco, CA 94104
Toll-Free: 800-445-8106
Phone: 415-434-3388
Website: www.caregiver.org
E-mail: info@caregiver.org

Freedom From Fear
308 Seaview Ave.
Staten Island, NY 10305
Phone: 718-351-1717
Website: www.freedomfromfear.org
E-mail: help@freedomfromfear.org

Imagery International
1574 Coburg Rd., #555
Eugene, OR 97401-4802
Toll-Free: 866-494-9985
Website: www.imageryinternational.org
E-mail: information@imageryinternational.com

International Society for Traumatic Stress Studies
111 Deer Lake Rd.
Ste. 100
Deerfield, IL 60015
Phone: 847-480-9028
Fax: 847-480-9282
Website: www.istss.org
E-mail: istss@istss.org

Iraq and Afghanistan Veterans of America
292 Madison Ave.
10th Fl.
New York, NY 10017
Phone: 212-982-9699
Fax: 212-982-8645
Website: www.iava.org

March of Dimes National Office
1275 Mamaroneck Ave.
White Plains, NY 10605
Phone: 914-997-4488
Website: www.marchofdimes.com

Mental Health America
2000 North Beauregard St.
6th Fl.
Alexandria, VA 22311
Toll-Free: 800-969-6642
Fax: 703-684-5968
Website: www.nmha.org

National Alliance for Caregiving
4720 Montgomery Ln.
2nd Fl.
Bethesda, MD 20814
Website: www.caregiving.org

National Alliance on Mental Illness
3803 North Fairfax Dr.
Ste. 100
Arlington, VA 22203
Toll-Free: 800-950-NAMI (6264)
Phone: 703-524-7600
Fax: 703-524-9094
Website: www.nami.org

National Child Traumatic Stress Network University of California at Los Angeles
11150 W. Olympic Blvd.
Ste. 650
Los Angeles, CA 90064
Phone: 310-235-2633
Fax: 310-235-2612
Website: www.nctsn.org

National Eating Disorders Association
603 Stewart St.
Ste. 803
Seattle, WA 98101
Toll-Free: 800-931-2237
Website: www.nationaleatingdisorders.org
E-mail: info@NationalEatingDisorders.org

National Headache Foundation
820 N. Orleans
Ste. 217
Chicago, IL 60610
Toll-Free: 888-NHF-5552 (643-5552)
Phone: 312-274-2650
Website: www.headaches.org
E-mail: info@headaches.org

National Multiple Sclerosis Society
733 Third Ave.
3rd Fl.
New York, NY 10017
Toll-Free: 800-344-4867
Website: www.nationalmssociety.org

National Organization for Victim Assistance
510 King St.
Ste. 424
Alexandria, VA 22314
Toll-Free: 800-TRY-NOVA (879-6682)
Website: www.trynova.org

National Psoriasis Foundation
6600 S.W. 92nd Ave.
Ste. 300
Portland, OR 97223-7195
Toll-Free: 800-723-9166
Phone: 503-244-7404
Fax: 503-245-0626
Website: www.psoriasis.org
E-mail: getinfo@psoriasis.org

National Sleep Foundation
1522 K St., N.W.
Ste. 500
Washington, DC 20005
Phone: 202-347-3471
Fax: 202-347-3472
Website: www.sleepfoundation.
org
E-mail: nsf@sleepfoundation.org

Nemours Foundation Center for Children's Health Media
1600 Rockland Rd.
Wilmington, DE 19803
Phone: 302-651-4000
Website: www.kidshealth.org
E-mail: info@kidshealth.org

PsychCentral
55 Pleasant St.
Ste. 207
Newburyport, MA 01950
Website: www.psychcentral.com
E-mail: talkback@psychcentral.
com

Rape, Abuse, and Incest National Network
2000 L St. N.W.
Ste. 406
Washington, DC 20036
Toll-Free: 800-656-HOPE
(656-4673)
Phone: 202-544-1034
Website: www.rainn.org
E-mail: info@rainn.org

Sidran Traumatic Stress Institute
P.O. Box 436
Brooklandville, MD 21022-0436
Phone: 410-825-8888
Fax: 410-560-0134
Website: www.sidran.org

Social Phobia
Social Anxiety Association
Website: www.socialphobia.org

Suicide Awareness Voices of Education
8120 Penn Ave. South
Ste. 470
Bloomington, MN 55431
Toll-Free: 800-273-8255
Phone: 952-946-7998
Website: www.save.org

Transcendental Meditation Program
Website: www.tm.org

World Federation for Mental Health
Ste. 101
12940 Harbor Dr.
Woodbridge, VA 22192
Website: www.wfmh.org

Yoga Alliance
1701 Clarendon Blvd.
Ste. 110
Arlington, VA 22209
Toll-Free: 888-921-YOGA
(921-9642)
Website: www.yogaalliance.org

Yoga Journal
Website: www.yogajournal.com

Index

Index

Page numbers followed by 'n' indicate a footnote. Page numbers in italics indicate a table or illustration.

521

526

divorce
 general-life stressors 271
 grief 10
"Does how much you eat affect how
 long you live?" (NIA) 436n
"Dogs and PTSD" (VA) 470n
"Don't Leave Childhood Depression
 Untreated" (FDA) 482n
domestic violence
 concrete supports 494
 stress 276
 trauma 297
domino effect, Alzheimer's brain 87
dopamine
 antidepressant 228
 atypical antidepressants 230
 defined 502
 drug abuse 277
 serotonin reuptake inhibitors 345
"DrugFacts: Understanding Drug
 Abuse and Addiction" (NIDA) 276
duloxetine, antidepressants 346
duodenum, acute gastritis 124
dysthymia, defined 502

E

early diagnosis, Alzheimer's disease
 85
EAP *see* employee assistance
 programs
Early Childhood Learning &
 Knowledge Center (ECLKC)
 publications
  children and teens 17n
  pregnancy 157n
eating disorders
 bulimic 245
 child traumatic stress 483
 cognitive behavioral therapy 185
 defined 502
 diabetes 104
 overview 234–8
 stress 25
"Eating Disorders— About More Than
 Food" (NIMH) 234n
eating habits *see* diet and nutrition
economic hardship, overview 446–58
ECT *see* electroconvulsive therapy

ED *see* erectile dysfunction
Effexor, bipolar disorder 230
electroconvulsive therapy (ECT),
 defined 502
EMDR *see* eye movement
 desensitization and reprocessing
emotional and thought responses,
 stress 35
"Emotional stress and heart disease in
 women: an interview with Dr. Viola
 Vaccarino" (NHLBI) 136n
employee assistance programs (EAP)
 assistance 444
 defined 502
 stress management 57
employee survey, job stress 443
emotional reasoning, cognitive
 restructuring 426
emotional intelligence, described 422
endoscopy, gastrointestinal 125
epileptic seizures, pets 371
epinephrine
 bipolar disorder 213
 defined 502
 diabetes 105
 post-traumatic stress disorder 138
 stress 99
erectile dysfunction, overview 107–13
"Erectile Dysfunction (ED)" (VA) 107n
erosive gastritis
 anemia 124
 defined 120
erythrodermic psoriasis, described 166
escitalopram
 antidepressants 229
 children 489
 depression 345
Eskalith (lithium), bipolar disorder 224
exercise
 Alzheimer's disease 91
 bulimia nervosa 236
 eating disorder 237
 erectile dysfunction 113
 grief 9
 headaches 132
 multiple sclerosis 150
 post-traumatic stress disorder 309
 relaxation techniques 390
 sleep hygiene 185
 see also physical activity